EXOTIC NO MORE

11/7/2022
15+ 176
193 - 208

11/13/2022
143 - 208
209 - 282

11/15/22
241 - 264
265 - 290

11/18/22
363 - 380
381 - 394

EXOTIC NO MORE

SECOND EDITION

Anthropology for the Contemporary World

EDITED BY **JEREMY MacCLANCY**

The University of Chicago Press ✕ *Chicago and London*

The University of Chicago Press, Chicago 60637
The University of Chicago Press, Ltd., London
© 2002, 2019 by The University of Chicago
All rights reserved. No part of this book may be used or reproduced in any
manner whatsoever without written permission, except in the case of brief
quotations in critical articles and reviews. For more information, contact
the University of Chicago Press, 1427 E. 60th St., Chicago, IL 60637.
Published 2019
Printed in the United States of America

28 27 26 25 24 23 22 21 20 19   1 2 3 4 5

ISBN-13: 978-0-226-63597-2 (cloth)
ISBN-13: 978-0-226-63602-3 (paper)
ISBN-13: 978-0-226-63616-0 (e-book)
DOI: https://doi.org/10.7208/chicago/9780226636160.001.0001

The University of Chicago Press gratefully acknowledges a subvention
from the Royal Anthropological Institute in partial support of the costs
of production of this volume.

Library of Congress Cataloging-in-Publication Data

Names: MacClancy, Jeremy, editor.
Title: Exotic no more : anthropology for the contemporary world / edited by
Jeremy MacClancy.
Description: Second edition. | Chicago : The University of Chicago Press, 2019. |
Includes index.
Identifiers: LCCN 2019000827 | ISBN 9780226635972 (cloth : alk. paper) |
ISBN 9780226636023 (pbk. : alk. paper) | ISBN 9780226636160 (e-book)
Subjects: LCSH: Anthropology.
Classification: LCC GN4 .E93 2019 | DDC 301—dc23
LC record available at https://lccn.loc.gov/2019000827

CONTENTS

INTRODUCTION

TAKING PEOPLE SERIOUSLY

Jeremy MacClancy

For far too long, social anthropology has often been seen as an academic discipline dedicated to the study of abstruse customs of out-of-the-way tribes. Extraordinary ceremonies in exotic settings, unusual behaviors in isolated communities—these have been seen by many as anthropologists' stock-in-trade. However, like so many stereotypes, this outdated image of anthropology is more misleading than revealing. For anthropologists have always set the world, and not just its more wondrous corners, as their geographical limit. Since the professionalization of the discipline in the late nineteenth century, there have been anthropologists working in Britain as well as in Papua New Guinea, in France as well as in Niger. It is just that much more work was done beyond the confines of Europe and that the potentially more sensational and more colorful instances of that work (especially those in particularly distant, even mysterious settings) have received far greater publicity.

Similarly, anthropologists have never restricted themselves to the academic investigation of the odd or the potentially entertaining, leaving the study of anything of any possible practical importance to others. From the relatively early days of the discipline, some anthropologists have dedicated themselves to research into matters of immediate relevance, such as nutritional practices, attitudinal surveys, and the fallacious presuppositions of racisms. In the 1920s the great American anthropologist Franz Boas played a major role in the intellectual attack on scientific racism. Once again, it just tends to be that the more eye-catching studies have gained more of the public's attention, skewing popular perception of the discipline in the process.

The aim of this book is to correct this imbalance and to reemphasize the public value of the discipline. Thus all the contributors strive to demonstrate exactly how today's social anthropology can make a large contribution toward the understanding of a wide range of practical social issues. In a series of essays covering a rich diversity of topics from socialisms to socio-natures, from counterterrorism to crack dealing, they seek to show how anthropologists today are committed, to a degree greater than ever before, to investigating contemporary social problems and to studying the West as much as the Rest. Even Aldous Huxley, writing in the mid-1930s during the rise of fascism, was well aware of the need to recalibrate anthropological efforts. In *Eyeless in Gaza*, he has one character argue that Europeans are not worse than indigenes: "They've just been badly handled—need a bit of anthropology, that's all!"

The first edition of this book, published in 2002, was reviewed generously, sold well, and as far as we can tell, was read widely. But that was seventeen years ago. The world has since turned, and anthropology with it. Some of the topics we chose then are still of overbearing importance, but have been nudged somewhat off center stage by newer, seemingly more pressing topics. For instance, this time round, we have chapters on counterterrorism, migration, hacking, museums, indigenous rights activism, etcetera. For a diversity of retained topics, new contributors have provided new chapters. Only about a third of the original contributors have written again, for this edition. And all of them have substantially, in some cases wholly, rewritten their contributions: because they've had to. As Jenkins points out in his piece on ethnicity and nationalism, he certainly didn't foresee in 2002 that politicians would return to openly playing the race card; that populism would rise and rise; and that the advent of IT would create echo chambers for the fabricators of "post-truths."

All too often many anthropologists, despite their best intentions, have hidden their insights and cloaked their findings in the thickest of prose. Their texts, weighed down with recondite terms, ugly neologisms, and an excess of polysyllabic abstract nouns, are usually difficult to read and harder to finish. This is as unnecessary as it is unwanted. If an idea is worth expressing, the chances are it can be most powerfully expressed in a simple manner. All the contributors to this book have done their best to uphold this principle, by trying to write their essays in an as clear, unpretentious, and jargon-free way as possible. A key purpose of this book is to put the anthropological message across. We want the taxpayers, who ultimately underwrite most of our costs, to know what we are up to, not dive for the dictionary before they have turned the first page. As González puts it in his chapter, "What anthropologists have learned over the past century and a half is too important to withhold from others, and too important to hide behind bloated or pretentious jargon."

The term *anthropology* can have a very broad set of meanings. For that reason I have to be clear from the outset. None of the contributors to this volume is primarily concerned with the distant past (that's archaeology) or with the effect of biological variables on human populations (biological anthropology). Instead, this book is exclusively about *social and cultural* anthropology. A note on academic dialects: until recently British anthropologists said they practiced social anthropology and nothing but; their US counterparts employed cultural anthropology and little more. Whatever real difference those names indicated in the past does not hold true today. If I had to switch jobs for a day with a colleague in, say, Reno, Nevada, I doubt either of us would have to change much our style of teaching or the content of our courses. Thus, as far as I can assess, the easiest way to forestall any lingering transatlantic confusion in terminology is to bring the two adjectives together. I regard that as a fertile cohabitation, not a shotgun marriage.

So, before going any further, what exactly is social and cultural anthropology and what is so distinctive about it?

FIELDWORK

Anthropology means taking people seriously. It means trying to understand how people interpret and thus act in the world. Anthropologists listen to what people say and watch what they do, and then try to make sense of their words and their deeds by putting these into context.

Since we all interpret the world within the terms of our own particular language, anthropologists have to learn the language of the people they are working with. But learning a language and getting to know people both take time, lots of it. So anthropologists have made *fieldwork* the core method of their discipline. This means living, day and night, with a group of people for a protracted period, usually about two years, at least for the initial study. It also means trying, as much as possible, to live like the locals: participating in daily activities while at the same time observing and asking questions.

The key consequence of adopting this approach is that the vast majority of anthropologists, unlike most social scientists, do not normally try to *measure* things. They might take account of the quantitative data (numbers, frequencies, percentages, etc.) generated by other specialists, for example when studying the cultures of science, but usually they do not try to create their own. Rather, they strive to gather qualitative information. So when starting a new study, their first task is not to devise a questionnaire but to make friends and to begin speaking in a foreign tongue. The idea is to get to know the locals before trying to learn what they know. For instance, as a postdoc, I went to live in a north Spanish village, to study the opposed ideologies of left-wing Basque nationalism and a right-wing regionalism, in the mid-1980s, a time when armed Basque groups were still active. To avoid suspicion in such a conflictive context, I didn't ask an ethnographic question for months. I wanted people to get used to me first, and thought I'd succeeded. Even so, after half a year there, in one gathering I was told to my face that I had to be a spy: why else would Thatcher, then prime minister, foot my bill?

One real power of fieldwork is that it allows anthropologists to take very little for granted. Since different peoples comprehend the world in different ways, what is common sense for one group may well be deep-set prejudice, if not nonsense, for another. Thus an anthropologist, newly arrived in the field, presumes very little and has to be prepared for even her most cherished preconceptions to be overturned. Over time she begins to discern the basic beliefs of the people she is living with, to apprehend their degree of order, and so be able to put the seemingly irrational into context.

By spending so much time in the field, an anthropologist has the opportunity to establish relations of trust and maybe even something approaching friendship with the people she is living with. This holds the promise of allowing her to discover whether things really are as they seem. Having gained the confidence of her hosts, an anthropologist can attempt to ascertain whether what people initially told her in fact corresponds with what they do and, if not, how they explain the gap between the two. Usually, people are all too ready to represent publicly themselves in a certain clear-cut way, while quietly upholding a much more nuanced set of rules.

A further power of extended fieldwork is that so much is learnt by serendipity. In other words, an anthropologist must try to be always ready for chance events, for unexpected things randomly happening in front of them. These accidental encounters may be surprising and at first incomprehensible. But by inquiring into what is going on and why, an anthropologist may well come to learn something about her hosts which she had never even suspected. In the late 1970s I was carrying out fieldwork in a coastal village on the island of Tanna, in the South Pacific archipelago of Vanuatu. The country was then in the throes of a classical anticolonial struggle, with most villages marked out as dedicated to either pro- or anti-independence parties. People allied to one party claimed not to cooperate in any way with those of another. One day, two months into my work, I was astonished to see a man from a politically opposed village bring his small boat into the bay, where he was met by a local to whom he gave some fish. When I asked what was going on, I was told, "But they are kin. And when these political troubles are over, we can all be brothers once again." Further questions over the next few days showed me that, though most kept up a front of political partisanship, many quietly maintained relationships which had existed long before political parties had ever been introduced to the area.

We put the chapter by Bourgois and colleagues first in our list, because they give a taste of what fieldwork is actually like: in their case, trying to make sense of a deadly logic underpinning the street-corner drug trade in a rundown section of Philadelphia. Some commentators are all too ready to blame the gun-toting victims for the violence they help perpetuate. In contrast, Bourgois and Hart unpeel the compounding contexts which make dealing drugs a rare entrepreneurial avenue to the American Dream for local youth: the closing down of factories, very high unemployment, artificially elevated drug profits, a steady stream of consumers, cheap armaments, and in-house training in violence while incarcerated. But working out how all of that articulates with seemingly illogical behavior by aspirant drug "big shots" took Bourgois and his team years.

The summary point of all of the above is that a clipboard-bearing social administrator who simply drops into a community, asks a predetermined list of questions, collects the answers, and then goes home at the end of the working day to tabulate her results mathematically is much, much less likely to have her prejudices unsettled, to be able to distinguish between local ideology and reality, or to witness an accidental but revelatory event. Instead, it is probable she will only confirm what she sought to establish in the first place, even if it is wrong, misguided, or prejudicial.

Of course, no discipline is a harmonious whole unto itself, with all its practitioners in complete agreement about the nature and aims of their subject. Social and cultural anthropology is no exception. For instance, two contributions to this book appear to disagree over a fundamental point. The Fortuns, in their chapter, say "the scientific bodies . . . with the authority to name divisions in geological time have not approved the name change" of the late Holocene to the Anthropocene. Lock, in her contribution, implies that they have. When I e-mailed with them, both the Fortuns and Lock took this apparent disagreement to be a statement of how complex science is today: whether the change has been definitively approved depends on which subcommittee(s) of which body or bodies one attends to. Both chapters make the point that science, though often presented as definitive, is an evolving product of debates generated by the supply of new data and new kinds of data in a dynamic culture of its own. In other words, this seeming divergence of opinion exemplifies, in practice, what all three contributors wish to portray.

Some anthropologists could disagree with my characterization of the discipline so far. They might wish to argue the plurality of social anthropologies that exist: comparative mythologists analyzing the stories people tell; cognitive anthropologists deploying a statistically based consensus analysis to explain abstracted patterns of shared knowledge; sociobiologists trying to integrate social and biological factors in their evolutionary approaches to the study of societies; social theorists bent on formulating abstract models of human behavior; and so on. In this book, it is true, the contributors emphasize, in chapter after chapter, the power and value of fieldwork-based ethnography rather than, for instance, engage in speculation about the nature of mental operations. But that is solely in order to achieve the aim of this book: to demonstrate the relevance of social and cultural anthropology to our understanding of the contemporary social world.

In recent decades, academics in other disciplines have begun to recognize the power and value of fieldwork as well. For instance, some sociologists and lecturers in cultural studies have adopted anthropological procedures: in their own terms, they practice "fieldwork" and they write "ethnography." This cross-disciplinary borrowing is potentially very flattering. Trouble is, in many cases what exactly the borrowers do is rather different from (and frequently less than) the anthropological approach of intensive interaction with a particular group of people, including learning their language, for a prolonged period of time. Thus, even though fieldwork and ethnography are no longer exclusive to social and cultural anthropology, they are still central to the anthropological enterprise. And it is this central place of fieldwork-based ethnography within social anthropology which continues to make it a distinctive discipline, with a distinctive contribution to the understanding of social concerns.

A further, major change of recent times is that most anthropologists today, whether studying people, ideas, or objects, do not stay in one particular place but practice multisite ethnography. If people move, anthropologists follow their movement to a new site, whether refugee camp, center for migrant labor, or tourist destination. Key questions that arise here are how people organize themselves socially in their new place of residence, however temporary it may be; what senses of culture do they wish to maintain or recreate; what kinds of relations do they negotiate with their host community? If ideas move from place to place, again we have to follow their path. For example, in my postdoc fieldwork I was interested in cultural dimensions of Basque nationalism, so I could not focus on life in just one place. Instead I journeyed to interview football fans, gastronomes, journalists, geneticists, curators, and political activists, among others. Similarly, we can view objects, shifted from site to site, as having their own "social life." The job of the anthropologist then becomes the tracing of this material biography. For example, to toot my horn yet again, when I studied the international market in what was then called "tribal art," I talked with local producers in Vanuatu, hung out with a dealer in the capital, attended auctions in London, then interviewed collectors and museum curators. By following the process through, from indigenous artifact to high art, I could track the successive ways objects were discussed, valued, and exchanged.

Work on all these various topics confirms that the long-standing conception of a culture as a fixed, clearly bounded, relatively static entity has to be forsaken for something much more fluid, much more dynamic: perhaps a collation of practices, a continuing creation of its practitioners, who may, at particular times, identify a certain set of those as characteristic of their way of life.

THE CONTENTS

Human activity cannot be boxed into neatly sealed compartments. The chapters of this book are therefore very loosely grouped. Any order to their sequence is more apparent than real. After Bourgois and colleagues on fieldwork, we engage with religion (Harding), examine "race" and genders (Harrison, Merry), broach politics (Jenkins on ethnicities and nationalisms, Hann on ideologies), progress to economics (Carrier), and then move on to some varieties of violence and human misery (González on counterterrorism, Andersson on migration, Gardner on the failures of development). Next come chapters on the environment (Fairhead and Leach), the medical consequences of meddling with it (Lock on toxicity), and the sciences of measuring that meddling (Mike and Kim Fortun). Kelty educates us on the phases of hacking, which segues into two chapters on rights: the clarifications and conundra of human rights (Buerger and Wilson) and the protracted campaigns for indigenous rights (Colchester and Griffiths).

We do not want all the contributions to this book to read like an analytical chronicle of gloom and doom from womb to tomb. So, the next five chapters are devoted to topics more commonly associated with "'high" or popular culture: Ginsburg on the media, Steiner on visual arts, Shelton on museums, Mac-Clancy on tourism, and Sakakeeny on music. A few readers might think these chapters the icing on our cake; as though the earlier contributions were the serious section of this book, and these five a concluding, light entertainment. Far from it. Each of this final five deals with core cultural institutions and practices. Each argues and demonstrates their deep sociopolitical, economic, and cultural entwinements in our lives today. Each of these five contributors investigates the transformative social and cultural practices their topic might afford. We are constantly reminded we live in a media-saturated environment, globally. Tourism is near all-pervasive: not to include it would give a lopsided view of today's anthropology and the world. Music is not just melody to our lives but a common mode for their refiguring. Appreciation of the visual is not elitist; aesthetics is a structuring structure for all our lives. Curators have dusted off museums: they are enjoying new levels of popularity, which their directors exploit in exhibits designed to make us rethink our attitudes and opinions.

Steiner takes a more individual cognitive track. In a series of sideways moves, more crablike than monorail, he opens out the dovetails between clocks, photos from around the world, our conceptions of ourselves and others, and their conceptions of us. He adds comments about the nature of tradition and modernity along the way. It's a worked-through demonstration of what anthropology can be so good at: unraveling different threads of our enmeshed lives to expose unexpected weaves, ones which tell us something important about ourselves.

THE NATURAL, THE CULTURAL, AND THE ANTHROPOLOGIST

Time and again the contributors show how anthropologists do not just make the strange familiar. They can make the familiar strange as well. In other words, they can both place seemingly unusual customs in their local cultural logics *and* draw out the cultural peculiarity of seemingly natural Western ideas. In this reflexive mode anthropology can act as a very powerful tool for understanding our own position in the world. For example, Carrier, Harrison, and Merry, in their chapters on economics, racisms, and sexuality respectively, demonstrate that though common Western ideas about "free" markets, human "races" and genders are made to seem perfectly "natural," they are in fact thoroughly cultural in their construction. This strategy of "naturalizing" the cultural is as widespread as it is insidious. For instance, as Merry shows, many Westerners still believe that it is a naturally determined fact that certain jobs are much more suitable for men, not women. Yet when a female anthropologist went to work in a car repair workshop, she found many activities did not require muscle. Loads could be lifted by tools and joists; heavy toolboxes could be wheeled, and then towed; spare tires didn't need to be carried, they could be rolled. Similarly, Carrier reveals how shaky the tenets of neoliberalism are. Its proselytizers argue the less fettered a market the better, for truly free markets self-regulate. In fact, there are no such markets: all so far documented are underpinned by social and cultural considerations. Financiers, of whatever level, are not 24/7 rational maximizers. In their deals they take social factors into account as well. As this pair of examples suggests, the power of the arguments deployed by Carrier, Harrison, and Merry resides in the fact that since many associate the normative with the natural, exposing the cultural fabrication of what appears "natural" does away with its normative consequence. To put that another way, the radical shift in position steered by the three contributors is from "because this is the way things are 'naturally,' this is the way things have to be" to "because there is nothing natural about the way things are, there is no natural reason why they have to continue so into the future."

Some anthropologists question not just the abuse of the idea of the "natural," but the very idea of "nature" itself. As Fairhead and Leach state in their chapter, these days many environmental anthropologists reject any people/nature binary, instead exploring "socio-natures," the inextricable intertwining of social and natural orders. Here, what was once viewed as irreducibly natural is now regarded as the product of repeated human intervention into the nonhuman world. Thus, forests come to be understood as historical entanglements of natural and cultural forces, as a form of socio-nature: looking at a landscape tells us as much about our forebears as about the local ecosystem. The same with soils: ecologists may class the Amazon as poor earth supporting rich but precarious vegetation, but local farmers seek the dark soils of the area, grounded traces of pre-Columbian civilizations' agricultural working of these lands. They are damp reminders that this rainforest is no virgin. Lock, in her contribution, argues in a parallel fashion. Our increasing knowledge of epigenetics has outdated any sharp division between the genome and social life, for human changes to the environment can have genetic, intergenerational consequences: detrimental ones. A medical anthropologist, Lock also highlights the concepts of "situated or emerging biologies," the inseparable entangling of the material human body with historical, economic, and sociopolitical factors. Her examples include the effects on North American locals of a leaden water supply; the transmission down the generations of toxins, thanks to mercury-polluted rivers, or the Vietnam War policy of mass-spraying Agent Orange. Her list could go on. As discussed in her chapter, are these situated biologies better classed as "exposed" ones, the human product of our species transforming the life around us into deadly toxic environments?

It is not just "nature" which is culturally constructed. Related arguments can be made about most other key concepts in Western society. For example, Harding, in her chapter, radically questions common understandings of world religions. She makes clear that, all too often, everyday notions of what constitutes "religion" are skewed by a Christian-oriented list of supposedly characteristic components: "sacred texts, a founding figure, a supernatural realm, rites, and places of worship, as well as beliefs." Yet, as she points out, some anthropologists argue that Islam, for instance, cannot be viewed in this manner without grave distortion. Rather, it should be regarded as a tradition of heterogeneous discourses; piety is not nurtured by following propositional beliefs, but by quotidian practices which foster the requisite sensibilities. Related comments can be made about Hinduism, a way of life even more decentralized, and with no identified founder.

Similar arguments about the fundamentally cultural nature of Western practices can be applied to that supposedly impregnable bastion of Western rationality: science. For though the great majority of scientists uphold their investigations as completely free of cultural bias, work by anthropologists suggests strongly that this is not the case. The Fortuns, in their contribution, demonstrate that scientists' pretensions of having a "culture of no culture" is a misleading representation, as work in laboratories is in fact shaped by very distinctive cultural forces. Indeed a succession of studies by anthropologists has made patent just how very deeply cultural values and beliefs shape the making of scientific knowledge. In today's world of large, complex, interdisciplinary projects, the Fortuns seek to discern the "thought style" of different kinds of scientists. They see this as a cultural frame, which "directs the perception of scientists, sharing what problems they investigate, what data they produce, and how they interpret those data."

Perhaps Harding and Fairhead and Leach provoke the most radical question. For they query the underlying perspective of conventional anthropology that there is only one reality. In that mainstream model, known as naturalism, anything which does not fit within everyday reality is classed a "belief." But this is to do violence to peoples who state there are multiple realities, shared by humans and other agents in this world, whether coresident animals, trees, spirits: whatever. And ethnographers not prepared to take this re-visioning on board are in danger of producing distorting ethnographies which reproduce, not rethink, fundamental Western categories.

GLOBALIZING ANTHROPOLOGY, LOCALIZING ISSUES

The groups of people with whom anthropologists work may be small, but the issues they deal with can be enormous. Just because one is studying the lives of a relatively restricted number does not mean that the ramifications of the analysis might not be very extensive indeed. For if the world is the ultimate geographical limit of anthropology, then nothing less than the nature of humanity is its ultimate intellectual limit. For instance, Hann, in his chapter on political ideologies, shows that comparative work on a series of small-scale ethnographic studies reveals how a diverse variety of ordinary people, as opposed to party leaders and policy makers, have understood the alternatives of socialism and capitalism and to what extent they have been able to identify these grand programs with their own, local ideologies. In much the same manner Jenkins, in his contribution on ethnicity, is able to reaffirm, thanks to a plethora of contemporary ethnographic studies, the essentially negotiated nature of ethnicity. Though some politicians or journalists would have us believe it is "primordial" or "natural," repeated anthropological work demonstrates that ethnicity can be negotiable and flexible from one social situation to another (though never *infinitely* so). In other circumstances, it may be non-negotiable. For those trapped within ethnic conflicts there may be no choice.

Formerly, many anthropologists wrote up their studies of local groups as though they were more or less isolated communities, in contact with their neighbors and aware of what was going on slightly further afield, but essentially ignorant of what occurred much beyond. This once-convenient conceit has long been viewed a distorting fiction. The ever-increasing spread of capitalist practices, the container revolution, the continuing growth of both labor migration and mass tourism, and the rise and rise of worldwide telecommunications have all contributed to the ending of any real sense of isolation. It is all too evident now that peoples are as affected by global forces as by local ones, and have long been so. Anthropologists have shifted their focus accordingly. The majority of contributors to this book emphasize how one cannot understand people's present predicaments without acknowledging broader frames as well.

Thus Ginsburg in her chapter on mass media argues that it is by now very, very hard to imagine doing fieldwork anywhere on earth without lending an eye to the accelerating proliferation of forms of mediation, which extend people's imagination far beyond the traditional horizon. For example, in northern Nigeria Hausa youth can choose their modes of popular culture: Hausa or Yoruba videos; Indian, Hong Kong, or American films; or videos of Quranic exegesis by local preachers. The Indian films in particular are so appealing that today regional writers, male and female, who produce pulp fiction pamphlets may well incorporate Indian styles of romance into indigenous Hausa reality. For Ginsburg, this ever-developing range of transcultural media allows Hausa youth to consider alternative modernities, and where might be the place(s) of contemporary Hausa within that spectrum. Steiner argues in a related fashion about photography and material culture. To use his examples, the meanings of neither a photographic print nor a clock are fixed. Photos are not innocent documents;

clocks can tell more than the time. And, in the hands of a skillful artist, both items can be deployed to multilayered ironic end, stimulating Westerners to re-think their ideas of others, and of themselves.

Globalization has a range of effects: extending the forms and processes of political expression; altering already-established identities; enabling new ones; and so on. At the same time, just because peoples throughout the world are subject to similar globalizing tendencies does not mean that they experience or interpret these forces in the same way. MacClancy, in his contribution on tour-ism, makes it clear that mass tourism does not always have to have a damaging effect on local cultures. In some cases the arrival of visitors can boost or even re-vitalize local ways. In parts of central Australia, for instance, the rise of a tourist market in Aboriginal artifacts freed the locals from year-round dependence on state handouts. Fortified with the cash from sales of their creations, they can now afford to readopt their "walkabout" lifestyle for several months of the year.

The effects of globalization are perhaps most clearly seen, however, in the created tensions between edicts of universal scope prescribed by agencies with a worldwide reach and the diversity of local realities. The United Nations would have us believe its Declaration of Human Rights articulates a universal set of claims. Buerger and Wilson demonstrate we need to think beyond this legal-istic box, and recognize that human rights are not universally applied; more commonly, they are achieved, after struggle, in partial, time-limited manners. Moreover, the influence of these rights goes beyond the legislative, into the social and normative. They can lead to shifting cultural attitudes and mores, as much as to legal victories and political triumphs. Anthropologists may thus view human rights as a culture of its own, with its own social life and practice. Colchester and Griffiths provide an extended case study of this: the continuing campaigns of the Forest Peoples Programme for the indigenous rights of forest dwellers. They show in a trio of examples that campaigns are slow, dogged, pro-tracted, negotiated procedures where teams of lawyers, anthropologists, and other specialists have to work in a continually self-reflexive, sensitive manner, to accompany embattled peoples in their struggle to secure a just future.

STUDYING ELITES, ENCOURAGING EMPOWERMENT

Formerly, anthropologists "studied down." That is, they worked with people who usually perceived anthropologists as coming from more prestigious or more powerful societies than their own. In the last three decades many an-thropologists, realizing how restrictive this focus is, have changed tack and started to "study up." These trendsetters work on previously uninvestigated elite groups, regarding them as cultures unto themselves with their own self-justifying logics and staffed by professionals who evolve their own ever-more elaborate languages in order to legitimate their claims to specialist expertise.

Several contributors address this central issue. González tackles it head-on because studying counterterrorism means studying the US government, or at least strong branches of it. One reaction of the George W. Bush administration to US military involvement in Iraq and Afghanistan was to create the Human Terrain System: embedded teams of anthropologists and other social scientists charged with learning locals' views and fears in order to win them over to the Allied side. But this style of counterinsurgency was broadly criticized, often did not produce the results desired, and was closed down within a few years. The Pentagon switched its focus to a computational strategy, the massive collation of big data for the development of predictive modeling programs. A few anthropologists have argued these programs need to be boosted by relevant sociocultural knowledge, which can get close to "Give us a job, General." Others contend the attempted incorporation of that kind of knowledge into a computer program is fundamentally flawed, and that relying on models, however all-embracing and therefore seductive, is a dangerously poor substitute for confronting reality.

Gardner, in her chapter, shows anthropologists must not just study development projects in terms of their success or failure, for the laudable aim of improving future interventions; they need also to research development as a world of its own, with both explicit and implicit objectives. For instance, some argue that development discourse furthers the power of states or global institutions such as the World Bank. Here the evident danger is that the implementation of a universalizing discourse which ignores local realities can lead to effects more damaging than alleviatory. An allied fear is that development policy may be created to legitimate, rather than orientate, practice. In this context, "success" and "failure" threaten to become but internal terms of evaluation, whose redefinitions may serve, above all, to perpetuate development teams, over the amelioration of local lives. Gardner treads a careful line. She recognizes the reality of these dangers but adjudges development like any "other areas of human endeavour: contingent, contradictory, and not always effective." Despite its structural flaws and self-serving logics, not all development is to be damned.

Andersson takes a comparable tack. In his assessment of approaches to migration studies over recent decades, he identifies shifts between research on powerful structures of the state and on the lived realities of migrants. Like Gardner, he views bureaucracies as monolithic in aspiration, not in practice, as migrants strive to act as grit in the mechanism, looking for ways to bypass, exploit, or confront would-be domineering systems of control. Desperate migrants may play the humanitarian card, obtaining the desired residence permit on grounds of compassion. Others, concentrated in camps like so much livestock, may see themselves as providing employment for the camp workers in an otherwise depressed area. So they assert agency, and threaten jobs, not by protesting, but by going on strike. Andersson sees ethnographers as perfectly placed to mine this middle ground, where high-level politics intersects, via meso-level structures, with social life-worlds. To put that another way, he wants to connect the phenomenal and the political; "seeing like a state" with "seeing like a migrant."

If there is a new-ish practice which aspires to the global, it has to be the Internet. Yet how can anthropologists best investigate this virtual concourse maintained by real people? One obvious avenue is to study consumers, especially those who feel more alive online than off, or who just dissolve any meaningful distinction between the two. Kelty cuts a different track, focusing neither on IT consumers nor on its producers, but on trickster intermediaries: hackers. The term itself is labile and can imply, in turn, criminal behavior, utopian intervention, or simply activism. Utilizing a very imaginative format, Kelty traces a certain periodicity to hackerdom, giving a rich account of how different versions of "hackers" wax and wane over time, like so many phases of the moon. He argues the broader issue illuminated by studying this evolving ecosystem of political technologies is the continuing tension between expertise and participation. Will further use and abuse of the Internet lead to technocracy or to a radicalized participatory politics? Are hackers the standard bearers for freedom in a post-truth era? If there is hope, does it lie in the "dark net," an unfortunately value-laden term for both illicit trade and anonymized whistleblowing?

A central consideration: a shift to "studying up" does not mean we start to forget those who are "down." In this book contributor after contributor emphasizes how anthropology often strives to question the status quo. Through the accumulated examples of their writings, they underscore how anthropology attempts to help empower the alienated and give voice to the otherwise unvoiced. Unlike almost any other discipline, anthropology can humanize institutional process, the effects of politics, and the work of nations. Anthropologists, by listening to, and then transmitting, the words of the marginalized, the poor, and the ignored, can bring high-flying approaches back down to ground and reintroduce the concerns of ordinary people into the equations of policy makers.

These activist efforts are not restricted to the most patently political of anthropological topics. For instance, Sakakeeny argues against the common view of music as a pleasuring bolt hole against the ravages of daily life. Using New Orleans bands as his example, he wants to reintegrate music in its political, economic, and social contexts. His ultimate aim is a public anthropology of music, which can contribute to "broader initiatives aimed at ameliorating suffering and building equity." Shelton, writing on museums, highlights the work of curators whose exhibitions query dominant concepts and mainstream modes of thought. These curators want visitors to their once-hallowed halls to rethink notions of gender, colonialism, art, the social construction of inequality, collecting, human/animal distinctions, and so on. They are turning formerly neocolonialist institutions burdened with promoting national identity into popular museums of resistance, contemporary sites of cultural critique. At the same time they relinquish claims to authoritativeness, collaborate ever more with source communities, and so hope to make their museums homes of a more democratic encounter.

THE MORALITY OF IT ALL

Colchester and Griffiths are profoundly aware of the morally difficult terrain they have to traverse. As they state, "As thoughtfully as possible, we try to avoid substituting our voice for those of the peoples themselves."

In the last three decades the ethics of anthropology have loomed ever larger: in the opinion of many, this development was very belated. One reason for this change was the increasing concern of many indigenous peoples at the way they were being represented and their determination to represent themselves, on and in their own terms. Other reasons appear to be professional reactions to recent cases of ethical misconduct in the discipline, the development of debates about the apparently competing claims of culture and rights, and the imposed implementation of ethical regulation, via institutional review boards in the United States and university research ethics committees in the United Kingdom. The broadened access to anthropological writings enabled by IT developments is probably another reason.

Anthropologists, on the whole, may wish to act in an ethically upright manner but know how ponderable that is, given the range of moralities they have to consider simultaneously: their own personal ethics, the codes of ethics of both their professional organizations and their universities, the legal codes of both their home countries and those where they do fieldwork, the moralities of the people whom they study, and so on. Anthropologists cannot suppose all these moralities will coincide on all questions nor, no matter how well trained they are, can they expect to have a ready solution to every dilemma their fieldwork brings up. In these troublesome but important contexts, where moralities are multiple and absolutes relative, many practitioners are conscious that the claims of a few to sport a badge of virtuous certainty, as though it conferred a halo of ethical superiority, are simply pretentious postures, to be dismissed or researched. As I wrote in a book I coedited on field ethics, "What is much harder, and more realistic, is for the would-be virtuous anthropologist to stake out an ever-negotiated claim as robust defender of the moral low ground."

González and Gardner in their chapters highlight the ethical dimensions of both anthropological knowledge and anthropological engagement beyond the strictly academic world. Some obvious questions here are: should a fieldworker, faced with appalling social injustice or worse, be content with penning cultural critique, or should they turn activist? Should an anthropologist, foreknowing the quandaries of working with the military, aid organizations, or similar institutions, comment from afar or attempt to change from within? Or should they be formulating their questions in an alternative manner?

These concerns do not go away, and they run through, though at times implicitly, many of the contributions to this volume.

This book, as I have stated above, concentrates on a particular style of social and cultural anthropology. Of course, there are several other kinds as well, many of them concerned with what appears at first sight to have a much more academically narrow focus: for example, comparative mythology, kinship and related systems, the nature of symbolism, the intricacies of indigenous cosmologies. But it is essential to remember that the boundaries of what is "socially relevant" research are constantly shifting, in tune with changing circumstances. What might appear abstruse scholarship one day may become material of great political import the next day. For instance, ethnographic work on the details of Australian Aboriginal conceptions of person and place became key in a whole range of court cases brought by indigenes against the appropriations of the Australian state. A version of this book published in thirty years' time would have a very different set of chapters.

In sum, there is a single point that all the contributors wish to put across: we anthropologists have no magic wand, but if we wish to comprehend better the social and cultural worlds within which we are both enmeshed and reproduce, then anthropological research holds serious potential. At its best, it can help us understand the present place of us and others in the world, nudge us to reconsider cherished concepts, and maybe even embolden us to action. In other words, anthropology can provide us with a stance, however shaky, from which to assess our landscapes.

SUGGESTIONS FOR FURTHER READING

MacClancy, Jeremy, and Fuentes, Agustín. 2013. "The Ethical Fieldworker, and Other Problems." In J. MacClancy and A. Fuentes, eds., *Ethics in the Field: Contemporary Challenges*, 1–23. Oxford: Berghahn.

    A collection of papers addressing questions of field ethics in all the anthropological disciplines, and transanthropologically.

CHAPTER 1

COMING OF AGE IN THE CONCRETE KILLING FIELDS OF THE US INNER CITY

Philippe Bourgois, Laurie Kain Hart,
George Karandinos, and Fernando Montero

It wasn't even supposed to happen like that. I was gonna smack him . . .
but he kept talking. I wasn't even gonna shoot him, but it just happened
too fast man. I don't know. . . . This the dumbest thing I ever did in my life.
—**Eighteen-year-old Leo, in county jail after shooting a disrespectful drug seller**

Raffy, the "bichote" [Puerto Rican slang for "big shot"/"drug boss"] is out on the
corner tonight and invites Tito and me to sit next to him on the stoop of an aban-
doned row home. Tito is Raffy's "caseworker," the local term for a bichote's second-
in-command, who is responsible for managing the shifts of sellers and lookouts on a
drug corner. We are surrounded by a half-dozen of his off-and-on-duty heroin and
cocaine sellers, wannabe sellers, and teenage and pre-teenage bored kids who are
all eager—like me—to be around the big shot boss. When he shows up on the block,
Raffy is always the charismatic nexus for action, money, power, potential, and risk.
He is also the only provider of local employment in this desolate neighborhood.
   A police car cruises slowly down the block. We tense up and avoid eye contact

while simultaneously trying to look bored and indifferent. The passenger-side officer rolls down his window and yells out, "Betta get off the block right now fatass!" Raffy jumps to his feet, muttering "Dickhead!" His riposte—meant for our ears only—is, however, a little too loud. The officer jumps out of the car, flushes red, and slaps his baton in his palm. "I heard that, fatass. Get the fuck outta here! A bunch of people I locked up been telling me about you. [Shouting] Go home Bitch . . . Right now!"

Raffy snaps his mouth shut, spins around and obediently starts walking toward the far corner. I hold my breath hoping the escalation will defuse, but after only a few steps, Raffy stops. A grin spreads across his face, and he slowly raises his fists above his head, pumping them in a boxer's victory salute. He is evoking the character of Rocky Balboa, Philadelphia's beloved movie icon whose billion dollar series of eight blockbuster films spanning the 1970s through the late 2010s was set in this very same neighborhood as it transitioned from all-white to nearly all Puerto Rican. The crowd of employees, wannabes, and young admirers breaks into laughter and starts following Raffy as he continues to walk up the block, in slow motion now, his fists raised above his head, pumping the Rocky salute in rhythm with each step.

Spittle flying from his mouth, the outraged officer blushes a deeper red and belts out another slew of "fatasses" and "bitches." Trailing after Raffy, he reholsters his baton and attempts to pump his fists to match Raffy's challenge, sputtering, "I'll fight you right now. . . . Right now." But like Raffy, he is extremely overweight, and his belly breaks through his uniform and bursts over his holster belt laden with pistol, Taser, baton, walkie-talkie, and other bulky accessories. This makes him stumble forward and the crowd roars with laughter. Someone starts chanting, "Dickhead! Dickhead!"

I notice that the caseworker, Tito, does not join the chanting. Instead he is hanging back at the edge of the scene, haranguing the youths in front of him, "Yo stop! Shut-up. You don't know what you're doin' . . ." He is clearly trying to deescalate the confrontation.

The driver of the patrol car has now jumped out as well and is loudly shouting for reinforcement into a walkie-talkie pinned to his left shoulder, making sure we can hear the potential disaster awaiting us. He glares out at the crowd and palm-slaps his baton, but the chanters have turned their back on him to follow behind Raffy, egging one another on in a parade of support. Trying to catch up, the irate officer struts down the middle of the street, fists still raised in a lame imitation of Raffy, but his taunts of "bitch" and "fatass" are drowned out by the crowd's chants of "dickheads."

Raffy reaches the corner first and the crowd backs away to allow the two officers, batons raised, to approach, but then immediately recloses in a circle around them with cell phones held out to video the scene. Raffy drops into a squat and goose-steps around the irate officer in a chicken dance, clucking and flapping his elbows. He then stands up, and announces during a momentary awed silence of the crowd, "Ok, officer, then meet me in the gym. We'll put on gloves. . . . Not out here on the street like bitches."

Two patrol cars screech around the corner and four more officers jump out, definitively breaking the stalemate. The crowd closest to the patrol cars jumps back and the calmer partner of the irate wannabe Rocky officer takes advantage of the momentary lull to grab Raffy's left elbow, twisting it expertly behind Raffy's back. Unmollified, the officer yanks Raffy up off his feet by his handcuffed wrists in an attempt to disloacte his shoulders. Instead Raffy adroitly uses the momentum to dive forward through the open back door of the patrol car. He ducks his head just in time under the door frame to avoid smashing it but thuds face first onto the back seat. Gasping for breath, he squirms upright in the seat with his handcuffed arms pinned behind him and manages to regain his composure. In fact, playing to the crowd, he opens his mouth widely in what looks like a full-throated, full-belly laugh, but we cannot hear him because the officers slam the door shut.

The crowd's show of solidarity, the plethora of cell phones videoing the scene, and Raffy's agility have saved him from the standard retaliatory outcomes of such confrontational arrests: a sprained handcuffed-wrist, a dislocated shoulder, a concussed head, a fractured rib, or just a routine black-and-blue All-American police beat-down.

The irate officer is on a roll now. He spins around to sprint after Wiwi, a sixteen-year-old wheelchair-bound hustler who makes the mistake of trying to rush to his home around the corner. Wiwi has a sunset "curfew condition" imposed on him from an arrest earlier in the week and the moon is already full in the dark sky. The officer grabs the right handle of Wiwi's wheelchair and drags him to the far side of the patrol car which has been flung open by another officer. He tries to throw the disabled adolescent directly from his chair into the back seat next to Raffy, but Wiwi is wearing a seatbelt and the entire chair lifts into the air. Both the officer and the disabled adolescent curfew violator fall backward on the pavement to the crowd's outrage.

Several adult onlookers have now raised their voices above the chorus of "dickheads," to protest, "Nah nah, Officer! He ain't doin' nothin'. He's just going home. The young bol [inner-city Philadelphia slang for young man] lives right here [pointing to the far corner]." The cop yells back, "I got every right to arrest him! I got him right here last week with bundles [wholesale packets of heroin] on him." Wiwi adds his teenager's cracking voice to the melee, "You got no right to arrest me in front of my own house." The officer laughs, "You cried like a little bitch in your cell last week. You gonna cry again now?" Sixteen-year-old Wiwi does, indeed, burst into flowing tears of rage.

Wiwi's mother pushes through the crowd, asking in a surprisingly calm but loud voice, "What seems to be the problem, Officer?" Without pausing for a response she

turns to Wiwi and raises her hand as if to slap him, but instead yells in Spanish,
"Callate, hijo *[Shut-up, son]." That appears to calm the officer down.*

*Wiwi, now, to his own mortification, sobbing, undoes his seatbelt and tries
to throw himself from his chair directly into the back of the open patrol car door
next to Raffy. He is shouting hoarsely, "OK, OK arrest me dickheads. My lawyer's
gonna . . ." His arms are not strong enough, however, and his wheelchair tips over.
His mother catches him just in time, jams him back down behind his seatbelt, and
wheels him home rapidly.*

why
were
they
arrested

*Two more patrol cars skid to a stop and the crowd retreats onto stoops and into
houses. The police make no more arrests. Instead, they pack themselves back into
their vehicles and screech off, in a stench of burnt rubber.*

*Tito, the young caseworker, has already started making multiple urgent phone
calls to "re-up product." This is his break to rise in the food chain. Sweating and
barking out orders, he announces, "We're opening back up." If a district attorney
presecutor throws the book at Raffy, he could get lucky and manage to take over as
bichote on this profitable block without having to pay rent.*

*Only minutes after the police have left, the usual stream of customers—most of
them white—is flowing by again, cash in hand. Many of the addicts look like walking war-wounded, or rather like emaciated Auschwitz survivors on the final death
march, limping covered in scabs and rags. A young white man with a white blood-
stained bandage wrapped around his forehead bargains with Tito to exchange a
"9 millimeter glock" for "a bundle [fourteen $10 packets] of dope [heroin] and a
bundle of powder [cocaine]."*

*During a lull in the selling, one of the hotter-headed "dickhead" chanters, who
is clearly jealous of Tito's move to take over the corner, brags, "We should'a beaten
up the cops—they was drawlin' [acting inappropriately]." This prompts an almost
conventional businessman's rebuke from Tito about the stupidity of having taunted
the police, "Nah, nah! They gonna be on our ass now. Hittin' the block. It's gonna be
hot. We won't even be able to smoke a blunt on this block no more."*

*The hothead ripostes, "Nah, they just angry at us 'cause we the outlaws and they
can't be." Tito cracks up laughing and slaps him a high five. A customer walks up
and they go right back to business, selling, play-boxing, and rolling blunts. Clouds
of marijuana waft into the chill of the late autumn night air as dollars and dope
pass rapidly from hand to hand.*

THE PUNITIVE MISMANAGEMENT OF INNER-CITY POVERTY

Surprisingly, a sympathetic judge dismissed the bogus assault charges filed by
the wannabe-Rocky officer and Raffy immediately returned to the block to take

back control of sales from his caseworker Tito. He started hanging out even more conspicuously, generously treating his sellers and the neighbors to sodas and hoagies. Tito, meanwhile, strategically quit as Raffy's second-in-command as soon as the humiliated police started raiding every day, several times a day. Within two weeks Raffy was arrested on drug charges two more times and a notoriously draconian judge sentenced him to a completely unanticipated sentence of 12.5 to 25 years in prison, for having violated his probation on a previous outstanding narcotics sales conviction compounded by the two new arrests. Meanwhile, another bichote, Panama Red, newly released from prison, and well-known for "liking to play with guns," burst onto the scene and took over. Wary of the police, however, Panama Red strategically stepped back and rented out the corner for $5,000 a week to a subcontractor, yet another ambitious wannabe bichote from the neighborhood who, sure enough, was arrested four months later.

The tempo of arrests then inexplicably slowed down as it always did in the mysterious sudden ebbs and flows of demoralized and incompetent inner-city police narcotics offensives. In Philadelphia, as in many large cities across the country, narcotics units are purposefully rotated out of neighborhoods every few weeks or months to prevent the institutionalization of petty corruption. The easy money and artificially high profits associated with illegal drugs render fragile the boundary between criminal perpetrator and law enforcement agent. The Philadelphia newspapers' investigative reporters—notably Wendy Ruderman, Barbara Laker, and Daniel Denvir, among others—documented dozens of examples of egregious police corruption and brutality scandals during our fieldwork years, including a Pulitzer Prize–winning series on one of the narcotics teams rotating through our micro-neighborhood. In 2017 the head district-attorney of the city was indicted on corruption and bribery charges.

Reassured that the police offensive had finally ended, Panama Red took over direct control of sales on the block. He hired two new caseworkers, one for the day shift and the other for the graveyard shift. For the next eighteen months, Panama Red managed to keep the block open 24/7 in a flagrant cat-and-rooster dance with incompetent police raids that arrested only the addicted customers and the lowest level sellers.

SCRAMBLING FOR UPWARD MOBILITY ON THE CORNER

We were initially baffled by Raffy's provocative response to the abusive police officer on the night of his arrest. Seasoned bichotes usually avoid spending time at their drug sales points lest they attract police attention or expose themselves to attacks by rivals. We were even more shocked when Raffy dared to continue to hang out so visibly at his sales spot, despite the likelihood of police revenge after a sympathetic judge released him. At the time we did not yet understand the economic, cultural, and personal stakes propelling Raffy to take such spectacular risks. We later learned that Raffy's performative visibility and risk-taking had been a desperate attempt to charismatically retain his fragile control of this valuable territory. It turned out that he was under active siege not only by Panama Red, who ultimately seized control, but also by an estranged partner, Lucas, who had formerly been in charge of supplying the cocaine. We also did not yet understand the culturally inscribed necessity of having a long-term credible reputation for violence and hypermasculine courage in order to mobilize supporters, called "riders" in Philadelphia slang, for back-up in times of conflict. Equally important was the need to impress or intimidate neighbors who otherwise might be tempted to serve as informants to the police.

Bichotes, caseworkers and even entry-level sellers cultivate obligations for assistive violence among networks of riders as a protection against future victimization. Rider relationships also have a pragmatic material valence. In the absence of public state legal services and sanctions for mediating economic disputes peacefully, the ability to mobilize a handful of loyal violent minions is the best way to enforce cash-only contracts in the multibillion dollar narcotics industry. Peace, however, is also good for business: it imposes the longer-term modicum of stability necessary for attracting a steady flow of customers and it keeps the police at bay. Ironically, one's reputation for being able to mobilize violence simultaneously imposes prompt payments of debts, enforces labor discipline, ensures product purity, attracts customers, and reduces one's chance of arrest. On days when the police did not raid our block, one hundred "bundles" (each consisting of fourteen $10 packets of heroin, usually weighing 0.03 grams) were often sold during a single shift. In other words, on many—if not most—days some $14,000 worth of cash in untraceable bills was changing hands without a single dollar going missing every eight to fourteen hours on the poorest Philadelphia street corners such as ours.

FIELDWORK AND THE NEIGHBORHOOD HISTORICAL CONTEXT

This whirlwind of bichote arrests and successions occurred early into the long-term participant observation fieldwork project that we carried out as a team from the fall of 2007 through 2013 with periodic follow-up interviews and visits through 2018, in the poorest corner of Philadelphia's Puerto Rican inner city.

FIG. 1.1.

We rented an apartment on a block with an active sales point and socialized with our neighbors, hanging out on stoops, in homes, and at the sales points. We accompanied the sellers through the criminal justice system and visited them in jail. Two of the co-authors, George Karandinos, who was an undergraduate student at the time, and Fernando Montero, a recent college graduate from Costa Rica, lived in the apartment for over four and three years respectively, and Philippe and Laurie visited regularly, often staying the night.

The neighborhood had been the nineteenth-century industrial heartland of Philadelphia. Its infrastructure was devastated since the 1980s by public- and private-sector abandonment. It was riddled with abandoned factories, decaying row homes, vacant lots, defunct railroad lines, and random piles of rubble and garbage. Ironically, Puerto Ricans began immigrating in large numbers to Philadelphia in the 1950s seeking factory employment precisely when the city's manufacturing sector was beginning its precipitous decline. Manufacturing jobs in the city dropped more than twelvefold between the early 1950s and the mid-2000s. During our fieldwork years, there were virtually no legal businesses offering any significant source of employment within ten blocks of our apartment, and almost half of the households in our census tract had annual incomes below the US federal poverty line. The multibillion-dollar global narcotics industry flooded into this economic vacuum during the crack epidemic of the late 1980s and then entrenched itself with the price of heroin dropping and its purity rising through the 1990s and 2000s—wreaking havoc along its path. Unemployed, second-generation Puerto Rican immigrants as well as new arrivals fleeing even more extreme poverty and violence on their natal island filled the entry-level rungs of this highly profitable, but high-risk retail endpoint of the global narcotics industry. Unemployed youth growing up on our block found themselves selling high-quality, inexpensive heroin and cocaine to primarily white customers in the shadows of factories that used to employ their grandparents. Their lives were devastated by an aggressive state response of chronic hyper-incarceration and law enforcement violence that further compounded the routinized occupational injuries of addiction and interpersonal violence.

Drawing from several thousand pages of fieldwork notes and transcriptions of interviews, we are trying to make sense of the maelstrom of deadly violence engulfing the young men we befriended. We are interested in linking the intimate experience of violence in the US inner city to the larger political, economic, and historical forces that turn US inner cities into concrete killing fields. These forces include, most importantly, (1) neoliberal globalization and financialization that has dramatically increased income inequality, (2) narcotics monopoly profits that are artificially elevated by illegality, (3) a global arms industry that thrives on ineffective US gun control laws, and, most visibly, (4) the carceral mismanagement of racialized poverty and unemployment. What follows is an account of how these forces play out in the lives of two brothers, Tito (Raffy's caseworker in the opening field note) and Tito's little brother, Leo, as they both came of age on our block. From their perspective, they were ambitiously seizing the only "actually existing" opportunities for a sliver of the American Dream in the segregated inner city into which they were born.

TERRITORIAL CONTROL AND "VIRTUOUS POWER"

We documented nearly a dozen bichote transitions within our micro-neighborhood during our six years of full-time fieldwork. These territorial successions became pressure cookers for violent confrontations that sometimes lasted several weeks or months with multiple rivals jockeying for control. The violent reputation and depth of rider relationships that each aspiring bichote was capable of mobilizing during these transition periods were crucial to the outcome. Successful bichotes, however, could not rely on brute force alone. Their longevity ultimately hinged on their ability to be recognized as a respected "leader among equals." They needed to cultivate a hegemony of what Venezuelan criminologist and social critic Andres Antillano calls "virtuous power." This second mode of legitimacy entailed reinforcing their territorial control with continuous and innumerable sociable, charismatic assertions of protective aggression and generosity. The most resilient bichotes interspersed their acts of expressive brutality—including, in Raffy's case, recklessly brave displays of comic self-respect—with performances of humility and generosity.

Had Raffy not been imprisoned with a twelve-and-a-half- to twenty-five-year sentence, he would likely have maintained his power, because he was respected by our neighbors. They admired him for preferring brave displays of old-fashioned fisticuffs rather than the spectacular, terrifying gunplay that Panama Red and many other bichotes favored. Tito also clearly respected Raffy for this blunt physical courage and proved it by loyally siding with him as his rider during the three-way divide-and-conquer tug-of-war between Panama Red, Raffy, and Lucas even though he had already strategically quit as caseworker to avoid arrest.

Tito: First, Panama Red's bols started taking the coke off of Lucas' sellers. Raffy was ready to fight but Lucas didn't want to ride and he started bitchin' to Raffy, "I'm just going to pay rent to Panama Red."

But when Panama Red started taking the dope off of Raffy's hustlers too, Raffy beat him up. No gunplay! Just knocked him to the ground with his hands [shadow boxing enthusiastically]. Knocked him right under his own truck!

After that, Raffy said "Fuck this, Lucas ain't riding, so I'm going to take the powder from him too." 'Cause he didn't really have no respect for Lucas at that point. So beef started bubbling up between Raffy and Lucas too.

Lucas got powdered up [high on cocaine] and came out the house at Raffy with his AK. At first he had the jawn [in Philadelphia slang, an indefinite noun defined by context, in this case referring to Lucas's AK-47 machine gun] pointed to the side and Raffy was like, "Yo nigga don't point that shit at me." But Lucas, I guess he had some courage from all that powder, and kept it pointed at Raffy, and that nigga started dancing. Like, "Oh shit!"—Ducking around, scared as hell, ready to dive.

Reenacting the scene, Tito opened his eyes wide and feigned a terrified adrenaline rush. He hopped from foot-to-foot, rocked his body, waved his arms, and shook his head.

But instead, Lucas went back into his house. I grabbed my ratchet [gun], and so did my brother Leo. It was me, Raffy, and Leo waiting for Lucas up the block, ready to put that shit full of holes.

Lucas came out and saw us waiting at the corner and he went right back in the house and didn't come out for days. But by then it was too late, Raffy was already locked up and Panama Red had this block poppin' with the fire dope. That nigga Lucas don't have no heart [spitting in disgust].

VIOLENCE AND INCARCERATION: TITO'S EXPERIENCE

None of this turmoil dissuaded Tito from his ambitions for upward mobility.

Tito: I don't even know what stamp [brand name of heroin] Panama Red's peoples be sellin' because the cops have been raidin' and I've gone up the food chain puttin' out my own work [drugs] on a corner over there now [motioning vaguely toward one of the active blocks parallel to us].

Tito had seized a new opportunity that opened up when the bichote on a neighboring corner was suddenly shot dead by the little brother of one of his caseworkers whom the slain bichote had failed to bail out after an arrest. The bichote's widow trusted Tito, having known him since he was a little boy. She also needed to act fast because one of her late husband's cousins was trying to take over the block by force. She offered Tito a low rent, only $500 a week—a tenth of what Panama Red received from his new renter on our block. Tito partnered with a friend who owned a brand-new .357 Magnum, and they eagerly agreed to a deal promising to defend the widow's corner from her cousin-in-law and pay her the rent faithfully. Business immediately boomed, only to come crashing to an end almost immediately when Tito accidentally killed his new partner in a drunken and benzodiazepine-addled celebration of their three-month anniversary as fledgling bichotes renting a bargain-priced drug corner. The judge, another notorious hard-liner, initially charged Tito with homicide—carrying a seventeen- to thirty-four-year sentence—despite the fact that everyone, including the arresting police officers, knew the shooting was a genuine accident and should have qualified Tito for a much shorter involuntary manslaughter charge of two and a half to five years.

We visited Tito in the county jail on multiple occasions. On the first visit, Tito walked into the visitor's room with his face covered in scratches and raised his shirt to reveal a deep crimson circular bruise in the center of his chest:

Tito: I just got in a fight with some black bol and look, the motherfucker bit me! We had words earlier at the phones, and he kept runnin' his mouth. But I let it go. I wanted to be peaceful, you know, I have a lot on my mind. I have to go to court tomorrow. But the nigga came into my cell and [making a punching motion] snuck me in the back of the head. Then he stood there lookin' at me like I wasn't gonna' do nothin'. Like I'm a pussy.

I guess 'cause I'm small and I'm Puerto Rican, and I came in here quiet, minding my business, people think they can fuck with you. That's what I get for trying to keep to myself. I know if I came in here like a savage then he wouldn'a done that.

Now I might end up killing this nigga, cus when I get mad I don't really know what I'm doing. And I get mad at any little thing. I just lose it; go into a rage.

The over-fourfold explosion in the size of the incarcerated population in the United States since 1980 has turned prisons into de facto gladiator schools that hone the fighting skills of inmates and sabotage their future ability to find legal employment. The structural brutality of overcrowded US jails dramatically raises the stakes for cultivating violent reputations and propagates racist prison gangs as each ethnic group scrambles for self-protection. Prisons oblige inmates to be aggressively violent in order to avoid victimization while simultaneously trapping them in a catch-22 feedback loop of solitary confinement, extended prison sentences, and punitive lockdowns. These cycles of fury and frustration are further exacerbated by the institutionalization of arbitrary bullying by often poorly trained and overwhelmed guards. In Tito's description of his first prison fight, for example, he mentioned with a shrug, "When I saw the bol was trying to stab me I asked the CO [Correctional Officer] 'don't lock us in' [the cell together] but the CO did anyway."

In this context of institutionalized brutality, it is easy to understand why Tito was obliged to fly into a "blind rage" and beat a fellow inmate into a pulp inside his jail cell. Tito is Puerto Rican and, as he points out, "small," in an African American–dominated, overcrowded county jail. As a baby-faced nineteen-year-old facing a long-term prison sentence, it is imperative for his survival, respect, and sanity that he does not become a mark for bullies.

Tito had no difficulty identifying the infrastructural context generating the extreme levels of interpersonal violence among his fellow inmates in the punitive maximum-security "lock-down" units. This kind of ostensibly interpersonal, but clearly institutionally fomented, violence is what late nineteenth-century French sociologist Émile Durkheim would have clearly identified as a "social fact." Each individual act appears to be precipitated by the idiosyncrasy of the personalities of the perpetrators but, from a sociological perspective, the systemic phenomenon of massive carceral interpersonal violence cannot usefully be understood as being the "choice" of individuals. From a contemporary theoretical perspective, Tito's fight can be interpreted as a manifestation of what anthropologist Paul Farmer has called "structural violence," or alternatively what Philippe Bourgois and Nancy Scheper-Hughes have categorized as "everyday violence or "normalized violence." These theoretical perspectives highlight the invisible forces of political economic inequality and the institutional and bureaucratic frameworks that generate the highly visible interpersonal criminal violence that has been routinized in the United States, a country whose firearm murder rate in 2010 was ten times higher than that of other comparably rich nations.

Tito understood the oppressive effects of structural forces, but his critical insight on punitive overcrowding in US jails did not stop the institutionalized brutality from seeping into his subjectivity and becoming a core component of his own conception of masculine self-respect:

Tito: This unit is crazy, man. A lot of people don't know what's going on yet with their case. They stressin'. They have that uncertainty. They don't know if they are going to go home soon, or if they ain't ever goin' home. Plus, we in close custody. They got us on lockdown half the time because of some shanking [stabbing]. There ain't shit to do. You just sit in your cell all day bored and frustrated. That's half the reason there is so many problems. We might kill each other over ten minutes on the phone. Or hot water in the shower, or whatever.

Out in the street I knew how to resolve a situation, you could talk to someone out there and maybe it didn't have to come to any violence. In here there is no choice. You can't just let them treat you like a bitch 'cause then everyone be sayin', "He a pussy. He ain't gonna do anything." And walk up in your cell, "Look nigga gimme all that, or I'm'a fuck you up." I done seen it too many times man.

No one is going to talk about me like that. All I have in here . . . [choking back tears] is my pride. I'm not letting nobody take that away from me! And my mama didn't raise no pussy.

We were concerned that Tito might not survive in county jail waiting for trial so we sought out Don Ricardo—a charismatic former bichote who had lived through a fifteen-year sentence for a road-rage murder committed in his early twenties. Against all odds, Don Ricardo had managed to reintegrate himself into the legal labor market in his early forties. He prided himself on his redemption as a just-above-minimum-wage, part-time janitor cleaning offices, and he maintained a prominent charismatic retired gangster presence on the block with his extended family. He frequently doled out advice to the young street hustlers who respected him for his past history as a successful, violent bichote. We were hoping to persuade Don Ricardo to call Tito and advise him to refrain from violence, but he cut us short:

Don Ricardo: Naaahh! I don't see nothing wrong with what Tito did. Tito did right to fight. He is going to have to fight a lot, especially in his weight class. Tito gotta show that he don't care how little he is. You can't show that you fear nobody.

If Tito keeps fighting like that, trust me, he'll be alright. He ain't gonna win all his fights, but he'll get his respect . . . make a reputation.

It's not just Tito's problem. The black people in the County [jail] — especially the Muslims [a racialized Philadelphia prison gang] — try to take your heart. Can't let them bully you or they're gonna call you Maytag [term for a feminized inmate]. You gonna be washing their underwear, dirty shitty underwear, and then you gonna be givin' that booty up. I seen smaller guys than Tito kill guys real quick during a prison lockdown. . . . Yo! It was a major riot. The whole prison went wild . . .

THE PUERTO RICAN COLONIAL DIASPORA AND THE GLOBAL DRUG TRADE

On the street, the stakes provoking high levels of violence on drug corners are most proximally raised by the circulation of automatic weapons, untraceable cash, and monopoly profit margins that are inflated by illegality. Less proximally, but no less important to understanding the specifically Puerto Rican vulnerability to violence and narcotics addiction in the US inner city, is that the island of Puerto Rico has been a formal colony of the United States since 1898. This hijacking of the island's political administrative system has disarticulated its economy, expelling over half of its population as cheap wage laborers to the US mainland. Literally driven by hunger, formerly rural unemployed Puerto Ricans desperately emigrated as cheap wage laborers to segregated inner cities like Philadelphia precisely when factories in the mainland United States were closing down to take advantage of even lower-cost, overseas tax-free production sites. This "globalization" process caused the "rustbelt" cities of the Midwest and Northwest to become especially vulnerable to drug epidemics since the 1980s.

Formal colonies are an anomaly in the twenty-first century and represent an international embarrassment to their imperial masters that is repeatedly condemned in the United Nations. Nevertheless, more than a century after its invasion by US Marines in 1898, Puerto Rico still remained (as of 2019) an "unincorporated overseas territory" of the United States. Although residents of the island have US citizenship and must obey federal laws and regulations, they cannot vote in US elections and their economy is subject to strict US federal oversight. Puerto Ricans receive the full legal rights of US citizenship only if they take up permanent residence in the US mainland.

In the 2000s, Puerto Rico's dysfunctional domestic economy finally imploded. The island's gross national product began a decade-long decline culminating in 2016 with the US Supreme Court thwarting the Puerto Rican governor's attempt to file for public sector bankruptcy. The US Congress imposed a seven-member "Control Board," nicknamed the *"junta,"* to oversee an economic austerity plan that prioritized debt payments to US creditors—including large obligations to multiple hedge and vulture funds—rather than disbursement of social welfare services and retirement pensions for Puerto Rican residents. According to the US Department of Labor reports, by the end of our fieldwork in the mid-2010s, over 46.2 percent of Puerto Ricans on the island lived below the US poverty line—more than three times the US poverty rate. Most importantly, legal labor force participation rates in 2017 dropped to 40 percent—more than one-third lower than that of the US mainland's rate of 62 percent, forcing an even higher proportion of the working-age population into an exceptionally violent underground economy. Murder rates on the island of Puerto Rico are approximately five times higher than those on the US mainland.

Ironically, it is the peculiarity of Puerto Rico's ongoing colonial status, with its US-imposed free trade–and–travel export/import model of economic development, compounded with the bad luck of the island's strategic geographical location in the Caribbean, which has turned both the island and its inner-city diaspora on the mainland into a profit incubator for the global narcotics industry. A disproportionately large share of out-of-work Puerto Rican youth desperately seeks employment in the workforce of the narcotics industry at its riskiest, inner-city endpoints such as the open-air drug markets of Philadelphia where we conducted fieldwork.

THE LEGACY OF CHRONIC INCARCERATION: LITTLE BROTHER LEO

This bleak, ongoing colonial history of dispossession manifests on inner-city corners, in the routinized everyday emergency of violent competition over monopoly drug profits at a great human cost of useless suffering. We watched Tito's little brother, Leo, who had just turned eighteen, follow ambitiously in the footsteps of his older brother, whom he admired so much. Immediately after Tito's incarceration, Leo took full responsibility for the outstanding rent owed on his brother's former corner and put out his own new "stamp" of heroin. Four months later Leo too was in jail, awaiting trial for shooting one of his employees. As an overly precocious teenager way out of his league, he, like his older brother, had climbed too fast into his fledgling bichote status. Surrounded by guns, money, and cash he overreacted to the pressure of being bullied, threatened, and disrespected by the slightly older and tougher peers he had hired to work for him. In the anxious boredom of his jail cell Leo reflected for long hours on why he had pulled the trigger. He was honestly befuddled at how he could have so stupidly shot a disrespectful worker when all he had meant to do was intimidate him into returning a $500 stash of stolen heroin.

Leo: Oh man, I got into some dumb shit. Real stupid! It was all over some nut-ass shit. I had this young bol, Adrian, out there hustling for me and I went around the corner to advertise my stamp [shout out his heroin's brand name to passersby]. When I go back, the work [cache of drugs] ain't there, so I'm like, "Adrian, damn, you're the only person sittin' here, like, what's up? Where the work go?"

[Imitating ostentatious innocence] "Oh, I didn't touch nothin'" . . . this-an'-that. Then he wanted to get all hype, so he called his peoples—all of his cousins. So I go back to my crib and I grab the strap [gun] and I come back.

[Head in his hands his voice cracking] I don't know, everything was just moving so fast, like. I ain't really know what to do. I was gonna smack the shit out of him. But he kept talking. I raised my hand at him but he dipped back.

And all his peoples was standin' there, I was thinkin' in my head, like [setting his face into a threatening frown], "Damn, if one of his peoples got a gun . . ." And Adrian like [taunting voice]. 'You a nut-ass nigga! You ain't gonna be treating me like a nut' . . . This-an'-that . . .

I'm like, "What!" And I pulled the jawn out.

But he was just like, "Nigga you not gonna do shit." And he came at me.

So I shot him, but just once so he could get away from me. That was the first time I ever shot somebody. And I thought I was gonna be like hesitant. But I didn't even hesitate. It was just like a spur of the moment thing.

Afterwards, from my crib I had called one of his peoples. He told me they found the dope and I told him, "Look, when Adrian get better, we could rumble [fist fight]."

But they told me Adrian was like almost dying in the hospital 'cause the bullet almost hit his main artery.

I'm thinking in the back of my head, "Damn, I didn't want all that to happen. . . . I just did some dumb shit."

Next thing I know, the police come running up in my crib. "Where the gun at?" And started rippin' the house apart.

Six months later Leo was in shackles awaiting transfer to a western Pennsylvania prison on a five-to-ten-year, plea-bargained sentence. As an eighteen-year-old he was objectively terrified that he would find himself cycling through prison for the rest of his life, trapped in the dead-end logic of the inner-city narcotics market in which he had tried so hard to be a charismatic overachiever.

Like his brother Tito, he was acutely aware of the structural forces propelling him to self-destruction. Terrified, as a high school dropout who had never held a legal job in his life, with a predicate felony record that extended back into his early adolescence, all he could do is blame himself for being "weak-minded":

> There's old-ass people in here with white hairs. And them niggas ain't changed. You really gotta be strong to change. And I ain't gonna hold [lie to] you, I'm kinda weak in my mind. I get sucked into doing dumb stuff.
>
>   'Cause it's like a chain reaction. You come home [from prison] and you go back right to the same thing. This lifestyle is just so addictive. Every little thing about it—especially when you got a corner. You just wake up and you got money. You walk around the block and your workers passin' you some money. Next thing you know [cocking his neck as if cradling a cell phone], "Yo, I'm done, come pick this money up." It's so easy. But it don't lead nowhere. Next thing you know you wind up killin' somebody 'cause he tried to kill you and you in this situation [shaking his shackles] ready to do more time. That's why I know I ain't gonna change if I come back to Philly.

THE DENSE POST-ADOLESCENT SOCIALITY OF INNER-CITY CONCRETE KILLING FIELDS

If being in prison was a scary prospect, being on the street was just as terrifying. On another one of our prison visits, Leo expressed ambivalent relief about having been incarcerated just in time to save his life, "If I wasn't in this predicament I probably would've got killed, not even knowing that they was looking for me to kill me." In an emotional confessional outpouring he described—barely stopping for breath—the dizzying details of multiple overlapping murders and threats of murder among his close-knit post-adolescent peer group of late teenage and early twenties wannabe-bichotes. They were trapped in the fickle camaraderie of his early childhood rider-relationships that were now embroiling them—sometimes inadvertently—into contradictory obligations for assistive violence across crisscrossing friendships that were polarized by ill-coordinated jockeying for fragile control of corners or derailed by momentary acts of jealous rage over jilted love.

It is impossible to keep track of the names of the victims and the perpetrators in Leo's account. Tellingly, despite their transition into early adulthood as bona-fide lethal gangsters, both the victims and the perpetrators still bear the affectionate diminutive baby boy nicknames bestowed on them by their mothers and grandmothers when they were adorable toddlers. It freezes in time an objective linguistic mark of the tragedy of growing up poor and

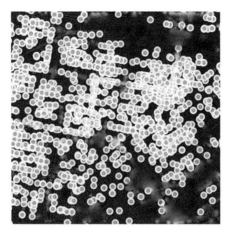

FIG. 1.2.   Firearm violence and injuries in the dozen square blocks surrounding our apartment, 2003–13.

too fast amidst guns, drugs, and chronic unemployment. What was often just a series of drug-addled impulsive or paranoid serendipitous miscommunications and petty squabbles became irrevocable acts of murder, turning the neighborhood into a killing field. Each shooting or insult traps a wider net of these sociable young men into obligations of solidary, rider violence. Figure 1.2 illustrates graphically the tragedy of easy access to unlicensed inexpensive automatic weapons in post-adolescent networks of small-time drug sellers such as Leo and his buddies.

Leo began with a story of a $50,000 contract that Gordo, an older, big-time supplier had put on his head when two kilos of coke "came up missing" from Gordo's garage. Gordo was a former boyfriend of Leo's mother, and Leo, as a child often ran errands for him. As an adult Leo sometimes passed by Gordo's house just to say hello and unfortunately one of those casual visits coincided with the timing of the stolen kilos.

Leo: But Gordo not my only problem. I was chillin' with Wiwi in his new car and we see my bols Dito and Nano in the Crown Vic [car]. Dito jump out, "Yo, let me get the gun, let me get the gun." Wiwi give him the ratchet, and Dito jump back into the car.

Twenty minutes later all you hear is bam, bam, bam, bam. And Dito come back around. He chillin', "Yeah, I just shot bitch-ass Lolo, because he wanna be smacking my baby mom. I hope that nigga die."

I'm like thinking, "Damn! You a vicious bol Dito. You crazy!" And that nigga look innocent as a motherfucker with his hazel eyes, but he got the devil in him, for real! Dito shot Lolo six times.

But Lolo didn't die and he didn't tell [the police] on Dito. He just walked in that bol's garage and shot him in front of everybody.

And Izzi too, that bol always be smilin'. He got big-ass teeth, just a funny lookin' goofy-ass nigga. But he one of the niggas that don't play either. He took his own man out on Somerset with a .357 [Magnum], and it wasn't over no bread, it was over some beef, "Oh, you tried to holler at my girl . . ."

They was walking and Izzi played cool with his bol and pulled back, and let his bol walk ahead of him. Now he's doin' life upstate. My other bol Litito got kilt over nothin' too. It was just the tension. . . . Words got thick.

Leo then proceeded to reenact a phone call he had received a week before his arrest from a close friend warning him that two of their other mutual friends were out to kill him. A few days earlier, bored, Leo had again gone cruising with a friend to pass the time of day. Unbeknownst to Leo, however, at that moment his friend was competing for control of a drug corner operated by several of Leo's other friends. When they saw Leo passing by in their rival's car they assumed he was in cahoots with their enemy:

Leo: [Imitating a gruff voice talking to him over the telephone] "Why you lookin' to kill Chinito?"

I'm like, "what you mean?"

[Gruff voice again], "Oh, then, why you runnin' around with a nigga that lookin' for my peoples?"

I told him, "What's up with that nut-ass shit! I didn't know nothin' about Chinito! Ya'll don't communicate. I didn't know ya'll niggas was goin' through shit. Next time, let a nigga know somethin' before I get shot for no reason!"

[Gruff voice again] "Alright. But Chinito's lookin' to kill you. And Lolo lookin' too. And I'm just keepin' it real, I was slidin' through your block every day 'cause I was tryna' check you out too."

George and Fernando, who were visiting Leo on this occasion, sat back in the uncomfortable plastic chairs of the jail's visiting room exhausted by the high stakes of trivial intrigue and the swirl of baby boy nicknames. They did not quite know how to respond, but Leo had only just begun. He poured out two more stories of horrific recent internecine shootings among his neighborhood friends. Despite his self-reflexive critique of the senselessness of "bein' kilt over nothin'—nut-ass shit," however, the primary lesson Leo drew from the kaleidoscope of deadly gun violence engulfing everyone around him was the need for

FIG. 1.3.

more fire power: "I don't wanna be caught slippin'. You can't let people think you sweet [weak]. That's why I was carrying my gun on me all day." The week before he shot his own worker for stealing his heroin stash, Leo had been staking out Gordo, "the bol who had put $50,000 on me": "I used to go to his girl's crib every night, strapped-up, ready to kill him. But he never showed up. I kept it on the tip [secret]. 'Cause if he know I know, he gonna be more of a fuckin' Jedi about killin' me first."

George shifted the conversation by asking Leo where he had obtained this last gun. This question opened the Pandora's box of the gun fetishism that seeps into adolescent masculine subjectivities in neighborhoods flooded with cheap, unlicensed, and very powerful and deadly automatic weapons. It is crucial to link this intimate account of what might look like sociopathic levels of deadly violence to political and economic forces: the predatory operations of the global firearms industry and the absence of functional gun control laws in the United States. Illegal firearms smuggling follows the same paths as illegal drugs except in the reverse direction, from north to south. The United States has the highest rate of gun ownership in the world. As we noted earlier, the colony of Puerto Rico is perfectly situated for the free flow of US-produced arms traffic to Latin America, saddling it with the tragic distinction of having the highest proportion of homicides committed by firearms (96 percent in the 2010s) of any

FIG. 1.4.

nation in the world simply because it is a conduit for legal and illegal trafficking of US small firearms coporations. Again, Leo's relationship to this propagation of corporately imposed firearm violence is profoundly embedded in peer group friendships and alliances.

Leo: I bought the jawn [weapon] off one of my homies. It was a big-ass chrome forty [.40 mm]. I put $300 and my bol Freddo put $300. We was sharin' it. It was real cheap 'cause somebody probably already done did something with it.

I'm a gun freak, I love them too much. Before this one, I had this shotgun that this bol had tossed on Allegheny Street when he was runnin' from the cops.

Later I sold it to Benny for like $80.

George: How do you get so many guns so easily?

Leo: I don't know. They just come to me. Like, [imitating a sales pitch] "Yo, I got a shotgun $100. Real cheap! . . . [Voice filling with energy] a nine [9mm] . . . a forty . . ."

And, I'm like [eyes lighting up], "I need that!"

George: You like guns too much.

Leo: [Nodding] I don't know why. I got to leave them alone . . . I had so many guns in the house, I'm surprised that my mom didn't just get rid of me [tears welling up and putting his head in his hands].

CONCLUSION: THE POLITICAL INFRASTRUCTURE OF VIOLENCE AND INCARCERATION

In the United States we often blame violent, addicted, or socially destructive behavior on the individuals who engage in it, framing such behaviors as "poor choices." Indeed, young men like Leo and Tito in North Philadelphia often blame themselves in just this way. From an anthropological perspective it is more accurate, and from a practical policy and political/humanitarian perspective, more productive, however, to situate these behaviors in the collective and historically situated context of what constrains the life chances of vulnerable individuals and pushes so many of them into self-harmful and community-destructive dead-ends. Unemployed Puerto Ricans living both on the island of Puerto Rico and in its colonial inner city diaspora are burdened with a politically imposed, disproportionately high level of suffering.

Specific ongoing dysfunctional state policies generate these extraordinary rates of firearm injury, interpersonal violence, addiction, mental and physical health disability, and "mass incarceration"—or more precisely what sociologist Loïc Wacquant and others now call "hyperincarceration"—of poor urban African Americans and Latinos that turn the United States into the nation with the most prisoners on the planet. Blatantly dysfunctional gun control policies in the United States flood inner streets with plentiful supplies of automatic weapons that sell for well below market rate and often well below their cost of production. The institutionally brutalizing effects of overcrowded carceral facilities turn rageful violence into a necessity for survival and self-respect. More complex, but not much less linear, is the way the war on drugs artificially elevates narcotics profits, raising the stakes of struggles over monopoly control of sales corners that have no legal means of mediation. This exacerbates the logic for expressive performance of violence.

The punitive law-enforcement response of zero-tolerance-to-drugs and racial profiling alienates residents by targeting addicts and local low-level street sellers in arbitrary sweeps that fail to protect the neighborhood's physical security. Ironically, the bichotes who successfully monopolize territory often metamorphose their brute force into what appears to be a virtuous power capable of maintaining a provisional order. Neighbors seek out their block's bichotes as the only available brokers to control the deadly collateral fallout of the violence that undergirds their narcotics profits. For ambitious young men like Tito and Leo in economically devastated neighborhoods, the classic immigrant's American Dream of upward mobility through intrepid entrepreneurship traps them into a destructive cycle of violence that they often insightfully condemn even as they reproduce it. Incarcerated as teenagers, many of them are determined to turn their lives around as twenty-something-year-olds, but they face formidable structural challenges:

Leo: I just don't want to go back to the same nut shit when I get home. Philly is like the fuckin' devil. I need to figure out a game plan to keep me away from the streets. I need to have a job before I get out of here. And I don't know how that's goin' to work. I ain't never had no job before.

ACKNOWLEDGMENTS

Research and alanysis was funded by National Institutes of Health grants: UL1TR001881, DA010164, AA020331, DA037820, DA038965. Portions of the ethnography and analysis were adapted from "Pax narcotica: Le marché de la drogue dans le ghetto portoricain de Philadelphie" *L'Homme* 219–20 (2016): 31–62; and "The Political and Emotional Economy of Violence in US Inner City Narcotics Markets," in *Ritual, Emotion, Violence: Studies on the Micro-Sociology of Randall Collins*, ed. Elliot Weininger, Annette Larean, and Omar Lizardo, 46–77 (London: Rougledge, 2019).

Photos 1.1 and 1.4 courtesy of George Karandinos.

Photo 1.3 courtesy of Fernando Montero.

SUGGESTIONS FOR FURTHER READING

Alexander, Michelle. 2010. *The New Jim Crow: Mass Incarceration in the Age of Colorblindness*. New York: New Press.

  Historical/legal analysis of contemporary mass incarceration and racism in the United States by a practicing civil rights advocate and litigator.

Bourdieu, Pierre. 2000. *Pascalian Meditations*. Translated by Richard Nice. Stanford, CA: Stanford University Press.

  Theoretical analysis by French social theorist of the reproduction of social inequality, including his most elaborate discussions of the useful concepts of cultural capital, symbolic violence, and habitus.

Bourgois, Philippe. 2003. *In Search of Respect: Selling Crack in El Barrio*. 2nd edition. New York: Cambridge University Press.

  Participant-observation ethnography among street-level crack dealers at the height of the US crack epidemic in East Harlem, New York City, foregrounding "US inner-city apartheid" and the impact of the political economy of de-industrialization as well as the colonization of Puerto Rico in the context of the rise of violence and the narcotics economy.

Contreras, Randol. 2013. *Stickup Kids: Race, Drugs, Violence, and the American Dream*. Berkeley: University of California Press.

Documents the lives of the author's childhood friends in the south Bronx as they become drug sellers and stick-up artists. Explores the brutal political economic as well as emotional forces constraining the lives of young men in the urban narcotics economy. Especially highly recommended.

Karandinos, George, Laurie Kain Hart, Fernando Montero Castrillo, and Philippe Bourgois. 2014. "The Moral Economy of Violence in the US Inner City." *Current Anthropology* 55 (1): 1–22.

Ethnographic presentation of the moral logics and structural forces that propel interpersonal violence in Philadelphia's Puerto Rican inner city.

Scheper-Hughes, Nancy, and Philippe Bourgois. 2004. "Introduction: Making Sense of Violence." In *Violence in War and Peace: An Anthology*, ed. Nancy Scheper-Hughes and Philippe Bourgois, 1–27. Oxford: Blackwell.

Introduction to theories of anthropological violence conceptualized as "the continuum of violence" that ranges from political economic structural inequality to corporeal violation and emotional suffering/trauma.

Wacquant, Loïc. 2010. "Class, Race, and Hyperincarceration in Revanchist America." *Daedalus* 139 (3): 74–90.

French sociologist's insightful analysis of the rise of the US carceral state in the historical context of institutional racism in the United States: From slavery to Jim Crow sharecropping to urban industrial and post-industrial ghettos.

CHAPTER 2

RELIGION

IT'S NOT WHAT IT USED TO BE

Susan Harding

To define is to repudiate some things and endorse others.
—Talal Asad

———————

Even though our definitions varied, anthropologists once had roughly the same sorts of things in mind when we spoke about "religion." Early in our history as a discipline, we used the term generally to refer to what was then known as "primitive religion," which included a diverse array of subtopics: animism, totemism, witchcraft, sorcery, magic, shamanism, myths, symbols, rituals, rites of passage, taboos, gods, spirits, ancestors, the afterlife: that is, any and all manner of beliefs and practices relating to the supernatural and/or the sacred in preliterate societies. After the 1960s, as we began to study more modern and complex societies, we gradually added a dozen or so "world religions" to our purview.

Many of us still use the term *religion* in this broadly encompassing way, if only for the convenience of relating to common-sense understandings, for example, when we are teaching an introductory course. However, over the past few decades the concept of "religion," as it has been understood in anthropology and related disciplines, has undergone a variety of critiques about the ways it was, and is, implicated in Western projects of domination. The anthropology of religion has responded to these critiques, but, in addition, new approaches to phenomena formerly known as "primitive religion" and to "world religions" have emerged, approaches that radically reconfigure our thinking about those phenomena, so much so that they cannot be integrated into the anthropology of religion as usual. The new approaches, which I will discuss here, are the anthropologies of ontology and secularism. First, however, I will say a little more about the events that motivated the critiques of "religion" in anthropology in the first place and how they reshaped the subfield of the anthropology of religion.

ANTHROPOLOGY OF RELIGION

A number of global transformations during the final decades of the twentieth century provoked anthropologists to rethink many of our basic concepts, religion among them. Escalating de-colonialization after World War II brought home anthropology's role in relation to colonialism. Though some anthropologists were already critics of colonialism, we began to realize how much our projects and concepts had lent themselves to colonial ends, and, indeed, how much our discipline arose out of the practice of colonial rule. We realized that we were speaking a "colonial discourse" that was integral to the apparatus of Western colonialism, and "religion" was one of its core concepts. Then, beginning in the 1970s, widespread religious resurgences around the world caught us, and most academics, by surprise, calling into question not only how we thought about religion in general but also how we understood the relationship of religion to history, economics, kinship, race, power, politics, and the state. Finally, the growing awareness of the global ecological crisis animated critiques of Western knowledge practices, both scientific and religious. If our knowledge practices were to be enlisted in finding solutions, we needed first to understand how they were part of the problem, for example, in the human-centric way they conceptualized nature and culture and the relationship between them.

The critique of anthropology as a colonial discourse opened up the anthropology of colonialism as a subfield, and among its topics was the role of religion, in particular, the role of Christianity, in European colonial and postcolonial projects around the world. Likewise, it opened up the roles of missionaries, and Christian missions in particular, as major topics within the anthropology of religion. In addition, the religious practices of local communities that anthropologists once studied as spontaneous and isolated expressions are now more likely to be examined in larger contexts, for example, in relation to complex political dynamics, capitalism, and, of course, missionary activity within the area under study. Anthropologists pioneered this new kind of work as early as the 1950s in studies of millenarian and revitalization movements. A few decades later, Michael Taussig's work in Andean highlands on capitalism, the devil, colonialism, and shamanism, as well as Jean and John Comaroff's work on British evangelical missionaries and the peoples of Southern Tswana in South Africa, established religion and colonialism as a major nexus of theoretical innovation within and beyond the discipline of anthropology.

The global religious resurgence in the later part of the twentieth century motivated and continues to motivate a reassessment of how we define religion and whether it makes sense to try to create a universal definition of religion. The default definition from the beginning of the discipline in the late nineteenth century to the present is belief-centered: religion, more or less, is defined as "belief in the supernatural." The terms may change—for example, to "ideas about ultimate reality"—but the presumption is that beliefs, whatever they are called, not facts, orient and motivate religious practices. Aside from undercutting the validity of what underlies religion, "belief," understood as a commitment to a creed, implicit or explicit, about the nature of ultimate reality, is a specifically Christian preoccupation, and thus to interrogate other practices in terms of that preoccupation is to remake them in the image of Christianity. Christianity as the model, or emblematic, religion is the outcome of the modern history of the concept, a history that is both theological and academic. The anthropological study of religion in preliterate societies emerged alongside the Euro-American "invention of world religions" as comparable traditions (composed of Christian-like components such as sacred texts, a founding figure, a supernatural realm, rites, and places of worship, as well as beliefs); and both intellectual projects, indirectly but powerfully, privileged science, Christianity, and European universalism.

With respect to introductory anthropology textbooks, conversations such as these within the anthropology of religion have not affected how "religion" is defined, but they have changed what gets discussed under the rubric "religion." Earlier textbooks focused most of their attention on preliterate religious practices, but now "world religions," though often in the form of local variations rather than ostensibly grand traditions, take up more, if not most, space in textbooks. In addition, the chapter or chapters on religion in anthropology textbooks now integrate into their discussions historical, economic, and political phenomena, such as missionaries; the effects of capitalism, socialism, and globalization; modern religious movements; religious diasporas; fusions of traditional and biomedical healing practices; secular rituals; social control; and violence. More advanced textbooks that focus only on the anthropology of religion have changed in similar ways, only more so, attending in some detail to the problems and politics of defining "religion" and proposing alternative definitions and conceptualizations. But the problems attendant with working under the universalizing rubric of religion have persisted enough to lead some anthropologists to develop alternative approaches to practices otherwise known as "religion."

ANTHROPOLOGY OF ONTOLOGY

The recent theoretical elaboration of "ontologies" has taken place outside the anthropology of religion literature. Anthropologists of ontology qualify the philosophical concept of ontology, which refers to the study of reality, by adding that "reality" is plural. The anthropological concept of ontology refers to a multiplicity of modes of existence, of worlds, that are enacted in and embodied through social practices. The anthropological literature on ontologies appears to cover some of the same ethnographic terrain as the anthropology of religion, namely, animism, shamanism, and myths, but it does not derive from, and only occasionally addresses itself to, that intellectual lineage. It situates itself instead in a philosophically inclined environmental anthropology as a critique of the West's concept of nature, the culture/nature dichotomy, and cultural relativism in Western science and epistemology. These are the primary conceptual targets of anthropological ontology, but, as we shall see, "religion" is implicitly targeted as well.

While anthropology has always been ontological in the sense of opening up "other realities," the discipline, like other modern academic disciplines, is grounded on a presumption that there is *in fact* only one real reality, namely, the natural, physical, material world. The "other realities" are cultural constructions. No matter how hard we try, we cannot make those "other realities" really real without risking our reputations because, as modern professional intellectuals, we have sworn an implicit oath to assume only one true reality that underlies them all. Hence, we end up undermining our ethnographically curated "other realities" by presenting them as socially constructed; they are always only ever versions of reality. It is this predicament that ontologists are trying to get out of, not by saying other versions are accurate representations of reality, but by turning our account—that is, that there is only one reality—into itself *a version of reality*. Ontologists make this intellectual move in order to make more room for other versions, the ones our version, in one way or another, marginalizes as "just culture."

Ontologists call the modern West's version of reality "naturalism." It is composed of a singular natural reality (mononaturalism) that is knowable accurately by science, and many cultural perspectives on nature (multiculturalism) that are representations of that reality. In order to break the West's intellectual monopoly on nature, ontologists have deliberately provincialized the West's naturalism. They have done so by "reinventing animism," not as culture or religion, but as ontology, and then have proposed "an animist critique of naturalism." Based largely on fieldwork among hunter/gatherer communities in the Amazon, they evoke an animist ontology that is "monoculturalist" and "multinaturalist." Spirit, soul, personhood, intentionality, subjectivity, and human culture itself in these communities are distributed among human and other-than-human persons. Humans recognize both themselves and animals as persons, and the animals recognize both themselves and humans as persons. Human and nonhuman interiority is shared (monoculture), and the species differ in the exteriorities (multinature). These are not beliefs or worldviews (terms that undercut their truth status); they are modes of existence and relating, ways of being and becoming, that instantiate distinct realities, hence the term *ontologies*.

Drawing on his own fieldwork among the Arawaté and on the work of many other ethnographers of Amazonian communities, Eduardo Viveiros de Castro describes their spiritually unified and corporeally diverse world and the shamans who mediate relations among species in predator/prey relationships. Each species is a "mere envelope (a 'clothing'), which conceals an internal human form, usually visible only to the eyes of the particular species itself and to certain trans-specific beings such as shamans." The body, the "clothing," is not merely an appearance that masks an essence, but is affectively endowed and activates the powers of the being, animal or human, it envelops. Thus, a shaman who puts on mask-clothing, say, the skin and teeth of a jaguar, assumes the identity, affects, and fierce capacities of the jaguar. "Shamanism is a cosmic diplomacy devoted to the translation between ontologically disparate points of view," and only shamans are able to desubjectivize, to neutralize the souls of, hunted animals so that they may be eaten safely. These aspects of Amazonian cosmology, Viveiros de Castro insists, are not cultural representations of reality. He wants us to understand them not as epistemology but as ontology, as ways Amazonians understand what counts as the world, that is, as what things really *are*. Rather than showing that Amazonians are humans "because they distinguish themselves from animals [as we do], we now have to recognize how *in*human *we* are for opposing humans to animals in a way [Amazonians] never did; for them nature and culture are part of the same sociocosmic field."

Although much of the ontological literature focuses on two ontologies, animism and naturalism, Philippe Descola recognizes other modes of human-nonhuman relationality and identifies different societies where one or another of these ontologies is foregrounded. He also suggests that the various ontologies are widely distributed, perhaps even universal, including in Western societies; however, they are differently valued and deployed in every society. Some ontological forms are marginalized or inhibited, and only one form gives "the scheme for which reality is perceived and acted upon." The prevailing ontology "isn't a representation or a construction. It's an *actualization* of properties against certain lines that are favored, or blocked, or inhibited according to the basic assumptions you make about the qualities of things, especially in regard to what [Descola calls] interiority and physicality." By way of example, Descola reports that when he gives public talks in Europe, "nice little old ladies" in the audience are not the least bit surprised by the notion that animals have souls. They say, "What's the big deal about animals having souls? My rose bush has a soul too." Descola concludes this is "a perfectly accepted notion in a way," but it's also blocked in the West. "It's never taken to its utmost consequences here" as it is elsewhere in the world, where "the idea that there might be some sort of interiority or intentionality, let's say, in the wider nonhuman realm" is commonly assumed.

The recent ontological conversation in and around anthropology is an avowedly ethical project. It would release the West from the grip of its nature/culture dualism and "make us over," enabling us "to pass through" barriers into other realities. By "becoming otherwise," we might generate a more "cosmopolitical" world that was more inhabitable for a wider variety of beings, both human and nonhuman. An ethical project, yes, but not one friendly to the concept "religion" because of that concept's inherent bias toward Christianity and other "great religions." Rather than trying to fit "ontologies" into the category of "religion," we might ask what religion looks like from the point of view of ontologies. "Religion," for anthropologists, is a form of culture, a social construction of reality, and thus another piece of the West's project of multiculturalism and mononaturalism. But Descola has gone still further, reimagining his framework of possible ontologies in "a quest for common ground" that would include world religions, not as religions, but as forms of ontology. His common ground is "figuration," "the public instantiation of an invisible quality through speech act or image." He would examine "the ontological pluralism of religious beings" (spirits, deities, ancestors, totems) and the different ways humans come to know them, proposing the study not of humans and their beliefs but of "the various populations of "incarnates" that peoples deal with when engaged in the kind of intercourse traditionally labeled as 'religious.'"

ANTHROPOLOGY OF SECULARISM

If the literature on ontology provincializes the concept of religion by ignoring or subsuming it and colonizing its territory, the recent anthropological literature on secularism, in response to both the critique of anthropology as a colonial discourse and the religious resurgences of the late twentieth century, shifts the analytic focus from religion to the practices and processes that define, transform, and regulate religion and religions in modern societies. Drawing on the work of the anthropologist Talal Asad and his collaborators, secularism in this literature does not refer to doctrines of separation of church and state or to unbelief but, instead, to the complex of political and legal practices, social conditions, and cultural presumptions that makes religion a recognizable social phenomenon and manages particular religions within modern nation-states. Religion and religions, both as concepts and as phenomena, are *inside secularism*, that is, inside state regimes that organize the religious and political order, not outside and opposed to them. Moreover, the establishment and the disestablishment of religion by states are relative terms, for in both cases — in states with and in states without an established religion — particular religions, as well as forms of a particular religion, are treated differently. The complex of laws, judicial rulings, policies, institutions, and ideologies that directly and indirectly govern religion within a nation-state establish the spectrum of religious normativity by privileging some religions and marginalizing others. In this context, "fundamentalist" religious resurgences (for example, among Protestants in the United States, Muslims in Egypt and Iran, Hindus in India, and Buddhists in Myanmar) are not atavistic outbreaks but efforts on the part of religious factions to renegotiate, in Elizabeth Hurd's words, "the most basic terms of the political and religious order" within a nation-state.

The broader secularism literature, which includes work in political theory, cultural, legal, and religious studies, history, and literature as well as anthropology, is grounded in an explicit critique of the concept of "religion," a critical history of the concept and the "invention" of "world religions," and a critique of the "secularization narrative," which predicted that religiosity and religion-as-a-civic-force would decline with the growth and spread of modern society. The literature includes a critique of anthropological notions of "religion," and the larger Euro-American discourse on religion and world religions. Until the early nineteenth century, European intellectuals used the term *religion* to describe only "true religion" — that is, Christianity, or belief in the Christian God — marking all other practices, including Judaism and Islam, as heresies or idolatry. Over the course of the nineteenth century "religion" was pluralized and came to include the three monotheistic Abrahamic religions of the West, still with a residual category of excluded others (heathens). Around the turn of the twentieth century, American as well as European intellectuals, now under the rubric of "world religions," added the traditions of Hinduism, Buddhism, Baha'i, and a half dozen or so other traditions to the list. Miscellaneous "others"—local, largely nontheistic and preliterate, traditions, the kinds that anthropologists studied most—were sorted into a still-residual, but no longer excluded, category labeled "other religions."

What at the time was presented and experienced as a process of discovery of "world religions" by missionaries, scholars, and (for lack of a better term) religious adventurers appears in retrospect to have been more a labor of social construction. They were not inventing "world religions" out of whole cloth, but they were selecting fragments of much more diverse, disjointed, and richly oral traditions so as to assemble something recognizable as a "world religion." These traditions, including Judaism and Islam, were made recognizable as religions by being made to resemble, as intellectual objects and, eventually, in social fact, Christianity. Euro-American world religionists, in collaboration with local religious intellectuals, identified sacred texts, a founding figure or figures, a clergy or priesthood of some sort, associated institutions, and, above all, beliefs, along with practices and rites motivated by those beliefs. Thus, Henry Steel Olcott, a cofounder of the American Theosophical Society, during his visit to Ceylon (Sri Lanka) in the 1880s, took it upon himself to write "a Buddhist catechism." He did so, in the words of Buddhist scholar Donald Lopez, on "an assumption deriving from the history of Christianity that religion is above all an interior state of assent to certain truths." Several decades later, another American Theosophist, Walter Evans-Wentz, chanced upon a text while traveling in the Himalayan mountains, asked a local English teacher to translate it, and published it as *The Tibetan Book of the Dead*, effectively converting it, according to Lopez, into the first and most famous Tibetan Buddhist "sacred text," even though it is "not really Tibetan, it is not really a book, and it is not really a book about death."

That the concept of "religion" is based on Christianity, which is centered on belief, has consequences beyond its mobilization as a model for the invention of world religions. Turning other peoples' lived traditions into beliefs also renders those traditions dispensable. As Talal Asad put it with regard to Islam, but in terms that can be applied to religion in general, and indeed to "culture," which is also a belief-centered concept: "The idea that people's historical experience is inessential to them, that it can be shed at will, makes it possible to argue more strongly for the Enlightenment's claim to universality: Muslims, as members of the abstract category 'humans,' can be assimilated or (as some recent theorists have put it) 'translated' into a global ('European') civilization once they have divested themselves of what many of them regard (mistakenly) as essential to themselves." This is one reason that Asad rejects all attempts to define "religion" in general, ostensibly universal but ultimately Christian-inflected, terms. Thus, for example, he and his collaborators have come to understand Islam as a heterogeneous discursive tradition in which piety is expressed not by adherence to a set of propositions or beliefs, but through everyday authoritative practices that cultivate pious sensibilities and dispositions that they regard as essential to themselves.

Anthropologists of secularism do not take religion and particular religions as their objects of study. They, along with scholars in related disciplines, focus instead on the complex of practices that define and evaluate *what counts as religious* within nation-states and are producing a growing literature on particular regimes and modes of secular rule. The secular regimes that coalesced with the emergence of modern nation-states vary enormously and have changed internally over time. This notion of "secularism" is not restricted to officially secular states, that is, states that do not have an official religion; it includes states with official religions, which also "regulate religion," official as well as unofficial. Regulation takes many forms: laws defining religious requirements for full citizenship or holding office, restricting blasphemy, and prohibiting particular religions or forms of religious expressions in public; institutions that train official clergy and administer public funds in support of certain religious buildings and practices; restrictions on, or the protection of, proselytization and the use of public space for religious purposes; policies that allow or prohibit religious control of or participation in public education; and literatures, technologies, civic institutions, and movements that challenge, sustain, or spread forms of religious normativity. The "regulation of religion" by governments is robust all along the spectrum from officially secular states to states with established religions and is amplified further by a raft of regulatory norms and myriad forms of social practice that, in effect, govern religion within a national society.

For the sake of illustration, let's look briefly at the two nation-states most renowned for their commitments to political doctrines of separation of church and state and of religion and politics, France and the United States, states in which one might expect to find very little or nothing resembling "the regulation of religion."

France traces its commitment to secularism to the French Revolution, culminating later in the 1905 law of separation that specified the official doctrines of French secularism, *laïcité*, as the separation of church and state, freedom of conscience, and "the absolute neutrality of the public and political realms." Mayanthi Fernando, whose work focuses on recent measures taken by the French state to manage "the Muslim presence," tells a different story, "one that takes *laïcité* as a sustained project of governmentality . . . , a story about the imbrication of religion and politics rather than their separation, about active state management rather than neutrality, and about the production and regulation of religious subjects rather than simply the guarantee of their freedom." During the nineteenth and twentieth centuries, church-state relations in France were reconfigured as Catholicism, Protestantism, and Judaism were brought into the administrative structure of the state via representative councils that would "help the state manage religious life." In addition, their legal and juridical arrangements and practices were subordinated to French law; and all three forms of diverse communal life were circumscribed into discrete, comparable entities, that is, into religions. The priority of Catholicism persists into the present through an array of special arrangements, for example, in the form of its holy days becoming public holidays; of state subsidies to private schools, most of which are Catholic; and of the public maintenance of religious buildings built before 1905, again, most of them Catholic.

In 2002, the French government created the French Council on the Muslim Religion as the representative body of Islam to help the state organize Muslim religious life. The inclusion of Islam was an outcome of a state campaign as well as a movement among Muslim activists, and its inclusion as a recognized religion was conditional. "After all," Fernando notes, "in order to be recognized, Islam must be recognizable — or made recognizable — as an acceptable religion." To make Islam an acceptable religion meant to secularize it, that is, "to turn it into a proper religion, one that restricts religiosity to the realm of belief, to private ritual practice, and to designated public spaces like mosques." Through a variety of government projects and regulations toward these ends, the state attempted to "disarticulate religion from culture and politics," in effect, to domesticate Islam. Fernando discusses an array of disciplinary techniques deployed by the French state to produce Islam as a proper religion and Muslims as proper (that is, secular in the sense of privately practicing) religious subjects. Among them are the ban on women wearing head scarves in spaces deemed public; the Institute for the Cultures of Islam, which works to create an *islam de France* by promoting cultural (that is, secular, not religious) activities as well as providing alternative prayer venues after street prayers were banned in 2011; and the establishment of the French Council on the Muslim Religion, which "seeks to cut the links between Muslim immigrants and their countries of origin, bringing Islam under the authority of the French state."

It is harder to think about secularism as "the regulation of religion by a nation-state" in the United States than it is in France (and many other countries), where one may look to specific central government agencies and a legacy of policies and law devoted to that project. The United States lacks both. Indeed, the notion that religion is not, and ought not to be, "regulated" in any way by government is widespread. Also, outside academic circles involved in re-thinking American "secularism," the meaning of that term is narrow and highly partisan: it refers either to the political doctrine of strict church-state separa-tionism (which opponents see as a program of state intervention in religion) or to "unbelief" (which opponents see as hostility toward religion and, in par-ticular, Christianity). A broader, more abstract, definition of secularism as, say, the processes that negotiate the basic terms of the political and religious order is perhaps more useful. This is so especially since throughout American his-tory those terms were being renegotiated at one or more levels and branches of government, in different parts of the country, and/or in the various forms of civil society governance in which both religion(s) and the state(s) have stakes: education; medicine and health care; family, sex, and gender; and race rela-tions. In effect this instability, this unruliness, is what the First Amendment's religion clauses, which enjoined the American government from establishing religion or prohibiting its free exercise, set in motion: a largely decentralized, nonbureaucratic, heterogeneous, fluid, and ultimately political (in the sense of its varying with who is elected and appointed to what governmental posts) regime of secular rule.

Until the 1940s, the religion clauses applied only to the federal government, which left church-state arrangements up to the various states and localities. Religion was, thus, diversely defined and organized: state and local govern-ments operated according to tacit definitions of what counted as "religion" and through myriad mechanisms (legal, governmental, social) that privileged some sorts of religions (Protestants) and marginalized religious others (Catholics, Jews, Mormons, Native Americans, "infidels"). During much of the nineteenth century, the effect of this decentralized regime of religious regulation was a "de facto Protestant civil establishment" in which white evangelical Protestants, in particular, flourished. The influence of evangelicalism was so pervasive that John Modern calls the antebellum religious-political order "evangelical secu-larism." Religion, as evangelicals understood it, was the outcome of conscious individual choice (not birth or obedience), and it was distinctly *not* private. White Protestant churches, ministers, and activists evangelized and organized frontier society; mobilized multiple social reform movements designed to cre-ate the nation in their (often conflicting) images; and infused popular literature and the curricula of the emerging systems of public education and private, de-nominationally affiliated colleges—that is, succeeding generations of Ameri-cans—with their particular "grammars of fear, desire, and expectation."

Pervasive, but not uniform, unitary, or uncontested. Alongside the de facto evangelical establishment, and accumulating force in certain places and over time, were contrary forces that would carry on the process of "disestablishment," of checking the power and influence of Protestantism, evangelical and otherwise, at the level of state and local governments, and in education and in civil society generally. Eight states had established churches when the Bill of Rights was ratified in 1789, and, by 1833, there were none. States and cities repealed blasphemy laws and religious requirements for public office. The Protestant grip on public school curricula and daily routines was lessened in some states and cities. Between the Civil War and World War I, institutions of higher education severed or curtailed their affiliations with religious institutions, and the emerging academic disciplines either purged themselves of theological concerns or translated them into nontheological language. The broad Protestant- and Republican-dominated national alliance that passed the Prohibition Amendment in 1918—perhaps the apogee of the evangelical establishment's power—broke up in the late 1920s. The nonevangelical parties in the alliance left the evangelicals behind and reassembled into a broader bipartisan and ecumenical alliance against "moralism" (specifically, evangelical moralism) in politics and repealed the Prohibition Amendment in 1933. Over the next half century, the federal government, along with many lower levels of government and institutions of civil society, including many religious ones, in some, but by no means all, parts of the country collectively engendered a political-religious order that was grounded in more a privatized notion of religion and a presumption that religion (specifically, evangelical moralism) and politics are, and ought to be, "separate." This regime of religious regulation has been called, simply, secularism or separationist secularism, but it could also be described as a de facto liberal Protestant (or liberal Protestant-Catholic-Jewish-science, still largely white) civil establishment, or, perhaps, "ecumenical secularism."

Whatever one calls it, this latter-day American secular regime did not entirely displace or replace earlier ways of experiencing "religion" and relating religion and politics. Indeed, it eventually motived a "religious resurgence" among partisans of the residual evangelical establishment and their newfound allies, especially conservative, or "traditional," Catholics. Seen as antimodern and separatist, these religionists sat out the mid-twentieth-century processes that secularized (privatized the religious expression of) their brethren, and they gradually assembled themselves into a national political force. Increasingly, from the 1960s on they objected to and resisted, more and less successfully, ecumenical reforms to public education curricula (such as teaching evolution and sex education) and daily routines (such as outlawing school prayer and Bible reading); reforms to local systems of race relations; and, most famously, a wide array of family, sex, and gender reforms, all of which, it could be argued, would further disestablish the de facto white conservative Christian political-religious order and modes of governance. The outcome of the past fifty years of heightened conflict over and renegotiation of the basic terms of the political-religious order is not settled. However, it is clear that efforts by the federal government, via the Supreme Court, to "separate church and state" have been stalled and in some cases turned back. According to the religious and legal scholar Winnifred Sullivan, the separation of church and state is now less often adjudicated by the Supreme Court than it is, once again, by partisan politics at federal, state, and local levels.

Perhaps the American nation-state has entered what will be a protracted and at times tumultuous period of dual sovereignty, in which both sorts of secularism, evangelical and ecumenical, govern and jockey for power and authority in different parts of the country, at different levels of government, and in different sectors of civil society. Or, perhaps, as some have said, pointing to recent Supreme Court decisions and legislative acts (such as the Religious Freedom Restoration Act), we've entered a new "accommodationist" regime of secularism in which the paramount concern is religious freedom and the accommodation of religion by governments wherever possible. Of course, not all religions, including no religion, are equal. It's a rough-and-tumble religious-political order in which some religions are better poised, or more inclined, to take advantage of the expanding raft of "religious accommodations"—court decisions, federal and state faith-based programs, aid and subsidies, expanded tax breaks, exemptions from workplace regulations, and other entitlements—and of "religious freedoms," such as religion-based exemptions for corporations as well as for individuals from regulations deemed offensive to their faith. Others might argue this is less a regime of accommodation than it is of proliferating entanglements. In any case, it's a recipe for dual (or multiple?) and endlessly dueling hegemonies of religious/political rule, yet another iteration of contemporary America's fractious body politic.

- Can cake seller refuse to sell to gay couple. I don't think so?

CONCLUSION

While these three anthropologies—of ontology, secularism, and religion— appear to share the turf of religion, the term *religion* has quite different, in some ways inimical, roles and resonances in each field. The anthropology of ontology is grounded in a critique of Western nature as constituting the one true reality, a critique that discounts all alternative realities as cultural (mis)representations, and it eschews the concept of religion insofar as it is implicated in this hegemonizing project. The anthropology of secularism begins with a critique of the religion concept, rejects the intellectual project of defining religion in universal terms, as if it were a natural object in the world, and focuses on the secularizing practices that produce religion as a concept and social form and that regulate religions, as well as on the traditions that resist those practices. To the extent that the anthropology of religion sees religion as a kind of culture and privileges a definition of religion centered on beliefs, it collaborates with both Western naturalism and secularizing practices. It will not be able to digest either of the other two anthropologies without rejecting its own conventional definition of religion and its de facto project of understanding practices called religious in ways that are ultimately compatible with Western presuppositions and hegemony.

The anthropologies of ontology and secularism have their own limitations. Both subfields reflect an awareness of the ways ontologies/religions are subject to and reflect dominant power arrangements, and they both discount cultural relativism and tolerance as modes of dealing with conflicts because those discourses are part and parcel of the apparatuses of knowledge and power that they are critiquing. But the anthropology of ontology stops short of analyzing the power arrangements that privilege some ontologies over others. Moreover, as critics have pointed out, its claim to have rendered its realities really real by theorizing them as ontologies is not entirely convincing, and indeed some of its renderings end up sounding too much like timeless, isolated wholes, that is, like the kind of cultures most anthropologists gave up theorizing long ago. The anthropology of secularism makes the analysis of the power arrangements that shape religion and religious life its primary focus, which, combined with its critique of Western assumptions and hegemony, has resulted in a remarkable and influential body of work regarding relations between relatively centralized nation-states and varieties of Islam. But its disavowal of universalizing concepts means that it does not present itself as a general approach to secularism or to other kinds of state/religion arrangements, so, in effect, it is at best an incitement to many anthropologies of secularism rather than a singular field that could contain them all. In addition, scholars of secularism confine their polities to human persons rather than pushing the boundaries of admissible beings in the way that ontologists have, and thus they risk reproducing the marginality of indigenous peoples and non-Western world religions whose relational worlds may include a lively variety of other-than-human persons.

Fortunately, in contemporary anthropology the borders between subfields are made for crossing. Recent works by James Bielo, Lucinda Ramberg, Eduardo Kohn, Marisol de la Cadena, and Anna Tsing, among others, transcend the limits of the subfields discussed here as well as of other lines of inquiry in and beyond anthropology. Terms such as "ontology," "cosmology," "tradition," "modes of existence," and "worlding" are being deployed theoretically in ways that loosen the grip of "religion" and make room for writing about a wider array of world-making practices, including those of science and Western naturalism. Such moves also open up more diverse relational worlds that are composed of other-than-human persons as well as humans. Finally, these approaches pre-sume agonistic modes of existence, admitting from the outset multiple, hetero-geneous, at times incommensurable, ways of being, becoming, relating, and negotiating. The term *religion* does not recognize the spirit or span of what's emerging in these new anthropological works. Political cosmologies or cosmo-politics might be better umbrella terms, but only as loose rubrics, not efforts to delimit a field of inquiry. The good news is that, in anthropology, religion is not what it used to be. And what it is becoming is multifarious, open-ended, and more finely attuned to the potentialities of other worlds, other beings, and other ways of being, both at home and abroad.

SUGGESTIONS FOR FURTHER READING

These references provide more background on, and alternative approaches to, recent developments in the anthropologies of religion and secularism: Michael Lambek, "Provincializing God: Provocations from the anthropology of reli-gion," in Hent de Vries, ed., *Religion beyond a Concept* (New York: Fordham University Press, 2008), and "Facing Religion, from Anthropology" http://aotcpress.com/articles/facing-religion-anthropology/. Fenella Cannell, "The Anthropology of Secularism." *Annual Review of Anthropology* 39 (2010): 85–100.

For further interventions in the "more-than-human" conversations going on in the social sciences and the humanities generally, see Richard Grusin, *The Nonhuman Turn* (Minneapolis: University of Minnesota Press, 2015).

Here are some additional ethnographies that deploy one or more of the ap-proaches discussed here: Susan Lepselter, *Resonance of Unseen Things* (Ann Arbor: University of Michigan Press, 2016); Saba Mahmood, *Religious Differ-ence in a Secular Age: A Minority Report* (Princeton, NJ: Princeton University Press, 2016); Amira Mittermaier, *Dreams That Matter: Egyptian Landscapes of the Imagination* (Berkeley: University of California Press, 2011); Stephan Palmié, *The Cooking of History: How Not to Study Afro-Cuban Religion* (Chicago: Univer-sity of Chicago Press, 2013); Aparecida Vilaça, *Praying and Preying: Christianity in Indigenous Amazonia* (Oakland: University of California Press, 2016).

REFERENCES

Asad, T. 2003. *Formations of the Secular: Christianity, Islam, Modernity*. Palo Alto, CA: Stan-ford University Press.
———. 2009a. *Genealogies of Religion: Discipline and Reasons of Power in Christianity and Islam*. Baltimore: Johns Hopkins University Press.

———. 2009b. "The Idea of an Anthropology of Islam." *Qui Parle* 17 (2): 1–30.

Bielo, J. 2015. *Anthropology of Religion*. London: Routledge.

Carrithers, M., M. Candea, K. Sykes, M. Holbraad, and S. Venkatesan, 2010. "Ontology Is Just Another Name for Culture." *Critique of Anthropology* 30 (2): 152–200.

Comaroff, J., and J. Comaroff. 1991. *Of Revelation and Revolution: Christianity, Colonialism, and Consciousness in South Africa*. Chicago: University of Chicago Press.

De la Cadena, M. 2015. *Earth Beings: Ecologies of Practice across Andean Worlds*. Durham, NC: Duke University Press.

Descola, P. 2013. "Presence, Attachment, Origin: Ontologies of Incarnates." In *A Companion to the Anthropology of Religion*, ed. Janice Broddy and Michael Lambek. Hoboken, NJ: Wiley-Blackwell.

Fernando, M. L. 2014. *The Republic Unsettled: Muslim French and the Contradictions of Secularism*. Durham, NC: Duke University Press.

Harding, S. 2000. *The Book of Jerry Falwell: Fundamentalist Language and Politics*. Princeton, NJ: Princeton University Press.

———. 2009. "American Protestant Moralism and the Secular Imagination: From Temperance to the Moral Majority." *Social Research* 76 (4): 1277–1306.

Henriques, D. 2006. "In God's Name: Religion Trumps Regulation as Legal Exemptions Grow." *New York Times*, October 8.

Holbraad, M. 2013. *The Relative Native: Essays on Indigenous Conceptual Worlds*. Preamble. By Eduardo Viveiros de Castro. HAU Books. https://www.haujournal.org/index.php/hau/article/view/hau3.3.032/455.

Holbraad, M., M. Pedersen, and E. Viveiros de Castro. 2014. "The Politics of Ontology: Anthropological Positions." *Cultural Anthropology* Website. https://culanth.org/fieldsights/462-the-politics-of-ontology-anthropological-positions.

Hurd, E. S. 2009. *The Politics of Secularism in International Relations*. Princeton, NJ: Princeton University Press.

Kohn, E. 2009. "A Conversation with Philippe Descola." *Tipití* 7 (2): 135–50.

———. 2013. *How Forests Think: Toward an Anthropology beyond the Human*. Berkeley: University of California Press.

———. 2015. "Anthropology of Ontologies." *Annual Review of Anthropology* 44:311–27.

Lambek, M. 2008. *A Reader in the Anthropology of Religion*. Malden, MA: Blackwell.

Latour, B. 2009. "Perspectivism: 'Type' or 'Bomb.'" *Anthropology Today* 25 (2): 1–2.

Lopez, D. S. 2008. "Belief." In *Critical Terms for Religious Studies*, ed. M. C. Taylor. Chicago: University of Chicago Press.

———. 2011. *The Tibetan Book of the Dead: A Biography*. Princeton, NJ: Princeton University Press.

Masuzawa, T. 2005. *The Invention of World Religions: Or, How European Universalism Was Preserved in the Language of Pluralism*. Chicago: University of Chicago Press.

Modern, J. L. 2011. *Secularism in Antebellum America*. Chicago: University of Chicago Press.

Ramberg, L. 2014. *Given to the Goddess: South Indian Devadasis and the Sexuality of Religion*. Durham, NC: Duke University Press.

Stengers, I. 2010. *Cosmopolitics I*. Minneapolis: University of Minnesota Press.

Sullivan, W. 2009. "We Are All Religious Now. Again." *Social Research* 76 (4): 1181–1198.

Taussig, M. 1986. *Shamanism, Colonialism, and the Wild Mana Study in Terror and Healing*. Chicago: University of Chicago Press.

Tsing, A. L. 2015. *The Mushroom at the End of the World: On the Possibility of Life in Capitalist Ruins*. Princeton, NJ: Princeton University Press.

Viveiros de Castro, E. 1998. "Cosmological Deixis and Amerindian Perspectivism." *Journal of the Royal Anthropological Institute* 4 (3): 469–88.

———. 2007. "The Crystal Forest: Notes on the Ontology of Amazonian Spirits." *Inner Asia* 9 (2): 153–72.

Viveiros de Castro, E. V. 2012. *Cosmological Perspectivism in Amazonia and Elsewhere*. HAU Books. https://haubooks.org/viewbook/masterclass1/cosmological_perspectivism.pdf.

CHAPTER 3

GENDER AND SEXUALITY

Sally Engle Merry

DEFINING GENDER

The difference between men and women has long seemed obvious. It is widely assumed that men and women differ in biological characteristics such as strength, size, and reproductive roles and that these differences affect behavior, such as men's capacity for leadership and decision making and women's for caretaking. Men are simply more rational, women more emotional. The idea that biological differences determine men and women's capacity for nurturance, aggressiveness, or violence was unquestioned.

Yet, anthropological perspectives on gender and sexuality challenge ideas that biology produces predictable differences in male and female behavior and temperament. Anthropological research shows that there is enormous variation in the way masculinity and femininity are understood in societies around the world. Moreover, it shows that biological differences do not determine what people do or what social positions they occupy. Men tend to be more powerful, not because of their biological characteristics, but because they control social institutions. It shows that gender is not a dichotomous category but a continuum. Individuals vary from those most identified with masculinity to those most committed to femininity in behavior and sexuality, with many in between. Anthropological research reveals how fluid gender really is in practice. At the same time, it shows how powerful ideas of gendered differences are in shaping what people do and in controlling their life chances. Gender inequality is pervasive around the globe, even though it takes many different forms.

The concept of gender has changed dramatically over the last forty years. Before the 1970s, most social scientists paid little attention to what women thought or did. In anthropology, for example, with some notable exceptions such as Margaret Mead, women were portrayed as part of the background or were neglected altogether. The first anthropologists to think about gender simply tried to talk to women and add them to the picture. Then they began to write studies of kinship in which women were agents rather than pawns and studies of politics that included women's struggles for power in the extended family.

Anthropologists who began to focus on women in the 1970s were primarily concerned with explaining women's universal subordination to men. One explanation was that women are culturally linked to nature and men to culture. Another was that women are subordinate because they are embedded in the family, the private sphere, while men are part of the public sphere of politics, jobs, and power. While these dichotomies were analytically useful, they were not universal. The nature/culture dichotomy was formed in the Enlightenment, while the private/public sphere was developed in nineteenth-century Europe. Anthropological studies of the diversity of women's and men's lives did not conform to these simple models. Women's subordination was less in small-scale hunter/gatherer societies and greater in societies where kinship was organized around a patrilineal descent group of men who brought in women as wives, for example. Some anthropologists searched for matriarchies—societies in which women exercised power—but found only myths that when women captured power they abused it and destroyed the society.

Feminist anthropologists have long sought to explain the widespread domination of men over women. Even though the distinction between the public sphere and the private sphere was a concept relevant only to modern society, deconstructing it was politically important to feminists. Women embedded in the private sphere were excluded from politics, power, and authority. Instead, they were situated in the protected sphere of the home and family where they were governed by men. This dichotomy justified the state's reluctance to intervene in the family, even in cases of violence. Understanding that men belong in the public sphere and women in the private sphere legitimated gender inequalities, an idea that feminists were eager to change.

Out of this intellectual ferment and political activism came several significant theoretical developments in anthropology and in social science more generally. Three theoretical insights are particularly important: the shift from sex to gender, from roles to performances, and from essentialized gender identities to intersectional ones. Each of these changes had a major impact on the way gender and sexuality are understood within contemporary anthropology. They show a progression from understanding gender and sexuality as biological and binary to a more complicated and culturally grounded analysis of gender as it is enacted in particular situations and contexts.

SEX TO GENDER

Anthropologists initially adopted the framework of sex roles and sex differences. Sex differences were understood to be rooted in biological features. Sex roles were expectations of behavior grounded in sex differences. As anthropologists looked more carefully at sex roles, however, it became clear that they were highly variable and were not based simply on biological differences. Instead, they were produced through social processes of learning and training that instilled ideas about what it means to be a man or a woman into each person's consciousness. Instead of referring to sex roles, anthropologists adopted the concept of gender to talk about the social dimensions of sex differences. This term expresses the idea that differences among men and women are primarily the product of cultural processes of learning and socialization rather than innate biological differences. Sex refers to genitalia while gender describes the social aspects of how men and women are expected to act. This term has now become international. For example, when the Chinese word for gender is translated back into English, it becomes "social gender."

However, even the concept of sex is less certain than this analysis suggests. A person's sex is also a product of cultural definition. For example, a study in Brazil of men who dress as women but work as male prostitutes suggests a very different division by sex than the conventional male/female divide based on genitalia. These men, referred to as *travesti*, enjoy anal penetration as a sexual experience. They seek to transform their bodies into a more feminine shape through hormones and silicone injections. When they have sex through anal penetration of other men, they are socially defined as men, and when they are penetrated by men, they are defined as not-men, as sharing gender with women. Similarly, effeminate gay men who enjoy anal penetration also acquire the identity of not-men, or women. Thus, in this context, the distinction between men and women, or more accurately between men and not-men, depends on the role a person plays in the sexual act, with the penetrator retaining a male identity and the penetrated taking on the not-men identity, or the gender of a woman. It is because they desire to be appealing as women that the *travesti* devote substantial energy to producing buttocks and female curves in their bodies, but they are clear that they are men, not women. Thus, not only is gender a culturally created and defined social position, but so also is sex. It cannot be seen as a clear biological category any more than gender.

Despite the Western assumption that sex is either male or female, anthropology shows that there are a wide variety of sexualities and forms of desire beyond exclusive heterosexuality. Nor do sex differences automatically determine gender identities. Some individuals are born with ambiguous sexual identities. Although they are typically assigned to the dominant cultural categories of male or female, some parents choose to raise their children as intersex individuals who are neither male nor female. They allow the child to choose its gendered identity at puberty. Although it is very difficult to grow up without being labeled as either male or female, there is a social movement to claim that intersex individuals have a human right to retain this identity. Sometimes a child is assigned to a gender at birth but comes to feel that he or she is in the wrong body. Some of the people who find themselves in bodies that differ from who they think they are decide to take on the opposite gender through dress and bodily performance, even to physically alter their bodies through sexual reassignment surgery. The transgendered person, either transman or transwoman, typically has a heterosexual relationship based on this identity. The term gender fluidity describes this situation of complex sexual and gendered identities.

ROLE TO PERFORMANCE

In a second development, anthropological theory shifted from role to performance. In the 1970s and earlier, anthropological research focused on exploring the discrete roles of women and men in every society. Roles were sets of expectations of behavior that evoked sanctions when individuals failed to conform. They were shared, expressed as norms, and relatively stable, although they were not necessarily always followed. Although societies differed in their sex roles, they shared an emphasis on the centrality of gender as the basis for the division of labor: the tasks each person was expected to do based on their identity. One study, for example, showed that all societies have a set of distinct male tasks and female tasks. Although they differ from society to society, there are some common patterns. Men tend to be responsible for tasks that require greater mobility and travel and are more dangerous, while women tend to have tasks that are more repetitive and closer to home such as food preparation and caretaking. The authors of this study described these patterns as differences in sex roles.

However, the concept of role proved too simple and static to describe the way gender operates in social situations. While it points to a set of expectations about how men and women should act, it does not account for what they actually do. It does not explain why people change the way they act depending on the context and those who are watching. Since the 1980s, anthropologists have theorized gender as a performance directed at some kind of audience. As a performance carried out in a particular situation, gender is expressed in different ways depending on the context. The same person can enact gender differently in front of different audiences, such as friends, families, or professors.

Gender is performed by tasks and activities. For example, a study of Chicana women in white-collar jobs in California argued that gender and race-ethnicity are not simply categorical statuses but accomplishments: identities produced through dynamic interaction and performance. As women do work, for example, they also "do gender." When their work activities are compatible with what they see as the essential nature of women, women can do work and gender harmoniously. Women in service jobs, for example, affirm themselves both as workers and as women. Employment in supportive service tasks enables them to do gender as they work. For these Chicana women, doing housework or child care allows them to accomplish both gender and race-ethnicity. Those who challenge traditional work patterns undermine their gender and culture-ethnic maintenance. Of course, the tendency to do work and to do gender in complementary ways maintains occupational segregation on the basis of gender and race as women seek jobs that reinforce the way they think about themselves and their membership in groups. At the same time, this process excludes them from the generally higher-paying jobs in which men do gender.

The connection between the performance of an identity and maintaining membership in a gender/raced group is a serious obstacle for those who wish to deviate from the norms of their gender and group. In the United States, women often have difficulty getting blue-collar jobs because they are thought to be unable to do "heavy" work. Male coworkers worry that women cannot pull their own weight in a work environment and that they will have to pick up the extra burden. Yet, blue-collar jobs in the trades, such as construction or car repair, typically are better paid than jobs open to women with similar training. A woman anthropologist decided to work as a car mechanic in California in order to explore the barriers that women face doing blue-collar work. Car repair seems to require strength, aggressiveness, and courage, traits associated with men but not women. Yet, the anthropologist discovered that many activities did not actually require strength. Heavy lifting was done with tools and hoists. Men often used physical strength when it was not necessary. For example, one woman riveted wheels to her heavy toolbox and towed it with a rope instead of carrying it. She noticed that some men gradually adopted this technique. When it was necessary to move tires from one part of the shop to the other, men would typically carry the tires, which are quite heavy, while women found it quite easy to roll them instead. The idea that strength was necessary was not always true.

The anthropologist also noticed that men showed they valued courage and risk taking by ignoring basic safety rules, such as using supports in addition to a jack when working under a car or detaching electrical wires when working on an engine. They often did not take the time to put on safety gear. While women would examine the problem before beginning work, men tended to rush into action, sometimes taking longer. They might use their strength to undo a bolt, breaking it off, rather than working more deliberately and effectively. Thus, the men are enacting an idea of gender as they do car repair work, seeing themselves as strong, courageous, and decisive. Yet, these are not essential to the work or even necessarily the best approach. Women appear to be unsuited to car repair work because these gendered qualities are culturally assumed to be necessary to be a productive worker. Risk taking and physical strength are not inherent to the work but reinforce the idea that this is men's work. Men carry heavy tool boxes not because it is necessary but because it shows that they are enacting male strength. Women have difficulty working in car repair shops because they are not doing gender at the same time as they work. Because car repair is a male gendered performance, women are usually excluded.

Doing violence can also be a way of doing gender. In many cases, men who control women through violence are seen to enact masculinity. Women who put up with violent assaults without complaint, and see it as deserved or inevitable, do femininity. But the woman who refuses to put up with male violence and takes her batterer to court risks defaulting on her female gender performance. She faces pressures from both his kin and her own. When a man uses violence against a partner whom he suspects of flirting with another man, he shows that he is a man who cannot be cuckolded, who is in control of his woman, who is a person of power and authority. When men batter women, they are performing masculinity not only for the woman but also for other men, who assess his masculinity by his performance. However, gender performances are refracted through race and class, so that notions of how to do masculinity in the face of a woman's apparent disobedience are shaped by racially and class-based cultural expectations. Masculinity is performed quite differently among young white street youth in the United States than it is among older middle-class African-American professionals, for example.

Through such performative expectations, women are also often excluded from positions of power and wealth. When employers in the United States seek to hire an executive, for example, they typically imagine the face of a white man, not that of a woman of color. Ideas about who fits into a particular role or job, based on gendered and racial performances, often operate consciously and unconsciously to exclude women on the basis of gender, color, and class. Such imaginaries are embedded in cultural conceptions and practices of gender and sexuality and can operate as habitual, unquestioned modes of thought. One of the projects of anthropology is to uncover such modes of thought and open them up to reconsideration and critique.

As theoretical work on gender developed in anthropology, it became clear that a dichotomous model of men and women was too simple. Research showed that male and female gender identities fall along a continuum from masculine to feminine. Some individuals are at either end, while many are closer to the middle. In some social situations, those in the middle face considerable pressure to conform to the ends, while those who refuse the terms of the continuum altogether and perform an ambiguous or ungendered identity such as an intersex one face sanctions and resistance. Those who change their gender performance, such as transmen or transwomen, often face hostility and sometimes violence. Analysis of the variations in the performance of gender from scholars working on queer identities played a critical role in moving anthropological theory toward a notion of gender that was not organized into binary roles but into fluid, variable performances. From the perspective of a performative model of gender, theories that assumed that differences between men and women were universal and biologically based were clearly inadequate.

ESSENTIALISM TO INTERSECTIONALITY

The third shift in anthropological theory about gender was from essentialism to intersectionality. Anthropologists labeled as essentialism modes of analysis that assumed that all males and all females had similar, biologically based identities. They critiqued this idea, arguing instead that a host of other identities based on race, class, ethnicity, nationality, disability, sexual orientation, and many other characteristics intersected with gender identities. Any notion that there is a single, stable identity of "woman" or "man" fails to recognize this diversity. Gender is shaped by the way it interacts with other identities such as race and class. The gendered identity of "woman" means something different for an upper-class urban educated secular wealthy white woman than it does for a poor, rural, evangelical Christian white woman living on welfare, for example. This is the intersectional model of gender.

Although this argument makes sense analytically since it recognizes the complexity and variability of women's life situations, it inhibits political orga-

nizing along gender lines. One strength of the 1970s and 1980s women's movement in the United States was its insistence that all woman share common problems, particularly that of male privilege and female subordination. While this
made good political sense, it ignored the diverse situations of women, particularly the differences between wealthy and poor women or white women and
women of color. It failed to consider intersectionality. For example, a major
issue in the women's movement of the 1950s and 1960s was women's inability
to work outside the home. But this was a middle-class woman's problem. Poor
women, single women, and many minority women had always done paid labor;
it was largely educated, middle-class white wives who were excluded. Thus, the
expectation that women should not work was not a universal problem but one
specific to women of a particular social class and marital status. Making claims
in the name of "women" obscured these differences and emphasized the demands of some women while ignoring those of others. For poor women, improved working conditions and better pay were more important than the right
to work at all.

The analysis of gender-based violence was similarly limited by a failure to
consider gender intersectionality. For example, the situation of a poor woman
being beaten by her husband is very different from that of an affluent woman
who has resources to escape the relationship. A woman with no income living
with a rich man is also imprisoned. A poor woman of color is especially disad-
vantaged in finding paths to escape violence and in seeking alternative housing
and forms of support. Moreover, she may hesitate to call the police for protection since it means turning a man of her community over to a criminal justice
system which she sees as oppressive and racially biased. As the number of incarcerated African American and Native American men mushrooms, women
partnered with these men find themselves reluctant to summon the police even
when they need protection from their violence. Immigrant women who are
battered face particular difficulties if their residence in the country depends on
their spouse. If they call the police or go to court, their partners may resist filing
the papers to make them legal residents. In the United States, despite some legal
protections for immigrant women who are victims of domestic violence, such
women are especially vulnerable. They may be socially isolated, lack the dominant language, and feel that their presence in the country is completely dependent on their partner's acceptance.

Clearly, women's situations vary significantly and seeing them as essentially
the same misses a great deal about each one. The early feminist movement in
the United States was largely white and middle-class, although some women of
color played critical roles in the antirape movement. In the last few decades, the
women's movement has developed a far more varied and nuanced understand-

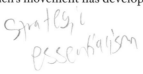

ing of the intersections among gender, race, and class. Anthropological theory has contributed to this rethinking.

Dismissing essentialism comes at a cost, however. One of the enduring challenges of the violence against women movement is the tension between the political benefits of seeing gender as an essentialized category versus the analytical value of an intersectional analysis of gender identities. The argument that all women are subordinated by gender-based violence is essentialist, yet it also fosters activism and support even by women who are not victimized. By defining violence as fundamental to the subordination of all women, violence against one woman becomes violence against all. Countering this violence is not just a matter of changing the life styles of the poor or alcoholics but of undoing the subordination of all women. This position was enormously effective for the battered women's movement in the 1980s and 1990s since it enabled activists to argue that battering is a problem for all women. Despite the political power of this position, it ignored the diversity of women's experiences with violence and the greater vulnerability of the poor. Women of color have increasingly argued that the battered women's movement is too focused on the situations of white women, and that approaches such as criminalization fail to take into account the very different life conditions of poor women of color. In other words, essentialism is both politically expedient and analytically flawed. A focus on essentialized "women" still prevails in international organizations such as the United Nations, however, because of its enduring political value.

GENDER-BASED VIOLENCE AND THE RESTRUCTURING OF MASCULINITY

In order to illustrate these three theoretical perspectives, the rest of this chapter presents an ethnographic study of a program for men who batter their partners. Batterer treatment programs seek to teach new conceptions of masculinity to men who are violent to their partners. They try to get men to behave with less violence by exploring their feelings and beliefs and encouraging them to analyze their own behavior. This description is based on my ethnographic research in the 1990s on Hilo, a small town in Hawai'i. The case study shows how a fluid, performative, intersectional conception of gender works to analyze a particular ethnographic situation.

Hilo is characterized by ethnic diversity, a plantation past, and contemporary poverty. Hawai'i was annexed to the U.S. in 1898 and remained a colony until statehood in 1959. Workers from all over the world were brought to the island to work on sugar plantations, but by the 1990s, the plantations were closing down, replaced by low-paid service jobs in tourism and agriculture, unemployment, and pockets of poverty. Many Native Hawaiians, displaced by US colonialism, have turned to subsistence strategies for survival. This is a post-plantation version of post-industrial society.

In Hilo, as in other American towns, the courts send most convicted batterers who stay with their partners to some form of counseling. Here, they are required to attend the program for six to eight months. Groups of ten to fifteen men meet weekly for two-hour discussions led by a male and a female facilitator. Men who fail to attend go to jail, at least in theory, although many are simply sent back to the program. The men attending this program are largely poor, unemployed, and uneducated. Both they and the women they batter are significantly poorer and less educated than the town's population overall. Many live on the fringes of the town's economy on their partners' welfare payments. Some camp in forests or on beaches and survive by hunting and fishing. They frequently talk about poverty, welfare, and survival by fishing, hunting, and odd construction jobs. They are often embittered by a colonial past and present poverty. Many suffer from emotional scars of childhood physical and sexual abuse. Three-quarters have had some experience with violence in their homes, either witnessing or experiencing abuse as children. Based on the stories they tell about their lives, many are afflicted with unmanageable rage, recurring difficulties with alcohol and drugs, and educational deficits. These are not the only people who batter, but they are the ones who end up in a court-mandated batterer intervention program.

The major focus of the batterer intervention program is the critique of male privilege and the reconstruction of masculinity. The program asserts that violence is learned behavior rather than psychopathology, thus focusing on the social and cultural determinants of violence rather than on the pathology of the individual. What is at stake in these classes is the definition of masculinity. The facilitators advocate a new image of masculinity, a more middle-class and egalitarian version that differs from that of most of the participants. The men are told that treating their partners with respect rather than violence will win them a more loving, trusting, and sexually fulfilling relationship and forge warmer relations with their children. Egalitarian gender relations are modeled by the male/female team of facilitators leading the group.

The men are taught a new vocabulary to express these new gender identities. Instead of calling the women in their lives "old ladies" or "cunts," they are told to refer to them as "partners." "Just a slap" becomes "physical abuse," and "battering" is expanded to include sexual violence, psychological battering, and the destruction of property and pets. The unfamiliar term *intimidation* (many asked for a definition of the word) is used to describe what they did when they smashed the windshield on their wife's car to prevent her from driving to town. "Male privilege" describes the assumption that men get to decide where women go, if they work, who their friends are, and that men need not consult their partners if they take drugs or buy themselves a new truck. After a few weeks in the program, men began to use these terms in conversation with each other, with me in interviews, and to judges in court. Attorneys and other court officials also noticed this new language, although they, along with program staff, were skeptical about how much it signaled a change in behavior.

In the group discussions, many of the men discuss how they use violence to hang on to their women. They constantly fear that their partners will abandon them for other men and are often vulnerable to jealousy and suspicion of the women they live with. They prevent their partners from leaving by puncturing their tires, stopping them from getting a job or visiting friends, and beating them if they go out without permission. When these men find that their wives fail to obey them or fight back in any kind of public setting, including the legal system, they feel humiliation and shame. When women do this, they spoil their performance of masculinity. At the same time, men sometimes report shame at their own battering behavior and acknowledge the loss of relationships with their partners and children.

The men describe their violence as part of their male identity. A Native Hawaiian in his twenties speaking the local pidgin, said that in the past, his idea was: "Be an asshole, be a jerk, bully—one of those macho guys, nobody can push you, act on impulse, be cruel—like I was to my nieces and nephews, make them afraid of me, my look. I don't want to do that anymore." Another man said, "Most men, when they're young, learn to be macho. Go into the service, learn to kill. It is hard to learn different."

By and large, this program adopts an essentialized view of gender. The men's curriculum refuses to see battering as a phenomenon of particular racial, class, or religious groups but views it as a universal product of patriarchy. The program articulates a uniform image of desirable masculine behavior: negotiated decisions between partners, equality, respectful language, and equal input into major decisions. Yet, this middle-class perspective is resisted by many of the participants. References to masculinity are a common aspect of group discussions but frequently differ from the model the facilitators are promoting. For example, a male facilitator suggested that the purpose of battering is to intimidate and punish partners, but a local part-Hawaiian man who works as a carpenter replied, "What do you do when you got no control? You gotta have control over your wife. Look, we gotta all pay taxes to the government. The wife and kids they gotta pay you too, gotta have respect, right?" Here the inescapable duty of paying taxes is equated to the duty of the wife to her husband.

This man says that the cause of battering is weakness. Later he observes that for him, male privilege is based on the Bible. "Woman is made as a helper. She helps you. God created man first and woman after. It's God's will. This is why we screwed up today—women are the king. When you go against God's will it gets screwed up."

Some men assert that violence is natural to men, even a source of pride and respect, and that women like it. The men talked about being a tough guy and having to keep the toughness up, not backing down, not being different from others. One man said, "She asked for it. She likes it. I need to prove I am a man." A young man said that his partner liked it when he gets angry and she asks for it. "I need to prove I am a man. Maybe she try to make me mad so she can tell you guys [directed to the facilitators]." He said his partner got mad because he was looking at girls, and she just slammed the door. If she hadn't slammed the door, he said, he wouldn't have hit her, but he did it to show her who is boss. One young man told a group that he thought women found macho men attractive. But going to the program is often seen as undermining this masculinity: "They say you are pussy-whipped." When told that the purpose of the program is to change beliefs, one man said, "We'll come home and say 'yes, dear.' And our wives will come here and say, What did you do to my husband?"

Men often present themselves as entitled to power because of their economic roles. "Women should stay home and take care of the house. Men are the breadwinners." Men talk a lot about the importance of having women at home when they come home from work, expecting them to have a dinner cooked and feeling frustrated and neglected if they don't, especially if they saw their mothers doing this for their fathers. Yet, the intake information from the program reveals that many of the women are supporting themselves by working or welfare and the men do not have significantly greater income. The men are often dependent on women for support. These images of legitimate violence reflect cultural ideals about gender identities.

For many men, violence is a justified reaction to woman's provocation and control. Her failure to obey him insults and humiliates the man so that he must assert his authority over her. One man asked the group, "Do you let your old lady go anywhere she wants? If so, you will be shamed." Men did not talk about their violence as discipline, but did describe it as a reaction to women's misbehavior and therefore justified. A middle-class white man said, "When I don't get angry like my father did, I feel I'm not doing right." Another said he beat his wife to show her he was angry and that "I'm the man."

Some men say they are not responsible for their violence because they cannot control their anger, reverting to a biological conception of gender that allows them to perform a violent masculinity with impunity. One man said that "it just came over me. I can't control my feelings, it just comes on me, don't know why. I do impulse things, snap fast." Another man said, "Before we learn this we never know nothing where all these things come from—actions, feelings—we just act, hit first." Some naturalize violence, drawing connections between physiological states (high blood pressure) and violence as a release of that pressure.

In the conversation about masculinity, some men resist the model presented by program staff by making jokes and saying things they know will be provocative to the facilitators, delighting and amusing the group. There is a good deal of joking and laughter in most group meetings as they play a more violent and sexualized masculinity to the group. The joking among the men refers obliquely to another cultural world in which this behavior is acceptable or, at least, is a way men bond together against women. The undercurrent of humor implies a different set of cultural assumptions about masculinity, not accepted in this group meeting but resonant in other spaces these men occupy. Sometimes one person becomes the center of these joking resistances, saying things the program leaders disapprove but eliciting laughter from the group. Clearly, they are performing a resistant conception of masculinity for the group audience. For example, a Portuguese man says he was drinking tequila and his wife didn't want him to drive, but he insisted and was weaving a little bit, at which all laughed. The female facilitator says, "This is dangerous; laughing minimizes it."

Some of those who last through the months of the program talk about changing conceptions of masculinity. One Native Hawaiian man, who lives in a camp on the beach and claims to be very tough, says, after a confrontation with a neighbor who made him angry, "I let this fucker live because of this class." He had a very violent past, but now thinks that the tough thing to do is to walk away from fights. "Before, I slap anyone who come in my face. Now I walk away, got the knowledge to walk away when I feel the tensions. I like that part." Another commented, "I never thought about all of this before—I never took it down. I just did things. And it is a matter of beliefs."

Masculinity is far more complicated than the vision which the program is trying to teach. In the face of its essentialized, uniform image, these men act out a subversive counterpoint of other ideas of masculinity, ideas which require obedience and respect from women and tolerate violence or yelling when they do not obey. Indeed, some men think women find this attractive. Masculinity is clearly defined intersectionally here, informed by men's ethnic identities and colonized histories. Yet, these men also recognize that this is a space where such violence is not acceptable, so they present themselves as different from other violent men in that their violence was minor and that the women deserved it. Or they say that they do not understand their feelings, they can't control them, and cannot stop themselves.

The stories they tell about their violence are clearly performances, directed to the facilitators and to the other men in the program. The facilitators present an idea of masculinity based on ideas of gender equality and respect, yet the participants counter with their own, subversive notions that women respect men who assert control over them through violence, that the violence is simply their response to women's provocations, and that they are in any case power- less to control their rage.

There is a class dimension to this change: the image of masculinity being advocated by the facilitators is that of the educated middle class while the group's resistance highlights the masculinity of the working class and the poor in this town. The different images of masculinity also draw from the history of class and ethnic resistance to white plantation managers' authority and con- trol. Humor and silence represent two potent modes of resistance to this recon- struction of masculinity. Yet, despite the obvious opposition of the participants, some of them find the discussions in this program appealing and welcome the possibility of a different masculinity that is more egalitarian and less violent.

CONCLUSIONS

Clearly, the men in these groups are performing a conception of masculinity for the group and the facilitators that is framed by class, ethnicity, and local histo- ries. Their performance of gender is shaped by particular contexts, such as the history of colonization, the plantation economy, and the contemporary absence of jobs. Here we see that gender is performed for audiences, that it appears natural, and that it is intersectional in the way it is defined by race, class, colo- nialism, and histories of violence. These linkages with race, class, and "local" identities render gender performances more resistant to change. The partici- pants joke and resist not just because they want to maintain male privilege but also to assert their ethnic and class identities.

Yet, at a moment of crisis such as being arrested for hitting a woman, gen- der ideologies can be opened up for reexamination. The encounter with the law as a result of actions that they consider normal male behavior, such as hitting women out of jealousy or driving drunk, sometimes disrupts gender identities. Although gender is typically taken for granted, at such moments it is subjected to questioning and debate. While these men resist the ideas of the facilitators, they are nevertheless willing from time to time to recognize alternative views and to reconsider their own. Clearly, the anthropology of gender and sexuality has moved far beyond biologically determined sex roles and developed a far more nuanced and fluid set of ideas that help to understand the way gender works in social life.

SUGGESTIONS FOR FURTHER READING

Abu-Lughod, Lila. 2013. *Do Muslim Women Need Saving?* Cambridge, MA: Harvard University Press.
> This is a useful anthropological critique of the Western-centric approach to reforming women's status.

Butler, Judith. 1990. *Gender Trouble: Feminism and the Subversion of Identity.* New York: Routledge.
> The fundamental text on defining gender as performance rather than as a feature of biology, it has transformed feminist theory.

Cohn, Carol. 2003. "Wars, Wimps, and Women: Talking Gender and Thinking War." Pp. 331–44, 1993, in *Masculinities: Interdisciplinary Readings,* ed. Mark Hussey. New Jersey: Prentice Hall, 2003.
> A wonderful example of the hidden use of gender ideology in everyday conversation.

Connell, R.W. 1995. *Masculinities.* Berkeley: University of California Press.
> An early effort to focus on the performance of masculinity, still less examined than femininity.

Crenshaw, Kimberle Williams. 1991. "Mapping the Margins: Intersectionality, Identity Politics, and Violence against Women of Color." *Stanford Law Review* 43 (6): 1241–1299.
> This article introduced the concept of intersectionality as a way of understanding the relationship between gendered identities and those based on race, class, and other factors.

Hodgson, Dorothy L., ed. 2011. *Gender and Culture at the Limit of Rights.* Philadelphia: University of Pennsylvania Press.
> This collection of articles examines gender ideologies and performances in a variety of countries through a human-rights perspective.

INCITE! Women of Color against Violence, eds. 2006. *The Color of Violence: The Incite! Anthology.* Boston: South End Press.
> As the movement against violence against women developed, there was concern that it focused only on the situation of white women, producing another intellectual movement focused on women of color, as represented in this book.

Kulick, Donald. 1999. "The Gender of Brazilian Transgendered Prostitutes." *American Anthropologist* 99 (3): 547–85.
> An important move to incorporate issues of sexuality and transgender identities into the analysis of gender.

Lewin, Ellen, and William L. Leap, eds. 2002. *Out in Theory: The Emergence of Lesbian and Gay Anthropology.* Champaign: University of Illinois Press.
> Traces the emergence of a LGBTI anthropological perspective.

Martin, Emily. 1991. "The Egg and the Sperm: How Science Has Constructed a Romance Based on Stereotypical Male-Female Roles." *Signs* 16 (3): 485–501.
> Fascinating analysis of the use of gendered metaphors to talk about the science of human reproduction.

Merry, Sally Engle. 2009. *Gender Violence: A Cultural Introduction.* London: Blackwell.
> A useful overview of the field of gender-based violence based on research on local movements and international human-rights efforts, including a discussion of the global movement against female genital cutting.

Rapp, Rayna. 1999. *Testing Women, Testing the Fetus: The Social Impact of Amniocentesis in America.* New York: Routledge.

An engaging analysis of the impact of identifying birth defects on women's reproductive experiences.

Smith, Andrea. 2005. *Conquest: Sexual Violence and American Indian Genocide*. Durham, NC: Duke University Press, 2015 reprint.

Smith provides an analysis of gender and violence focused on Native Americans.

CHAPTER 4

UNRAVELING RACE FOR THE TWENTY-FIRST CENTURY

Faye V. Harrison

Anthropological studies of race and racism in relation to the cultural, political, and economic forces that coconstruct them over historical time and geographical space have proliferated over the past few decades. In good part, the heightened interest is a response to intensifying racial tensions and identities in many parts of the world. In the history of humankind, race has come to be a significant dimension of positioning and power. As an ideologically charged distinction in social stratification, race is a culturally encoded social classification applied to people presumed to share common physical or biological traits. Racial categories have been used to mark purported natural differences even in contexts of relatively ostensible homogeneity. In such cases, racially designated populations are believed to share, at least in part, some socially salient ancestry and heritable characteristics construed to be of social consequence to the dominant social order.

Racially stratified societies vary in the extent to which socially salient ancestry, perceived appearance, and sociocultural status (e.g., education, income, wealth, religion)—along with varying combinations of these—are used as criteria for assigning race. Whenever race becomes salient, it operates in complex matrices of inequality and power shaped by interlocking axes of class, gender, sexuality, nationality, and sometimes even religion. Never an innocuous designation, race does not exist apart from the structural racism that (re)produces it. Racism is much more than prejudice, doctrine, or worldview, though these may be significant aspects of it. Racism is a nexus of material relations within which social and discursive practices perpetuate oppressive power relations between populations presumed to be essentially different. Racism involves whatever sentiments and actions that, intended or not, produce and sustain this oppression. A dehumanizing or more tacitly infrahumanizing force, it is a violation of human rights and human dignity.

SITUATED KNOWLEDGE AND EMBODIED EXPERIENCE OF RACE

As a sociocultural anthropologist, I have studied comparatively forms of social inequality in which race is a significant axis of power. The topic of race has proven to be particularly significant in my career. My ethnographic specialty area has been the Caribbean and the broader African diaspora. In settings such as these, where peoples of African descent predominate or figure prominently in pluriethnic and multiracial societies, sociocultural definitions and legal codifications of racial and related color and ethnic distinctions have historically played a major role in "naturalizing" starkly unequal and unjust distributions of wealth, power, and prestige over the past five centuries of colonial and now postcolonial or neocolonial order. This enduring global nexus of relations is constituted by what Peruvian sociologist Aníbal Quijano refers to as the "coloniality of power" which permeates capitalist modernity. Worldwide, this mode of domination has favored the interests, worldview, and structural location of strata of people descended mainly from West Europeans and their allies around the world. From the vantage points of subordinate segments of racially stratified societies (such as indigenous peoples and African descendants in the Americas), structured racial inequalities are often experienced as profoundly problematic assaults on their dignity, life chances, and human rights. However, race may also be experienced as an identity that is embraced and mobilized in everyday life as well as in more broadly based struggles for civil and human rights, socioeconomic mobility, and political empowerment.

In other contexts, race operates as an unmarked, taken-for-granted, and adamantly denied dimension of lived experience in which the injuries of racism are disguised and displaced upon more socially acknowledged and politically charged axes of difference such as class, ethnicity, or religion. Especially at a postcolonial, late modern juncture when flagrant forms of racism may have been widely discredited and their heinous consequences exposed, race is often the ugly, embarrassing undercurrent of ethnic conflicts that rises to the surface only when tensions explode. The language of difference in many such contexts deploys terms that emphasize fundamental cultural differences. These are cases of what scholars sometimes call cultural fundamentalism or cultural racism.

My decision to study anthropology as a university student and to become a professional anthropologist may well have been influenced by the profound impact of race and racism on my formative experiences as a US citizen of African descent. Stigmatized in an especially injurious manner, African origins and "blood" have symbolized to many Euro-Americans the social bottom and an ever-threatening contagion to an imagined white purity. The greater social salience of African heritage relative to my other ancestries is consistent with a sociocultural logic that anthropology has helped me understand. According to hypodescent, a culturally contingent mode of reckoning descent, individuals with sub-Saharan African heritage have historically been incorporated into the category to which their racially subordinated ancestors were assigned. This classificatory practice has historically relegated people of any publicly known African origins to more precarious life chances and structural locations.

As I reflect upon my lived experiences, I cannot escape the hard social fact that, like many of the ethnographic subjects whom anthropologists have investigated, I live a racially marked existence. The racial distinctions around which my natal community's collective life was organized and devalued, diminishing the extent to which black lives mattered, impelled me to think critically and comparatively about social and cultural differences. Being an inquisitive youngster who grew up during the era of "Jim Crow" segregation (or what is now sometimes called "American apartheid"), I was inspired by the civil rights movement and other progressive movements that overlapped with or followed it. I yearned to be able to think beyond the limits of folk theory and common sense. Moreover, I was eager to see and travel beyond the local, regional, and national boundaries that restricted most people's understanding, including that of my own family and the teachers who encouraged me to follow my dreams.

In my youth, my curiosity about race and racism prompted me to raise questions about how the United States fit into the larger world of human social and cultural diversity. Why had one of the most rigid systems of race relations developed in the United States? Do the so-called racial democracy and racial harmony that Brazilian and other Latin American societies tout really exist, and, if so, do they represent a model that US Americans or South Africans should emulate? I eventually learned that these kinds of questions as well as the many others I would come to ask are amenable to the kinds of inquiry that socio-cultural anthropologists undertake, which are modes of investigation that take ordinary people's voices and everyday lived experiences seriously as clues for interpretation and explanation.

HIGHLIGHTS FROM THE ORIGINS AND EVOLUTION OF RACE AS A CONCEPT AND PHENOMENON

The only race is the human race!

Ironically, while my youthful interrogation of race and the culturally and po-litically mediated processes of racialization may have led me to anthropology, the anthropology I encountered in the 1970s and 1980s was largely silent on the question of racial inequality and the ideological and material relations that constitute and sustain racism. However, a few anthropologists continued the tradition of antiracism that had been so much a part of the Boasian school of thought that informed prominent trends in the discipline during the first half of the twentieth century. Franz Boas and his associates and students (e.g., Ruth Benedict, Gene Weltfish, Melville Herskovits, Zora Neale Hurston, and Ashley Montagu) played a strategic part in dismantling scientific racism and defining the parameters for an antiracist mode of inquiry. Boas's work was probably informed by his experience as a German Jew, whose stigmatized "subracial" status was problematized by anti-Semitic folk ideologies that were eventually elevated by Nazism. The German anthropology of that time, which drew on the trajectory of scientific racism in the United States, played a key role in legiti-mating those unconscionable ideas.

In addition to Boasianism and its legacy, anthropological inquiry has also been influenced by other antiracist and anticolonial projects, particularly those advanced by such intellectuals of color as W. E. B. Du Bois, whose con-tributions have been too frequently unrecognized. Beyond the United States, racially subordinate intellectuals in other national and world contexts have also interrogated dominant discourses on race and racism in their societies and in the world. For example, in 1885 the Haitian ethnologist Antenor Firmin pub-lished a comprehensive critique of scientific racism, based on an alternative mode of evidence-based analysis in his *anthropologie positive*. Recent research on twentieth-century Brazil has documented an extensive trajectory of Afro-Brazilian social and political thought that interrogated the national ideology of racial democracy and offered an array of perspectives that were silenced. The sociopolitical climate created by more recent movements for racial jus-tice in Brazil and throughout Latin America has made it possible to reclaim this intellectual history and resist the epistemic violence and *epistemicide* that buried it. The racialized, gendered, and heteronormative biases of knowledge production and canon formation have been underscored especially in projects that antiracist feminists have undertaken to rescue the intellectual history (or "*her*stories") of Afro-descendant women in various parts of the Americas.

Just before I was introduced to anthropology as an undergraduate student, a vigorous debate on the biology and biologization of race occurred during the 1960s, perhaps paralleling and informed by the struggle against racial discrimination both in the United States and internationally. Due to its operational ambiguity, arbitrariness, artificiality, and erroneous and harmful assumptions, the concept of race declined in usage in both biological and cultural anthropologies. Intense debates over race's scientific status led many anthropologists to adopt a "no-race" position. To rid the field of its biological determinist baggage, many anthropologists jettisoned any notion of race, embracing the culture-centered concepts of ethnicity and ethnic group as alternatives. Unwittingly, this turn inhibited much-needed interrogations of racism. It took decades to close that problematic gap.

Many biological anthropologists attempted to make a conceptual shift away from species and sub-species thinking to clinal or cline-based approaches (which examine cross-cutting gradients of populations varying in gene frequencies). However, a sizable minority of physical anthropologists continued to use the race concept in relatively uncritical ways. A fuller break from the legacy of scientific racism has been blocked by formidable societal influences. For example, neoconservative foundations such as the Pioneer Fund encourage research that demonstrates genetic determinants for academic achievement (notably IQ), upward mobility, and violent crime. Also corporate interests have shaped the outcome of some pharmaceutical research and promoted the creation of racially specific markets. In criminal justice, immigration control, and the war on terrorism, the US state increasingly relies on technologies of genetic surveillance to predict probable suspects on the basis of race, as it has come to be recoded in terms of DNA, the results of whose testing are more fallible than typically assumed. The normalization and legitimacy of these trends are now being questioned by anthropologists, including critical biological anthropologists, attentive to power dynamics and struggles over conflicting interpretations and interests in the application of scientific and technological innovations in society. Drawing on elements of human variation studies and sociocultural anthropological perspectives on the racialization of difference, critical biological anthropologists are helping to produce a new synthesis that permits investigations of the interplay of biology, culture, power, and race that transcend the limits of earlier kinds of reductionist, binary thinking.

By the mid-1990s, the social and intellectual construction of race and the dynamics of racism reemerged as major interests in anthropological analysis. A growing body of work illuminated how race operates as a dimension of socially defined difference intersecting with ethnicity along with other axes of inequality and power. Anthropologists and other social scientists documented how race encodes social and cultural differences presumed to be unbridgeable and unchanging and how this encoding has pathological effects on the dominant national body. Ethnicity and race have come to be thought of as interrelated but distinct dimensions of identity formation, and, depending on the context, one dimension can modify or take precedence over the other. More anthropologists now realize that, despite the state of considerable biological knowledge disproving the notion of natural races, racism as an oppressive, discriminatory force of structural inequality and power remains prevalent and persistent with the resilient capacity to alter and disguise its form in response to changing social, political, and economic conditions. Moreover, owing to contributions from critical biocultural research, we also know that racism is a major environmental stressor whose embodiment results in health disparities that negatively impact the lives of biopolitical subjects. Consequently, the reality of living with and against racism has a significant biological dimension, which is something that sociocultural anthropologists, especially medical anthropologists, can no longer ignore. This approach is qualitatively different, however, from biodeterminist thinking.

Many anthropologists and historians have argued that race and racism are not transhistorical phenomena existing in all societies and cultures at all times. Rather, they arose in the historically specific context of Western colonial expansion, world capitalist development, and the resultant form of modernity. While racism in one form or another assumes nearly global proportions today, these far-reaching perimeters derive largely from the roots and routes of global capitalism's tumultuous history. This is not to say that ideas and prejudices about physical differences were insignificant before the rise of the transatlantic slave trade and the historically unprecedented racial slavery that emerged in the hemisphere that Europeans mapped as the New World. Evidence suggests that folk classifications stereotyping physical traits existed in some precolonial societies. However, it seems that those categories were largely local and particularistic in their significance and impact, not operating in contexts of sustained racial stratification. With the emergence and consolidation of colonial empires and the modern world-system, the salience and scope of classification systems based on phenotype or appearance grew, changing into global racial taxonomies with concrete implications for denying the humanity of whole segments of the world's population. At that juncture in world history and human social development, prejudice based on phenotype or color (as a metonym) came to be institutionalized through its convergence with slavery and the formal elaboration of ideas by intellectuals, particularly scientists, who accounted for social differences in terms of inherent biophysical differences. Racial classifications have reflected the political processes that alienated populations of whole continents from their lands and transformed them into a supply of coerced labor. Contemporary racial categories continue to index the histories of those colonially subjugated populations and deny their descendants access to the more privileged and secure segments of the labor market as well as to higher levels of organizational and structural power.

RACE RECONFIGURED IN CONTEMPORARY GLOBAL RESTRUCTURING

Many scholars have observed that during current conditions of globalization human societies are becoming more tightly integrated into a nexus of intercultural and transnational fields of power, knowledge, and commodification. Advanced telecommunications, the increased mobility of capital and labor, and rapid flows of culture and commodities compress time and space across an uneven political and economic geography, giving the impression that, in some respects, the world is becoming smaller and more accessible. The world as "global village," however, is not set against an idyllic background. Unlike the principles of reciprocity and redistribution which may have played a major part in governing everyday life in the typical village of the ethnographic record, the global community is marked by a decentralization of capital accumulation and an upward reconcentration of wealth in the hands of a few. Within this global community we also find a heightening of differences and a deepening of identity politics, often along life-threatening lines of conflict. In many instances, these volatile lines of differentiation relate to shifting dynamics of race as they interact with and mediate those of class, ethnicity, nationality, and gender. Beyond the implications of deepening class disparities, the contemporary reconcentration of wealth intensifies patterns of racialization, which play a major role in shaping global dynamics. Along with the global system's logic of uneven and unequal economic restructuring, there is a tendency toward cultural fragmentation and its effects on identity. Manifested in this process is the weakening of national identities and the emergence of new ones based on ethnic, racial, language, and religious differences and loyalties. Movements based on these distinctions have increased all over the world in both the global north and south.

Racial meanings and practices are fluctuating and contradictory. They range in visibility from subtle, hidden subtexts to flagrant acts of hate speech and genocidal violence. Racial tensions are not at all confined to racial orders like the United States and South Africa, in which the most blatant forms of racial formation have developed in contexts of white supremacy. As studies of inter-group tensions in Fiji, Sri Lanka, and Rwanda reveal, racialization, the social processes that give rise to new racial identities or the transformation of old ones, is not limited to societies structured around the (immediate) dominance of populations socially defined as white. While in the overall global scheme of things, whiteness in its cross-cultural varieties has certainly come to be a prin-cipal locus of domination, there are other racisms that ultimately feed into the structural power of whiteness, its privileges, and its accompanying Euro-centric way of life. Sustained and promoted by what Arturo Escobar describes as "global coloniality" or "imperial globality," white privilege does not simply refer to the advantages of people with white phenotypes. More significant is the promotion of a way of life and the structures of power that undergird it. These structures privilege elites and middle classes around the world who defend the values and interests of Western modernity at the expense of the vast majority of the world's peoples. Escobar claims that one of the most injurious features of coloniality and modernity in many parts of the world, Latin America included, is antiblack racism. The racial and ethnic dynamics of indigenous struggles are interrelated and warrant being addressed in the context of mutually constitu-tive structures of alterity.

Some researchers invoke the concept of "global apartheid" to characterize the troubling gaps in wealth, power, military control, and life expectancy that are widening as neoliberal logics of global restructuring proceed. This state of affairs implicates multiple axes of difference and inequality and unleashes con-siderable structural violence. Structural violence disproportionately assaults impoverished people in the southern hemisphere, where material relations and processes, which also produce uneven and unequal development in the "north," are most concentrated. For the most part, those most adversely affected are people whose subordinate positions within international fields of power and political economy have historically been rationalized in terms of class and na-tion as well as race. Howard Winant observes that even at this historical junc-ture, virtually all over the world darker skin tones still correlate with the brunt of social inequality and structural violence.

Despite racialization's global reach, there is no overarching uniformity in racial formation. Anthropologists, with their multisited and multifocal research orientation, contribute a great deal to our understanding of the diversity of racial formations as they have unfolded historically and are still being recon-figured around the world today according to logics of neoliberal globalization.

MAKING ASIAN TRENDS VISIBLE

Since much of the scholarship on race and racism colors racial domination white, correlating it with European descent, it is important to signal the role that some categories of nonwhites have played in racializing the international division of labor. For instance, Aihwa Ong's classic ethnographic accounts of female industrial workers in Malaysia implicate Japanese economic interests in helping to create conditions under which women in the global south have become model racialized subjects within a new colonial frontier for capital accumulation. Anthropologists have observed the relatively liminal location located between the "Civilized White" and the "Barbarous Black" that the Japanese occupy in the global racial hierarchy. During the apartheid period in South Africa, Japanese visitors and migrants were classified as "honorary whites" while Chinese were assigned to the "colored" category, reflecting China's "Third World" position in the global hierarchy at that time. Symbolically aligning themselves with whiteness and what it represents in terms of wealth, power, cultural capital, and racial superiority, sectors of the Japanese mainstream denigrate the black Other in popular or mass culture. John Russell argues that the bias against blackness is clearly exhibited in depictions of figures in blackface. Even former President Obama was caricatured in "Barackface."

On a different note, Dawn-Elissa Fischer's research shows how elements of Japanese youth subculture express a considerably different view of racial alterity. In Japanese hip hop, the narrative strategies, tropes, and symbols of blackness are deployed to "flip the script" on Western hegemony, white supremacy, and Japanese state ideology promoting homogenized constructions of Japanese identity. The actors in this vibrant sphere of popular cultural production are heterogeneous and include mixed heritage Japanese, *hafu*. They perform black tropes to contest the racial subordination of Koreans, Chinese, Filipinos, ethnic hybrids, and other stigmatized segments of Japanese society, such as the indigenous Ainu and the Burakumin. Hip hop has provided a receptive counterpublic space for revitalizing these disparaged minorities' identities at a moment when, as Yasuko Takezawa observes, racialization is being exacerbated with the deepening of neoliberal conditions. Buraku-identified persons comprise a stigmatized outcaste traditionally employed in occupations considered impure and tied to death—executioners, morticians, butchers, slaughterhouse workers, street cleaners, and leather workers or tanners. Takezawa explains that popular beliefs have held that Buraku blood lines are polluted. Out of fear of discrimination and, in the worst cases, fear for their lives, many Buraku have changed their names, hidden their origins, and "passed" into the mainstream. In 2012 a scandal erupted when the family background of a mayoral candidate in Osaka City was exposed in the media.

In an era of racism without races, purported racial differences among ethnically and socially diverse people who cannot actually be distinguished by physical criteria are (re)produced through nonvisual modes of representation that emphasize multisensorial perceptions of how radically different these particular racialized Others supposedly sound, smell, and feel upon touch, which is to be avoided. The Ainu and Burakumin, who often live and work in economically marginal circumstances, are reputed to be filthy and foul-smelling, as though these descriptors are intrinsic to their identity. Fortunately, these prejudices are not uniformly shared within Japanese society. This is reflected in the outcome of the 2012 Osaka mayoral race, which the Buraku candidate won with the help of campaigners and electors committed to equality and social justice.

The western side of Asia is also of interest. Smadar Lavie has boldly interrogated the racialization that Mizrahi Jews face in Israel. The Mizrahi population, with origins in western Asia and northern Africa, comprises the majority of the Israeli citizenry. According to her feminist ethnography, working poor and often welfare-dependent Mizrahi single mothers have confronted the state's bureaucratic torture and drastic retrenchment of welfare benefits in protests against Israel's intersectional injustices, which she conceptualizes in terms of "GendeRace." Her analysis revolves largely around the mass protests that Vicky Knafo catalyzed when she wrapped an Israel flag around herself and marched 205 kilometers to Jerusalem from Mitzpe Ramon, a remote desert town. Her pilgrimage and subsequent encampment across from the capitol attracted many other protesters and media attention along the way. Lavie argues that despite mass political protests such as that associated with the nearly month-long "Knafoland," the agency of Mizrahi women in opposing intra-Jewish oppression has been constrained. The Ashkenazi-controlled state's mobilization of a divine cosmology legitimates its policies and practices, and Jewish unity is enforced by censoring and repressing dissent.

GLOBAL AFRICAN LANDSCAPES

The continent of Africa figured prominently in the history of European colonial expansion and the rise of the modern world system. Processes of racial formation were integral to conquest and the colossal abduction and transoceanic enslavement of Africans. The focus of most historical and anthropological inquiry has been on the transatlantic reach of the African experience into the Western Hemisphere; however, more recently, attention on the trans–Indian Ocean diaspora has grown considerably.

Although not the only motor force, slavery drove much of the dispersion of

East Africans (from the Horn of Africa to Mozambique and Madagascar) across the Indian Ocean to a multiplicity of island and mainland destinations. The Red and Arabian seas were also important waterscapes and trade routes in the formation of the Old World African diaspora. For many centuries, this sphere of the slave trade was dominated by Arab merchants, with Indians playing a lesser role. By the late seventeenth and early eighteenth centuries, European agents (French, Portuguese, British) had grown more significant. Kwesi Prah argues that the magnitude and severity of Arab-controlled slavery in various "Afro-Arab borderlands" persist today with the unlawful capture and enslavement of black bodies in places like Mauritania and Sudan. United Nations–facilitated discussions on racial slavery as a crime against humanity still emphasize the transatlantic world of the past, neglecting other histories and contemporary trajectories of imperial expansion and exploitation.

Not surprisingly, studies of post-apartheid South Africa have been a major focus in Africanist studies of racism. Anthropologists are interested in the post-conflict transition and reconciliation process, reconfigurations of citizenship across racial, ethnic, and class divides, as well as the transformation of ethnic/racial identities and the terms of belonging. For example, the Griqua, a multi-heritage Khoekhoe and Khoe-San rural population classified as "colored" under apartheid, have remade themselves as indigenous in recent phases of their long-standing struggle for land and autonomy. In another context, colored and Afri-kaner farmers compete in their respective claims to indigenous identity. They are rivals in the attempt to secure control over the production of rooibos tea and the cultural ownership of it as a traditional use value that is now an important commodity. The meanings of the rooibos plant have long been tied to a historically deep landscape whose political ecology is currently threatened by climate change and troubling intergroup relations. *caused by colonialism*

Beyond South Africa, the rest of the continent has received little attention in the study of race and racism. The assumption has been that racelessness has prevailed since the end of the colonial period in largely racially homogeneous societies. However, Jemima Pierre reveals that the politics and political economy of race have been integral both to African countries' colonial existence and to their postcolonial development. Popular meanings of whiteness, the common preference for lighter complexions, the prevalence of skin bleaching practices (much to the detriment of public health), and, in the context of Ghana in particular, the government's promotion of political and cultural Pan-Africanism since the early independence period. In more recent decades, Ghana has promoted a form of heritage tourism and expressions of cosmopolitan blackness that attract visitors and ex-patriots from the African diaspora in the Americas and Europe.

Kristin Löftsdottir's perspective on development in the lives of the WoDaaBe Fulani pastoralists in Niger reveals a somewhat complementary view of racialization. In light of the overlap between global processes and race making, international development is a key site where the meanings and representations of whiteness are engendered and reproduced. Through development's lived practices, cross-cultural encounters, and visual representations, historical memories of colonial racialization are reinvested, and new racialized identities are constructed. These processes operate via the mobility of people, commodities, and images as well as the ideas and desires appropriated within local contexts.

NEW IMMIGRANTS, REFUGEES, AND ESTRANGED CITIZENS IN EUROPE AND NORTH AMERICA

Under conditions of postcoloniality and the post–Cold War era, once-established cultural relations, boundaries, and distances are being disrupted and renegotiated. Extensive economic restructuring, political realignments, and policy shifts in the North and South are rendering race making and race relations a more volatile front of power and cultural struggle. In the increasingly multicultural nation-states of the North, the meanings and practices of contemporary forms of racism are being used to mobilize xenophobic attacks against immigrants, refugees, and asylum seekers. Across Europe and North America (notably the United States), immigrants, especially "visible immigrants" from parts of the developing world, have come to represent destabilizing and parasitic ethno-racial outsiders, whose place within the host countries has grown more tenuous. This precarity, in both political and economic terms, has been deepened by the current refugee crisis in Europe.

The extent to which everyday reactions to immigrants, particularly from Africa and the Middle East, are perceived as threatening and are subjected to racist backlash has varied across national boundaries and across intranational regions with divergent patterns of economic development, modes of political organization, and histories of migration. However, since September 11, 2001 (9/11), in the aftermath of Al Qaeda's terrorist attacks on the United States, along with subsequent acts of terror in Europe, Islamophobia has grown. Both government and popular anxieties around "homeland security" and "terror" have given rise to a sociopolitical climate that has made Arabs and Muslims, both immigrants and long-standing non-immigrant citizens, susceptible to racial profiling, immigration monitoring, and hate crimes. In the most conservative public discourse, the Islamic religion has been conflated with radical Islamist ideology and terror. Within this context, the US government administration, via a controversial 2017 executive order, imposed a "Muslim ban" on travel from six predominantly Muslim countries (Syria, Iran, Yemen, Libya, Somalia, and Sudan). Panic responses to the perceived Muslim threat has resulted in the consolidation of a "terror-industrial complex" whose infrastructure encodes the racialized culpability and scapegoating of Muslims, particularly those with origins in the Middle East and South Asia.

The terror-industrial complex is tied to two other sectors of the US penal system: the immigrant detention complex and the prison industrial complex. These three interlocking domains disproportionately target different segments of racially stratified US society, both immigrant and minoritized racial subordinates who have been cast outside the boundary of national belonging despite their formal citizenship status. The mechanisms of surveillance, punishment, and violence operative across these spheres are transnational in scope, mediated through an alliance between states and corporations, to which carceral functions are outsourced. Businesses such as the Corrections Corporation of America and the Wackenhut Corrections Corporations manage for profit prisons in the United States, United Kingdom, and Australia. A wide spectrum of mainstream corporations in clothing and hi-tech manufacturing, telemarketing, food processing and packaging, and agriculture super-exploits inmates as cheap laborers forced to work for slave wages. This is not a mere metaphor, because the US Constitution upholds the legality of enslavement in the sphere of incarceration in the first section of the Thirteenth Amendment.

Racial profiling and too often lethal policing practices that contribute to the carceral regime's law and order, immigration control, and national security objectives are not only controversial issues in the United States. As Didier Fassin elucidates in the French context, in the aftermath of the 2005 state of emergency imposed on Paris' outer-city *banlieux*, where working-class immigrants (largely North and sub-Saharan Africans and Roma) are concentrated, the state imposed a legal-political measure that authorized the police to deploy unlawful and immoral practices they would never consider using in other communities. In that context of urban unrest, expanded policing, with its racializing effects, reflects the power to make, as Walter Benjamin theorized, the exception the rule.

Xenophobia and nativism do not only affect Muslims. In Europe, Roma, Travelers, Jews, and Eastern European migrants are often targeted. According to the controversial decolonial thinker and activist Hourida Bouteldja, anti-Semitism has been shrouded or softened by "positive racialization" in France. This has led to the State's commemoration of the *Shoah* (Holocaust) while not treating "the transatlantic slave trade, colonial history, and the Gypsy holocaust" on equal terms. This has provoked resentment from other segments of the minoritized population. "Philosemitism," Bouteldja claims, is a tactic for exploiting a buffer group in order to control other subordinate groups.

In the US context, new waves of immigration from the global south have destabilized traditional assumptions about the society being predominantly white, leading to a crisis of identity for many Euro-American citizens, especially segments of the lower-middle class and working class fearful and resentful about the risks of downward mobility. They are prone to scapegoating immigrants and racial minorities, a nativist tendency manipulated in right-wing politics. In the context of current demographic shifts, Mexican and Central American immigration has become a major preoccupation, with the stereotyping of undocumented migrants whose presence supposedly warrants the building of a wall to keep them and their criminality out. Many of these migrants, however, seek employment in the United States because subsistence at home has declined under the impact of policies such as the North American Free Trade Agreement (NAFTA). While free trade has had some success, it undermines peasants' competitiveness by flooding the market with less costly, mass-produced, and subsidized produce from US agrobusiness.

NEORACISMS

While biodeterminist conceptions of race, whether nineteenth-century or contemporary variants, emphasize natural and biological differences, many current perspectives on race are couched in a language of culture, ethnicity, and nationalism. Consequently, in many settings around the world today, there is "racism without race"; that is, there are public discourses on irreconcilable, unchangeable, and virtually heritable sociocultural differences without any explicit acknowledgment that "races" exist or that "racial" distinctions continue to be socially and politically significant. In these supposedly colorblind, raceless contexts, which are often difficult to interpret or decode, a concept of culture (whether linked to ethnicity or nation) and a broader, culture-centered idiom within which it is embedded serve as an ideological device that defines social differences as essential or natural and, hence, reconfigures racial boundaries.

Anthropologists debate whether the xenophobic, anti-immigrant situations in Western European countries such as France and Germany represent instances of "neoracism," in which race is masked but remains a vital force, or cases of "cultural fundamentalism," in which a real shift in the conceptual structure of difference making has been made to usher those societies into a truly "postrace" era. The latter argument perhaps has some appeal, because traditional racist discourses, biologizing discourses, do not always have legitimacy in those political contexts, not even in the eyes of some right-wing activists. These politicos tend to conceptualize difference in terms of bounded, incommensurate, and spatially segregated cultural entities that cannot be evaluated in terms of an explicit hierarchy or relations of superiority and inferiority. In the United States, a comparable race evasive, colorblind discourse has gained popularity among growing sectors of conservatives, while others still cling to ideas about the determinative role of IQ and genes in leadership, class mobility, and academic achievement.

In the current US context, race-evasive idioms highlighting culture and sometimes class, that dimension of social stratification about which Americans usually have little to say, have gained considerable political utility. Colorblind conservatives acknowledge the existence of race and racism only when they think whites are the target of "reverse racism" emanating from government policy and racial minorities' insistence on "making race an issue." Whereas a language of cultural deficits and pathology frames arguments about the problems impoverished blacks and Latinxs supposedly impose on American society, a limited notion of class is sometimes used to privilege the legal personality and give a competitive edge to working-class whites over racial minorities situated across the class spectrum. This discursive tactic, deployed according to the logic of white nationalism, evades the persistent obstacles that racism presents to blacks and other racial minorities, regardless of their class position. It ignores the fact that the class privileges enjoyed by upper- and middle-class blacks do not immunize them from institutional and cultural racism. For instance, studies document that racial redlining still deprives African Americans of mortgages that whites of comparable economic circumstances (e.g., income and occupation) have no difficulty getting. This white-centered discourse, then, marginalizes racial oppression by privileging the injuries that whites suffer from class subordination. The injuries that blacks, who are disproportionately represented at the social bottom, suffer from class tend to be attributed to the absence of appropriate "family values," "personal responsibility," or a "culture of achievement" rather than to the outcome of structured class disparities mediated by race. There is little recognition in US public discourse that class intersects with race and that the constraints or opportunities, oppressions or privileges, associated with class are exacerbated or enhanced by race's structural power. Race-evasive discourses, whether centered on notions of culture or class, divert public attention from the persistence of racial oppression while serving to reproduce it.

The discursive shift away from explicit conceptions of racial hierarchy to those of cultural nationalism or class, however, has not been accompanied by changes in material conditions. While American neoconservatives may argue that post–Civil Rights US society is free from racism, that public policy should be completely colorblind, and that racial minorities have no constitutional rights to the government protections and sponsorship encompassed within affirmative action policies, disparate outcomes in infant mortality, incarceration and death penalty sentencing, wealth accumulation, and many other domains of everyday life demonstrate that racial inequalities persist as a concrete reality warranting careful examination and explanation.

INTERROGATING IDEOLOGIES OF RACIAL DEMOCRACY AND MIXEDNESS IN LATIN AMERICA

Latin America and the Caribbean have long been reputed to be much more fluid than systematically oppressive racial orders such as the United States and South Africa. In many places, appearance and social markers such as class and acculturation to Eurocentric norms have been believed to weigh as much as or, in some situations, even more than ancestry in determining sociaracial status. Particularly in the Caribbean and in those parts of Central and South America where there was a sizable African presence historically, tripartite classifications differentiating white, brown, and black along with variations of a more complexly graded color continuum have represented intriguing contrasts to the historically bipolar definition of race in the United States.

At least that used to be what we thought. As Eduardo Bonilla-Silva points out, now the Latin American model of pigmentocracy and *mestizaje* (mixedness) seems to have migrated to the United States. The region south of the United States has long been represented as a home of valorized mixedness and "racial democracy," once presumed to be an alternative to racism. However, as Peter Wade argues, though many Latin Americans continue to deny that racism exists in their societies, the categories of black, white, and indigenous retain social significance despite the existence of ambiguous and blurred boundaries between graded color categories.

More recent work, such as Tanya Golash-Boza's research in Peru, reveals that intermediate racial categories do not exist everywhere. There was no "*mulato* escape hatch" in the area where she did her fieldwork. Although an extensive color terminology existed, those labels were largely descriptive and did not function as racial classifications. Robin Sheriff made similar observations among Afro-Brazilian *favelados* (slum residents), who code switch from one discursive register to another when speaking about matters related to race and color in various semantic contexts. She found that an extensive array of descriptive color terms was used in everyday conversation, but descriptive discourse is only one of three major registers. The other two were a pragmatic discourse sensitive to etiquette and inclined toward euphemistic expressions, and a classificatory discourse on race, organized in largely bipolar terms.

Are these instances of relatively bipolar (or tripolar in cases in which the indigenous are also salient) conceptions of race the outcome of recent changes in which the socioracial continuum and "calculus," as Marvin Harris characterized it decades ago, have been reconfigured and resignified in ways that have been influenced by recent black movements and their race-cognizant identity politics? Or perhaps color and race have been redefined by what Charles Hale describes as neoliberal multiculturalism, an outcome of the cultural processes entwined with the restructuring of governance and citizenship in societies that now acknowledge and administer claims to the constitutionally codified cultural, social, and territorial rights of indigenous people and Afro-descendants? Latin America's new multiculturalism, a double-edged sword, expands the space available for ethno-racial blocs without relinquishing the established nexus of power aligned to Latin variants of white supremacy.

Antonio Sérgio Alfredo Guimarães hypothesizes that there indeed has been a significant shift from assigning social classifications in terms of color categories (with the potential of stretching to accommodate individual social class status) to classifications based on a notion of race, which is much less affected by social class status. Since the 1990s, he claims, the Brazilian classification system has two added new features. First, an explicit reference to race appears on the census and in the media; and, second, the "generic stretching" of categories because of individuals' social position has ceased. Moreover, more emphasis is now given to family and ancestral origins as well as to cultural traditions. As a consequence, middle-class *mulatos* and *mulatas* are now commonly labeled "black" or "Afro-descendant" in the language of the contemporary antiracist human-rights movement. The salience of categories punctuating mixedness for individuals of recognizable African descent has declined in the public sphere, as has the legitimacy of the ideology of whitening. The meaning of color, therefore, has changed, but Guimarães points out that racialized meanings for color were always implicit in the traditional color continuum. Those implicit meanings informed the race consciousness of the 1980s and the 1990s. Consequently, common attributions of the rise of the black movement to US cultural imperialism are unconvincing.

Another study that concurs with this view is Paulina Alberto's intellectual and social history of Afro-Brazilian perspectives on racial democracy. Her comparative regional approach points to the variations within Afro-Brazilian social and political thought in three main regions of the country: Salvador, Bahia; Rio de Janeiro; and São Paulo. Dating back to the turn of the twentieth century, we see, Afro-Brazilian intellectuals in the south defined themselves as black, even when admixture was discernible. The population, cultural life, and economic pattern that shaped São Paulo were affected by an influx of European immigrants. The Brazilian state promoted European immigration to improve the nation's development and modernity profile by whitening the population. Alberto convincingly argues that discourses of racial identity in Brazil have not been uniform or uncontested across time and space.

Traditional arguments for racial democracy in Brazil and related ideologies in other parts of Latin America have been the outcome of nationalist ideologies that marginalized both indigeneity and blackness to the extent that they failed to melt into these nations' exaltation of mixing and whitening. Rather than being the democratizing agent it is often claimed to be, *mestizaje* coexists with and mediates discrimination and exclusion. Arlene Torres and Norman Whitten view *mestizaje* as an ideology that reveals uneasiness with black and indigenous ethnic-bloc formation. In their view, *indigenismo* commemorates the indigenous contribution to the nation without embracing indigenous self-determination or sovereignty. *Indigenismo* appropriates some symbols of the indigenous historical past while excluding present-day indigenous people from key aspects of national affairs. In some settings, social movements have offset this traditional state of affairs (e.g., Evo Morales' Bolivia), where indigenous agendas have made significant interventions in local and national politics and in transnational human-rights norms.

In some settings, US military occupation, neocolonial rule, and/or corporate presence have facilitated the process of associating whitening with advancement and darkening with backwardness. In some of these settings, notably prerevolutionary Cuba and the contemporary Dominican Republic, ideologies and practices of whitening have been accompanied by especially negative evaluations of blackness. Antiblackness is associated with the demonization of Haitianness in the Dominican Republic.

INDIGENOUS AND BLACK AS MUTUALLY CONSTITUTING CATEGORIES OF RACE AND ETHNICITY

Although some anthropologists of Latin America used to think of "black" as a racial classification based on unmalleable somatic differences and "Indian" as an ethnic category based on manipulable cultural signs such as clothing, language, and place of residence, Peter Wade's work reveals that this division is artificial and spurious. He points out that although phenotypic traits cannot be manipulated in the same way that cultural criteria can, physical appearance is, nonetheless, perceived in culturally specific ways, and it is culture that makes phenotype socially significant. In much of Latin America, it is asserted that money whitens. Hence, upwardly mobile economic status can potentially alter the way one is labeled. Whether the label signals a pragmatic or euphemistic identification or a racial classification is the question that requires more social inquiry, recognizing the different registers of race and color discourses. Although the boundary between Indian and Mestizo may be crossed by manipulating cultural signifiers, "Indian" is both a racial and an ethnic category in view of its place within the colonial history, out of which the region's discourse on race emerged. Racism impacts indigenous peoples as well as Afrodescendants, albeit in different ways, as shown in Jonathan Warren's ethnography of indigenous resurgence and movement building, which he places clearly within the context of antiracism. Other scholars who recognize the salience of race and racism in indigenous people's lives are Marisol de la Cadena and Mary Weismantel. The most recent trends in the anthropological literature now make it clear that "black" and "Indian" should be treated not as concepts of different types but as mutually constituting cultural categories. Moreover, Mark Anderson's ethnography of the Garifuna, who, in some situations, identify as both black and indigenous, demonstrates that these two categories can also be fused. As complementary modes of sociopolitical navigation, indigeneity represents a normative model of collective rights, while blackness imparts a diasporic status of subaltern cosmopolitanism.

In exploring the different ways that Afro-descendants and indigenous people have been incorporated into Latin American nation-states, Wade explains that, for the most part, *indígena* have been seen as essentially different from their observers, whereas descendants of Africans have been viewed more ambiguously, as both inside and outside the society of their masters and observers. Owing to their institutionalized identity and their visibility in national policy, indigenous people have been granted certain legal protections by the state (e.g., autonomous communities, reserves). Blacks, on the other hand, have been usually seen as ordinary, second-class citizens in class society and are assumed not to have culture *sui generis*. However, Afro-descendants with historical claims on ancestral territories, such as Maroons (descendants of self-manumitted blacks who ran away from slavery), have had varying levels of success in collectivist claims to distinctive culture and territorial rights. While new constitutions in countries like Brazil, Colombia, and Ecuador legally codify their collective status within pluriethnic nation-states, there is still a big discrepancy between de jure rights and the de facto practices for implementing and enforcing the law.

RACISM AND ANTIRACISM IN BRAZIL TODAY

In Brazil the resurgence of black identity politics has stimulated anthropologists to reexamine the realities of race and racism in that country. Recent research addresses questions related to cultural citizenship, political subject formation, and rights, including those to land and life itself. Ethnographies illuminate how people navigate racialized and racializing landscapes reconfigured by the contradictory effects of new social movements and state apparatuses driven by neoliberal logics. These studies document the major shift in Latin American racial politics from the valorization of race mixture and whitening to a growing recognition of the legitimacy and desirability of black and indigenous rights.

Feminist ethnographers are making important contributions through their studies of sex tourism, reproductive justice, and black women's sociopolitical mobilizations in social movements and civil society. These issues are examined in communities vulnerable to being displaced and put under siege by the encroachments of real estate and tourist developers as well as of state and state-sanctioned violence from police, death squads, and malign negligence with its ill effects on social conditions, environmental sustainability, and spiritual well-being. Keisha-Khan Perry's examination of a coastal favela in Salvador, Bahia, illuminates the activism and leadership of black women who serve as the "foot soldiers" of a movement combating racism, sexism, and other aspects of the "war on the poor," as John Gledhill emphasizes.

Beyond neoliberalism's intensified war on the poor, João Costa Vargas argues that a genocidal continuum is at work inflicting social death and police lethality upon a population that is disproportionately black. Drawing on Nancy Scheper-Hughes' idea of genocidal continuum, Vargas illuminates the multiple modalities of violence that cumulatively inflict genocide. He insists that individual intentions should not be a major criterion for genocide when social analysis amply demonstrates the effects of a wide spectrum of threatening conditions, including sterilization, infant mortality and morbidity, flagrant inequalities within schools, economic marginality and dislocation, lethal policing, and mass incarceration. He argues that these conditions constitute a genocidal continuum, a predicament foundational to black racial subjection in Brazil and across the black diaspora.

Substantiating many of Vargas's claims, Christin Smith adopts Cameroonian political theorist Achille Mbembe's notion of necropolitics to illuminate the regime of death that operates in disproportionately black favelas in Salvador. In these settings, police and death squads, largely immune from prosecution, execute drug dealers, activists, and innocent people on the streets and in their homes. The war against crime and drugs is the rationale, but the motivation in many instances, she argues, is political and political-economic. She shows how paradoxes of black citizenship and acts of spectacular violence make black communities vulnerable to displacement, environmental degradation, and other iniquities. Indeed, she argues that it is through violence that racial boundaries are constructed and maintained, particularly in contexts where race is purportedly fluid, ambiguous, or of little or no social significance, as Brazil's national ideology has long claimed. In her view, black racial identity, as typically understood, is not necessary for antiblackness to perform its labor. Race is less an identity than a social relationship engendered by encounters that mark bodies as being outside the social contract and moral order. An example is the 2007 case of Sirlei Dias de Carvalho Pinto, a domestic worker, who personally identified herself as *parda* (brown, mixed race). As she was on her way home from her job in Tijuca, an affluent neighborhood in Rio de Janeiro, a group of upper-middle-class youth savagely beat her up and later claimed they thought she was a prostitute. Drawing on popular stereotypes of black women, they "scripted" her as a prostitute "out-of-place" and, therefore, culpable for being one of the nation's "internal enemies."

Smith offers an insightful look at the collective resistance to antiblackness in her analysis of React or Die!/React or Be Killed!, a movement roughly parallel to #BlackLivesMatter in the United States. Her ethnography also examines street theater activists whose popular consciousness-raising activities make social injustices and human-rights violations more legible. She poignantly demonstrates how their performances provides a forum for ordinary Afro-Brazilians to come to voice in protesting the various forms of discrimination, violence, and disciplining that subjugates them and reproduces white supremacy.

FINAL REFLECTION

Whether in arenas of academic research, public debate within nation-states, or the deliberations within the United Nations' human-rights committees over states' obligations under the International Convention on the Elimination of All Forms of Racial Discrimination (ICERD), it is imperative that the confusion over what constitutes something as "racial" and "racist" be offset by conceptual tools that anthropological inquiry can provide, at least in part. More scholars and activists have come to recognize that the models of race and racism that evolved from North American experiences do not exhaust the discursive and material structures of racial formation that developed in the past and are still unfolding in the present world. To the extent that race intersects and entangles with other dimensions of inequality, power, and identity, it commonly ebbs and flows as an invidious undercurrent that gains its greatest visibility when tensions heighten. However, even nasty intergroup situations may be rationalized in idioms that deny the relevance, power, or existence of race. Current reconfigurations of racism demand careful scrutiny with investigative tools that anthropologists can help to offer as a public intellectual service to the world of the twenty-first century.

REFERENCES AND SUGGESTIONS FOR FURTHER READING

Alberto, Paulina. 2011. *Terms of Inclusion: Black Intellectuals in Twentieth-Century Brazil.* Chapel Hill: University of North Carolina Press.

This is an important study of black intellectualism in three of Brazil's major regions. It reveals the variations of perspectives on racial democracy among African descended Brazilians who participated in the public sphere.

Alvarez, Sonia E., and Kia Lilly Caldwell, eds. 2016. "African Descendant Feminisms in Latin America, Part I: Brazil." *Meridians: Feminism, Race, Transnationalism* 14(1).

This is a historic collection of writings of black Brazilian feminists and US scholars on black feminism in Brazil.

Alvarez, Sonia, Kia Lilly Caldwell, and Agustín Laó-Montes, eds. 2016. "African Descendant Feminisms in Latin America, Part II: South and Central America and the Spanish-Speaking Caribbean." *Meridians* 14(2).

A historic collection of Afro-Latin American (Afro-Hispanic), feminist writings, typically unavailable in English.

Anderson, Mark. 2009. *Black and Indigenous: Garifuna Activism and Consumer Culture in Honduras.* Minneapolis: University of Minnesota Press.

This ethnography elucidates how Garifuna activists in Honduras draw on both black diasporic and indigenous models in building their activist strategies for change.

Appadurai, Arjun. 1996. *Modernity at Large: Cultural Dimensions of Globalization.* University of Minnesota Press.

This book compiles Appadurai's most significant essays on globalization and modernity.

Baker, Lee. 1998. *From Savage to Negro: Anthropology and the Construction of Race, 1896–1954.* Berkeley: University of California Press.

This is an important contribution to intellectual history, with a focus on anthropology's role in constructing and deconstructing race.

———. 2010. *Anthropology and the Racial Politics of Culture.* Durham, NC: Duke University Press.

This book examines the different ways that American Indians and African Americans were treated in the history of anthropology with respect to questions of culture and race.

Baliber, Etienne. 1991. "Is There a 'Neo-Racism'"? In *Race, Nation, Class: Ambiguous Identities*, by Etienne Balibar and Immanuel Wallerstein, 15–28. New York: Verso.

Banton, Michael. 2002. *The International Politics of Race.* Cambridge: Polity.

This is an informative book on how racism and antiracism have been dealt with in the United Nations human-rights regime. The difficulties in monitoring the compliance of various nation-states (e.g., the United States, selected European countries, and Australia) with the antiracism convention are examined.

———. 2015. *What We Now Know about Race and Ethnicity*. New York: Berghahn Books.

Bonilla-Silva, Eduardo. 2001. *White Supremacy and Racism in the Post–Civil Rights Era*. Boulder, CO: Lynne Rienner Publishers.

———. 2014. *Racism without Racists: Color-blind Racism and the Persistence of Racial Inequality in America*. Fourth edition. Lanham, MD: Rowman & Littlefield.

> This sociological study is widely consulted in anthropology for its insights into contemporary colorblind ideology and policies.

———. 2008. "The Latin Americanization of Racial Stratification in the US." In *Racism in the 21st Century: An Empirical Analysis of Skin Color*, ed. Ronald E. Hall, 151–70. New York: Springer Science.

Caldwell, Kia L. 2007. *Negras in Brazil: Re-envisioning Black Women, Citizenship, and the Politics of Identity*. New Brunswick, NJ: Rutgers University Press.

> This is an exemplary black transnational feminist ethnography on black Brazilian women's agency and organizational capacity building.

———. 2017. *Health Equity in Brazil: Intersections of Gender, Race, and Policy*. Urbana: University of Illinois Press.

> Study of black Brazilian women's human-rights advocacy and activism around health policy.

Cultural Anthropology Hot Spots. 2015. *#BlackLivesMatter: Anti-Black Racism, Police Violence, and Resistance*. Bianca C. Williams, ed. Posted June 2, https://culanth.org/field sights/696-blacklivesmatter-anti-black-racism-police-violence-and-resistance.

> A poignant collection of essays on antiblackness and resistance to it in US society and in other national/transnational contexts.

———. 2016. *Refugees and the Crisis of Europe*. Mayanthi Fernando and Christiana Glordano, posted on June 28, https://culanth.org/fieldsights/911-refugees-and-the-crisis-of -europe.

> This post offers timely reflections on refugee and immigrant crisis in Europe from perspectives informed by ethnographic research.

De la Cadena, Marisol. 2010. "Indigenous Cosmopolitics in the Andes: Conceptual Reflections Beyond 'Politics.'" *Cultural Anthropology* 25 (2): 334–70.

Drake, St. Clair. 1987. *Black Folk Here and There: An Essay in Anthropology and History*. Vol. 1. Los Angeles: Center for Afro-American Studies, University of California-Los Angeles.

———. 1990. *Black Folk Here and There: An Essay in Anthropology and History*. Vol. 2. Los Angeles: Center for Afro-American Studies, University of California-Los Angeles.

> This is a classic work in two volumes addressing the history of and the sociology of knowledge on the evolution of antiblack racism. The study offers an interrogation of the meanings of blackness in the Old World African diaspora before the era of colonial expansion when slavery was racialized and linked to skin color prejudice and ideas of heritable differences.

Escobar, Arturo. 2008. *Territories of Difference: Place, Movements, Life*, Redes. Durham. NC: Duke University Press.

> This is a theoretically provocative ethnography written from the perspective of the ontological turn, with the epistemology and ontology "otherwise" grounded in the lives and social movements of Afro-Colombians of the Pacific coast.

Fanfán-Santos, Elizabeth. 2016. *Black Bodies: The Politics of* Quilombolismo *in Contemporary Brazil*. Austin: University of Texas Press.

Fassin, Didier. 2013. *Enforcing Order: An Ethnography of Urban Policing*. Cambridge: Polity Press.

Fischer, Dawn-Elissa. 2013. "Blackness, Race, and Language Politics in Japanese Hiphop." *Transforming Anthropology* 21 (2): 135–52.

Friedman, Kajsa Ekholm, and Jonathan Friedman. 2011. *Modernities, Class, and the Contradictions of Globalization: The Anthropology of Global Systems.* Lanham, MD: AltaMira Press.

Garner, Steve. 2017. *Racisms: An Introduction.* Second edition. London: Sage.

    Features up-to-date information on trends in scholarship and public life, including the impact of social movements and activists such as Hourida Bouteldja; she sheds light on the asymmetry between Islamophobia and anti-Semitism in French politics.

Gledhill, John. 2015. *The New War on the Poor: The Production of Insecurity in Latin America.* London: Zed Books.

    Through case studies of Mexico and Brazil, this book presents a nuanced analysis of state securitization and assaults on the poor.

Golash-Boza, Tanya. 2010. *Yo Soy Negro: Blackness in Peru.* Gainesville: University Press of Florida.

Goodman, Alan H., Yolanda T. Moses, and Joseph Jones. 2012. *Race: Are We So Different?* Malden, MA, and Oxford: Wiley-Blackwell.

Gravlee, Clarence. 2009. "How Race Becomes Biology: Embodiment of Social Inequality." *American Journal of Physical Anthropology* 139:47–57.

Guimarães, Antonio Sérgio Alfredo. 2012. "The Brazilian System of Racial Classification." *Ethnic and Racial Studies* 35 (7): 1157–1162.

Hale, Charles. 2006. *Más que Un Indio: Racial Ambivalence and Neoliberal Multiculturalism in Guatemala.* Santa Fe: School of American Research. (SAR) Press.

    This book exemplifies recent trends in the study of race in Latin America under neoliberal conditions.

Harris, Marvin. 1970. "Referential Ambiguity in the Calculus of Brazilian Racial Identity." *Southwestern Journal of Anthropology* 26:1–14.

    This is a classic anthropological study of the color/racial continuum in Brazil.

Harrison, Faye V. 1995. "The Persistent Power of 'Race' in the Cultural and Political Economy of Racism." *Annual Review of Anthropology* 24:47–74.

———. 2005. "Introduction: Global Perspectives on Human Rights and Interlocking Inequalities of Race, Gender, and Related Dimensions of Power." In *Resisting Racism and Xenophobia: Global Perspectives on Race, Gender, and Human Rights,* ed. Faye V. Harrison, 1–31. Walnut Creek, CA: AltaMira Press.

———. 2008. "Global Apartheid, Foreign Policy, and Human Rights." In *Transnational Blackness: Navigating the Global Color Line,* ed. Manning Marable and Vanessa Agard-Jones, 19–40. New York: Palgrave Macmillan.

———. 2012. "Race, Racism, and Antiracism: Implications for Human Rights." Guest essay in *Race: Are We So Different?* by Alan H. Goodman, Yolanda T. Moses, and Joseph L. Jones, 237–244. Malden, MA, and Oxford: Wiley-Blackwell.

Hartigan, John, ed. 2013. *Anthropology of Race: Genes, Biology, and Culture.* Santa Fe: School for Advanced Study Press.

Ho, Christine G. T., and James Louky. 2012. *Humane Migration: Establishing Legitimacy and Rights for Displaced People.* Sterling, VA: Kumarian Press.

Ives, Sarah. 2017. *Steeped in Heritage: The Racial Politics of South African Rooibos Tea.* Durham, NC: Duke University Press.

    An ethnography on the traditional commodity associated with indigeneity; it focuses on claims to indigenous identity by Cape Colored and Afrikaner groups.

Jayasuriya, Shihan de S., and Richard Pankhurst, eds. 2003. *The African Diaspora in the Indian Ocean*. Trenton, NJ: Africa World Press.

> This is an important volume on trans-Indian Ocean African diaspora, its historical development and contemporary conditions.

Jung, Moon-Kie, João H. Costa Vargas, Eduardo Bonilla-Silva, eds. 2011. *State of White Supremacy: Racism, Governance, and the United States*. Stanford, CA: Stanford University Press.

Lavie, Smadar. 2014. *Wrapped in the Flag of Israel: Mizrahi Single Mothers and Bureaucratic Torture*. New York and Oxford: Berghahn.

> A provocative ethnography of Israeli gendered racism targeting Mizrahi women.

Löftsdottir, Kristin. 2009. "Invisible Colour: Landscapes of Whiteness and Racial Identity in International Development." *Anthropology Today* 25 (5): 4-7, October.

Loveland, M. T., and D. Popescu. 2015. "The Gypsy Threat Narrative Explaining Anti-Roma Attitudes in the European Union," *Humanity and Society* 40 (3): 329-52.

Mbembe, Achille. 2003. "Necropolitics." *Public Life* 15 (1): 11-40.

Mullings, Leith, ed. 2009. *New Social Movements in the African Diaspora: Challenging Global Apartheid*. New York: Palgrave Macmillan.

Newman, Katherine, and Ariane De Lannoy. 2014. *After Freedom: The Rise of the Post-Apartheid Generation in Democratic South Africa*. Boston: Beacon Press,

Nyamnjoh, Frances B. 2016. *#RhodesMustFall: Nibbling at Resilient Colonialism in South Africa*. Mankon, Bamenda, Cameroon: Langaa Research & Publishing Common Interest Group (RPCIG).

> A postcolonial perspective on the resilience of colonialism and racism in South Africa, as seen through the #RhodesMustFall student campaign.

Ong, Aihwa. 2010. *Spirits of Resistance and Capitalist Discipline: Factory Women in Malaysia*. Second edition. Albany: State University of New York Press.

Paschel, Tianna S. 2016. *Becoming Black Political Subjects: Movements and Ethno-Racial Rights in Colombia and Brazil*. Princeton, NJ: Princeton University Press.

> A comparative, multisited study of movement building in Brazil and Colombia.

Perry, Keisha-Khan. 2013. *Black Women against the Land Grab: The Fight for Racial Justice in Brazil*. Minneapolis: University of Minnesota Press.

> A feminist ethnography on working poor black women's leadership in a grassroots movement against displacement of an ancestral community in Salvador, Bahia.

Pierre, Jemima. 2012. *The Predicament of Blackness: Postcolonial Ghana and the Politics of Race*. Chicago: University of Chicago Press.

> Theoretically sophisticated study of racial formation and racialization in Ghana as a cosmopolitan postcolonial state.

Prah, Kwesi Kwaa. 2006. "Introduction: Racism in the Global African Experience." In *Racism in the Global African Experience*, ed. Kwesi Kwaa Prah, 1-20. Cape Town: Centre for Advanced Studies of African Society (CASAS).

> This essay provides the historical and conceptual framework for a compilation of papers written from African and African diasporic perspectives.

Quijano, Aníbal. 2000. "Coloniality of Power, Eurocentrism, and Latin America." *Nepantla: Views from the South* 1 (3): 533-80.

> This article is an important intervention by a leading Peruvian and Latin American sociologist, whose thinking on coloniality, modernity, and decoloniality has influenced the work of many anthropologists.

Rana, Junaid. 2016. "The Racial Infrastructure of the Terror-Industrial Complex." *Social Text* 34 (4): 111–38.

Rana's article elucidates the racialization of South Asian and other Muslims in the context of the war on terror in the United States and transnationally.

Reiter, Bernd, and Kimberly Eison Simmons, eds. 2012. *Afro-Descendants, Identity, and the Struggle for Development in the Americas*. East Lansing: Michigan State University Press.

Roberts, Dorothy. 2011. *Fatal Invention: How Science, Politics, and Big Business Re-create Race in the Twenty-first Century*. New York: New Press.

Critical examination of the use and effects of new genomic technologies on reinventing race.

Ross, Fiona C. 2003. *Bearing Witness: Women and the Truth and Reconciliation Commission in South Africa*. London: Pluto Press.

———. 2010. *Raw Life, New Hope: Decency, Housing, and Everyday Life in a Post-apartheid Community*. Cape Town: 24 University of Cape Town Press.

Russell, John G. 1991. "Race and Reflexivity: The Black Other in Contemporary Japanese Mass Culture." *Cultural Anthropology* 6 (1): 3–25.

———. 2015. "Historically, Japan Is No Stranger to Blacks, nor to Blackface." *Japan Times*, April 19. http://www.japantimes.co.jp/community/2015/04/19/voices/historically-japan -is-no-stranger-to-blacks-nor-to-blackface/#.WWBsBITytqQ. Accessed on July 29, 2017.

Santos, Beatriz dos. 2014. "Black Women and Their Situation of Discrimination and Vulnerability in Brazil." In *Feminism: Perspectives, Stereotypes/Misperceptions and Social Implications*, ed. Pearche Stroud, 49–68. New York: Nova Science Publishers.

A black Brazilian anthropologist's perspectives on African diasporic feminism and on the forms of racialized gendered or gendered racist discrimination black women confront.

Schweotzer, Erwin. 2015. *The Making of Griqua, Inc.: Indigenous Struggles for Land and Autonomy in South Africa*. Wien, Germany: LIT Verlag.

This ethnography draws on Jean and John Comaroff's notion of "Ethnicity, Inc." to examine the process of post-apartheid identity formation associated with struggle for land reform and autonomy.

Sheriff, Robin E. 2001. *Dreaming Equality: Color, Race, and Racism in Urban Brazil*. New Brunswick, NJ: Rutgers University Press.

Sheriff's book is an important intervention in studies of race and racial democracy; it elucidates three different registers of discursive practice—descriptive, pragmatic/euphemistic, and classificatory. The latter acknowledges polar designations of racial difference.

Smedley, Audrey, and Brian D. Smedley. 2012. *Race in North America: The Origin and Evolution of a Worldview*. Fourth edition. Boulder, CO: Westview Press.

This is now a classic intellectual and social history of race in the United States. Most recent edition brings psychologist B. D. Smedley on board with his analysis of the health disparities implicating the racial worldview.

Smith, Christin A. 2014. "Putting Prostitutes in Their Place: Black Women, Social Violence, and the Brazilian Case of Sirlei Carvalho." *Latin American Perspectives* 41 (1): 107–23.

———. 2016. *Afro-Paradise: Blackness, Violence, and Performance in Brazil*. Chicago: University of Illinois Press.

An ethnography on racism in Brazil, with a focus on Salvador, Bahia; its analysis of antiblack violence is sophisticated, organized around the consciousness-raising role that street theater performance plays.

Stolcke, Verena. 1995. "Talking Culture: New Boundaries, New Rhetorics of Exclusion in Europe." *Current Anthropology* 36 (1):1–24.

Sturm, Circe. 2002. *Blood Politics: Race, Culture, and Identity in the Cherokee Nation of Oklahoma*. Berkeley: University of California Press.

This is a study of Cherokee racial identity that takes into consideration the contested relationship black freedmen and women have to and within the Cherokee nation.

Takezawa, Yasuko, ed. 2011. *Racial Representations in Asia*. Kyoto: Kyoto University Press.

This volume examines questions of race and racialization in Asia, mainly East Asia.

Thomas, Deborah, and Tamari Clarke. 2012. "Globalizing Race." Guest essay in *Race: Are We So Different?*, ed. Alan Goodman, Yolanda Moses, and Joseph Jones, 234–37, 243. Malden, MA, and Oxford: Wiley-Blackwell.

Torres, Arlene, and Norman Whitten Jr. 1998. "General Introduction: To Forge the Future in the Fires of the Past: An Interpretive Essay on Racism, Discrimination, Resistance, and Liberation." In *Blackness in Latin America and the Caribbean: Social Dynamics and Cultural Transformations*. Vols. I and II. Norman E. Whitten Jr. and Arlene Torres, eds. pp. 3–33. Bloomington: Indiana University Press.

Vargas, João H. Costa. 2011. *Never Meant to Survive: Genocide and Utopias in Black Diaspora Communities*. Lanham, MD: Rowman & Littlefield.

This book applies the concept of genocidal continuum to the black diaspora, based on evidence from the United States and Brazil, highlighting continuity with earlier human-rights petitions.

Vargas, João H. Costa, and Jaime Alves Ampara. 2010. "Geographies of Death: An Intersectional Analysis of Police Lethality and the Racialized Regime of Citizenship in São Paulo." *Ethnic and Racial Studies* 33 (4): 611–36.

Wade, Peter. 2010. *Race and Ethnicity in Latin America*. Second edition. London and New York: Pluto Press.

Warren, Jonathan. 2001. *Racial Revolutions: Antiracism and Indian Resurgence in Brazil*. Durham, NC: Duke University Press.

Important intervention in conventional indigenous studies; situates new movement politics in context of antiracism.

Weatherman, Thomas, and Morgan Hoke. 2017. "Critical Biological Anthropology: A Model for Anthropological Integration." In *The Routledge Companion to Contemporary Anthropology*, ed. Simon Coleman, Susan B. Hyatt, and Ann Kingsolver, 283–302. London and New York: Routledge.

This chapter provides an overview of recent trends in research representing the new biocultural synthesis in anthropology.

Weismantel, Mary. 2001. *Cholas and Pishtacos: Tales of Race and Sex in the Andes*. Chicago: University of Chicago Press.

Whitten, Norman E., Jr., and Arlene Torres. 1992. "Blackness in the Americas." *North American Congress on Latin America* 25 (4):16–22, 45–46.

Williams, Erica Lorraine. 2013. *Sex Tourism in Bahia*. Urbana: University of Illinois Press.

Winant, Howard. 2004. *The New Politics of Race: Globalism, Difference, Justice*. Minneapolis: University of Minnesota Press.

CHAPTER 5

IMAGINED BUT
NOT IMAGINARY

ETHNICITY AND NATIONALISM IN
THE EARLY TWENTY-FIRST CENTURY

Richard Jenkins

It seems almost inconceivable that not so very long ago scholars such as Ernest Gellner and Eric Hobsbawm were cheerfully proclaiming the decline, if not the actual end, of nationalism: modernity would render such ideologies irrelevant. Today, however, whether in Myanmar, the South Asian subcontinent, West Africa, Central and Eastern Europe, Russia, Britain, or the United States—just to offer some highly visible examples—calls to arms in the name of nation (and, indeed, ethnicity) ring out as loud and clear as they have at any time during the last two centuries.

With this in mind, in this chapter I offer two general perspectives on ethnicity and nationalism, which may look a little contradictory but, actually, aren't. The first of these, perhaps unsurprisingly, is that ethnic and national identities continue to mean a great deal to the individuals who claim them. Attachments of this kind, which are often perceived to be "natural" or involuntary, are something for which, and about which, humans remain prepared to fight. The second is that the meanings and power of ethnicity and nationality are not, however, dictated by history or by the blind passions of the "blood." They may not be infinitely malleable, but they are nonetheless made and manipulated by human beings, as individuals or collectivities, in response to their perceived needs and in pursuit of their interests.

Bearing in mind that second point, the particularities of events and their consequences since the turn of the millennium necessarily loom large over any contemporary discussion of ethnicity and nation. Four such sets of events, in particular, cannot be ignored. The attack on the Twin Towers in New York in 2001, the subsequent "war on terror" in Afghanistan and Iraq, and the resultant long collapse of the Middle East into chaos and carnage, not least in Syria, is the first such chain of events. Second, we are in the middle of an international refugee crisis, the scale of which is almost beyond comprehension, as is the depth of suffering of the people who are on the move. Third, the gradual reemergence of a strong and confident Russia from the mess of the immediate post-Soviet period has been powered politically by "United Russia" nationalism. The annexation by force of the Crimea, Ukrainian national territory, fomented further conflict in eastern Ukraine and encouraged growing and strident populist nationalism elsewhere in Eastern and Central Europe.

These three passages of history feed into the fourth matter of which we need to be mindful here. Historians will remember 2016 as the year in which populism, largely but not only right-wing, emerged from minority obscurity to upset political apple carts: the narrow vote in favor of the United Kingdom leaving the European Union—so-called Brexit—and the victory of Donald Trump in the electoral college that decides the US presidency are merely the most conspicuous manifestations of this trend. Developments in France, Austria, Hungary, Poland, and the Netherlands suggest that there may yet be more to come. The "populist turn," if we can call it that, matters here because once again things are being said, and political arguments made, that had for decades appeared to have been retired in disgrace from mainstream public discourse.

And there is more to this than something called "populism." In the supposedly "advanced" western world of Europe and America it is perfectly acceptable to claim and identify with *ethnicity*, and even *heritage*. It remains acceptable to do so despite the collective guilt inspired by a history of slavery, colonialism, and genocide that has, for the moment anyway, banished *race* and *tribe* to an uneasy closet of disreputability. Neither the progress of modern "rationality" nor the shape-shifting of postmodernism's celebration of infinite difference has undermined the power of ethnic and national identity to move people and to shape their lives. However, while "race" may be in quarantine, as a potent idea it has not gone away; the word may be rarely uttered, because there is no real need for it to be uttered. It merely has to be hinted at, in the shadowy form of a convenient Other.

populism = appeal to ordinary folks who feel resentful towards elites

"Race," and, to be more precise and more plain-spoken, *racism* have returned to center stage in the increasingly theatrical politics of Europe and the United States, which are both cause and effect of populism. The election in 2008 of Barack Obama, the United States' first African American president, precipitated a concerted "birther" movement, aiming to out him as not authentically American by birth and therefore ineligible to hold office. The thought of a black president was apparently more than some people could stomach. During the 2016 presidential campaign, the Republican Party's candidate, Donald Trump—who had himself publicly fueled doubts about the authenticity of Obama's passport—persistently described Mexican immigrants as criminals and rapists and declared all Muslims wishing to enter the United States to be suspect. As Mendelberg has shown, playing the "race card," whether overtly or covertly, has a long history in American politics, but in Trump's hands it has become less subtle and determinedly unapologetic.

In the United Kingdom the race card has also been played. During the European Union referendum campaign of 2016, many of the politicians and journalists arguing for a "leave" vote were unembarrassed about persistently using immigration as the peg on which to hang their arguments; playing on public anxiety in the United Kingdom about immigration arguably produced the eventual outcome, a narrow victory for the leavers. Two separate images capture the spirit of this strategy. In one, a photograph of Syrian refugees in a long queue at the Croatia-Slovenia border in 2015 was used by the United Kingdom Independence Party (UKIP), with the caption "Breaking Point: The EU has failed us all" encouraging voters to "break free of the EU and take back control of our borders." Without explanatory comment or context, it conjured up a veritable tsunami of Them, coming to swamp the national Us. The other is not a visual image but a scary number: 12 million Turks were waiting to come to Britain, according to the British *Sunday Express*, while a Leave campaign poster said that "Turkey (population 76m) is joining the EU." That these were both lies apparently didn't matter. The Turks—a people who have long been portrayed as a malevolent alien demon lurking on the European margins—were coming. The Muslim hordes were waiting at the gate.

The point is not simply that whether what is said is inaccurate or misleading is beside the point in the "post-truth" hall of mirrors of the new populist politics. Politicians and journalists have always had an uneasy relationship with the truth, and ends have always justified means. What works for them at the time is all that matters. To combine the two general perspectives that I offered in my opening paragraph, in attempting to mobilize "'the people" along perceived ethnic or national lines, manipulation has always been grist to the demagogue's mill. So no surprises there.

The more important point, for the purposes of this chapter, is that whereas since 1945 playing the race card brazenly and explicitly has been confined to the unrespectable margins of extreme right-wing politics in the democracies of Europe and North America, it is no longer either marginal or disreputable. "Extremism" has been mainstreamed, and its rehabilitation has probably not finished yet. This has happened in at least three ways. First, a range of convenient Others has been developed, some old, some new, some specific, some all-purpose: Muslims, Mexicans, Moroccans, immigrants, refugees, non-natives. All are rhetorically useful, and none are tainted by guilty histories of slavery, colonialism, or genocide. Second, an emboldened popular press, largely dominated by right-of-center proprietorial interests, has taken freedom of speech to mean freedom to lie and to say what would have been unsayable not too long ago. Third, the echo chambers of social media, and the Internet more generally, allow "fake news" to circulate unchallenged while cyber-anonymity encourages racism and ethnic abuse to proliferate and flourish.

How?

Less dramatically, in many places around the world — from the transnational arenas of the European Union, to the internal politics of the People's Republic of China, to the orderly municipalities of social democracies such as Denmark — ethnic and national identity are among the most crucial bases of claim and counterclaim about who gets what, and how much. Ethnicity, nation, origin, and culture seem, at least for the time being, to have replaced class conflict as the motor of history.

Ethnicity and nation are, however, not only a matter of violence or the politics of collective entitlement. It must also be recognized that ethnicity — whether racialized or not — and national identity do, for many people, offer a source of the intangible collective good offered by "community." As the Scandinavian social democracies demonstrate, for example, we should not simplistically reduce national pride or patriotism to xenophobia, ethnic chauvinism, or cynical political calculation (albeit that they may also be present). There is still a wide range of other, more benign possibilities.

There are also other positives: the marketing of Irishness, in tourism and elsewhere, is one such example. Sport, too, offers pertinent illustrations of the complex salience of ethnic and national identity in the modern world. There is an increasing flexibility of national identification in terms of sponsorship or team membership. The pursuit of individual career advantage and prestige, combined with the quest for national sporting success, has produced many "national" sportswomen and -men who have but recently been nationalized.

So, as I argued in my opening remarks, there are two interpretations of ethnic — or national — identity. On the one hand, it can be seen as a fundamental, perhaps even an irrational, emotional force. This is the basis of its rhetorical attraction for the new populism. On the other, it appears to be a negotiable, perhaps even superficial, personal resource. These opposing points of view begin to converge, however, if we recognize that ethnic or national attachments, far from withering away in the face of increased internationalism, are at least as important in the global arena of the early (Christian) twenty-first century as they have ever been. In order to understand why this might be, we have to start with a very basic question.

WHAT IS IDENTITY?

Similarity and difference are the touchstones of human social identity, positioning us with respect to all other people. They tell us who we resemble and from whom we differ. They provide us with at least some idea of what we can expect from others and what they can legitimately ask of us. They are the latitude and longitude that provide us with a functioning, if somewhat imprecise, orientation to the social environment that we must daily navigate.

It makes both logical sense and social sense to say that without similarity there can be no difference, and vice versa. This is one of the basic principles of all classification systems. It should not, however, be understood as merely a version of the static binary oppositions so beloved of structuralist approaches to language and culture. It is, rather, a dynamic relationship between two complementary aspects of a social process (identification) and its product (identity). Within this ongoing relationship of call and response — and call and response again, and again, and again . . . — neither difference nor similarity is determinate or dominant.

Each of these axes of identification is imagined, a product of the human imagination. This does not mean, however, that they are imaginary in the sense that an illusion or a fantasy is imaginary. Far from it. Identification — similarity and difference perpetually feeding back on, and emerging out of, each other — is massively consequential, both in our mundane everyday individual experience and in the historical social construction of human collectivities. Depending on the context, identification affects everything from which side of the street we can walk on to what we can eat and what we like to eat; from who we can mate with to how we understand our place in the cosmos; from how we live to how we die. Everything. To paraphrase a deservedly famous remark of the American sociologist W. I. Thomas, if we define situations as real, then they are real in their consequences. We define identity as real. Without the work of the imagination that is identification we could not relate to each other consistently or predictably, and human society as we understand it would be impossible.

One of the central themes of social identification is membership, what the British anthropologist Anthony Cohen talked about as "belonging." This is not the lumpen togetherness of "potatoes-in-a-sack," but, rather, the shared *sense* of belonging that comes about through participation in a common symbolic world (in other words, culture). The feeling of similarity that this participation conjures up creates the space within which individual and other differences may coexist under a symbolic umbrella of community: community and belonging are thus imagined but not imaginary.

Whatever its roots, "belonging" immediately conjures up positive, warm images of inclusion, mutuality, and security. These may have as their foundations a range of social contexts: in the emotional hothouse of kinship and family; in more negotiable friendship or economic networks; in a local sense of shared residence and place; in more impersonal and formally defined citizenship; in a common history; or in a more diffuse sense of apparently shared "way of life" (language, religion, technology, cuisine, etiquette, and the myriad other things that constitute everyday practical cultural competences). All of these and more may contribute, in different contexts—and to differing degrees of significance depending on the context—to the idiom of identification that we call ethnicity.

But of course something else may also be evoked when we talk about ethnicity. Inclusion breeds exclusion. It cannot be otherwise. As with similarity and difference, logically and socially the one entails and requires the other. We know who we are—Us—at least in part because we know that we are not Them. This does not mean that conflict is inevitable, or that They must provide the negative to Our positive, but it does generate a fertile field of fraught possibilities. It is therefore not surprising that conflict and ethnicity can be seen feeding off each other as far back as there is a historical record to consult: the Old Testament story of the Israelites' invasion of the Promised Land is, for example, as much a catalog of ethnic conflict as the Vinland Saga's report of the first encounters between the Vikings and native North Americans.

Ethnicity—much as social identification more generally—is neither a "good thing" nor a "bad thing." It simply is. It is difficult to posit a human social world without it. For better or worse, processes of *ethnic* identification appear to be integral to the frameworks of meaning and significance—culture—that allow humans to know the world, to conjure up that world's meaning, and to recognize themselves in the process of doing so. If this is true, the most promising approach is not to cast a superior eye over ethnicity's apparent irrationality, or bemoan the obstacles to progress and civility that it presents, but to attempt to understand it on some, at least, of its own terms.

WHAT IS ETHNICITY?

When the ancient Greeks talked about *ethnos*—the root of our modern word *ethnicity*—they had in mind a community living and acting together in manner that we usually translate today as "people" or "nation." This evokes an image of a collectivity with at least some manners and mores, practices and purposes— a way of life—in common. In other words, a group whose members share something in terms of culture; thus the Norwegian anthropologist Fredrik Barth has defined ethnicity as "the social organization of culture difference." Ethnicity is not, however, an abstract, collective phenomenon. As we have already seen, it matters personally, to individuals. In this sense, to quote another anthropologist, this time Clifford Geertz, an American, ethnicity is "personal identity collectively ratified and publicly expressed."

Ethnicity is thus one way—perhaps, after kinship, the most ubiquitous way—of classifying humans into collectivities. This necessitates judgments that certain people are similar to each other, and, in this, different to others. Ethnicity draws on the cultural differences and similarities that the participants in a situation regard as significant, in order to build and dramatize these social boundaries. However, the ways in which culture is socially organized into ethnicity are neither obvious nor straightforward. People may appear to differ enormously in terms of culture and yet be able to identify themselves as ethnic fellows: think, for example, about the variety that is subsumed within Jewishness. Nor does apparent cultural similarity preclude strong ethnic differentiation. Viewed by an anthropologist from Mars, I have no doubt that Protestant Anglo-Americans and Protestant Anglo-Canadians look very similar; I have even less doubt, however, that they do not see things this way (not yet, anyway).

These examples suggest a need for selectivity; that our understanding of ethnicity cannot simply depend upon a crude model of cultures seen "in the round." Some cultural themes or identificatory criteria offer more grist to the ethnic imagination's mill than others: language, notions of shared descent, the inventiveness of tradition and history, locality and coresidence, and religion, these have all proved to be particularly potent ethnic markers. Even so, a common language, for example, or shared religious beliefs and practices don't necessarily do the trick in themselves. Nor do shared space and place. Although living together may be a potent source of shared identification, space and place can also divide people. They can be a resource to compete for. Even the minimal interaction that is necessary for a sense of difference to emerge takes up space: it needs a terrain. Thus it is that lines may get drawn in the sand; that borders and boundaries may come to constitute arbitrary and culturally defined group territories.

Since the first edition of this book there has been a scholarly debate, inspired by Rogers Brubaker, about the reality of the groups to which the label "ethnic" routinely attaches. Brubaker proposed that ethnicity is a shared *sense* of "groupness,", rather than membership of a well-defined, bounded corporate ethnic group. It is thus largely a cognitive phenomenon, an *idea*. He is right, of course, but largely tilting at a windmill: since Barth's seminal contribution, and indeed before, the internalized "groupness" that he describes, emerging out of the ebb and flow of everyday interaction, has been the dominant anthropological model of ethnic identification and ethnic groups.

These points suggest that ethnicity is not a matter of definable degrees or obvious kinds of cultural similarity or difference. It is not possible, for example, to offer a check list that would enable us authoritatively to determine whether or not members of Group A are *really* ethnically different to members of Group B, or whether Group C, for example, is an ethnic group or some other kind of collectivity. Enumerating cultural traits or characteristics is not a useful way to understand or identify ethnic differences. Anthropologists cannot classify the world of humans in the same way, for example, that lepidopterists might classify butterflies. Our subjects have a voice, and the baseline is whether a group is *seen* by its members to be different, not whether it "really" is (whatever that might mean).

Self-definition is not all that matters, however. It is also necessary that a group should be seen to be distinctive—itself—by others. In at least two senses there can be no such thing as unilateral ethnicity. First, ethnicity involves ethnic *relations*: connections and contacts between people who are seen to be different, as well as between those who are seen to be the same. A sense of ethnicity can only arise in the context of relationships and interaction with others. As I have already argued, without difference, there is no similarity. Defining *us* implies—if nothing stronger—an image of *them*. This is true of all social identities.

Second, it is difficult to imagine a meaningful identity—ethnic or whatever—that is not accepted and recognized by others. When the rising star of American golf Tiger Woods appeared on the Oprah Winfrey TV show in the United States in 1997, he insisted that, despite being claimed and fêted as such, he was neither black nor African American. He was, he suggested, "Cablinasian," a mixture of *Ca*ucasian, *bl*ack, North American *In*dian, and *Asian*. His tongue was at least partly in his cheek, but there was something serious in his rejection of a crude category of identity—black—and his insistence that, if descent in these terms matters, and in US society it surely does, it is anything but a simple matter. It will, however, come as no surprise that Cablinasian hasn't caught on as an authentic ethnic identity in its own right, if only because it has not been accepted as such by others. It is not enough to assert, "I am an X," or "We are Xs," for either of these things to become so. And, as more recent, and more serious, events in the United States have shown, "black lives matter," as do black deaths: being "black" is not something that can be self-defined away.

VARIETIES OF ETHNICITY

So, what kind of thing does count as "being an X" in the contemporary world? What kinds of social identities are ethnic? If we look at actually existing situations, many of the answers to this question appear to be pretty straightforward. In the United States, for example, Chicanos, Sioux, Irish Americans, African Americans, Italian Americans, Jews, Koreans, Chinese, Navajo, Mexicans, Cajuns, Aleuts, Hawaiians, Pennsylvania Dutch, Chippewa, and Ukrainians— arbitrarily chosen from many possibilities—are all recognizably "ethnic," in one sense or another. But what, for example, about the Amish, or the Mennonites, or the Mormons? Or, perhaps even more interesting, what about New England Yankees, or Texans, or people from New Orleans, or Southern whites in general? Are they ethnics? My answer, looking from outside, would in all of these cases be differing degrees of the affirmative. But given the strong association in the United States and elsewhere between the words *ethnic* and *minority*, their own answers—certainly in the case of the Yankees, the Texans, and the Southern whites—might be a resounding "No."

Looking at a range of relationships of similarity and difference may help to clarify matters. Take, for example, the somewhat unsubtle and incomplete, sequence shown in the diagram, which draws its general inspiration from a range of anthropological and other studies of Sicily and the *Mezzogiorno*, the "barbaric" south that, in the eyes of many northern Italians at least, is the nearest available Other between them and north Africa. Similar hierarchical models could be drawn up for anywhere in the world. There is nothing particular about Italy in this respect: it has been chosen somewhat arbitrarily here, reflecting my own ethnographic reading. You may like to try the exercise for wherever you live or 'come from'; in the process, you might also like to think about what it means to 'come from' somewhere.

HIERARCHIES OF SIMILARITY AND DIFFERENCE: VARIETIES AND LEVELS OF SICILIAN IDENTITY

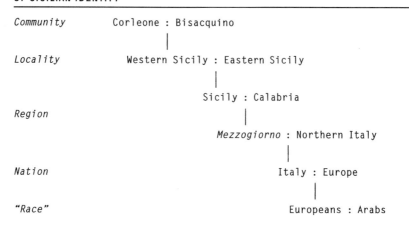

Community	Corleone : Bisacquino
Locality	Western Sicily : Eastern Sicily
	Sicily : Calabria
Region	
	Mezzogiorno : Northern Italy
Nation	Italy : Europe
"Race"	Europeans : Arabs

What does the model mean? Most immediately, it attempts to capture on the page something of the situational variability of identification: in one context my village provides my most important identity; in another it is that I am from the south; in yet another it is that I am an Italian. I may be able to emphasize this or that facet of my identity, depending upon what is to my advantage; however, I may not wish to or be able to. And if I come from Corleone, say, I can, depending on the context, mobilize all of the identities represented by the left-hand poles of the oppositional pairs in the model. Those that I differ from at one level, I can share something with at the next. Exclusion becomes inclusion.

The next point to note is that the words *ethnic* and *ethnicity* do not appear anywhere in the above scheme. And yet, in terms of the broad definition offered above—and in terms of our everyday understandings—much of the similarity and difference that is represented here looks, to say the least, something like ethnicity. The diagram thus suggests some questions. Where does ethnicity end and communal identity, or local identity, or regional identity, or national identity, begin? What is the relationship between community and locality, or locality and region? And what are the differences between all of these things? Where does "race" fit in with them?

As I have already suggested, context is important, but in each of these cases, it is difficult to define exhaustively and precisely the characteristics of the identificatory idiom in question. Criteria such as language, religion, descent, territory, and history or tradition have more or less salience at different "levels" of identification. Sicilian community identity—the village and the town— depends for its boundaries largely upon territory, family and descent, and tradition or history (which may all be combined in the local institution of the feud, or *vendetta*). By contrast, although such things undoubtedly serve to signify the difference between western and eastern Sicily, this difference is also very publicly visible in the daily use of language, that is, dialect. Even more marked linguistic differences provide a fault line of identification with respect to the regions of Calabria and Sicily, and the north and the south more generally. But here, at the regional and subnational levels, other factors such as shared cuisine, public interactional etiquette, and a nebulous notion that there are different "ways of doing things" are also significant.

At a greater degree of collective abstraction, national identity involves, in the first instance, a formal package which includes citizenship, a passport, political rights and duties within and without the national borders, and so on. Where the informal powers of others to accept or reject identity have been important previously, this is the unambiguous domain of formal power and authority. And even here, other things are involved too: language, food, and in the Italian case a contrast with much of the rest of the European Union on the basis of, among other things, religion. This recedes in significance, however, beside the dramatic sense of religious difference—embedded in a powerfully symbolized and inventive historical tradition—which serves to draw a line between Europeans and Arabs. Nor is it just religion that is believed to matter in this case. Putative descent reenters the frame in the shape of "race," the belief in distinctive populations sharing common ancestors in the remote past, human stocks with their own characteristics. From this point of view, Italians are very different from Libyans, for example. They are not the same "kind" of people. And although "racial" categories draw upon the visible features of bodies to assert the "naturalness" of particular similarities and differences, let us remember that "race" is culturally defined, not natural. Hence my use of quotation marks to remind the reader that it is a contested and problematic concept.

In this respect, and in others, this diagram represents, of course, only part of the hierarchical model of identification that could be constructed with respect to Sicilian identity. One could, for example, add in the relationships of similarity and difference between Italians and the other "Latin" peoples of the Mediterranean basin, between the peoples of the western and the eastern Mediterranean, between southern and northern Europe, between Sicilians and Sicilian Americans, and so on. This would begin—but only begin—to give us a picture of the multidimensional relationships of ethnic identification that are involved in "being Sicilian."

Further complexity emerges if we turn the model on its head. As presently presented, the eye proceeds down the page. In effect, this means beginning at the Sicilian town or village level, and thus implicitly adopting the point of view of a very local Sicilian Us. There is another way to do it, however. We could begin from a northern Italian perspective and go in the other direction, up the page, in which case everything appears in a different light. A member of the

Northern League, or a Padanian nationalist, for example, would doubtless emphasize the similarities between Sicilians rather than the differences and have a different understanding of what they are. Such "external" categorizations of Sicilian identities are important in that they are part of the social terrain and environment within which those identities arise, change, and have their meaning. These categorizations have political, economic, and other consequences that contribute in no small part to whatever it means, in any context and at any point of time, to be Sicilian. Thus in order to understand the complex social processes of Sicilian identification, it is necessary to adopt many points of view other than those of Sicilians themselves.

Community, locality, region, nation, and "race": are they even the same kind of thing? The answer is no, and yes. No, in that they appear to be about different things, with each evoking its own particular combinations of criteria of similarity and difference. No, in that some of these criteria are easier to negotiate around or away than others; locality or citizenship, for example, are more flexible than versions of the criterion of descent, such as family or "race." No, in that some of them find expression through organized ideologies such as nationalism and racism—political philosophies that assert how the world is and how it ought to be—while some do not. But yes, in that the criteria of similarity and difference in each case are definitively cultural. Yes, in that they all contribute to the social organization of a broad and distinctive genre of collective identification, which is not reducible to either kinship or social class, to pick only the most obvious (gender seems to me to involve altogether different principles of individual and collective identification). And yes, in that they all offer the potential for political organization and ideologizing.

So, instead of searching in vain for ever-more exclusive and exact definitions and distinctions, perhaps we should keep our options as open as possible. A more satisfactory approach may be to suggest that communal, local, regional, national, and "racial" identities can all be understood as locally and historically specific variations on a general and ancient theme of collective identification, ethnicity. Each of these variants says something about "the social organization of culture difference": even closely neighboring villages may have some small differences—with respect to patron saints, perhaps, special items of food, the use of particular words, festivals—between them. In the process each contributes to the symbolization and imagination of belonging and similarity. Each of them also says something about "the cultural organization of social difference." They are, if you like, culturally imagined and socially consequential, a way of putting things which recognizes that distinguishing between "the cultural" and "the social" makes only limited sense, at best.

Communal, local, regional, national, and "racial" identities also offer the possibility of "collectively ratified personal identity." In Sicily, as elsewhere, it may make a considerable difference *personally* to people which village they be-long to. It is, after all, individuals who belong. It may also make a considerable difference to people in their judgments of others *as persons*: as potential part-ners in whatever enterprise is in hand, as adversaries, or merely as objects of safe indifference. Even at the most abstract level of identification, "being Ital-ian" involves more than the possession of a passport and voting rights (and to judge from recent Italian political history the latter may not be very signifi-cant at all). Indeed, it is possible to be a citizen of another country—the United States, Australia, the United Kingdom—and still "be" an Italian.

WHY ETHNICITY MATTERS

A broad understanding of ethnicity can thus encompass and deal with social identifications which reflect and express similarity and difference defined ac-cording to community, locality, region, nation, and "race." Adopting an anthro-pological point of view encourages and requires us to generalize in this way. As an intellectual enterprise, anthropology tries to take the broadest, the most holistic, view of whatever social situation or context is the focus of attention. As a characteristically comparative enterprise, anthropology also needs sensitiz-ing concepts that travel well—kinship and religion are other good examples—rather than concepts which are too locally specific.

But anthropology has other emphases too: on culture and meaning, on local perceptions and knowledge—viewed from a generalizing and comparative per-spective—and on the routines of everyday life. This means that an anthropolo-gist's ideas of "what is going on" must, at the very least, be forged in a process of dialogue with the local people whose social universe is being studied. What *they* think is going on has to be taken seriously: it is the baseline from which we proceed. This is the main reason why anthropologists continue to insist upon long-term fieldwork, and face-to-face contact, as the mainstay of our research.

So far in this chapter I have concentrated upon the ways in which ethnic identification is a contextually variable and relative process. If we listen to people, this is one of the most important things that we learn about ethnicity: that it may be negotiable and flexible from one situation to another. But it is not the only thing that we learn: depending on cultural context and social situation, ethnicity may be non-negotiable. There may not be a choice. And when eth-nicity matters to people, it has the capacity to *really* matter, to move them to action and awaken powerful emotions.

This returns us to my opening theme of two contradictory images of ethnic and national identification. We are now better placed to understand that these images are only apparently contradictory. On the one hand, that ethnicity may be negotiable or flexible does not mean that it is *infinitely* negotiable or flexible. Some aspects of ethnic identification are less malleable than others. It is one thing to get a new passport, change one's religion, move and live somewhere else, or even adopt a new way of life; it is quite another thing to disavow one's family or to shuck off the physical attributes that may embody a particular identification. And lest the latter be misunderstood, this careful choice of words does not necessarily refer to the "natural" characteristics of "race": it could just as easily mean a tattoo, male circumcision, or some other ethnically significant body modification.

And this is before we consider whether or not a change of self-identification will be validated in its appropriate context. The power of other people may be decisive. In the north of Ireland, for example, it is one thing to "turn"—as changing one's religion is described locally—on marriage to a member of the "other side." It is quite another, however, for that to be accepted by one's spouse's family and community. Hence the well-known phenomenon of individuals converting under these circumstances, only to become more enthusiastically "bitter"—to use another local expression—than their spouse, in-laws, and new neighbors. There are some kinds of identity that it is no one's *right* to change; that change has to be performed, validated behaviorally, and believed by others.

On the other hand, that ethnicity can be a source of powerful affect and meaning does not imply that it is either "primordial" or "natural." This common misunderstanding has been a source of some futile debate, in anthropology and elsewhere, between "primordialists" and "constructionists," between what Marcus Banks has evocatively described as models of "ethnicity in the heart" and "ethnicity in the head." There are several important things to bear in mind about arguments of this kind. First, how much ethnicity and its variants matter, and to whom, differs from epoch to epoch and place to place. There is no human consistency with respect to the strength of ethnic attachments, although that there are ethnic attachments—according to my general definition—does seems to be consistent. Nor do we need to resort to notions of essence and nature to explain why, when ethnicity matters to people, it matters so much: the nature and content of primary socialization, the affective power of symbols, local histories, and the local consequences of identification are probably sufficient to account for this.

What matters, anyway, is not actually whether ethnicity is a personal and cultural essence with which we are born and about which we can do nothing. What matters is that many people, in many situations, fervently believe this to be so and behave accordingly. That national feeling and identity are of this noble order—rooted in language, collective psychology, culture, and place—is the central tenet of many local brands of nationalism, with philosophical roots in the European Romantic tradition and practical political roots going back at least as far as the 1848 bourgeois revolutions. Whether it is true or not, this is certainly consequential.

Which brings me to one last point. Nationalism, for example, something so apparently timeless that it can be described as primordial, generally turns out on closer inspection to be decidedly modern. This is only "generally," because some nationalisms arguably have a long history, while the general collective idiom of ethnic identification is positively timeless. But part of the apparently ancient gloss of nationalism comes from an appeal to a vision of lost greatness. "United Russia," "Make America Great Again," and "Take Back Control" may be slogans that purport to be forward-looking and, on their own terms, progressive, but they all look backward: to the unity of the heroic Tsarist empire, to a time when America was the big kid on the block, and to Britain's stolen mastery of its own destiny. All of which the modern cargo cult that is nationalism promises to return.

So modern ideologies of nationalism, which argue that nationhood and national sentiment are governed by natural law and justice, are precisely that, modern ideologies. Their usefulness in legitimating domination, appropriation, and mass violence sits uncomfortably alongside their potential to inspire liberation. This is perhaps the real contradiction at the heart of any discussion of ethnicity and nationalism in the modern world. It is certainly the most consequential. It is why we should need to approach these things on their own terms at the same time as thinking critically about them. It is a powerful argument for an open-ended anthropological understanding of processes of ethnic identification that can accommodate their fluidity as well as their intractability. That they are imagined but not imaginary.

ACKNOWLEDGMENTS

Although I am responsible for the shortcomings of the original chapter, and this revised version, these would have more numerous without the careful attention and advice of Simon Holdaway, Jenny Owen, and David Phillips, to whom I am most grateful.

SUGGESTIONS FOR FURTHER READING

The following introductions to the academic literature on ethnicity and nationalism can all be recommended:

Banks, M. 1996. *Ethnicity: Anthropological Constructions*. London: Routledge.
Cornell, S., and D. Hartmann. 2007. *Ethnicity and Race: Making Identities in a Changing World*. Second edition. Thousand Oaks, CA: Pine Forge.
Eriksen, T. H. 2010. *Ethnicity and Nationalism: Anthropological Perspectives*. Third edition. London: Pluto.
Gingrich, A, and M. Banks, eds. 2006. *Neo-Nationalism in Europe: Perspectives from Social Anthropology*. New York: Berghahn.

The general theoretical arguments about social identification on which this chapter is based can be found in:

Jenkins, R. 2014. *Social Identity*. Fourth edition. London: Routledge.
————. 2008. *Rethinking Ethnicity*. Second edition. London: Sage.

For the reader interested in looking further at the Sicilian case, there is a wealth of good literature, most of which has focused on some or other aspect of *mafia* behavior. Two good places to start are:

Cole, J. 1997. *The New Racism in Europe: A Sicilian Ethnography*. Cambridge: Cambridge University Press.
Schneider, J., and P. Schneider. 2005. "Mafia, Antimafia, and the Plural Cultures of Sicily." *Current Anthropology* 46 (2005): 501–20.

REFERENCES

Barth, F. 1969. "Introduction." In *Ethnic Groups and Boundaries: The Social Organisation of Culture Difference*, ed. F. Barth. Oslo: Universitetsforlaget.
Brubaker, R. 2004. *Ethnicity without Groups*. Cambridge, MA: Harvard University Press.
Cohen, A. P. 1985. *The Symbolic Construction of Community*. London: Routledge.
Geertz, C. 1973. *The Interpretation of Cultures*. New York: Basic Books.
Gellner, E. 1983. *Nations and Nationalism*. Oxford: Basil Blackwell.
Hobsbawm, E. J. 1990. *Nations and Nationalism since 1780*. Cambridge: Cambridge University Press.
Mendelberg, T. 2001. *The Race Card: Campaign Strategy, Implicit Messages and the Norm of Equality*. Princeton, NJ: Princeton University Press.

CHAPTER 6

SOCIALISM

ETHICS, IDEOLOGIES, AND OUTCOMES

Chris Hann

Why do we have to have rich and poor? Why? Why can't
everybody have a little bit? What's wrong with that? That
mother-fucking Gorbachev is to blame for this mess.
—Bulgarian villager in 1992, quoted in Creed (1998, 270)

INTRODUCTION

When the American anthropologist Gerald Creed began his research in Bulgaria in the mid-1980s, Comrade Todor Zhivkov had held power unchallenged
for more than thirty years. Bulgaria seemed as stable as all the other socialist
regimes in the vast region known as the Soviet bloc or the Second World (sand-
wiched between the First World of Western capitalism and a Third World of
more or less impoverished postcolonial states). Creed investigated transformations at village level. There were good economic as well as ideological reasons
for bringing peasants together to form larger farming units, but socialist collectivization had been imposed crudely "from above" and was therefore un-

welcome to villagers. As elsewhere in Eurasia, it obliterated earlier forms of cooperation and created new structures of bureaucratic and political power.

Creed goes on to tell a more complex and less familiar tale of how these villagers accomplished a further revolution in the following decades. They "domesticated" socialism through their everyday activities, focused on personal plots and family contracting. Collective farm ideology was progressively modified and the villagers reaped the material benefits. Creed revisited the village after the momentous political changes of 1989–90, and listened to local people's views on the respective merits of socialism and capitalism. Opinions differed, as they do in most human groups, but the majority held a positive view of socialism. They wanted to retain the security and relative equality that socialist policies had brought them. Villagers critical of socialism while it had lasted nonetheless identified strongly with its ideals as they understood them (primarily in terms of development and an ethic of social justice). Many continued to vote for communist candidates when alternatives were available. Nor was this nostalgia short-lived. When Creed returned for more fieldwork in the new century he documented, in addition to economic dislocation and political instability, intangible losses which he summed up as "cultural dispossession." Bulgaria has been a member of the European Union since 2007, but economically it remains a basket case, heavily dependent on the remittances of labor migrants. Most other states of the former Soviet bloc have experienced similar problems, including the Russian Federation itself. Poland was exceptional in the sense that its socialist governments were never strong enough to impose collectivization. But through its strategies of rapid industrialization, here too the state greatly expanded the options available to its citizens. When factories were privatized and closed or downsized in the 1990s, power holders were accused of neglecting their elemental duty to provide for the well-being of citizens.

Similar scenarios are replicated on other continents. The glory days of Cuba's socialist revolution were long gone by the time of Fidel Castro's death in 2016. Subsidies from oil-rich Venezuela could not compensate for the massive economic shock experienced when the island's umbilical cord to the Soviet bloc was severed after 1990. Without gradual concessions to market principles, the Cuban economy would have collapsed altogether. Given the difficult circumstances of everyday life, foreign commentators found it hard to understand the respect and even affection shown for Fidel Castro. In their external eyes he was a dictator, but in the eyes of most Cubans he was an inspirational figure whose revolution had transformed the social structure of their island and brought schools and hospitals that were the envy of the rest of the continent. Cubans, too, are apprehensive of an acceleration in cultural dispossession as new leaders rebuild relations with the United States.

Could their future lie in some hybrid combination of planning and market such as the "market socialism" of China or Vietnam? Communist parties have held on to power in these Asian states, following the introduction of radical economic reforms in the 1980s. Growth rates have been high, and hundreds of millions of citizens have significantly improved their standard of living. But alongside the emergence of new middle classes, seemingly preoccupied with consumption and indistinguishable from the middle classes of capitalist countries, social inequality has generally increased. When the Communist Party becomes enmeshed in the world of business and its top cadres are able to transmit wealth as well as privileges to their offspring, the socialist ideology proclaiming this party to be the vehicle of the working class (in alliance with the peasantry) loses credibility. The slogans of the elites ring hollow in this situation; but for the powerless, resigned complicity is a more likely strategy than revolutionary opposition, especially if they too have some access to new paths of embourgeoisement.

I begin this chapter with these concrete examples because such case studies are the hallmark of modern sociocultural anthropology. But ethnographic investigation is not an end in itself. Socialism raises larger questions about human nature and community. In the narrower sense, socialism was a political movement launched in the nineteenth century in Western Europe in the wake of the dislocation caused by capitalist industrialization. In the course of the twentieth century this countermovement imposed alternative models of modernization on much of the planet. Long after the ideological heat has cooled down, the pantheon of Marxist-Leninist-Maoist socialism remains familiar. Even lesser Gods such as Fidel and Che Guevara are global icons. In the United States, long considered immune to socialism, a self-styled democratic socialist called Bernie Sanders mounted an impressive showing in the presidential electoral campaign of 2016. Is there perhaps more to socialism than ideological militancy, secret police, and repression? I shall argue that it is the modern form of a seemingly universal ethical impulse to contain social inequality, the rational secular successor to witchcraft accusations, beliefs in the justice of divine kings, and religious principles such as "love thy neighbor." To implement this impulse in densely populated industrial societies is not easy; yet there are good reasons to suppose that the future of our species and our planet depends on reaching global agreement on some new form of socialism—a form that meets the needs of humanity more adequately than any of the Marxist-Leninist-Maoist variants.

SOCIALISM AS A POLITICAL IDEOLOGY

The word ideology is loaded: *other* people have ideologies, we in the West have democracies and civil societies. Anthropologists point out that ideals such as "open society" and "transparency international" are also ideological. Ideology is a feature of all human communities. As anthropologists such as Eric Wolf have shown, it is most effective when it merges invisibly into the realms we call religion, cosmology, or simply "culture." Certain forms of the state, however, propagate ideology in systematic ways to mobilize their populations through public rituals. In modern conditions, states have the power to inculcate specific doctrines through their control over education and the mass media. Fascism and many varieties of nationalism conform to this pattern, but Marxist-Leninist-Maoist socialism is the paradigmatic case.

While philosophers, political theorists, and other intellectuals have written many erudite books about socialism, anthropologists tend to begin by asking what it means for ordinary people in their everyday lives. This is not well documented. Most of the literature on socialism falls into one of four categories. Within the Second World (as the socialist *other* used to be known), ideology was reproduced through endless propaganda texts, including hagiographies of the founding fathers and contemporary leaders. In the nonsocialist countries, academic studies tended to give socialism a bad press: political scientists applied concepts such as "totalitarianism," and economists had little trouble in proving that centrally planned economies would never work. Third, there was a charitably disposed "Western left," an orientation that was often marked by gross naivety and overlooked actual conditions in the socialist countries. Fourth, within the bloc itself, some dissident intellectuals succeeded in attracting the attention of the West; but they were not always to be trusted in representing the views and aspirations of their fellow-citizens, the ordinary consumers of socialist ideology.

The upshot was that, until the end of the Cold War, marked symbolically by the collapse of the Berlin Wall in 1989 and of the Soviet Union just a few years later, the images that most Westerners held of socialism were an unreliable mixture of journalistic caricature and myth. Anthropological research offers a corrective. Its premise is the most basic anthropological move: to acknowledge that the institutions and values of the modern West have no universal validity. Socialism was an attempt to organize human communities according to principles that differ from those of political liberalism and capitalist market economies. The methodological premise is that, through fieldwork, anthropologists are in a position to analyze how abstract ideological principles interact with distinctive local traditions to shape human lives.

The ideologists of Marxism-Leninism, above all in the era of Joseph Stalin, aimed at nothing less than the creation of a new belief system, a future-oriented worldview for new people ("socialist man"). Other models of socialism, however, for example on the African continent in the early postcolonial decades, paid more attention to the past—to the evocation of traditions of social harmony in an age when modern markets did not yet threaten. Regardless of whether the main focus of idealization was the future or the past or some combination of the two, socialist ideology always encountered subversive factors. Karl Marx and Friedrich Engels proclaimed (in *The German Ideology*) that the "ideas of the ruling class are in every epoch the ruling ideas," but in practice there is always some room for contestation and resistance. Socialism is no exception. It is not difficult to represent its doctrines to mass audiences since, behind the more technical language of historical materialism and modes of production, the core ideas of equality and mutuality are very widely distributed in human communities. This wide resonance is rooted in an aversion to inequality that appears to be a unique characteristic of *homo sapiens*, as cognitive scientists have suggested. This explains how an ideology with very specific origins in Europe in the early phase of industrialization could later be adapted, at least superficially, in virtually every part of the world. The collapse of "actually existing socialism" must thus be distinguished from the deeper resilience of socialist ideals. The work of Gerald Creed shows that socialism in Bulgaria has a "robust history." When postsocialist governments set about implementing more dogmatic models of capitalist society than Westerners themselves possessed, it becomes easier to understand why the core ideas of socialism are reasserted by angry citizens such as the Bulgarian villager quoted above.

One hundred and seventy years have passed since Marx and Engels in the *Communist Manifesto* urged the workers of the world to unite. They offered a comprehensive philosophy of history, focused on the emergence and development of capitalism but engaging with earlier epochs and, since they were committed revolutionaries, with the future as well. They saw the bourgeoisie as a progressive class whose temporary dominance would inevitably give way to socialism, and ultimately to the withering of the state in a communist utopia. The successes of this movement in the industrialized countries of Western Europe were limited. In Russia, however, the Bolshevik Party, playing the vanguard role theorized explicitly by Lenin, was able to seize power in dramatic circumstances in 1917. Marxism-Leninism became the political ideology according to which the Soviet Union and its allies organized their societies until the sudden collapse of the bloc more than seventy years later.

This ideology was imposed by elites which rejected the bourgeois institutions of party political competition and freedom of association. Power was concentrated in the state, which was controlled by the monopolistic Communist Party. But how was this power to be exercised and justified? The personalizing of power in the hands of old men and the capriciousness of its exercise were sources of weakness rather than strength. The early phases of socialism were accompanied almost everywhere by violence, and the later phases by the stench of corruption. How could loyalty and commitment be maintained? Martin Holbraad has argued for the case of Cuba that the revolution is rooted not so much in ideology but in a "political ontology" which differs radically from liberal theory and renders the revolutionary cause immune to profane refutation. When the state, the people, and the person are conceptually fused, internalized notions of self-sacrifice and martyrdom provide a moral authority that trumps all ethnographic evidence of human imperfection (such as undignified graft, caused by shortages of housing and other goods).

But the question remains: how is this revolutionary ontology sustained among ordinary "flesh and blood" citizens, especially after the charismatic revolutionaries have departed the scene? While Western democracies decentralize power through the market and through regular contested elections, socialist states were compelled to develop alternative techniques of legitimation. The quasi-religious elaboration of Marxism-Leninism as an ideological system was an attempt to meet this need. It was more than a body of political doctrine. It was the core of a meaningful world of cultural symbols representing not only the organization of a national society but the nature of human beings and the scheme of the universe.

How was this ideology disseminated? Ideological language differs from that of everyday speech. It is formulaic, based around a few central slogans (though initiates who study hard can develop proficiency in an elaborate system of knowledge comparable to a theology). Ideological oratory is frequently incomprehensible to many of those obliged to listen to it. In this respect the language of Marxism-Leninism resembles the formal language of powerholders in many 'traditional' societies. Much of its repertoire was drawn from the works of the founding fathers. Concepts such as Lenin's "democratic centralism" (to describe the organization of the Communist Party) were presented as science but taught with the rote methods of the catechism. Selected texts were published in lavish complete editions, some of which found their way to the offices of the managers of factories and collective farms (*kolkhozy*). The holy books might even be displayed in the living quarters of ordinary workers, where it was just as well that they were not read (*kolkhozniki* might not have appreciated Marx's disparaging comment on "the idiocy of rural life"). Ideological language was constantly monitored and new terms were introduced from time to time. The language of armed struggle against the capitalist foe eventually gave way to the language of "peaceful coexistence." But as Alexei Yurchak has demonstrated, the shift away from ideological language that marked the years of *glasnost'* and *perestroika* in the 1980s was followed swiftly by the collapse of the entire edifice of Soviet socialism.

Ideologies are disseminated through many kinds of rituals and symbols. Lenin was a rationalist and an atheist who would doubtless have deplored the construction of his mausoleum in Red Square and the deliberate fostering of a cult with overtones of more conventional religious movements. But he was also a hard-nosed politician, and there is little doubt that his cult, together with the widespread adoption of new symbols such as the hammer and sickle and the construction of a new ritual calendar, had long-term political payoffs in the Soviet Union. These innovations helped ordinary people to make sense of their social order. People learned that they had a social system of which they could be proud. Whatever economic or political difficulties they might face, at some deeper level they had the consolation that they were morally superior to the degenerate imperialists of the West. Ritual creativity was extended from the public sphere of flags and Mayday parades to encroach deep inside the private sphere of life-cycle rituals, including name-giving ceremonies and funerals.

OUTCOMES

Throughout Eurasia there was remarkable uniformity in the symbols used by powerholders to justify the rule of the working classes. From Peking to Prague the same photographs of Marx and Lenin were carried in the same sort of parades and the same quotations from the *Communist Manifesto* appeared on the front page of the party newspaper. Similar techniques and inventions were successfully deployed in other parts of the world. In Hanoi and Havana the similarities to the original Soviet model were strong; indeed, they outlived the original. Elsewhere socialism is often more variable and elusive. The Green Book of Libya's Colonel Qaddafi was quite different from the Red Book of Chairman Mao, and also from other models of socialism in the Islamic world. Postcolonial states such as Tanzania and Zimbabwe were attracted by the emancipatory rhetoric of socialism, but outcomes on the ground were diverse. The common elements were a rejection of certain imperialist legacies, including free markets and party political competition, and a concomitant appeal to indigenous alternatives. But the Western-educated leaders of socialist movements in the Third World often had trouble maintaining their personal integrity in the face of a global political economy that allowed them little or no room to realize their aspirations.

There is no easy way to measure the strength of a political ideology, any more than there are easy answers to questions about the strength of religious belief in modern societies. Some became devout believers in the churches of Marxism-Leninism and Maoism. Others became committed opponents. The great majority were somewhere in between. This variation corresponds to the fate of socialism's invented rituals, some of which were more successful than others. Most Eastern Europeans had little difficulty in adapting to secular, socialist weddings, though some preferred to combine the secular ceremony with a traditional church service. The latter option was not open to those who worked for the state, and such constraints could lead to tensions, even within families. An entirely secular funeral presented greater problems. In the Hungarian village where I did fieldwork in the 1970s, the Communist Party secretary admitted to feeling uncomfortable when carrying out this ritual. He was seldom called upon to do so, not even for deceased party members. In Bulgaria, by contrast, secular funerals became routine.

Socialist rituals were most successful when they could be grafted onto tradition, as when a portrait of Mao was added to the shrine of the lineage ancestors in East Asia. Despite the internationalism of the founding fathers, the most powerful nonsocialist elements proved to be those of the nation and nationalism. Soviet rituals commemorating the sacrifices made for the Fatherland in the "Great Patriotic War" undoubtedly struck deep chords throughout society, because they managed to link the larger solidarities of nation and state to personal and familial meanings. Elsewhere it proved harder to graft socialism onto the *sacra* of the nation, especially in smaller states where nationwide antisocialist rebellions had been quashed. I found mixed responses to socialist ideology in my comparative work in Hungary and Poland between 1975 and 1982. By this time, more and more people were judging their system by its own ideals and finding it to be deficient. Even though egalitarianism was seldom highlighted in official ideological publications, the core moral values of socialism were linked by ordinary people to a high degree of social equality; by the 1980s, disillusion in this regard was widespread. The interminable speeches at the Communist Party congresses were boring: people preferred new forms of entertainment, if possible Western, on their newly acquired televisions.

I also found that relatively few citizens formulated explicit challenges to Marxism-Leninism. Even when the number of sincere believers was in steep decline, socialism encompassed a body of diverse ideas which had something to offer to most social groups. For example, young people could value the emphasis placed on sport and communal outdoor activities, while ignoring the explicitly political messages. Workers and peasants benefited initially from unprecedented opportunities for social as well as geographical mobility, followed by new opportunities to accumulate goods as the regimes gradually shifted away from a narrow bias toward heavy industry to promote consumption and raise living standards. The old bourgeois intelligentsia was the most significant loser in this process, yet many of those who inherited cultural capital profited from the subsidies given by socialists to the arts and to higher education and research. People in all walks of life showed a measure of critical detachment from their regime in everyday life, without necessarily calling its ideals into question. For example, they often told jokes that turned on central political dogmas of the ideology (Example: What is the definition of capitalist society? Capitalist society is based on the exploitation of man by his fellow man! And what is the definition of socialist society? Under socialism it is precisely the other way around!). Hans Steinmüller has documented the persistence of such patterns in contemporary China. They are by no means restricted to urban intellectuals: irony and cynicism are widespread in the countryside, among local state officials and their clients alike.

Comprehensive rejection of the system was rare and largely confined to groups such as churches and sects that were persecuted. Gypsies frequently resisted socialist efforts (even when well-intentioned) to turn them into disciplined factory workers, because this was so antagonistic to their traditional values and culture. But even those with an unambiguous aversion to the political dogmas of socialism, such as dispossessed descendants of the old bourgeoisie, were not immune to the influence of socialist values. How could they have been, given the conditions in which they lived, the air that they breathed?

Even within Eurasia, Marxism-Leninism was everywhere refracted by specific cultural and institutional factors. Hungary and Poland are neighbors in east-central Europe and their political and cultural traditions have many common features. Yet by the 1970s the differences seemed more striking than the similarities. In Hungary, the legitimating role of an abstract ideology declined following the introduction of the "new economic mechanism" in 1968. Instead, greater emphasis was placed on individualism and economics, as in most capitalist countries. The party secretary I mentioned above was an agronomist by training, but he was not employed in the socialist sector of the village cooperative. As in the Bulgarian community documented by Gerald Creed, some agronomists were charged with assisting villagers to maximize their household production, all in the interests of the national economy. My friend rationalized this as a legitimate adaptation of socialist principles. After all, collectivization was not even mentioned in the texts of the founding fathers, so there was no need to be too rigid in repressing private farmers. Hungary remained a one-party system, but pragmatic market-oriented modifications were generally welcomed, and this was conducive to regime stability as well as to the accumulation of private wealth.

In Poland no such flexible adaptations proved possible. Collectivization was never fully implemented (though the peasantry remained suspicious of regime intentions). Successive Communist Party leaders were afraid to experiment with "market socialism" and a perceived ideological rigidity estranged the population from power holders to a much greater degree than in Hungary. Opposition was mobilized by a powerful institution with deep historical roots among the people, which socialist ideology in Poland simply could not contain: the Roman Catholic Church. The image of the Black Madonna of Częstochowa which adorned the lapel of *Solidarity* leader Lech Wałęsa was a much more potent symbol than the image of Marx, Lenin, or a red socialist star in the lapel of a party functionary.

If neighboring socialist countries in Central Europe could develop in such different directions, what can we say about the export of socialist ideology to other parts of the world? One fruitful approach is to investigate how socialist ideas can or cannot connect with other elements in the society. For example, when socialism was implemented in a country such as Laos it necessarily became entangled with the specific cultural traditions of Buddhism, including ideas about personal "merit making." The constraints of this well-established religious ideology made it extremely difficult for the peasantry to accept a collective basis for the organization of agriculture. However, there were fewer constraints to inhibit relatively smooth adaptations to collectivization in the case of Russian peasants or Siberian reindeer herders. These groups have experienced particularly severe problems in the postsocialist era, since they had little precedent for the concepts of private ownership and entrepreneurship on which their survival has come to depend.

The appeals launched by socialist leaders to the collectivist traditions of the people were generally romantic and simplistic (and sometimes plain false and self-serving). In Tanzania, for example, elite efforts to promote a distinctive African socialism were not notably successful, especially when they implied, as in *ujamaa* villages, a tradition of working the land on a communal basis. In reality, here as in most agricultural societies, while land might in some sense have been collectively owned, it was very seldom *worked* communally. While certain activities required labor cooperation, most plots, most of the time, were the responsibility of just one household (or even one person). Socialist policies that overlooked such complexity were likely to provoke resistance. In East Africa and elsewhere field studies have shown that, behind a rhetoric of socialist equality, earlier power structures often remained intact; alternatively, a "new class" of literate officials became dominant.

Both the ambitions and the limitations of socialism as a modernizing ideology can be seen in gender relations. Even though Marx himself had little to say on the subject, many socialists have asserted the desirability of full gender equality. Realities have been very different. In China, Chairman Mao proclaimed that women held up half the sky. While he was in power women certainly came to undertake more work than previously outside the home, but they seldom lost their subordinate position within it and only rarely could they exercise equal power in the public sphere. Although the government of China still styles itself socialist, it has in recent decades modified or dropped numerous elements that were in conflict with centuries of patriarchal custom. While some observers speak of increasing individualization and detect convergence with global norms, anthropologists of China have shown that patriarchy persists in many culturally specific ways, not least as a result of state intervention in birth control. The role of kin in providing social support continues to differ from the typical domestic patterns of Western capitalist societies.

The case of Germany is particularly instructive because it allows for direct comparisons between socialism and the "free West." After the Nazi period, in which the political, cultural, and indeed racial unity of the German *Volk* was the primary ideological principle and Joseph Goebbels its best known expositor, Germany was partitioned by the victorious allies. For almost half a century, until 1990, the German Democratic Republic espoused a rather rigorous version of Marxism-Leninism, with highly centralized political and economic controls and all the usual ritual symbolism. The controls extended to Orwellian language: for example, the wall erected in Berlin in August 1961 to prevent East Germans from defecting was called the Anti-Fascist Protection Wall. Meanwhile the Federal Republic operated much as other Western pluralist democracies.

Even though East Germany performed quite well in comparison with other socialist countries, the Federal Republic was always much more powerful economically. This was the principal factor which led the majority of East German citizens to vote in favor of reunification when given the opportunity in 1990. However, the early enthusiasm soon gave way to disillusionment on both sides. The former East Germans were classified as *Ossis* and they became objects of criticism, pity, and ridicule for *Wessis*. They were perceived as greedy in wanting to receive all at once the privileges of a higher standard of living, which could only come in the form of federal subsidies, since large sectors of the old socialist economy were uncompetitive in the new context. The *ossis* were in turn bitter about what they perceived to be the arrogance of the *Wessis*. They resented being cast as second-class citizens, complained about capitalist colonization and exploitation, and continued to invoke elements of an egalitarian socialist ideology to assert their dignity.

The economic, social, and political problems of German reunification have been studied by many social scientists, but the extent to which the values of the old ideology have been preserved and continue to influence behavior can only be revealed through in-depth anthropological studies. For example, Birgit Müller has documented the emotional attachments that many East Germans experienced toward their work brigades, especially when these micro-level units of sociality were swept aside following privatization and the imposition of new forms of labor discipline. The institutions of socialism had radical effects on everyday social relations and the life course. East Germany provided childcare facilities which enabled women to return to work very soon after giving birth and put them in a better position to pursue careers on equal footing with men. Their rights and capacities have not been enhanced by reunification, which has led to an erosion of these distinctive socialist institutions in the family sphere. (This is not to say that earlier gender models were entirely swept aside under socialist ideology in East Germany. On the contrary, the women who went out to work in factories and offices continued to bear the primary responsibility for cooking, cleaning, and general household maintenance when they went home. As in Maoist China, this element in socialist ideology certainly had a significant impact on divisions of labor, but the deeper structures of power and value in society could not be so readily altered.)

A population such as that of East Germany, exposed to relatively high doses of ideology over a long period, may suffer withdrawal systems when the treatment is suddenly interrupted. Where new political and economic opportunities have opened up, people hurry to take advantage of them, but in areas where "the transition" has proceeded less smoothly, notably in regions of high structural unemployment, people may turn in frustration to other ideologies to find an explanation for their predicament. The source to which people most commonly turn is nationalism: right-wing extremism and suspicion of foreigners are disproportionately prevalent among the *Ossis*. But this pattern is by no means specific to Germany, or to Europe. In many other parts of the world, too, the gaps left by receding socialist ideologies have often been filled by more or less malignant forms of nationalism.

The majority of today's East Germans have not been mobilized in this way. Rather, they have become more or less satisfied capitalist consumers. From having the highest rates of voter participation in the socialist years, the eastern districts of Germany now have the lowest. Does this mean that capitalism is non-ideological? Are the slogans of "private property," "market economy," and "civil society" mere incantations, just like the jargon of Marxism-Leninism in previous generations? Although the similarities are clear enough, it is important to see that the nature of the ideology has changed: the domination of a narrow political class has been replaced by more diffuse, less visible forms of domination. The ideology of the market is less "transparent" than a centrally controlled political ideology and this makes it harder to grasp and to contest. For anthropologists of an anarchist disposition, all forms of domination and ideology are equally pernicious. But it is hard to conceive human social organization without some forms of hierarchy and corresponding ideologies of legitimation. Even egalitarian hunter/gatherers and utopian communes cannot dispense with ideology in this fundamental sense.

CONCLUSIONS

A century has passed since the Russian Revolution. Was twentieth-century socialism simply a horrible failure? From an evolutionist's perspective, the answer is affirmative. Marvin Harris declared in 1992 that the socialist variety of industrial society was obviously unable to compete with the capitalist varieties. He was referring to materialist efficiency, but for many critics the ethical shortcomings of socialism have been even more serious. The distinguished British historian Eric Hobsbawm never left the Communist Party. At the end of his long life, when the USSR had disintegrated and the devastation wrought by Stalin could be assessed from new perspectives, Hobsbawm would still explain patiently to interviewers that these huge sacrifices had been justified in the larger scheme of things, i.e., to save the world from Fascism. Few could go this far. The British Communist Party lost many of its leading intellectuals after the Soviet invasion of Hungary in 1956. But Hobsbawm's many detractors failed to recognize the ethical basis of his loyalty. For him, socialism meant ideals of emancipation and popular sovereignty that could not be delivered by any alternative bourgeois program (such as "human rights").

The positions taken by sociocultural anthropologists tend to be more nuanced, partly because even this most universal of ideologies was always subjected to local modifications that the ideologists themselves could not fully control. Those who document such complexities are liable to be criticized by those who prefer to see things in black and white, such as the ideologists themselves, or their intellectual opponents in "dissident" groups. In the past I was sometimes regarded as an apologist for Hungary's "goulash socialism," and more recently I have been accused of exaggerating postsocialist nostalgia. This is the uncomfortable obligation of the anthropologist. To report that many elements of socialist society were widely endorsed and are nowadays sincerely mourned is not to excuse the violence and hypocrisy of generations of self-serving power holders.

In African and other postcolonial societies, self-styled socialists did not achieve as much as they hoped and expected. Their efforts may nonetheless have resulted in more equal societies than those which followed untrammeled capitalist paths. Cuba, in spite of an American blockade since 1960, managed even in the "special situation" after 1990 to provide better health, education, and pensions for its population than many European societies. Maoist China offered virtually all of its citizens better nutrition and subsistence guarantees (and also literacy rates) than did democratic India, with its greater reliance on markets. Yet we should never forget that many millions died in the disruption of the early decades of socialism in China, as they had earlier in the Soviet Union. No easy ethical judgements are possible. Here I simply suggest that anthropological studies which reveal how ordinary people understood the alternatives of socialism and capitalism and how far they "internalized" their own ideologies may add something of value to the statistics of economists and demographers, to the prejudices of politicians and the stereotypes of journalists.

Eastern European societies voted against their previous rulers as soon as they were given opportunities to express their views freely in 1989–91. My friend the party secretary in Hungary lost his job and was unable to find a new one. However, he has remained loyal to his party and a generation later he still has friends and sympathizers in his village. Postsocialist governments did not dare to dismantle overnight a welfare net that commanded mass support. After brief experiments with "shock therapy" (notably in Poland), many countries in Eastern Europe voted the direct successors of the communist parties back into power. Under the impact of a capitalism that often takes on very crude and extreme forms, many people feel nostalgia for the security they had in the past. It is more than nostalgia. As Caroline Humphrey found in the mid-1990s when she revisited Buryat collective farms in Siberia, "there is a kind of gut loyalty to this former everyday life, which older people especially cannot abandon."

Some people draw explicitly on what they recall from Marxist-Leninist ideology when commenting on their postsocialist predicament. The socialist condemnation of "speculation" (*spekulacja*) is still heard in Russia whenever a new trader or entrepreneur is thought to be making unreasonable profits, and especially when the profit goes to a dealer rather than to the manufacturer. This could be seen as a long-term success of socialist ideology, one which continues to inhibit the development of new social forms based on the tyranny of markets. Of course, the underlying antimarket sentiment is much older than Marxist socialism and goes back at least to Aristotle.

We can conclude that the ideology of Marxism-Leninism was most successful when it managed to insinuate itself into older streams of values. The "labor theory of value" is not a socialist invention, but its incorporation into socialist ideology helped power holders to justify their programs to peasants who were themselves deeply committed to a strong work ethic as a moral dimension of economy. Privileging the downtrodden, ordinary people of every epoch, including our own, socialism might be theorized as a variant of *populism*. The connections are historically tangled. They will be firmly rejected by most enthusiasts of socialism, for whom contemporary populists mystify social relations ideologically, in the classic sense of Karl Marx. Thus Donald Trump attracts voters by lambasting socialism (always a bogey in the USA). Yet far from serving the interests of the American people, the policies pursued by this populist president have primarily benefited elites and accentuated capitalist inequalities.

Socialism is much more than a modernist political current deriving from Enlightenment ideals of emancipation and progress. It embodies the deepest aspirations of all human communities: ideals of fairness, empathy, and equal treatment. This is why socialist ideas continue to influence minds and to have material, political, and ethical consequences all over the world. With our species struggling to constrain social inequality and sustain our environment, the next round of socialist revolutions could be just around the corner.

SUGGESTIONS FOR FURTHER READING AND REFERENCES

Creed, Gerald W. 1998. *Domesticating Revolution. From Socialist Reform to Ambivalent Transition in a Bulgarian Village.* University Park: Pennsylvania State University Press.
    A rich case study, focusing principally on the socialist period but with useful 1990s updating.
———. 2011. *Masquerade and Postsocialism: Ritual and Cultural Dispossession in Bulgaria.* Bloomington: Indiana University Press.
    The author revisits the country of his earlier field research and focuses on the folk tradition of mumming to paint a bleak picture of the postsocialist condition.
Graeber, David. 2011. *Debt: The First 5000 Years.* New York: Melville House.
    The remedy to the problems of capitalist domination and violence that have dogged the history of modern humans is seen by this author to lie in "everyday communism," but this is grounded in idealized anarchism rather than in any version of socialist ideology.
Hann, C. M., ed. 2002. *Postsocialism. Ideals, Ideology and Practice in Eurasia.* London: Routledge.
    Includes numerous studies of Eastern Europe and a sample of non-European studies, including China and Africa.
Harris, Marvin. 1992. "Distinguished lecture: Anthropology and the Theoretical and Paradigmatic Significance of the Collapse of Soviet and European Communism." *American Anthropologist* 94:295–305.
    A distinguished representative of the school of "cultural materialism" delivers a verdict on socialism that epitomizes the Western liberal preconceptions of most Anglophone approaches.
Holbraad, Martin. 2013. "Revolucion o muerte: Self-Sacrifice and the Ontology of Cuban revolution." *Ethnos* 79 (3): 365–87.

Combining his ethnographic experience of Cuba with his expertise in anthropology's "ontological turn," the author shows how dissatisfaction with the empirical facts of Cuba's late socialist society is reconciled with a resilient belief in the revolution's ideals.

Humphrey, Caroline. 1998. *Marx Went Away but Karl Stayed Behind.* Ann Arbor: University of Michigan Press.

A postsocialist updating of an outstanding study of Siberian collective farms, showing how socialist ideology was essentially integrated into a specific cultural system.

Malewska-Szałgin, Anna. 2017. *Social Imaginaries of the State and Central Authority in Polish Highland Villages, 1999–2005.* Newcastle: Cambridge Scholars Publishing.

Provincial citizens in the Carpathian foothills of Poland remain imbued with a world-view that has much in common with that of the preindustrial peasantry. Today's "post-peasants" complain that their postsocialist governments have betrayed their responsibilities, notably to provide jobs. They reject liberal democracy—not in favor of socialism, which remains ideologically unacceptable, but in favor of virulent populism.

Müller, Birgit. 2007. *Disenchantment with Market Economics: East Germans and Western Capitalism.* Oxford: Berghahn.

Based on fieldwork shortly after German reunification, the author shows how East German workers struggled to adapt to their new Western bosses.

Steinmüller, Hans. 2013. *Communities of Complicity: Everyday Ethics in Rural China.* Oxford: Berghahn.

Analyzes how Chinese villagers draw on a variety of moral frameworks to deal with dislocation and uncertainty of a socialist system now radically different from that of the Maoist era.

Verdery, Katherine. 1996. *What Was Socialism and What Comes Next?* Princeton, NJ: Princeton University Press.

The most comprehensive attempt by a Western anthropologist to construct a general model of socialism, illustrated primarily with reference to the author's own work in Romania.

Wolf, Eric R. 1999. *Envisioning Power: Ideologies of Dominance and Crisis.* Berkeley: University of California Press.

Combines analyses of Kwakiutl, Aztec, and Nazi cases with stimulating general reflections on key concepts, including ideology and culture.

Yurchak, Alexei. 2006. *Everything Was Forever, until It Was No More: The Last Soviet Generation.* Princeton, NJ: Princeton University Press.

A sophisticated linguistic-philosophical analysis of how the observation of formal conventions in performances maintained socialist ideological hegemony, before illusions were rudely dispelled under Mikhail Gorbachev.

CHAPTER 7

ECONOMY

James G. Carrier

In 2008 the system of global finance froze up and it took massive efforts by governments in many countries to produce something like stability. Even with those efforts, much of the world entered the Great Recession, the most severe economic decline since the Great Depression of the 1930s. These events led to a great deal of interest in the economy, much of it focused on the financial sector, what firms in the sector did and how they got us into this mess.

Because the Great Recession started in the financial sector, that focus is understandable, but it ignores other questions that might be more basic. What do people in places like Western Europe and North America think the economy is? How do they think it operates? How accurate is that thinking? These questions deserve attention, because people's understanding of the economy shapes their expectations about how those in the financial sector, and elsewhere, will behave and why. This in turn affects whether people think that collectively they can affect that behavior, or instead should accept it as natural and inevitable or even laudable. Moreover, the accuracy of those understandings affects how likely people are to experience things like the financial crisis and the Great Recession again in the future.

Since the emergence of the discipline in its modern form early in the twentieth century, anthropologists have studied people's economic orientations, practices, and institutions, and they have used what they learned to address larger questions about economic life generally and about how we might think more clearly about it. In this chapter I lay out some of what anthropological work on the economy can tell us about how economies operate. I do so by using that work to reflect on the understanding of economy and the people in it that is influential in Western countries, governments, and central banks.

THINKING ABOUT ECONOMY

The predominant way that economy is understood in Western societies is neoclassical economics, less commonly called microeconomics or even ECON 101. While these names point to aspects of the formal discipline of economics, there are important parallels between the underlying assumptions and orientations of the prevalent view of economy in Western societies and in neoclassical economics. This becomes apparent if we consider some of the basic elements of the economics.

In neoclassical economics the economy is the aggregate of market activity, and that activity is people making choices in the market. The most familiar market choices are likely to be those made by ordinary consumers with limited resources, effectively money, and a range of wants or desires they hope to satisfy. Seeking that satisfaction, they enter the market, which can be an abstract entity like the automobile market or a physical space like a farmers' market. There they confront a variety of things for sale which would help satisfy one or more of those wants. They then decide which, if any, of those things are worth the money required, and buy accordingly. The economics assumes that when they make their decisions about what to buy, market actors are rational maximizers: they want to satisfy as many of their wants as they can while spending as little of their resources as they can. Although I do not focus on them in this chapter, sellers are like ordinary consumers, though their resources are the wares they bring to market to transact for money. Like those consumers, they are rational maximizers, seeking to get as much money as they can while selling as few of their resources as they can.

In addition to being rational maximizers, market actors are autonomous because they are not linked or obligated to those whom they confront in the market, and they are self-centered because the wants they seek to satisfy and the resources they command are their own and no one else's. As Adam Smith, often called the founder of modern economics, put it: "It is not from the benevolence of the butcher, the brewer, or the baker, that we expect our dinner, but from their regard to their own interest." So, in our dealings with our fellows we "address ourselves, not to their humanity, but to their self-love, and never talk to them of our own necessities, but of their advantages."

Those who think in terms of this view are prone to see it as natural, reflecting people as they really are, or perhaps as they really are underneath it all. Smith, for instance, said that market transactions are the result of a "propensity in human nature," which is "the propensity to truck, barter, and exchange one thing for another." One implication: markets and the market orientation are reflections of human nature, so we should accept and even celebrate that people are this way. For some, that becomes the basis of a political stance often called neoliberalism: that is, broadly, advocates think market choice is desirable; it ought to be extended to more areas of life; things which hinder that choice are undesirable and ought to be reduced or eliminated. So, where markets already exist they ought to be free of whatever restricts the freedom of market actors to transact to satisfy their wants, and where markets do not exist they ought to be encouraged or even required to emerge. Advocates argue that this would be good for individuals because it would allow them to make their own decisions about how to use their resources rather than having those decisions made for them by others. They also argue that this would be good for people generally because markets encourage competition and innovation. Together, they say, these mean greater efficiency and lower cost, so that people can satisfy more of their desires with the resources they have, as well as the development of new things which satisfy their desires.

This influential common view of economic activity and the economy as a whole has a number of features. In the following, I describe anthropological work relating to the more important of them: first, the idea that the economy is the market.

FORM AND SUBSTANCE

In focusing on consumers' market choices and transactions, the conventional model is concerned with the form of economic decision and action: the weighing of costs and benefits of alternatives in the market. Drawing on Karl Polanyi's work, many anthropologists think this "formalist" view of economy a reasonable, but restricted, approximation of a certain sort of economic activity. Instead, they argue the economy is more than this, that it is better to approach economies and economic activities from a "substantivist" perspective: this sees economies in terms of the substance of what is going on—the satisfaction of wants.

The substantivist approach extends the notion of economy to include everything that people do with objects from the point of production to that of consumption, when consumers' wants are satisfied. Much of this occurs outside of the markets which are the focus of the conventional view. For example, people take purchased foodstuffs home from the market and turn them into meals, which are eaten. These satisfy the wants of household members, but are likely to be invisible to those who are focused on the market. A limitation of the conventional view is that it ignores those who do not survive by their own market activities but depend on those who do. When I was young, my father ran a small business; my mother helped with the paperwork but was not paid; my brother and I went to school. In our household, only one of the four occupants survived through the market transactions formalists would focus on. For a substantivist, however, we all were involved in the circulation of things to satisfy our wants.

When a substantivist view takes into account those who do not survive through their market transactions, it encourages us to see things can circulate among people in other ways. Polanyi describes three forms of circulation: first, reciprocity, where individuals or sets of people give to and receive from each other repeatedly, creating a cycle of gift and countergift; second, exchange, the direct exchange of objects between transactors (for example, a buyer in a market exchanges money for a seller's wares); third, redistribution, where a number of people give to a central figure, who distributes the accumulated objects to those who have given (for example, when a person holds a party and asks invitees to contribute food or drink, which the host lays out for guests to consume). More significantly, one can see governments doing this, receiving taxes from those in the country, then distributing the revenue in various ways. These three forms of circulation can all exist in the same society and be ways that people satisfy their wants. However, in different societies one or another of them is likely to be the most important empirically and in people's understanding of themselves: in Western societies, exchange is the most important.

In these three forms, people are related to each other in different ways. In the exchange form, transactors are relatively autonomous and, leaving aside possible differences in their resources and desires, are relatively equal. In the reciprocity form, people are not autonomous, but obligated to each other because of the history of their transactions. In the redistribution form, marked inequality is probable. Those who contribute may all be equal, but they are likely to be inferior to the party who receives the contributions and carries out the redistribution.

Because so many anthropologists are substantivists, anthropological work on economy is often at odds with the conventional view. This is appropriate: even in societies where markets are economically central, they are not the only way objects circulate among people, nor the only way people satisfy their wants. Moreover, the broader scope of substantivism allows anthropologists to consider aspects of the circulation of objects difficult to discern from the conventional perspective.

TRANSACTION SPHERES AND ORIENTATIONS

The conventional view that economic actors are autonomous individuals suggests that all we need to do, and perhaps all we can do, is think in terms of individuals, with their desires and resources. Many anthropologists have reservations about this. That is because they see patterns in economic activity, which suggests that more is going on than autonomous individuals transacting simply to satisfy their personal wants in impersonal markets.

A sign of this is what are called spheres of exchange. Where these exist, people do not freely exchange different things against each other in the way that the conventional model supposes. Rather, only certain sorts of things can be exchanged against each other, each sort marking a distinct sphere. The original work on spheres of exchange was done by Paul Bohannan in an African society with three spheres. He said that one was a subsistence sphere, effectively ordinary foodstuffs and other items of daily consumption. A second was a prestige sphere, involving valuable items like brass rods and cattle. The third sphere was female relatives of marriageable age, the basis of marriage relations and alliances. Bohannan said that these different things were exchanged in spheres because those from one sphere were not supposed to be transacted against those in another sphere: brass rods should not be exchanged for ordinary foodstuffs, for instance. Such transactions were rare, caused comment, and required an explanation.

Spheres of exchange, then, exist when people generally think that certain sorts of things should not be transacted against other sorts and when such transactions are uncommon. This occurs even in Western market-based societies. In many of those societies, for example, sexual activity is not supposed to be transacted against money. That is prostitution, and in many places it is a crime. The same is true of a vote or a university degree: paying someone to vote in a particular way is a crime in most places, and paying a university to give you a bachelor of science degree, for example, is a wrong even if it is not necessarily a crime. Further, as Richard Titmuss found, many people hold that blood should not be transacted against money. It is so important that, instead, it should be given for free. As these examples suggest, in Western market-based societies there are things that are special, in the sense that they should not be transacted against money in the same way that we transact loaves of bread or rides in a taxi. Rather, they circulate in other spheres or cannot be exchanged at all.

The idea of spheres of exchange directs attention to different sorts of objects and the ways that they circulate. A related idea directs attention to the orientation of those doing the circulating. That is the idea of the difference between short-term and long-term orientations, developed by Jonathan Parry and Maurice Bloch. They argued that transactions that reflect a short-term orientation are the ways that people satisfy their immediate needs, such as buying groceries or taking a bus somewhere. In such transactions people are expected to be relatively self-centered, approximating to some degree the autonomous market actor of neoclassical economics, and the transactions involve little formality or ceremony.

Transactions involving a long-term orientation are different. In these, people are transacting in light of important interpersonal and social values that those transactions celebrate and affirm. The most important transaction for people in many societies is buying a house, and that is not only because houses are so expensive. It is also because the transaction reflects those important values, especially in the United States, with its stress on home ownership. There, owning a home marks one as a mature and responsible person able to look after oneself and one's family, and those undertaking the transaction are likely to make a special effort to consult those close to them and seek to accommodate their wishes. Less spectacularly, giving gifts at Christmas and on birthdays reflects the durable relationships among close relatives, who are the people most likely to give and receive such gifts. Appropriately, such transactions are more formal and involve more ceremony than transacting money for groceries in a supermarket: objects usually are specially wrapped and given at a special time, such as Christmas morning or at a birthday party. Charitable giving expresses similar social values, whether a large endowment to a university, for instance, or a smaller contribution to a local charity. The degree of formality is likely to vary with the size of the gift. In all cases, however, such a transaction is seen as different from the routine transactions of ordinary life, and its social purpose is likely to be recognized by governments, which commonly give such gifts favorable tax treatment.

The ideas of spheres of exchange and of the difference between short-term and long-term orientations are related. That is because the different spheres appear to be associated with more short-term or more long-term goals. Ordinary daily necessities define one of the spheres described in this section and their acquisition illustrates the short-term orientation of satisfying routine, daily wants. On the other hand, items of prestige, gifts, and donations define other spheres and their transaction expresses a longer-term orientation toward collective values, people's standing in their group, and their relations with those close to them.

Together, these ideas produced by anthropologists studying economy raise questions about the common view of the economy. People in the market, with their money and desires, are still there, but the inadequacy of reducing all economic activity to what they do is obvious in several ways. For one thing, people's wants are satisfied through more than just market transactions. For another, people want to do more than satisfy their present desires. They also want a pleasant and respectable life with their relatives and among members of their group. Achieving these things means that they enter into relations and transactions with people that are difficult to accommodate in the image of the autonomous market actor.

MARKET, ACTORS, AND SOCIETY

Another important aspect of the common view of economy arises from its microscopic orientation toward the decisions of individual transactors maximizing their satisfactions in the market. As noted in the previous section, that focus diverts attention from things outside of the moment of market choice, such as important relationships and values. Diverting attention in that way has the effect of elevating the economic over the social, economy over society. While neoclassical economics generally ignores the social, neoliberalism does more. Margaret Thatcher, the prime minister who brought the first wave of neoliberalism to Britain early in the 1980s, is widely reported to have said that there is no such thing as society, there are only individuals and their families.

Like the economists and the neoliberals, Thatcher's stance treats well-being as based on the economy, and her rejection of the idea of society treats it as based only on the economy. This view is illustrated by the attention commonly paid to gross domestic product (GDP), effectively the market price of all that is bought and sold in a country. To see GDP as indicating the strength of an economy, even a country, is to reduce what is important in people's lives to that buying and selling, so that people and their relationships are invisible. Even the GINI coefficient, which is a measure of the degree of concentration of wealth in a population, is only a small sign of interest in what anthropologists commonly address, which is the relation between economic activity, including market activity, and its larger context.

Elevating economy over society is justified in part by the claim described above, that market activity is natural, the expression of an in-built human propensity. Because people are naturally inclined to buy and sell, it follows that the market will expand by itself if it is not hindered by external factors. Put differently, it follows that all that the social realm does is hinder the market. Anthropologists generally reject this view and point to the ways that the spread of market relations and orientations frequently is induced and even coerced by powerful interests and governments in the face of significant popular opposition, whether in Britain in the nineteenth century, in many countries in Central and Latin America in the 1980s, or in Western Europe and North America in the present, where there is widespread opposition to free-trade agreements of various sorts.

An important basis for the rejection of this view is in the work of Polanyi, whom I have already mentioned as the author of the distinction between formalist and substantivist approaches to economy. He was a historian, and one of his interests was the changing strength of market thought and practice in Britain in the nineteenth century, which he described in *The Great Transformation*. He said that their spread was in many ways a result of actions by powerful sets of people and the British government. Further, he said that a result of that spread was the emergence of a countermovement, as people sought to defend valued social practices and institutions from the disruptive effects of markets. In other words, he and the anthropologists influenced by him do not see market orientation and activity as occurring naturally when it is not stifled by things other than the desires and resources of market actors. Rather, they see them as shaped by the forces at work in the larger realm that contains those transactors and influences their behavior.

The creation of policies and practices that induce people to think of themselves in market terms can involve a process that Danny Miller and I have called virtualism. The name is based on an analogy with the virtual reality of computer games played using goggles that display the game directly in front of the player's eyes. What the player sees is the result of the computer program that generates the game. However, it covers so much of the player's field of vision that it seems real. So, it is a virtual reality. Neoliberals who see the world in terms of the neoclassical model are seeing the results of the logic of that model, but it covers so much of their mental field of vision that they mistake it for the world itself. When they then use that vision to shape policy, their virtual reality gets turned into virtualism, as they seek to induce the world to conform to that vision.

An example of seeing the world in neoclassical terms is the claim that markets reflect the judgment of a mass of market actors and so are more rational than any individual or regulatory body. That claim reflects the logic of the neoclassical model and supporting anecdotes rather than a body of empirical research, and indeed it is difficult to imagine how the claim could be assessed empirically. The main policy implication of this claim is that markets ought to be left alone, a view that was accepted by governments in many countries late in the twentieth century. The result was reduced regulation of financial markets and institutions in particular, which unfortunately seems to have contributed to the financial crisis of 2008 and the Great Recession. This example shows how a virtualizing vision can influence governments, leading them to act in ways that are intended to bring the world into line with the vision, the sort of action that Polanyi described for Britain in the nineteenth century.

It is not just government which can act in ways that induce people to conform to the idea of market rationality. Alexandra Ouroussoff presents an instance of other bodies that do so, one involving firms, risk, and rating agencies. To survive, firms need to borrow money, and if they are to flourish they need to borrow at competitive rates of interest. Rating agencies investigate firms that seek to borrow and assess their credit-worthiness. If the firm is considered by the rating agency to be investment grade it will be able to borrow at a competitive rate, but if it is considered to be less creditworthy it will be rated lower than that and will have to pay a premium to borrow. As Ouroussoff explains, a key concern of rating agencies is whether a firm treats risk in the way that the prevailing model says that a competent rational maximizer must do. That is, as something to be quantified, managed, and reduced to a minimum. However, she found that some people who run firms saw the nature of business differently. They held that risk handled intelligently should be embraced as a source of profit, which is different from the rating agency view that it should be avoided as a source of loss. Resisting the agency view effectively, however, costs time and money. One successful firm that she described set up what amounted to parallel sets of accounts, one to show to the rating agency and one that reflected what the firm actually was doing, and a shadow system of internal communication where things could be said without leaving records that the rating agency could see.

Ouroussoff describes how people can find themselves under pressure to conform to aspects of the market model, or at least appear to conform. This indicates that when people act as the model describes, we may be seeing the result of political and commercial pressure rather than the result of some basic aspect of human nature. There is other research that leads to the same conclusion.

That research relates to the idea that market actors are autonomous. There are such actors; some potential buyers and sellers confront each other free of any obligation and are concerned only with the transaction at hand. However, as Ronald Dore pointed out, this is an unstable state of affairs. Studying firms in the United Kingdom and Japan, he found that when companies first dealt with each other commonly they were autonomous in this way. If those initial dealings were satisfactory they were likely to be repeated. When those dealings went on for an extended period of time, however, that autonomy disappeared. Instead of being orientated only toward the rational calculation of value for money as they were initially, firms began to think in terms of being fair to each other in their dealings. Autonomy, that is, came to be replaced by a sense of mutual obligation.

The sense of obligation that Dore found conflicts with the idea that market actors are rational maximizers, and the logic of the market model dictates that those who want to maximize must try to avoid that obligation. One way to do this is to reduce the likelihood that there will be repeated economic transaction between people or firms. Efforts to reduce such transactions, and so induce people to conform to the conventional view, are illustrated in Susana Narotzky's description of what she was told of banking practices in Ferrol, in northern Spain. She said that bank staff tended to stay in the same branch for a long time and got to know their customers over the course of many transactions. The result was that customers often came to trust members of staff, who in turn valued that trust. Staff felt an obligation to honor that trust by treating customers well, not selling them products that were inappropriate. When banks began to sell complex financial instruments during the housing bubble that began in the 1990s, such employees were reluctant to try to sell those instruments, which were highly profitable and the source of a growing proportion of banks' income. Many banks got around that problem by introducing new policies that obliged staff to change branch regularly. This made it less likely that they would deal with the same customers over an extended period, more likely that they would see customers as anonymous strangers to whom they felt no obligation, and more likely to encourage them to buy products that banks were trying to sell.

I said that one of the justifications for elevating economy over society, the market over other realms of life, is the claim that market activity is a reflection of human nature and hence ought not to be constrained. In the preceding paragraphs I have described anthropological and other work that indicates that market activity and ways of thinking do not rest in any obvious way on human nature, but are instead shaped and even brought about by powerful sets of people. We should be cautious, then, about accepting the neoliberal view that denies or denigrates the social realm and that urges us to consider markets, market mentality, and market activity on their own.

In the remainder of this section I present other anthropological work that shows how unwise it can be to consider markets and market actors in isolation from the social and other activities that surround them. One way that those activities affect what goes on in the market has been reported in studies of peasants in Latin America, and the processes that researchers have described exist in market economies as well. For instance, Stephen Gudeman and Alberto Rivera studied peasant households of small-scale farmers who produce foodstuffs intended primarily for household consumption, but who also seek to produce a surplus that they will sell to get the money required to buy things that they need but cannot produce themselves. Household members live off household resources and they work without pay. The effect of this is that they end up selling the surplus that they produce for less than would be demanded by a commercial farmer who must pay those who did the work of growing the crops. In other words, market prices, and hence market transactions, are affected by things that go on in the social realm.

The same sort of relationship between households and the market exists in Western Europe and North America, although it takes a somewhat different form. Commonly in those places members of households do things like cook and clean for each other, and they do so as part of their obligations to each other. Because they are not paid for the work they do, what they produce costs less than it would if it were purchased in the market. Most obviously, a meal prepared at home costs less than the same meal bought in a restaurant. Preparing such meals, and the rest of the domestic work that people in the household do, is part of what sustains the household members who work for pay. As a result, they can sell their labor for less than would be the case if all household activities were purchased at market rates. In this way, activities in the social sphere affect what goes on in the market because they subsidize the firms where household members work.

The integral relationship between the market and the broader social world is not limited to the ways that social activities can affect market transactions. In addition, those transactions can affect things outside of the moment when they occur, an effect that is difficult to see if we restrict ourselves to the conventional market model. For instance, consumers who buy heavier vehicles with larger engines will use more fuel and produce more emissions than those who do not, and so affect others in society. Some of the broader consequences of people's market decisions are described by Jane Collins in her consideration of the American retail firm Walmart.

As Collins notes, Walmart prospered by offering low prices and was able to do so by keeping costs down. To keep them down it built its stores in low-cost areas outside of towns, it paid workers little, and it bought much of its wares from inexpensive suppliers overseas. The result was that at the point of market transaction they offered things at low prices. Viewed more broadly, however, these low prices had effects that were less fortunate and that were not visible to those focused on the transaction. Collins identifies two sorts of effects.

One is fairly straightforward. Paying low wages meant that those who worked for Walmart had less money than workers in more conventional firms, and that tended to depress wages and retail sales in the area more generally. Buying from inexpensive overseas sources rather than in the United States meant that Americans generally had less money because there were fewer jobs in manufacturing, which tended to pay better than service jobs. For a noticeable number of people, then, Walmart's low prices had the effect of reducing their income. The other effect that Collins identifies is more subtle. She says that in their advertising and practices the firm encouraged the idea that simply seeking low prices for what one consumes is what makes a virtuous consumer. This displaced common older views that saw consumers as more than just rational maximizers seeking their own advantage. In those views, they were virtuous if they assured that merchants behaved responsibly by treating their staff and neighbors well, sold safe products, and described them honestly.

CONCLUSION

I began this chapter by asking how people in Western countries understand economy and how accurate that understanding is. As I noted, these questions are important. The answer to the first is likely to influence people's sense of whether they can affect the economic world in which they exist. The answer to the second indicates how likely they are to experience things like the Great Recession again in the future.

The understanding that I described, which I called the conventional market model, is the neoclassical economics that has dominated popular thought and governments since around 1980. That is a model of academic economics, but its basic orientation resembles popular thought with its focus on value for money for the consumer confronting objects in the supermarket aisle or in product advertisements. That model sees economy as buying and selling in the market by autonomous people with their personal resources and desires. It is a highly simplified model of an important aspect of collective life, and many academic economists and neoliberals see that simplification as a virtue, for it appears to provide clear answers to problems in the world.

As the research described in this chapter indicates, anthropologists tend to think differently. The discipline prides itself on seeing things holistically, in terms of their context rather than simplified and in isolation. That research shows that we can understand economies, the people in them, and what they do only if we place them in their context. Doing so is unlikely to produce the clear answers that neoclassical economics offers. It can, however, give us a better sense of what the problems in the world might be.

The autonomous rational maximizer of the conventional market model turns out to be a powerful tale that we tell ourselves, one with important consequences. Like all such tales it has an element of truth in it. However, the research described in this chapter shows that it, again like all such tales, obscures as much as it reveals.

SUGGESTIONS FOR FURTHER READING AND REFERENCES

Bohannan, Paul. 1955. "Some Principles of Exchange and Investment among the Tiv." *American Anthropologist* 57:60–70.

    The classic account of spheres of exchange.

Carrier, James G., ed. 1997. *Meanings of the Market: The Free Market in Western Culture.* Oxford: Berg.

    A critical consideration of the model of the free market,

Carrier, James G., and Daniel Miller, eds. 1998. *Virtualism: A New Political Economy.* Oxford: Berg.

Collins, Jane. 2015. "Walmart, American Consumer-Citizenship and the Erasure of Class." In *Anthropologies of Class: Power, Practice and Inequality*, ed. James G. Carrier and Don Kalb. Cambridge: Cambridge University Press.

Dore, Ronald. 1983. "Goodwill and the Spirit of Market Capitalism." *British Journal of Sociology* 34:459–82.

Gudeman, Stephen, and Alberto Rivera. 1991. *Conversations in Colombia: The Domestic Economy in Life and Text.* New York: Cambridge University Press.

    An account of peasant households and of the notion of the house economy in Western thought.

Harvey, David. 2005. *A Brief History of Neoliberalism.* New York: Oxford University Press.

    The classic exposition of neoliberalism.

Mauss, Marcel. 1990 (1925). *The Gift: The Form and Reason for Exchange in Archaic Societies.* Trans. W. D. Halls. London: Routledge.

    A presentation of the idea of gift transactions, which is an inspiration of much economic anthropology.

Narozky, Susana. 2015. "The Organic Intellectual and the Production of Class in Spain." In *Anthropologies of Class: Power, Practice and Inequality*, ed. James G. Carrier and Don Kalb. Cambridge: Cambridge University Press.

Ouroussoff, Alexandra. 2010. *Wall Street at War: The Secret Struggle for the Global Economy.* Cambridge: Polity Press.

Parry, Jonathan, and Maurice Bloch, eds. 1989. *Money and the Morality of Exchange.* Cambridge: Cambridge University Press.

    Includes a consideration of short-term and long-term orientations in economic activity.

Polanyi, Karl. 1944. *The Great Transformation: The Political and Economic Origins of Our Time.* New York: Farrar & Rinehart.

    A study of the emergence of liberal economy in the 1800s, especially in Britain.

———. 1957. "The Economy as Instituted Process." In *Trade and Market in the Early Empires: Economies in History and Theory*, ed. K. Polanyi, Conrad M. Arensberg, and Harry W. Pearson. Glencoe, IL: Free Press.

    Distinguishes the formalist and substantivist approaches to economy.

Smith, Adam. 1976 (1776). *An Inquiry into the Nature and Causes of the Wealth of Nations.* Chicago: University of Chicago Press.

Thompson, E. P. 1971. "The Moral Economy of the English Crowd in the Eighteenth Century." *Past and Present* 50:76–136.

   A classic discussion of moral economy.

Titmuss, Richard M. 1971. *The Gift Relationship: From Human Blood to Social Policy*. London: Allen & Unwin.

CHAPTER 8

ANTHROPOLOGY, TERRORISM, AND COUNTERTERRORISM

Roberto J. González

During the twenty-first century, few topics have attracted as much global media attention as terrorism. Although terrorism is a centuries-old concept, its meaning has shifted over time. For many people, the attacks on the World Trade Center and the Pentagon on September 11, 2001, brought fear and anxiety. If such horrific acts could strike New York and Washington, what could possibly prevent terror from hitting London, Beijing, Paris, or Mumbai? Since 9/11, government officials in places as diverse as Brussels, Islamabad, Riyadh, Madrid, Nairobi, and Ottawa have committed themselves to developing or supporting counterterrorism efforts.

But what exactly *is* terrorism—and for that matter, what is a terrorist? Increasingly, the terms have come under criticism because they impose moral judgement. The saying "one man's terrorist is another man's freedom fighter" encapsulates the problem: when a person describes those who perpetrate political violence as terrorists, he or she also vilifies them. In North America and Europe today, terrorism typically refers to violence carried out by groups or individuals perceived to be espousing radical Islam—not to violence carried

or the state violence

out by, say, neo-Nazis or white nationalists who kill African American church-goers. For this reason, investigative journalist Glenn Greenwald has called terrorism "the most meaningless and manipulated word," a useless propaganda term. Some suggest abandoning it altogether.

Anthropology is a discipline that is well suited for developing a more sophisticated and critical understanding of terrorism and counterterrorism. Because anthropologists are trained to question basic assumptions, terms, and categories, they are in a good position to rethink conventional understandings of indiscriminate political violence and efforts to stop it.

At different historical moments, government agencies have been keenly interested in ethnographic knowledge because many anthropologists spend years living in small-scale societies, immersing themselves in cultures that are organized very differently from their own. This intimate knowledge of the Other can potentially make the anthropologist a source of understanding and human empathy—a diplomatic figure able to bring greater awareness and appreciation of cultural difference.

But this knowledge can also make the anthropologist a source of strategic information for military planners and intelligence agents. In *Cold War Anthropology*, his groundbreaking book on the hidden history of the discipline, David Price has carefully documented how anthropologists have been witting and often unwitting accomplices to those inclined to use culture as a weapon. The fact that anthropologists have a legitimate reason for traveling to out-of-the-way places potentially gives them the perfect cover for conducting espionage, and over the years many researchers have been solicited to conduct spy work. For more than a century, the discipline has struggled with the moral and ethical dilemmas surrounding the uses and misuses of anthropological knowledge.

In some cases, anthropologists have succeeded in helping policy makers and the general public gain a clearer and more nuanced understanding of the motivations behind violent extremism, including attacks that have been labeled as terrorist acts by the mass media and policy makers. But as we shall see, anthropologists haven't always done so. In fact, some have uncritically adopted the perspectives, goals, and language of counterterrorists and counterinsurgents fighting the "war on terror." (The phrase "war on terror" was first used by President George W. Bush on September 20, 2001, just days after the 9/11 attacks. It has come to refer a wide range of initiatives, from the international military assault on suspected terrorists to surveillance programs aimed at detecting terrorist plots.) In this chapter, I will examine a few ways in which anthropology, terrorism, and counterterrorism have intersected in recent years. Rather than provide an exhaustive survey of the topic, I will focus upon a few illustrative examples. The chapter begins with a brief historical overview of the origins of the word "terrorism" and its transformation over time. The next section examines how anthropologists responded in the aftermath of 9/11, particularly to the US-led invasions of Afghanistan and Iraq. It gives special attention to the US Army's Human Terrain System, a counterinsurgency program that embedded social scientists with combat units. This is followed by a discussion of computational counterterrorism—a series of efforts that seek to integrate "big data" (including ethnographic information) for predictive modeling—and its relationship to drone warfare in various regions of the world. The next two sections summarize new anthropological research that might potentially transform counterterrorism into a preventive, rather than a corrective, endeavor by addressing the root causes of violent extremism. The chapter concludes with a few thoughts about the need to communicate critical anthropological insights about terrorism to much wider audiences.

TERRORISM AND ITS TRANSFORMATIONS

The term terrorism has no universally accepted definition, but when it is used in the United States or Europe today, it typically means something similar to the US State Department's definition, dating back to 2001: "The term 'terrorism' means premeditated, politically motivated violence perpetrated against noncombatant targets by subnational groups or clandestine agents, usually intended to influence an audience."

This definition is remarkably different from the original definition of terrorism. In a widely read 2003 article, anthropologist Scott Atran reminds us that the idea of terror as the use of violence to achieve political goals was first articulated during the French Revolution. The antimonarchical Jacobins, a ruling coalition that supported the Revolution, embarked on a Reign of Terror from 1793 to 1794 in which they mercilessly killed thousands of potential opponents, sometimes publicly beheading them with guillotines. The Jacobins divided the world between pro- and antirevolutionaries, and they believed that only they could save France from total destruction at the hands of Europe's monarchies. When the term "terrorism" entered the English language, it thus referred to violent acts perpetrated by a ruling national group—in other words, the state—against its perceived enemies, most of whom were civilians.

Since that time, the meaning of the term has alternated. At times, it has been primarily associated with state terrorism, such as the practices of Nazi Germany or of the Soviet Union under Stalin's leadership. In other periods, politicians and the media have used it to describe the actions of groups or individuals using violence to destabilize national governments, as in the case of anarchists in the late 1800s or anticolonial guerrillas (or "revolutionaries" or "insurgents") in the 1950s and 1960s. In North America and Europe, the pendulum has not swung significantly for the past fifty years, at least not among journalists and policy makers: they tend to use the term *terrorism* only if political violence against civilians is carried out by nonstate actors, or by groups threatening already established nation-states. State terrorism appears to be a taboo topic.

If we use academic journals to roughly gauge anthropological interest in terrorism, we can detect similar shifts in meaning. The term *terrorism* first appeared in *American Anthropologist*, the flagship journal of the American Anthropological Association, in 1892. The term arose in an article on the evolution of law by James Welling, specifically laws surrounding the appropriate use of torture in Europe from ancient times to the end of the eighteenth century. The term *terrorism* appears only once in the article, in reference to physical torture used by the state to extract confessions from an accused criminal. The term did not appear again in *American Anthropologist* until more than a half century later, in a 1943 article by W. M. Krogman. Once again, the reference was to state terror, specifically the Nazis' "hysterical, political, nationalistic attempts to bolster an ideology founded in ruthlessness, nourished by terrorism." The term also appeared that same year in an article by E. O. James that appeared in *Man*, a British journal published by the Royal Anthropological Institute.

During the 1960s, a few anthropologists such as Alex Weingrod began to use "terrorism" to describe violence perpetrated by groups other than states, though it still seldom appeared in journals. By the late 1970s and early 1980s, anthropologists were often using the term in a way that resembles contemporary popular usage — at times with explicit reference to groups such as the Palestinian Liberation Organization, the Front de Libération Québecois, and the Irish Republican Army.

In the 1990s, anthropologists such as Carole Nagengast began looking once again at the nation-state's use of terror as a means of controlling its own citizens. Jeffrey Sluka's edited book *Death Squad: The Anthropology of State Terror* signaled the arrival of a critical anthropological approach to the study of state-inflicted terror from a global perspective. Ethnographic accounts from Spain, India, Argentina, Guatemala, Northern Ireland, East Timor, and the Philippines pointed to an unsettling fact: far more civilians were subjected to political violence by state actors than by nonstate actors. State-supported death squads and paramilitary forces were much larger in size — and more lethal — than small groups and individuals typically labeled as "terrorists" by Western journalists and politicians. Such work also marked a refusal on the part of anthropologists to accept the conventional meaning of terrorism.

ANTHROPOLOGY AND THE "WAR ON TERROR"

Days after the 9/11 attacks, the US Congress granted President George W. Bush broad authority to use force against those deemed by him to be terrorists—and so began what came to be known as the "war on terror." (See fig. 8.1.)

Anthropologists responded in a variety of ways in the following months and years, sometimes very publicly. For example, Catherine Lutz placed the attacks in historical context, noting that the United States has been in "a permanent state of war readiness" since the 1940s but that for many Americans this has not been visible because conflict has been outsourced to the global south through proxy wars. David Harvey, Talal Asad, and others strongly condemned the attacks and then made an impassioned appeal for the United States to refrain from retaliating or continuing flawed policies overseas. William Beeman wrote numerous op-ed pieces, including one that articulated the dangers of engaging al Qaeda in a short-sighted war of revenge and another that explored the West's historical exploitation of the Middle East. Janet McIntosh and Wade Davis critiqued the inability of US leaders to come to terms with America's role of cre-

FIG. 8.1.   US leaders responded to the attacks of September 11, 2001, by declaring a war on terrorism. The deadliest attack occurred at the World Trade Center towers in New York City. Photo by Michael Foran, courtesy of Creative Commons. © Michael Foran 2001.

ating the conditions that led to the 9/11 attacks. Several other anthropologists, including David Price, Hugh Gusterson, and Laura Nader, condemned the curtailment of academic freedom and the stifling of dissent. (To see these commentaries, as well as others, see my 2004 edited book, *Anthropologists in the Public Sphere: Speaking Out on War, Peace, and American Power.*)

By contrast, some anthropologists offered to directly support the "war on terror" by participating in the US Army's Human Terrain System. The mission of HTS was to provide real-time cultural expertise and ethnographic data to military commanders by embedding social scientists (preferably anthropologists) in combat units in Iraq and Afghanistan.

The Human Terrain System was the brainchild of cultural anthropologist Montgomery McFate. David Price notes that McFate's Yale doctoral dissertation on British counterinsurgency campaigns in Northern Ireland "reads as a guide for militaries wanting to stop indigenous insurgent movements . . . [a study] designed to make those she studied more vulnerable to cooption and defeat." In her dissertation, McFate rhetorically asked: "Does good anthropology contribute to better killing?" In 2005, McFate tried rewriting the history of anthropology by arguing that before the Vietnam War, the discipline had a "fruitful" and mutually beneficial relationship with military and intelligence agencies—a relationship worth rekindling, in her view.

The meteoric ascent of HTS paralleled and was accelerated by the rise to power of General David Petraeus, a staunch supporter of the program. As a commander in Iraq, Petraeus became known for a strategy that relied upon "securing" the population by interacting with civilians and paying off local tribal leaders in exchange for political support. Top Pentagon officials were impressed with the strategy, which was soon codified in a new Army field manual, *FM 3-24: Counterinsurgency*, in late 2006. (See fig. 8.2—the account of HTS that follows is based on several of my previously published articles, including "Human Terrain: Past, Present, and Future Applications," which appeared in *Anthropology Today*, and "The Rise and Fall of the Human Terrain System," published in the online journal *CounterPunch* in 2015.)

Counterinsurgency warfare had an air of theoretical legitimacy—indeed, Petraeus surrounded himself with a team of advisers with doctoral degrees in political science and history who referred to counterinsurgency as "the graduate level of war." Many brigade commanders fell into line once the Petraeus Doctrine was established as the Army's preferred method for fighting insurgents. Criticizing counterinsurgency—or HTS—was a bad move for officers seeking to advance their careers. Congressmen and women generally liked the new approach because it appeared to be succeeding (at least in Iraq) and because many viewed it as less lethal. And HTS fit perfectly with the narrative that

FIG. 8.2. US Army Major Robert Holbert speaking with local school administrators during a cordon and search in Afghanistan. Holbert was a Human Terrain team member attached to the 82nd Airborne Division. Photo by Staff Sgt. Michael L. Casteel, US Army, courtesy of US Department of Defense.

Petraeus had crafted with the help of compliant reporters: counterinsurgency is the thinking man's warfare.

However, HTS encountered a series of obstacles. The program met organized resistance from hundreds if not thousands of anthropologists. In 2007, less than a year after the first Human Terrain Team was deployed to Afghanistan, the American Anthropological Association issued a sharply worded statement in which it expressed disapproval of the program, describing it as an "unacceptable application of anthropological expertise." Nonetheless, a modest number of anthropologists joined HTS and were deployed to Iraq and Afghanistan.

The program was also beset by tragedy. Between May 2008 and January 2009, three young social scientists who were employees of the program—Michael Bhatia, Nicole Suveges, and Paula Loyd—were killed in action.

Later it became clear that the company was on a hiring binge and inadequately screening HTS applicants, most of whom were academics with no substantive cultural knowledge of Iraqi or Afghan culture. Very few could speak or understand Arabic, Pashto, or Farsi. As early as 2009, reports of racism, sexual harassment, and payroll padding began to emerge, and in 2010, an Army investigation found that the program had severe problems. To make matters worse, the investigators found that many brigade commanders considered HTS to be ineffective. In the wake of these revelations, McFate resigned from the program.

By the end of 2014, HTS was terminated. Given its spectacular growth and the Army's once insatiable demand for embedded social scientists, we might ask: Why did HTS meet such a sudden demise?

One reason had to do with the scheduled pullout of US troops from Iraq and Afghanistan. As early as 2012, HTS's management team was desperately searching for a way to market the program after a US troop pullout. Apparently, none of the military's branches or combatant commands were interested in funding the program beyond fiscal year 2014.

Another factor that undoubtedly damaged HTS's survival was Petraeus's spectacular fall from grace during his tenure as CIA director. As reports of his extramarital exploits and reckless handling of classified information were publicized in 2012, some journalists began to acknowledge that the news media's enthusiasm for counterinsurgency warfare was due in large part to an irrational idolatry of Petraeus, who had built a personality cult. In a remarkably candid confession, *Wired* magazine's Spencer Ackerman admitted in 2012: "The more I interacted with his staff, the more persuasive their points seemed. . . . In retrospect, I was insufficiently critical [of counterinsurgency doctrine]. . . . Another irony that Petraeus's downfall reveals is that some of us who egotistically thought our coverage of Petraeus and counterinsurgency was so sophisticated were perpetuating myths without fully realizing it."

By 2013, a new wave of criticism began to surround HTS. *USA Today* correspondent Tom Vanden Brook published a series of excoriating articles based upon documents that the newspaper had obtained through the Freedom of Information Act. Independent reporter John Stanton cultivated a network of HTS insiders and published dozens of reports about the seedier aspects of the program. Journalist Vanessa Gezari published a riveting exposé in 2013, entitled *The Tender Soldier*. In it, she writes: "The Human Terrain System lied to the public and to its own employees and contract staff about the nature of its work in Afghanistan. . . . [It] would prove less controversial for what it did than for its sheer incompetence."

Criticisms of HTS continued in 2014, when US Representative Duncan Hunter, a Republican member of the House Armed Services Committee, launched a one-man crusade against the program. His frustration was palpable: "It's shocking that this program, with its controversy and highly questionable need, could be extended. It should be ended," he told *USA Today* reporter Tom Vanden Brook. On September 30, 2014, the program was officially terminated.

Some argue that HTS was a good idea that was badly mismanaged. It would be more accurate to say that HTS was a bad idea that was badly mismanaged. Cultural knowledge is not a service that can be provided by contractors and consultants, or taught to soldiers using a training manual. The Human Terrain System was built upon this flawed premise.

In the meantime, McFate has moved on: she currently holds multiple academic and governmental positions, including the Minerva Chair at the US Naval War College and the Executive Board member of the Federal Coordinating Committee for the US Department of Homeland Security Study of Terrorism and Responses to Terrorism.

FROM COUNTERINSURGENCY TO COMPUTATIONAL COUNTERTERRORISM

As HTS faded into obscurity, the Pentagon underwent a broad shift in priorities, away from cultural intelligence and toward geospatial intelligence. As noted by geographer Oliver Belcher in 2013, the latter "marks a real move towards conducting human terrain intelligence at a distance within strategic centers of calculation in Washington, DC and Virginia." Counterinsurgency appears to have been a passing fad.

By 2014, the rapidly growing fields of computational social science and predictive modeling had become fashionable—they aligned neatly with the Obama administration's sweeping embrace of "big data." Many Pentagon planners would prefer to collect data from mobile phone records, remote sensors, biometric databases, and drones equipped with high-resolution cameras than from human social scientists.

Yet the potential value of anthropological approaches was recognized by those developing predictive modeling programs. For example, the final report of one sociocultural modeling workshop, edited by Dylan Schmorrow in 2010, discussed "thick ethnography" and ways in which thick description might be incorporated into behavioral modeling: "The involvement of more social scientists requires that social scientists become re-educated . . . cultural anthropologists should not be discounted. Rather, actual working workshops in which ethnographers partner with modelers to build a few prototypes are needed." A different part of the report noted that "far more [social scientists], particularly anthropologists, should be part of the endeavor." By 2010, the director of the Department of Defense's nascent Human Social Cultural Behavior modeling program recognized that the department had a significant gap in the area of "sociology/anthropology for irregular warfare and support ops." The message was clear—sociocultural knowledge needed to be a necessary part of high-tech counterterrorism.

Sometimes anthropologists have worked directly for modeling and forecasting companies. For example, shortly after Robert Popp founded the company National Security Innovations (NSI) in 2007, he hired Indiana University–Fort Wayne anthropologist Lawrence Kuznar as chief cultural sciences officer. National Security Innovations describes itself as a "human behavior analysis" company and has been awarded approximately one hundred contracts since its creation, the majority of which have been awarded by Pentagon agencies or defense contractors.

The extent to which Kuznar has been involved in NSI's forecasting projects is not clear. If anything, it seems that Kuznar has been circumspect about forecasting. Among Kuznar's most interesting papers is a 2008 piece which includes a cross-cultural comparison of prediction. In the concluding section, he notes: "Prediction, in the form of divination, is nearly universal in human societies, and often appears to provide a degree of psychological assurance used to deal with uncertainty and randomness, rather than provide any scientifically defensible predictions about the empirical world." He warns that "when beliefs in predictions become dogmatic and not adjustable in light of new data, the benefits of prediction are lost and whole societies can be destroyed due to a collectively held fantasy."

But not all anthropologists have been so critical. Take for example UCLA archaeologist Jeffrey Brantingham, who has played a leading role in using computational social science for prediction and forecasting. Brantingham has used Department of Defense–funded research on predictive modeling to create a new company, PredPol (short for "predictive policing"). He sits on the company's board of directors and serves as its chief of research and design.

Nearly a decade ago Brantingham began collaborating with a UCLA colleague, mathematician Andrea Bertozzi, to develop algorithms designed to predict when and where crimes are likely to occur. In 2006, the National Science Foundation awarded them a grant for "Mathematical and Simulation Modeling of Crime Hot Spots," which focused upon predictive modeling for urban policing. The project was conducted in Los Angeles and used historical data to forecast future crimes.

The Pentagon was also interested. Brantingham and Bertozzi were awarded several Department of Defense grants beginning in 2006, when they received funding for a proposal entitled, "Spatio-temporal Event Pattern Recognition." Soon their research was comparing California gang violence to Iraqi insurgent attacks, and by 2010 they were awarded Department of Defense fund-ing to study "Dynamic Models of Insurgent Activity" and "Information Fusion of Human Activity and Social Networks." Later, Brantingham and Bertozzi were awarded grants from the Army Research Office, the National Geospatial Intelligence Agency, and the Air Force Office of Scientific Research for related projects.

Brantingham has made occasional references to the ways in which anthropology informs his predictive models. He is quoted in a 2010 article by Steve Wolpert for *US News & World Report*: "Criminal offenders are essentially hunter/gatherers; they forage for opportunities to commit crimes . . . the behaviors that a hunter/gatherer uses to choose a wildebeest versus a gazelle are the same calculations a criminal uses to choose a Honda versus a Lexus. . . . An insurgent who wants to place an IED (improvised explosive device) in a particular location will make the same kind of calculations that a car thief will use in choosing which car to steal." It is worth exploring this claim in more detail. Brantingham uses Charnov's prey selection model to argue that thieves prefer Hondas over Lexuses because it requires less energy expenditure—and therefore greater reward—relative to expended effort or energy. In much the same way that foragers (hypothetically) prefer wildebeests over antelopes. Though anthropologists might be skeptical of such a claim, the editors of *Crime Science Journal* were impressed, and they published an article summarizing Brantingham's work. (See fig 8.3.)

A more critical anthropological view would question the validity of Brantingham's analogy. For example, ethnographic accounts of Hadza hunting practices in Tanzania indicate that foragers are not rational-choice robots. Their hunting expeditions are deeply embedded within patterns of cooperative work, reciprocal food-sharing, and notions of masculinity as noted by Frank Marlowe in his 2010 book *The Hadza: Hunter-Gatherers of Tanzania*. It would seem likely that the motivations of car thieves are equally complex and culturally embedded, but Brantingham's model does not account for these nuances.

Beyond the private sector, there have been other efforts to create modeling and forecasting programs as counterterrorism tools. Nexus7 was among the most secretive. The program, developed by the Defense Advanced Research Projects Agency (DARPA), was described by *Wired* magazine reporter Noah Shachtman as "a war-zone surveillance effort [that] ties together everything from spy radars to fruit prices in order to glean clues about Afghan instability." According to Shachtman, it gathered "hundreds of existing data sources from multiple agencies" to create "population-centric, cultural intelligence." According to one report, DARPA contracted three companies to implement Nexus7: Potomac Fusion, Data Tactics Corporation, and Caerus Associates.

FIG. 8.3. Predictive modeling is sometimes used to create simulation programs designed to increase cultural awareness in complex situations. Here US Army General Martin Dempsey demonstrates a virtual Afghan village used for training military personnel. Photo by Sgt. Angelica Golindano, courtesy of US Army.

Nexus7 is unusual in that it was deployed for military operations in Afghanistan from the beginning. DARPA has historically functioned as an agency supporting basic research for technologies that might get used years later. With Nexus7, DARPA played a much more assertive wartime role. Department of Defense documents describe Nexus7 as a rather ordinary package of data extraction and forecasting software, but it has apparently functioned as a full-blown spy program for trawling massive amounts of intelligence data to find pockets of instability in Afghanistan and to determine which villages or neighborhoods support the Kabul government or the Taliban.

Nexus7 was championed by David Kilcullen, a well-known counterinsurgency theorist who served as a close adviser to General Petraeus in Iraq from 2007 to 2008 and to the International Security Assistance Force (ISAF) in Afghanistan 2009 to 2010. He founded Caerus Associates, a defense company that was awarded Nexus7 contracts. Kilcullen, who has a PhD from the School of Politics of the University of New South Wales, wrote a doctoral dissertation on insurgency in West Java and East Timor based on multidisciplinary fieldwork methods including anthropological techniques and analysis. In the 2010 book *Counterinsurgency*, Kilcullen developed the idea of creating quantifiable "metrics" to measure progress in Afghanistan, such as percentage of reported IEDs that are found, voluntary reports from Afghan informants, transportation prices, progress of NGO development projects, tax collection records, and the prices of exotic vegetables. Kilcullen argued that such metrics, when pooled together, might give military planners a powerful tool for accomplishing their missions.

Predictive modeling programs are disconcerting. What will happen when such programs become more acceptable for use in real world situations? In 2014, Kerry Fosher, an anthropologist working in the national security sector, wrote: "We do not have the basic science that would allow us to render complex cross-cultural practices into computer algorithms, nor does the nature of knowledge about culture allow it to be parsed for storage in databases. Yet, we continue to fund these projects as though such scientific realities were irrelevant. Projects are described as though it is just a matter of getting the programming right and then we will have the ability to store information about culture, to analyze it, to predict behavior."

Hugh Gusterson raised an even more troubling critique in an article by Farah Stockman that appeared in the *Boston Globe* in 2010: "Are we going to detain someone if a computer predicts that he will become an insurgent? The real danger of models is their seductiveness. They can be so realistic and powerful that it is easy to forget they are just a model, and then start to rely on them more and more."

ANALYZING THE CULTURAL PSYCHOLOGY OF EXTREMISM

So far, this chapter has focused primarily upon anthropologists' efforts to give military and intelligence agencies exactly what they wanted: quasi-ethnographic data, sometimes qualitative (as in the case of HTS), and sometimes quantitative (as in the case of "metrics" or "data points" for predictive modeling). Broader questions beyond the frame provided by military and intelligence agencies are not asked when anthropology is applied in such an uncritical fashion. Under such circumstances, flawed assumptions may go unchallenged and bad situations can get much worse. Now let us turn our attention to anthropological work that provides critical analyses of the so-called war on terror by examining the root causes of disaffection and alienation that lead some people to engage in political violence—including the policies, actions, and inactions of nation-states.

Anthropologist Scott Atran has criticized the wasteful use of taxpayer dollars on pseudo-scientific counterinsurgency and counterterrorism programs. "Millions are spent, and mostly wasted, on speculative gaming, counter-narratives,

FIG. 8.4. ISIS originated in the tribal areas of Iraq and Syria, but the group has successfully recruited thousands of men and women from dozens of countries, including European countries. Photo in the public domain, courtesy of Wikimedia Commons. Photographer unknown.

and modeling this or that, but nary a penny on scientific attention to what is actually happening on the ground," he told reporter Tom Bartlett in 2016. Atran very publicly critiqued the Human Terrain System before the US Senate Armed Services Committee in 2010, noting that "the possibility that social scientists themselves would have to fire their weapons and perhaps kill local people . . . is guaranteed to engender academia's deep hostility."

Atran has spent much of his career conducting research on cognition and classification. More recently, he has focused on human motivation—for example, what motivates people to take up arms and join ISIS (the Islamic State of Iraq and Syria; see fig. 8.4). In the article by Tom Bartlett mentioned above, he rhetorically asked, "What propels people from 100 countries to come to this place to blow themselves up? There's something in human beings that this appeals to; otherwise it wouldn't work."

Atran's research has called into question fundamental assumptions typically made by military planners and policy makers. For example, in a 2003 article published in the journal *Science*, he argued that suicide bombers in the Middle East are not psychopaths, nor are they typically impoverished or uneducated— in fact, they "generally are not lacking in legitimate life opportunities relative to their general population." He has conducted interviews with people espousing political violence against civilians in a number of countries, including Indonesia, Pakistan, Iraq, Israel, and Palestine.

Cross-cultural and historical examples often illuminate Atran's analysis. He has argued that those who are branded as "radical Islamists" by Western politicians "are much closer in spirit and action to Europe's post-Renaissance Counter-Reformation . . . its clearest historical model [is] in the Holy Inquisition," not in any previous Islamic movements. "The idea that religion must struggle to assert control over politics is radically new to Islam," he wrote in 2003, and it is not a popular idea among the majority of the world's Muslims.

In 2016, Atran published an article with significant implications titled "The Devoted Actor," based upon on interviews with ISIS fighters and Kurdish *peshmerga* in Iraqi Kurdistan. Atran and his colleagues developed a theoretical model called the "devoted actor framework," which is grounded in psychological anthropology. It hypothesizes that people who are willing to make extraordinary sacrifices for a cause are often driven by sacred values that are embodied in tight social networks of "imagined kin." Furthermore, the devoted actor's self-identity becomes subsumed with that of the collective group.

Yet for Atran, the key variable is not so much religion; what matters most is the promise of glory, esteem, and friendship. In his 2010 book *Talking to the Enemy*, he argues that extreme violence and self-sacrifice may be carried out "for friends — campmates, schoolmates, workmates, soccer buddies, body-building buddies, paint-ball partners — action pals who share a cause." In other words, the motivation may be comparable to what drives young American men to join the US Marine Corps: "Maybe they die for dreams of jihad — of justice and glory — and devotion to a familylike group of friends and mentors who act and care for one another, of 'imagined kin,' like the Marines." The devoted actor framework might also apply to certain messianic cults, particularly those in which the members are willing to commit collective suicide in the name of a greater cause.

Atran's argument — that those attracted to groups like ISIS may be doing so more for camaraderie and glory than out of religious conviction — undermines conventional assumptions about so-called jihadi terrorism. For example, policy makers and the media typically frame violence perpetrated by Muslims — the 9/11 attacks, ISIS beheadings of Western journalists, etc. — as a manifestation of an epic "clash of civilizations," to use a phrase popularized by historian Samuel Huntington in the 1990s. According to this idea, the twenty-first century will be a period inevitably marked by deepening tension and conflict between the world's great religions. Atran's point is all the more compelling because ISIS recruits often know very little about Islam. In fact, many appear to be either relatively recent converts or young Muslims who were not raised to be devoutly religious. For Atran, both "homegrown terrorists" and ISIS recruits are motivated by a lack of opportunity — and a lack of hope. He offered the following suggestions for an effective, if ambitious, counterterrorism strategy in 2009 before the US Senate Armed Services Subcommittee on Emerging Threats and Capabilities:

> In the long run, perhaps the most important anti-terrorism measure of all is to provide alternative heroes and hopes that are more enticing and empowering than any moral lessons or material offerings. Jobs that relieve the terrible boredom and inactivity of immigrant youth in Europe, and with underemployed throughout much of the Muslim world, cannot alone offset the alluring stimulation of playing at war in contexts of continued cultural and political alienation and little sense of shared aspirations and destiny. It is also important to provide alternate local networks and chat rooms that speak to the inherent idealism, sense of risk and adventure, and need for peer approval that young people everywhere tend towards. It even could be a 21st-century version of what the Boy Scouts and high school football teams did for immigrants and potentially troublesome youth as America urbanized a century ago.

Some aspects of Atran's work are controversial among anthropologists. Atran's research is partially funded by grants from the Minerva Initiative, a US Department of Defense program that was created in 2008 for the explicit purpose of funding social science research in narrowly targeted areas. Some might question whether Atran's partial reliance upon Pentagon funds might be contributing to a warped version of social science that neatly eliminates a broader critique of American empire. As noted by David Price in 2008 shortly after the creation of the Minerva Initiative, "Minerva doesn't appear to be funding projects designed to tell Defense why the US shouldn't invade and occupy other countries; its programs are more concerned with the nuts and bolts of counterinsurgency, and answering specific questions related to the occupation and streamlining the problems of empire." One might also ask why Atran's research among violent extremists has not included white nationalists like Dylann Roof, the young man who killed nine people at the Emanuel African Methodist Episcopal Church in Charleston, South Carolina, in 2015.

Another issue has to do with the ethics of Atran's work, most notably his interviews with captive ISIS soldiers. One of the foundational ethical concepts in anthropology is that of voluntary informed consent—the notion that an anthropologist should only conduct research among people who have freely granted permission to do so, after being informed of potential risks. Since Atran's research participants include prisoners captured on a battlefield who are being monitored by armed guards, it is difficult to imagine how Atran would be able to obtain truly voluntary consent.

Despite these concerns, Atran's research might change the way some policy

makers view terrorism. To his credit, he has made a concerted effort to publi-
cize his work by writing commentaries for the general public, appearing frequently on TV news programs, and speaking before US congressional committees about his research. As public attention is directed increasingly toward
the rise of ISIS and deadly attacks on civilians in urban centers across Europe
(Paris, Brussels, Nice) and the US (Boston, San Bernardino, Orlando), Atran's
perspectives could potentially lead to creative ideas for reducing violent extremism, not only among those claiming to be waging war for Islam but also among
those acting in the name of white supremacy or other extremist ideologies.

TERROR AND TRIBAL SOCIETY

Akbar Ahmed is another scholar whose work demonstrates the potential power
of an anthropological approach to terrorism. Ahmed has had experience not
only in academia, but also in government: in the past he has served as a political agent for South Waziristan and as the Pakistani high commissioner to the
United Kingdom.

Among his best-known books is *The Thistle and the Drone*, based on an analysis of forty case studies conducted by a research team studying groups on the
margins of global society, ranging from Somalis in the Horn of Africa to Bed-
ouin tribes in the Middle East. Like Atran, Ahmed critiques Huntington's "clash
of civilizations" thesis, but their approaches and emphases are different. For
Ahmed, the US-led "war on terror" has been manipulated by many national
governments (which he refers to as "the center") to wage war against tribal
peoples living in rural areas ("the periphery"). Consequently, the post-9/11
period is characterized not so much by struggles between Muslim and Christian civilizations as suggested by Huntington, but by struggles within predominantly Islamic nation-states. In *The Thistle and the Drone*, Ahmed notes:

> The war on terror has been conceptualized as a triangle formed by three points—
> the United States, the modern state within which the tribes live, and al Qaeda. . . .
> The third point, however, is actually not al Qaeda. . . . It is the tribal societies that
> have directly or indirectly provided a base for al Qaeda and other groups advo-
> cating violence. Many of these peripheral groups had been clamoring, or even
> fighting, for their rights from central governments for decades. A small number
> of al Qaeda operatives, in Afghanistan and elsewhere, found these tribes to be
> receptive hosts.

The main organizing principle of tribal society is the segmentary lineage
system, which has been of interest to anthropologists for many years. Ahmed

defines it as a kinship system based primarily on patrilineal descent from a common ancestor, a system that contains within it "pyramid-like structures of clans and subclans . . . the operative level is the subsection, consisting of several extended families, which is part of a larger section, which, in turn, is part of an even larger clan." Tribes tend to be highly egalitarian (and often acephalous, that is, without leaders) and have territorial rights defined in segmentary terms. They also characteristically have strict codes of honor.

Ahmed begins by examining the collapse of what he calls "the Waziristan model" of tribal society, named for the federally administered tribal areas of northwest Pakistan. A series of tragic interconnected events have chipped away the foundations of Pukhtun tribal life in Waziristan over the past four decades, beginning with the Soviet invasion of Afghanistan in 1979 and the subsequent US arming of the Afghan mujahideen in the 1980s, continuing with Pakistani president Pervez Musharraf's military invasion of the province in 2004, and ending with the relentless, ongoing US drone strikes which escalated during the presidency of Barack Obama and has continued apace during the Trump administration. (See fig. 8.5.)

Out of the chaos, disaffected Taliban from various tribes formed a coalition, the Tehrik-e-Taliban Pakistan (TTP) in late 2007. The group systematically destroyed the authority of Pukhtun tribal elders and the code of honor (*pukhtunwali*), then sought to replace it with its own vaguely defined notion of an Islamic state. At the same time, TTP leaders created their own warped version of *pukhtunwali* that emphasized disproportionate revenge and violence directed at civilians. Members of the TTP beheaded elders, sent suicide bombers to gatherings of tribal leaders opposed to the Taliban, and (ironically) began attacking mosques as a way of challenging the authority of traditional religious leaders. The Pakistani military's response further ripped apart Waziri Pukhtun society, while the US drone war on the region added fuel to the fire by killing hundreds of civilians.

Given this situation, perhaps we should not be surprised that tribesmen tell Ahmed, "Every day is like 9/11 for us."

Ahmed's analysis of forty tribal societies relies heavily upon an updated version of the structural functionalism so popular among British anthropologists more than a half-century ago, though unlike most of the classic structural functionalists, Ahmed's analysis is diachronic. Not only is he concerned with the tribe as an institution, but he is equally interested in processes of change and conflict. In this sense, his approach might be said to draw from political economy, and his use of the terms center and periphery can be seen as an explicit link to that theoretical framework. Ahmed's analysis reveals that contrary to popular belief, twenty-first-century terrorism is not rooted in Islam; it stems from the troubled relationship between central governments and tribal peoples

FIG. 8.5. The use of unmanned aerial vehicles, or drones, has increased dramatically in recent years. Here two airmen load a Hellfire missile onto a Predator drone in Afghanistan. Photo by Sgt. Sabrina Johnson, Air Force; courtesy of US Department of Defense.

living in the periphery. As he argues in *The Thistle and the Drone*: "[It] is the result of the failure of the modern state to deal effectively and peacefully with the periphery. The center is marked by poor governance, corruption, and incompetence. It is applying short-term callous tactics to exterminate 'terrorists.' But the center has no long-term strategy to maintain its own integrity while including the periphery in the nation with its identity and rights respected."

Far from helping to reduce violence, US intervention in countries such as Pakistan, Yemen, Somalia, Afghanistan, and Iraq (among others) is further poisoning the relationship between those countries' central governments and the tribal periphery. "Central governments around the world still cannot provide a satisfactory explanation for the violence or are merely manipulating the United States into supporting their efforts against the periphery," he notes. Central government officials claim to be attacking religious extremists, but use this as a pretext for continuing to destroy tribes living within their borders. The US-led war on terror has therefore become a global war on Islamic tribal societies.

In the months following the 9/11 attacks, several anthropologists predicted some of the transformations described by Ahmed. For example, David Price wrote a commentary in which he observed that the vague and overused term "terrorism" led to its rapid adoption by Russian leaders to describe Chechnya's separatists, by Chinese leaders to describe Uighur protesters, and other peripheral populations. For Price, the "war on terror" threatens indigenous peoples and ethnic minorities around the globe. Another example is a commentary by Nazif Shahrani, who counseled the eventual formation of a new Afghan government based on the stability of past models: "The international community should encourage the creation of a government that recognizes the crucial role of the local and regional communities in self-governance, as existed in earlier eras." (See my edited book *Anthropologists in the Public Sphere* for reprinted versions of these commentaries.) — self plug

To find peace, argues Ahmed, central governments must grant tribal societies meaningful political and economic autonomy, and the right to preserve their cultural heritage and their languages. Tragically, global economic integration—that is, corporate capitalism—has tended to do the opposite. As central governments have opened the doors to foreign investors seeking natural resources, they have recklessly allowed settlers and profiteers to colonize the peripheral lands of tribal peoples in Xinjiang, Mindanao, Baluchistan, and many other regions across the world.

More recently, Ahmed has made insightful and related observations about ISIS. He notes that the group has its origins in the tribal areas of Syria and Iraq, regions that, like Waziristan, have been upended by war and instability. The tribal peoples of these areas have been brutalized by the national governments of Syria (under Bashar al-Assad) and Iraq (particularly under Nouri al-Maliki), and ISIS, like the TTP in Pakistan, found it possible to establish a firm foothold in the region at least partly due to neglect and even repression. Yet policy makers in the United States tend to attribute the rise of ISIS solely to radical Islam, falling back once again on the "clash of civilizations" thesis, as if the broken relationship between central governments and peripheral tribes—and the sheer chaos left in the wake of the US occupation of Iraq—had nothing to do with the situation.

Like Scott Atran, Ahmed has taken a keen interest in "homegrown terrorism." Ahmed argues that young Muslims in Western countries who are attracted to violent extremism do so as the result of a number of factors: social marginalization, discrimination, and racism; outrage at US foreign policy and a sense that Islam is under siege; a relative dearth of influential elders; and parents' poor cultural understanding of the societies in which their children are living. In *The Thistle and the Drone* he writes, "Many young Muslims find the answer that they are seeking from forceful Islamic voices, either in person or on the Internet, preaching hatred of the West and quoting certain selective verses of the Quran." The implications are clear: helping disaffected youth would require a multipronged strategy that would only be effective if substantial changes occurred across multiple institutions: national and international governmental policies would have to change, but so too would the practices of Islamic religious institutions and immigrant Muslim families.

ON THE FRONT LINES

As should be evident by now, anthropology has much to contribute to a more lucid understanding of terrorism and counterterrorism. All of the anthropologists mentioned in this chapter would probably agree on one thing: the discipline should not sit on the sidelines while self-proclaimed "experts" with few substantive qualifications—the pundit class—monopolize public discourse on issues of vital national and international significance. (An outstanding collection of anthropological articles critiquing some of the United States' best-known "experts," including Samuel Huntington and Thomas Friedman, is the 2004 book *Why America's Top Pundits Are Wrong*, edited by Catherine Besteman and Hugh Gusterson.) If we avoid participating in public forums, we run the risk of making ourselves irrelevant, viewed by others as a fascinating but ultimately useless discipline that is oddly disconnected from the world, or perhaps as too aloof to care about it. What anthropologists have learned over the past century and a half is too important to withhold from others, and too important to hide behind bloated or pretentious jargon.

Anthropology needs to be on the front lines, but on its own terms. This means that academic and practicing anthropologists need to make a renewed effort to share their insights with policy makers and politicians while resisting the temptation to slavishly and unquestioningly serve their needs. In other words, it is vital to maintain a high degree of autonomy, especially when dealing with and addressing powerful institutions and individuals. Academic and practicing anthropologists also need to do a better job of communicating the results of their research to the general public—after all, without a knowledgeable citizenry, there is little hope that social problems will be adequately addressed—but at the same time, they must avoid oversimplifying complex issues. And as anthropologists pursue front line work, they must remain cognizant of the discipline's basic ethical principles: do no harm, be open and honest, obtain informed consent from willing research participants, carefully weigh competing ethical obligations, and make research results widely accessible.

Terrorism (to use that problematic term once more)—whether secular or religious, whether inflicted by states or by nonstate actors—is an intractable problem that appears to be getting worse. But anthropologists are already providing a more complete and informed understanding of the phenomenon. Here are a few critical insights that suggest a need for different approaches.

State terror is terrorism too. Any serious examination of terrorism must

172 ROBERTO J. GONZÁLEZ

include a historical analysis. For more than two centuries, the term *terrorism* has referred to indiscriminate violence against civilians perpetrated by states, not just nonstate actors. In the contemporary era, many states have undertaken actions and military offensives that exemplify this, from Syria to Sri Lanka to Israel. A strong argument can be made that the United States has also perpetrated state terrorism in recent decades—we need look no further than ongoing drone wars that have killed thousands of men, women, and children and terrorized entire regions of the world. More research is needed to explore possible connections between state terrorism and the rise of violent extremism among nonstate actors.

Terrorism is not an Islamic phenomenon. In North America and Europe today, "experts" and the media nearly always buy into the "clash of civilization" thesis described earlier in this chapter, assuming that violent extremism is an expression of global jihad. The problem is that such an assumption excludes other forms of violent extremism. For example, in recent decades right-wing zealots—terrorists if we use the US State Department's definition—have attacked a number of federal buildings in the United States, including the 1995 Oklahoma City bombing that killed 168 people. That tragic attack was perpetrated not by a Muslim, but by Timothy McVeigh, an antigovernment extremist who was raised as a Catholic. There are many other examples.

Religion is not the primary motive for terrorism. Friendship, loyalty to a group of peers, fame and glory, the promise of adventure—these forces tend to be much more compelling and attractive motivational forces than religion. These might potentially be channeled in a wide variety of ways, including participation in competitive team sport, involvement in a rock-and-roll band, membership in a street gang, commitment to military service, or dedication to a group espousing violent extremism. Rather than "drain the swamp they [terrorists] live in," as former US Defense Secretary Donald Rumsfeld vowed to do in 2001, counterterrorism initiatives might begin by providing meaningful and attractive options to young people living desperately hopeless lives.

The "war on terror" isn't working. One problem with conducting a war against terrorism is conceptual. Terrorism is not a thing: it's a tactic. How then does one go to war against it? Given the impossibility of the task, national governments have decided to pursue suspected terrorists and their supporters. In practical terms, this often translates into drone warfare directed at tribal societies. As noted earlier in this chapter, it is a strategy that has not only been ineffective but has exacerbated previously existing conflicts between central governments and peripherally located tribes. Countering violent extremism can be effective only if the root causes are addressed.

Although these observations alone will not bring an end to violent extremism or terror inflicted by nation-states, they do demonstrate how anthropological perspectives can lead to a more enlightened understanding of a troubling global phenomenon. Culture matters. Anthropology matters. Without a fuller appreciation of the cultural contexts in which violence occurs, there is little hope of countering it.

SUGGESTIONS FOR FURTHER READING

Ahmed, Akbar. 2013. *The Thistle and the Drone: How America's War on Terror Became a Global War on Tribal Islam.* Washington, DC: Brookings Institution Press.
> This widely read book radically reframes the so-called "war on terror" as an assault on Islamic tribal or indigenous peoples who inhabit rural regions of the Middle East, North Africa, and Central and South Asia.

Giroux, Henry A. 2015. *America's Addiction to Terrorism.* New York: Monthly Review Press.
> This book's central argument is that the United States is a leading purveyor of terrorism today, through such mechanisms as officially sanctioned torture, foreign economic policies promoting brutal austerity policies, and the militarization of domestic police.

Price, David. 2016. *Cold War Anthropology: The CIA, the Pentagon, and the Growth of Dual Use Anthropology.* Durham, NC: Duke University Press.
> This book provides a fascinating history of anthropology during the Cold War— a period in which the discipline underwent rapid expansion to meet the needs of the national security state.

Rubinstein, Robert A., Kerry Fosher, and Clementine Fujimura, eds. 2012. *Practicing Military Anthropology: Beyond Expectations and Traditional Boundaries.* West Hartford, CT: Kumarian Press.
> This volume, edited by anthropologists who have experience practicing anthropology within national and international military organizations, is aimed at demystifying military anthropology.

Sluka, Jeffrey A., ed. 1999. *Death Squad: The Anthropology of State Terror.* Philadelphia: University of Pennsylvania Press.
> This collection of essays is a searing analysis of the role played by nation-states and their paramilitary death squads in inflicting terroristic violence upon civilians. A wide range of examples include cases from Punjab, Kashmir, Argentina, Guatemala, Northern Ireland, Indonesia, the Philippines, and East Timor.

REFERENCES

Ackerman, Spencer. 2011. "How Special Ops copied al-Qaida to kill it." *Danger Room* (Wired blog). September 9. http://www.wired.com/2011/09/mcchrystal-network/all/.

Ahmed, Akbar. 2013. *The Thistle and the Drone: How America's War on Terror Became a Global War on Tribal Islam.* Washington, DC: Brookings Institution Press.

American Anthropological Association. 2007. "Executive Board Statement on the Human Terrain System Program." October 31. http://www.aaanet.org/issues/policy-advocacy/statement-on-HTS.cfm.

Atran, Scott. 2003. "Genesis of Suicide Terrorism." *Science* 299:1534–1539.

————. 2009. "Pathways to and from Violent Extremism: The Case for Science-Based Field Research." Statement before the US Senate Armed Services Subcommittee on Emerging Threats and Capabilities. http://www.artisresearch.com/articles/Atran_Statement_Bef ore_the_Senate.pdf.

————. 2010. *Talking to the Enemy: Faith, Brotherhood, and the (Un)Making of Terrorists.* New York: Ecco Press.

————. 2016. "The Devoted Actor: Unconditional Commitment and Intractable Conflict across Cultures." *Current Anthropology* 57 (Supplement 13): 192–203.

Bartlett, Tom. 2016. "The Road to ISIS." *Chronicle of Higher Education*, May 20. http://www .chronicle.com/article/The-Scientist-Who-Talks-to/236521.

Belcher, Oliver. 2013. "The Afterlives of Counterinsurgency: Postcolonialism, Military Social Science, and Afghanistan 2006–2012." Unpublished PhD diss., University of British Columbia.

Besteman, Catherine, and Hugh Gusterson, eds. 2004. *Why America's Top Pundits Are Wrong.* Berkeley: University of California Press.

Fosher, Kerry. 2014. "Cautionary Tales from the US Department of Defense's Pursuit of Cultural Expertise." In R. Albro & B. Ivey, eds., *Cultural Awareness in the Military*, 15–29. London: Palgrave Macmillan.

Gezari, Vanessa. 2013. *The Tender Soldier: A True Story of War and Sacrifice.* New York: Simon & Schuster.

González, Roberto J., ed. 2004. *Anthropologists in the Public Sphere: Speaking Out on War, Peace, and American Power.* Austin: University of Texas Press.

————. 2007. "Human Terrain: Past, Present, and Future Applications." *Anthropology Today* 24 (1): 21–26.

————. 2015. "The Rise and Fall of the Human Terrain System." *CounterPunch*, June 29. https://www.counterpunch.org/2015/06/29/the-rise-and-fall-of-the-human-terrain -system/.

Greenwald, Glenn. 2010. "Terrorism: The Most Meaningless and Manipulated Word." Salon .com, February 19, http://www.salon.com/2010/02/19/terrorism_19/.

Gusterson, Hugh, and Catherine Besteman, eds. 2009. *The Insecure American: How We Got Here and What We Should Do about It.* Berkeley: University of California Press.

James, E. O. 1943. "Review of *Lamps of Anthropology* by J. Murphy." *Man* 43 (Nov.-Dec.): 137–38.

Kaplan, Fred. 2014. *The Insurgents: David Petraeus and the Plot to Change the American Way of War.* New York: Simon & Schuster.

Kilcullen, David. 2010. *Counterinsurgency.* Oxford: Oxford University Press.

Krogman, W. M. 1943. "Review of *Man's Most Dangerous Myth: The Fallacy of Race* by Ashley Montagu." *American Anthropologist* 45:292–93.

Kuznar, Lawrence. 2007. "Rationality Wars and the War on Terror: Explaining Terrorism and Social Unrest." *American Anthropologist* 109 (2): 318–29.

————. 2008. "Anthropological Perspectives on Rare Event Prediction." In Nancy Chesser, ed., *Anticipating Rare Events.* Department of Defense White Paper, 17–24. http://www .dni.gov/index.php/newsroom/press-releases/198-press-releases-2014/1003-iarpa-launc hes-new-research-program-to-significantly-improve-adaptive-reasoning-and-problem -solving.

Marlowe, Frank. 2010. *The Hadza: Hunter-Gatherers of Tanzania.* Berkeley: University of California Press.

McFate, Montgomery. 2005. "Anthropology and Counterinsurgency: The Strange Story of Their Curious Relationship." *Military Review*, March–April, 24–38.

Nagengast, Carole. 1994. "Violence, Terror, and the Crisis of the State." *Annual Review of Anthropology* 23:109–36.

Price, David. 2009. "Anthropology, Human Terrain's Prehistory, and the Role of Culture in Wars Waged by Robots." *CounterPunch*, October 1–15; 16 (17): 1, 4–6.

———. 2016. *Cold War Anthropology: The CIA, the Pentagon, and the Growth of Dual Use Anthropology*. Durham, NC: Duke University Press.

Schmorrow, Dylan. 2010. "A View of Defense Department Science and Technology." Unpublished slide presentation. https://www.navalengineers.org/SiteCollectionDocuments/2010%20Proceedings%20Documents/UHSI%202010/Presentations/Day%201/Schmorrow.pdf.

Shachtman, Noah. 2011. "Inside DARPA's Secret Afghan Spy Machine." *Danger Room* (Wired blog), July 21. http://www.wired.com/2011/07/darpas-secret-spy-machine/all/hearts minds ii.

Sluka, Jeffrey A., ed. 1999. *Death Squad: The Anthropology of State Terror*. Philadelphia: University of Pennsylvania Press.

Stockman, Farah. 2010. "Knowing the Enemy, One Avatar at a Time." *Boston Globe*, May 3. http://www.boston.com/news/nation/washington/articles/2010/05/30/knowing_the_enemy_one_avatar_at_a_time/.

US Department of State. 2001. United States Code, Title 22, Section 2656f(d). https://www.law.cornell.edu/uscode/text/22/2656 f.

Weingrod, Alex. 1962. "Reciprocal Change: A Case Study of a Moroccan Immigrant Village in Israel." 64:115–31.

Welling, James C. 1892. "The Law on Torture: A Study in the Evolution of Law." *American Anthropologist* 5 (3): 193–215.

Wolpert, Steve. 2010. "Can Math and Science Help Solve Crimes?" *US News & World Report*, March 2. http://www.usnews.com/science/articles/2010/03/02/can-math-and-science-help-solve-crimes.

Vanden Brook, Tom. 2014. "Military Social Sciences Tab up to $726M Since 2007." *USA Today*, January 2. https://www.usatoday.com/story/nation/2014/01/02/human-terrain-system-waste-fraud-abuse-sexual-racial-harassment/4290977/.

CHAPTER 9

THE ANTHROPOLOGICAL BORDERLANDS OF GLOBAL MIGRATION

Ruben Andersson

It was a breezy day when the patrol car stopped at the topmost point of one of Europe's most fortified borders. From the hills of Ceuta, a Spanish enclave on the North African coastline, views stretched from the Moroccan forests on the other side of the border fence to the blueness of the Strait of Gibraltar just north of us. My Civil Guard cicerone looked up toward the imposing barrier, squinting in the midday Mediterranean sun. "There you'd cut yourself well," he said, matter-of-factly: coils of razor wire clung to the double, six-meter-tall fence blocking undocumented African migrants' path into this tiny slice of the European Union. Moroccan sentry boxes, manned by green-uniformed auxiliary forces, lurked behind the mesh, but no migrants were anywhere to be seen. The last time a migrant died here had happened while my cicerone was on holiday: ensnared in the teeth of the concertina wire, the migrant was but one more death in a tally of thousands at the borders of the Union.

In the days after our border "tour," I spoke to one of the men who had made it across. Sipping his orange juice at a café in central Ceuta, Amadou told me how he had been lying in wait on the Moroccan side of the fence, scanning it, watching the guards' routines. The sniffer dogs had spotted him, and he had been expelled to the faraway Algerian border, but he made it back on foot through the forests. Eventually, his time had come. He knew what kind of clothes to use to avoid snagging on the wire; how to scale the fence with deft movements; and how to stealthily make it past the internal walkway between the fences, pushing his way through the last barrier into Spain. To survivors such as Amadou, migration was a battle of wits and a struggle between life and death. Like many other West Africans on the overland trail toward Europe, he called himself an adventurer. Stuck within the enclave of Ceuta, waiting for his chance to cross into Europe proper, his adventure was not yet over—as indicated by the protest echoing down Ceuta's narrow streets that day, staged by other stranded migrants fed up with their indeterminate wait in this man-made limbo on the doorstep to the continent.

I start this chapter on migration with these brief vignettes to highlight the stakes involved in how we define, research, and discuss migration within and outside academia. Migration is one of the most visible political topics of our time, but only in some of its manifestations: racialized Others scaling fences and crossing maritime borders on unseaworthy boats capture headlines and steer political debate. Yet most migration, and most mobility, remains far more humdrum and invisible. In Spain, one survey in the past decade indicated only about 1 percent of the country's migrants had arrived undocumented by sea. At the official border crossings in Ceuta's fence, Moroccan day workers and daytrippers lined up each morning for a visit to this slice of Spain, whose very existence depended on their labor and custom: further along the snaking fence, in a gated opening, impoverished Moroccan porters lugged huge parcels of goods into Morocco under the stern gaze of the border forces, in an officially sanctioned "irregular" trade that likewise sustained the enclave's economy. The civil guard showing me around his dominions was himself a migrant from northern Spain, stationed for a few years in Ceuta; a prospect he did not relish, as the very fence he was in charge of enclosed his family inside the enclave. The Moroccan forces in their sentry boxes were likewise brought in from elsewhere, doing their dire tour of duty in the forested hinterlands of the barrier, while many among Ceuta's inhabitants were migrants or descendants from Andalusia across the Strait.

The kind of migration that had the bright spotlights of fences and camera flashes cast upon it was, then, but a small fragment of the broader picture of mobility at this ancient crossroads of Europe and Africa. The crossing of adventurers such as Amadou was gendered and racialized as a masculine battle between black African migrant and white European border guard, between fence and flesh, while most movements took place away from the public gaze.

When we study migration as anthropologists, this partial *hypervisibility* of certain migrants and invisibility of others must be one of our starting points. We may begin by taking apart the commonsensical notion of "the migrant," to shift our gaze and see what lurks beneath. Who is this migrant everyone frets about, and why and how has he (or sometimes she) been framed and treated in specific ways?

Anthropologists are sometimes described as tricksters, straddling borders between different groups, and between insider and outsider perspectives; yet in a field so replete with border crossings of all kinds as international migration, this position can be an uneasy one. As we drove away from the fence that day, and in coming weeks during my fieldwork in Ceuta, doubts lingered over my enterprise; and as I started work as a volunteer in the reception center for migrants who had made it across the fence, these doubts grew. "Ah, so you are studying us?" one West African resident asked me in eloquent French one day in the lower reaches of the "camp," as migrants called their temporary home. Indeed, the camp was a ready-made site for research delegations and journalists to come and interview stranded migrants in near-captive conditions; a situation not lost on this questioner and the migrants protesting down in central Ceuta against their stay in "Guantánamo" (as they called it). I return to my response to his question below, yet the challenge was clear: in a world where certain people on the move are stigmatized through their very mobility as unwanted migrants, how can we as anthropologists avoid falling back on our colonial history of studying "natives" and Others on the other side of the fence of global power structures? Is an "anthropology of migration," insofar as it exists, itself complicit in that very state-imposed division between citizen and migrant, insider and outsider, researcher and researched?

"Migration studies" has turned into a vast field of study in recent years well beyond the reaches of our discipline, in parallel with the rise of the political prominence of migration. Development economists, demographers, and geographers have traced global "stocks" and "flows," pinpointing structural reasons why migration may persist despite state restrictions. Segmented labor markets, in which richer nations fill lower slots in domestic employment hierarchies with marginal outsiders, may bolster international migration; global imbalances wrought through unequal trade arrangements may create pathways between global "centers" and "peripheries"; and migratory networks themselves spur fresh generations of movers. In these fields of study, migration is treated through a behavioral, often positivist lens: these are the migrants, and these are the causes behind their movements, which can be ascertained with some level of (preferably mathematical) generalizability. Creating typologies, building formulae, crunching statistics to obtain predictive capacity is in the interest of scholars, and understandably so. However, it is also in the interest of "receiving states," not least Western ones, which have since colonial times wanted to map the whereabouts of the global poor even as they actively appropriated their labor. The result is that migration has often been treated as a "problem to be solved," and scholars have all too often been willing to help frame it as such.

This state-centric focus on stocks, flows, and risks is quite alien to anthropology, given the discipline's preference for holistic studies of communities. As anthropologists did start studying migration, they brought their ethnographic toolkit as they set to work on forging intricate accounts of the subjective, social, and cultural factors involved in migration processes. This has greatly enriched our understanding of the role of movement in people's life-worlds, while also complementing the state perspective on migration that behavioral approaches often take for granted. Yet until quite recently, anthropological studies did not fully question how migration and migrants have become such commonsensical categories of state intervention and scientific scrutiny, and with what consequences. That larger task of defamiliarizing what we take for granted, at which anthropology tends to excel, has only gradually come into focus in migration scholarship—and we urgently need more of that fundamental questioning, not least as migration (in some of its guises) keeps redefining politics on both sides of the Atlantic.

FROM INTERNAL TO TRANSNATIONAL MOVEMENT

A brief look back toward the emergence of migration studies as a field is one good way of starting to defamiliarize the "migrant." For a long time, migration scholars, whether in anthropology or beyond, were principally concerned with *internal* migration, that is, movement within the borders of nation-states, or within colonial dominions. Migration had already in colonial times been framed as a problem to be solved by politicians, officials, and scholars, yet it was also an evident source of riches for the colonizers. In French West Africa, forced migration and punitive taxation pushed workers from the dusty hinterland of the Sahel toward the plantations and colonial hubs on the coasts, while in southern Africa, the demand for mass labor in mining helped reshape local societies. While the economic benefits of such movements were clear, officials still cast an anxious eye on these new generations of footloose Africans. As British social anthropologists set out to study such migratory patterns in the 1930s and 1940s, they initially came to reflect official anxieties in their concern with "detribalization" and its potential for tearing at the social fabric of "traditional" societies.

As other disciplines started studying migration in Africa and other poorer parts of the world, they similarly came to reflect or reinforce the official ambivalence toward migration, advising officials on how rural outflows could be managed or halted while also arguing for the economic benefits of mobility. Development economists considered how rural people might get drawn into the underbelly of the urban economy, even when actual job prospects were scarce. While such studies largely saw migration as beneficial, supplying labor where it was needed and in the long run equalizing economic prospects, the pendulum was swiftly swinging the other way. By the 1960s, Marxist-influenced scholars were treating migration as one prominent form of exploitation leading to "underdevelopment" in formerly colonized nations. Based on world systems and dependency theories, such studies saw formerly self-sufficient rural areas as gradually transforming into exploited peripheries of the "world economy." Capitalism red in tooth and claw tore into self-sufficient rural livelihoods while cash and consumerism infringed on local economies. Powerful states and capitalist forces combined to foment crisis through exploitation both inside and outside their own countries, which in turn "uprooted" people who saw little choice but to set off on the highway to modernity. John Steinbeck, whose *Grapes of Wrath* may still be the most powerful novel written on migration, set the tone in describing the migrations of "Okies" amid the Dust Bowl of the US Depression era, and how their lives were torn up by the landowners waiting to see them go West: "We're sorry, said the owner men. The bank, the fifty-thousand-acre owner can't be responsible. You're on land that isn't yours. Once over the line maybe you can pick cotton in the fall. Maybe you can go on relief. Why don't you go on west to California? There's work there, and it never gets cold. Why, you can reach out anywhere and pick an orange. Why, there's always some kind of crop to work in. Why don't you go there? And the owner men started their cars and rolled away."

As rural residents were displaced across the capitalist "semi-periphery" of the world system, labor-heavy industries in the West (or colonial enterprises elsewhere) could tap into the productivity of labor without having to pay for its reproduction. New generations were brought up back home, schooled (sometimes) and readied for a fresh bout of exploitation depending on the vagaries of global demand. They were, to scholars writing in this vein, a global reserve army of labor.

Amid their hard-hitting critique of capitalism, these Marxist-influenced scholars often ignored the liberating potential of movement: how, even though movement is tied up with economic exploitation, it may also allow individuals to shape their lives anew in a testament to the strength of the human spirit, as seen for instance in how young West Africans talked about the dangerous journey toward Europe as an "adventure" of personal trial and transformation.

These ambivalences around migration, its benefits versus its drawbacks, its liberating and exploitative potential, its personal and socioeconomic dimensions, have been inherited by more recent generations of scholarship in anthropology and beyond. Migration still alternately appears as an uprooting and exodus, or as a life project forged under the inevitable conditions of contemporary globalization.

Anthropologists ended up leading the way in foregrounding some of this complexity in an influential set of postwar studies of African urbanization, yet as that stream petered out, the discipline had for quite some years little to say about migration. This changed in the 1990s, when it was again to be a principal conduit for rethinking the complexity of migration's meanings and consequences, but now on an international rather than a national scale. This move came through the paradigm of transnational migration.

By the 1990s, the bulk of wider migration scholarship had shifted away from internal to international migration, reflecting as in earlier times political priorities in Western states over the nature of the migration "problem." Yet this very shift toward the international scale was itself interrogated by anthropologists and other scholars with a good ear to the ground. In an influential article from 1995, Nina Glick Schiller, Linda Basch, and Cristina Szanton Blanc started by implicitly taking issue with the Marxist view on migration above: "Contemporary immigrants can not be characterized as the 'uprooted.' Many are transmigrants, becoming firmly rooted in their new country but maintaining multiple linkages to their homeland." To these authors, *transmigrants* were those whose daily lives depended on constant connections across borders, and whose public identities related to more than one nation-state. Through their actions and networks, such transmigrants unsettled state categories of migration and belonging. The authors urged scholars to do the same, tearing free of the inherited "methodological nationalism" that, they argued, made us see migration through a narrow nation-state prism.

As the transnational paradigm spread well beyond anthropology, it encountered skepticism in some quarters: are all international migrants equally transnational, or only a small elite? How can we begin to quantify and test the "transnationalism hypothesis"? Yet despite such questions, empirically valid and simplistically positivist by turns, the transnational paradigm remains, to this day, the most significant theoretical contribution of anthropology to studies of migration, challenging researchers of all kinds to rethink our categories of analysis. Moreover, a transnational perspective forces us to consider migrants' own perspective on their mobility. Instead of seeing migration "like a state," to paraphrase anthropologist James Scott, we need to "see like a migrant" to reveal other ways of belonging that do not neatly map onto the narratives of immigrant "integration," migration "pressures," and the like that keep defining policy debate and much of mainstream migration research.

Consider, in this vein, Susan Bibler Coutin's powerful study of the struggles for residency experienced by migrants from El Salvador in the United States. Coutin shows how the seeming simplicity of a citizenship process may stage a clash between state-imposed ideas of singular incorporation into the nation and migrants' own "cultural logics of belonging," which may see no contradiction between obtaining citizenship and forging *stronger* relations with their "homelands." Indeed, the first act of many "naturalized" Salvadorans is to reconnect back home. In the words of one of her informants, an asylum applicant: "The day that I receive [legal permanent residency] papers, that very day, I'm catching a plane to go to El Salvador again. It's been eleven years since I've seen my parents."

Instead of seeing citizenship in the United States as a zero-sum game with their existing nationality, Coutin found Salvadoran migrants "articulated an *additive* model of citizenship" at odds with the official version. In the words of one member of a Salvadoran organization promoting citizenship, "Becoming citizens, we don't lose anything. We remain Salvadoran at heart." In citizenship ceremonies replete with pomp, flag waving, and lofty speeches directed at scores of "new Americans," Coutin found a fluctuation "between the tedium of bureaucratic processing and the mysticism of a religious conversion." Through their intricate rituals, the ceremonies tried to forge similarity out of difference, blending foreign practices into melting-pot America in a great feast of unity. Yet this idea of individual, generic absorption into the archetypal "nation of immigrants" was not necessarily shared by the Salvadorans waiting in line: instead, they often articulated a fear of never being seen as "fully American." Through their new legal status, they were, however, sometimes able to forge life opportunities that made the most of their dual national identity, in a peculiar symbiosis between national ideas of singular belonging and multiple forms of dependency across borders.

In sum, through a transnational lens on these struggles, Coutin shows that despite the seeming clash between the logics of exclusive national membership and global interdependency, the very national membership categories that deny global interconnections can paradoxically help facilitate more such connectivity. The nation-state "box" is a real social phenomenon, a dominant presence in Salvadorans' everyday lives. Yet at the same time Salvadoran migrants are, through their navigations of the system, able to forge a lived experience that straddles and to some extent eludes its legal, physical, and metaphorical walls.

In parallel with the transnational turn, some scholars were proposing a radical shift in focus in how we study society that dovetailed with transnationalism. To these scholars, social sciences had an inbuilt "sedentary bias," treating sedentary life as normal and movement as aberrant, outside the "national order of things." To rectify this, they proposed a mobilities paradigm that sees human migration as just one form of mobility underlying broader social changes, together with the mobility of capital, of goods and of ideas, all of which should take center stage in the study of social life.

The mobility and transnational paradigms were both important break-throughs, in helping to unsettle what we mean by "migration" as well as the ways in which scholars and states have tended to place it in opposition to the sedentary or nation-state norm. As an alternative, both paradigms offered a view of movement as a fundamental part of human existence. Yet both were also products of their time. The 1990s and early 2000s saw a swirl of optimistic policy thinking on the "development potential" of migration and remittances, reinforced by powerful actors such as the World Bank and international development agencies. After this period, when rather triumphant assertions of migrant "agency" and of mobility as an unstoppable force had rung down the halls of academia and of international organizations, a rude awakening was to follow.

FROM SUBJECTS TO STRUCTURES

If in the 1990s, anthropologists had, crudely put, concentrated on studying global "scapes" and "flows," in the 2000s many shifted their attention to structures of violence, immobility, and power. Given developments after 9/11, this move is not hard to understand. Mobilizations around border security, fear of migrants, the war on terror, and national sovereignty were reshaping politics in powerful Western states, and scholars were facing up to the latest in sentiment on migration. Instead of "seeing like a migrant," some researchers embraced Scott's challenge of "seeing like a state"—shifting the gaze toward powerful structures and regimes, while ethnographically displacing the object of study "upward," toward state and "state-like" agents shaping and controlling migrations.

The shift was present in the transnational and mobilities camps, too. Although the original paradigms had always worked against the backdrop of the state, their proponents now addressed powerful structures more explicitly and systematically. Anthropologists faced head-on a central political quandary: "How are scholars of migration, travel, tourism and refuge to understand the rapid glamorization and then demonization of categories of mobile people?" In response, some proposed a shift in focus toward "regimes of mobility." By casting an ethnographic eye on state power, international regulatory frameworks, and the surveillance of movement, their aim was to explore how the privileged movements of some related to the stigmatized movement of others in an unequally mobile world.

The anthropologist Michel Agier took on such a challenge in his book on the worldwide proliferation of camps for migrants and refugees, *Managing the Undesirables*. Camps, to him, served as a means for richer states to contain and regulate the (im)mobility of undesirable Others: his starting point is the very division of mobility into celebratory and stigmatized forms, rendered in his opening lines as clean and visible versus dark and invisible worlds, lurking in the global shadows behind tall walls. Tucked away in perennial refugee camps such as Dadaab in Kenya or holding sites on the periphery of the West itself, the global "undesirables" are subjected to forms of governance that defines them at once as helpless victims and threatening subjects who need to be contained and controlled. Stuck in the "straightjacket of the victim identity," camp residents are treated as nameless individuals, marooned in limbo-like spaces where time seems to have stopped. Life in camps becomes parenthetical, the future receding from view, with deep consequences for personal identity and well-being. "No one knows who I am" is a frequent complaint among encamped refugees; and so is the complaint no one cares about their existence, with little information forthcoming on when (if ever) they will escape across the wires of encampment.

Agier's methodology further questioned what "being a migrant" or refugee involved: "Taking 'refugees' as the object of research . . . would mean confusing the object of research with that of the intervener who creates this space and this category." This intervener, onto which researchers needed to shift their gaze, was what Agier called "humanitarian government," or the structures of the United Nations and state agencies (plus other institutions) put in place both to care for and control migrants and refugees, while fixing and defining certain roles for them. Indeed, caring for "vulnerable" refugees in camps was in itself a means of migration *control*, facilitating the containment of those who should not move, especially not toward those Western states that helped fund the camps in large refugee host nations.

Another key thinker on care and control, Didier Fassin, also deployed the term humanitarian government at the time, albeit with different emphasis. In his study of the rise and eventual razing of the Red Cross–managed Sangatte camp on the outskirts of Calais in France, long a site of attempted clandestine crossings across the Channel into the United Kingdom, he delved into the "bio-politics" of migration control and its construction of deserving and undeserving Others. Instead of seeing unwanted migrants as simply set aside from society, hidden in its shadows, he showed the deep enmeshment of, and even confusion between, the humanitarian and the political in France. The Sangatte camp, a repurposed warehouse, was both a site of containment and a site of humanitarian action, where the state security police parked a bus day and night at the entrance while the Red Cross tended to those who had made their makeshift life amid the prefabs inside the gates.

If the camp space helped make visible certain migrants, other, less visible spaces outside the camp equally brought to the fore the interaction between political, security and humanitarian concerns. Fassin takes the case of Marie, a twenty-five-year-old Haitian woman working her way through the French asylum system. Her father, a political dissident, had been murdered, her mother thought to have been killed; Marie herself was a survivor of rape. As her application for asylum came to naught, she faced social isolation; depressed, she was admitted to hospital. The doctors who saw her were aware of amendments to the French Immigration Act recognizing the possibility of a residence permit for undocumented immigrants who faced severe health problems and who had no access to effective treatment at home. Her depression was however not a strong enough "humanitarian reason" to build such a case, yet when Marie was found to be HIV positive, her chances improved: the case became "legally easy" and she obtained her permit. As Fassin concludes, "What she had not been able to get as a right had finally been given to her by compassion."

Studies such as those of Agier and Fassin foreground powerful structures and systems for the control of mobility. Agier denounced such structures' "absolute power over life," illustrated through mundane acts such as the distribution of essential goods, such as soap bars, in camps. However, he also emphasized how anthropologists must sift for those "grains of dust that jam the machinery"; the contradictions, tensions, and conflicts inherent in any system of control. He saw these points of friction in refugees' own strategies of rendering themselves invisible to the authorities; in the self-organization of non-official camp-like spaces such as the "ghettoes" of undocumented sub-Saharan migrants in North Africa; and in staff complaints about residents' "manipulation" and resistance. Fassin took this further, in bringing in deeply human stories such as that of Marie to show how, amid the tightening constraints of migration politics, tactical openings could be exploited by those with few other options. Yet he also recognized how, by engaging in such tactics, migrants may come to reinforce the official "biopolitics" by taking recourse to the humanitarian victim role.

This move back toward the *subject* of migration was a well-needed one, as the tension already identified in earlier generations of scholarship between a structural and an individual, life-centered view on migration kept reproducing itself. While the analytical move toward states, regimes, and forms of "government" in Agier's sense was a salutary development after the fervor around agency and mobility, it also risked rendering human movement as a process exclusively in hock to power, in which people on the move become controllable and trackable ciphers of all-powerful systems.

THE PHENOMENAL AND THE POLITICAL

As my fieldwork wore on in the "camp" of Ceuta in 2010, I recognized many of the dynamics traced by Fassin and Agier. The camp was a peculiar place. It was labeled a "temporary reception center," yet mobility had switched to stasis. The average stay before transfer to the Spanish mainland (for deportation or freedom) had grown to 1.5 years and was growing longer. Police, who occasionally entered the camp for deportation round-ups, explained to me how the camp, and Ceuta itself, served as a deterrent to further entrants. The longer people were kept as collective punishment, the fewer would try to arrive from across the imposing fences and around the enclave's sea perimeter (or so went the theory). Red Cross workers within the camp fulfilled the "care" function, treating residents as "vulnerable" yet failing to see how their main vulnerability was *structural*, stemming from prolonged encampment itself. With no chance to work and ensconced on the very geographical margins of the enclave up in Ceuta's hills, some encamped migrants were going mad, worried residents reported; others lashed out in anger, launching the protest against "Guantánamo" that reverberated down the central streets that summer.

It was clear, however, that the camp was far from a successfully self-contained world and "space of exception." Rather, it was brimming with social and political activity. Some residents had skirted camp rules in mounting satellite cables, providing TVs for their bunk rooms; others used Internet dongles to connect to the outside world that the camp was trying to keep them away from; yet others refused camp existence and built their own ramshackle communities in the hills above it. In the bushes outside the fenced perimeter female residents, rendered socially invisible by the authorities and the media (and to their detriment treated as "vulnerable" migrants par excellence), had set up makeshift food stalls, selling West African stews for a euro a plate. Meanwhile, residents hotly contested their political predicament, and I as a camp volunteer was poised in the middle as momentum started to build for the protest. At one gathering on the benches set amid the prefab bunk rooms, questions came thick and fast: "If you come back after a year and I am still here, would you be happy?" one resident asked. Others chimed in: "It's a prison." "We are treated like savages." "It's the slave trade all over again." The older man who had questioned my presence also spoke up. He was a veteran of the migrant circuit: he bared his thigh to show two big round scars from a bullet fired by border guards on an earlier entry attempt across the fences in 2005. "Look above," he said, pointing toward the horse-riding center that had been constructed right above the camp and regularly sent clouds of dust down over the parking lot. "Here they keep some beasts next to others." *"Aucun blanc peut vivre ici"* ("No white person can live here"), someone added. It was an unstoppable barrage of statements and questions, all converging around the racialized exclusion, containment, and even exploitation they (quite correctly) saw themselves as subjected to.

As several migrants remarked, the camp brought funds and employment to the crisis-ravaged local economy, meaning the longer migrants were kept stranded, the bigger the benefits of this "human trading." At one point, a female long-term resident lashed out at the Red Cross worker I accompanied on her rounds of the bunks: "I could do your job!" Yet for the workers, such complaints fell on deaf ears: the migrants were objects of intervention of a peculiar kind, set aside from society and vulnerable in their outsider role. When the protest eventually unfolded, migrants tellingly called it a "strike," not a protest: they saw themselves as "working for" the camp authorities by "doing time." By exiting the camp and refusing to play by the rules, they withheld the vital labor that sustained the camp structure and its punitive economy.

The strike itself made migrants visible in a peculiar way: as angry, even threatening. Migrants, I saw in my research, sometimes tactically played their own peculiar role in what is sometimes labeled the "spectacle of migration" in order to achieve their aims. In a similar vein, migrants I met outside Ceuta, on the trails toward North African coasts, often talked about themselves as "illegal" or (in French) *clandestin,* as they emphasized how their life chances and even identity were bound up with the night raids, patrols, random checks, fences, legal exclusions, and desert crossings that constituted their obstacle course through the Euro-African borderlands. Yet even as they sometimes played into official categories, migrants' own notion of the dangerous journey as an "adventure" put a radically different spin on their movements than the official framing in terms of illegality. In sum, as legal routes into the West have diminished for certain kinds of migrants, and as formidable barriers have gone up, new subject positions are being created in direct interaction between official attempts at control/containment and the agency and willpower of people who feel they have nothing to lose.

Anthropology is extremely well placed to explore this intersection of high politics, meso-level structures, and social life-worlds, combining some of the strengths of the analytical trends traced in the previous sections. In Israel, anthropologist Sarah Willen has traced the everyday strategies of "illegalized" African migrants, in an evocative ethnographic attempt of "linking the phenomenal and the political." To evade law enforcement, migrants would dress in layers of clothing that hid their skin or turn weekly rhythms upside-down, skirting the sharp gaze of day. I heard similar stories among "adventurers" in Morocco, Senegal, and Mali. One migrant recounted how he had managed to cross the Sahara tucked in under contraband cigarette packets in a truck, ren-

dering himself "thinglike" and transportable away from the gaze of border officials. Another recalled how, as he was being deported back through the desert
in a cattle truck by Algerian forces, his body rocking from side to side with each
bump in the road, he felt animalized. "Am I really a goat? A cow?" he asked
angrily, echoing the critique of the encamped migrants in Ceuta. Other writers
on precarious migrations have observed similar trends elsewhere. Coutin, following Central Americans toward the United States, has shown how undocumented journeys unfold in a blank space "outside the law," hidden and invisible,
while Shahram Khosravi, in his autoethnography of traveling without papers
from Iran to Sweden, perceives the border not as simply a juridical line but as a
physical, phenomenological barrier. Crossing it, he says in an echo of Amadou
at the fences in my opening vignette, is a performance in which breath, bodily
composure, dress, and comportment may in an instant define one's life chances.

All these studies get at the central contention of this section—the need for
anthropology to keep developing analytical frames that link life-worlds and
structures, the phenomenal and the political. Migration and mobility are aspects of human existence in which the encounter between powerful structures
of state and market and laboring, struggling, desiring people is often jarringly
laid bare, and ethnography provides a tool for shining a light into that conflictive, productive, and sometimes destructive encounter.

Yet the initial question remains: what kinds of migration are we contributing
to make visible in our studies? The question of the Ceuta camp resident remains
unanswered: "So you are studying us?" I was there to study the *system* for the
containment, care, and control of "unwanted" migration, not the migrants and
their experiences, and had responded to him in this vein, saying I was studying
the camp itself. Whether this response satisfied him is another question, however, and my ambivalence lingered. In the deeply politicized field of migration,
our choices of study sites and themes need to be closely motivated and analytically as well as ethically accounted for, hopefully arriving at a different view.

MOVING BEYOND MIGRATION?

Anthropological studies of migration and mobility have, in many respects, developed similarly to those of other fields. As Buerger and Wilson's chapter in
this volume shows, the study of human rights has moved toward more "systemic" perspectives that consider human rights itself as a cultural and social
field for practitioners. In migration we have seen a similar move, toward considering structures of power and the social and cultural worlds of migration officials, camp workers, border guards, and other groups which contribute to the

formation of such (political) structures. At the same time, the "trickster" role of anthropology remains its strength, as ethnographers have managed to straddle the worlds of officialdom and the lived experience of migration regimes.

It may be worth formulating these shifts in starker terms. Given the visibility of (certain kinds of) "migrants" in the public and political spheres today, I would argue for a need to further *de-center the migrant* in studies of migration and (im)mobility. The bulk of migration research, in anthropology and other disciplines, remains fundamentally concerned with "the migrants": the causes behind their movements, the consequences of these on "receiving" societies, and the like. Despite the gradual shift toward more structural and systemic perspectives, researchers are still principally gazing toward specific migratory subjects, leaving other parts of the global mobility picture relatively invisible. De-centering the migrant, in this context, does not mean ignoring the real struggles of those who are made visible as (unwanted) migrants; instead, it can in an ethnographic vein build on their own analyses of their situation. As migrants in Ceuta and elsewhere challenged my research focus, I came to shift the gaze in my ethnography toward the systemic aspects of their predicaments, or what I came to call the multifaceted "industry" of border and migration controls developing at and beyond Europe's southernmost edges. Migrants' analysis of the "trading" and tribulations offered by this system was thus put center stage, but so was their own daily struggle with its various manifestations, from the ambivalent interventions of camp workers to the deterrence strategies of police and border guards. Equally, I could have shifted focus to those who did *not* move internationally and so fell outside powerful states' purview: families back home and traders in West Africa, say, whose patterns of im/mobility are both tied up with deep regional histories and with more recent political attempts from Europe to "manage" migration at a distance. Or I could have shifted focus to the vast data systems for risk-profiling international movers now at work in advanced economies, yet which rarely receive enough scholarly attention because of their invisibility relative to the "spectacle" of controls at physical land and sea borders.

Mobility may be the stuff of social life, as the mobilities paradigm has insisted, yet which *kinds* of mobility and immobility receive political, media, and scholarly attention is a question we need to confront as we step onto the treacherous terrains of today's conflictive "age of migration."

SUGGESTIONS FOR FURTHER READING

Agier, M. 2011. *Managing the Undesirables: Refugee Camps and Humanitarian Government.* Cambridge: Polity.

Andersson, R. 2014. *Illegality, Inc.: Clandestine Migration and the Business of Bordering Europe.* Oakland: University of California Press.

Castles, S., M. Miller, and H. de Haas. 2013. *The Age of Migration: International Population Movements in the Modern World.* Fifth edition. Basingstoke: Palgrave MacMillan.

Coutin, S. B. 2003. "Cultural Logics of Belonging and Movement: Transnationalism, Naturalization, and U.S. Immigration Politics." *American Ethnologist* 30 (4): 508-26.

Fassin, D. 2005. "Compassion and Repression: The Moral Economy of Immigration Policies in France." *Cultural Anthropology* 20 (3): 362-87.

Glick Schiller, N., L. Basch, and C. Szanton Blanc. 1995. "From Immigrant to Transmigrant: Theorizing Transnational Migration." *Anthropological Quarterly* 68 (1): 48-63.

Glick Schiller, N., and N. B. Salazar. 2013. "Regimes of Mobility across the Globe." *Journal of Ethnic and Migration Studies* 39 (2): 183-200.

Steinbeck, J. 1993. *The Grapes of Wrath.* London: Everyman's Library.

Urry, J. 2007. *Mobilities.* Cambridge: Polity.

Willen, S. 2007. "Toward a Critical Phenomenology of "Illegality": State Power, Criminalization, and Abjectivity among Undocumented Migrant Workers in Tel Aviv, Israel." *International Migration* 45 (2): 8-38.

CHAPTER 10

ANTHROPOLOGY AND DEVELOPMENT

Katy Gardner

For generations anthropologists have regarded development with suspicion. Seen as at best intellectually dull and at worst ethically dubious, those either working *in* development or studying it (anthropologists *of* development) are viewed with disdain by purists who insist that anthropologists should focus their attention on areas of human meaning and action untouched by the bothersome interference of planned change. Yet, as we shall see, development and anthropology have much to offer each other. It is not simply that the insights and methods of anthropologists can contribute to development. It is also that development has increasingly become a fertile ground for anthropologists studying broader theoretical issues concerning governance, the workings of late capitalism, gender, ethics, morality, and gift exchange, to name but a few of the areas concerned. Indeed, it is fair to say that some of the most interesting anthropological research in recent years has been concerned with development. In what follows I describe three approaches taken by anthropologists who are, in their various ways, engaging with development as a field of study. Some of these ways are positive, in that the anthropologists believe that development is a good thing, though with improvements to be made. Others are negative: development is a bad thing, to be condemned, usually as a form of postcolonial power play or evidence of the dastardly workings of "neoliberalism." Finally there is work which does not take a moral position but simply reveals development and all that it involves as an object of ethnographic study, as intriguing, "other," contradictory, and ultimately as understandable as a village, kinship system, or religious cult.

First, though, what *is* development, and why do anthropologists find it so troublesome? For the purposes of this chapter I will restrict my discussion to what Gillian Hart calls "Big D" development. This is, quite simply, planned change, from vast schemes of agricultural modernization such as the Gezira Scheme in Sudan, in which around ten thousand square kilometers were irrigated in the 1920s in order to produce commercial cotton, to small-scale projects implemented by local NGOs such as micro-credit or literacy schemes. Big D development is analytically different from what is referred to as "economic development," which usually means economic growth—growth in the wealth of a country via increased production. Other indices of development involve measures of "human development" such as a growth in literacy or life expectancy rates, a reduction in maternal deaths and child malnourishment, and so on. Other measures are less quantifiable. The economist Amartya Sen has talked about development as freedom and a realization of human capabilities; for others happiness has become the goal. What all these various perspectives share is a belief in progress, in life and society improving over time via processes of modernization, enrichment, emancipation (from what are seen as oppressive traditions), and empowerment, the ability of people to exercise individual agency. In many versions of development the processes that bring progress are assumed to be similar to the experience of countries such as Britain or the United States over the nineteenth and twentieth centuries. Industrialization, modernized infrastructure, the commercialization of agriculture, urbanization, and so on take place alongside the overall uplift of the population, which in the last hundred years in the northern hemisphere has become better-educated, healthier, and accustomed to hot water, electricity, and buying food in supermarkets. Democracy and a modern, noncorrupt state are usually assumed to be at the heart of the process.

Although development isn't any single thing, what is clear is that it is a *process*, a future state which a group of people or a place is moving toward. While economic growth, urbanization, and commercialization are to an extent spontaneous, the result of chance and particular global or local conditions, Big D development involves a belief that progress or "betterment" can be planned and implemented via policies, schemes, and projects which it is hoped will help move a place or society from A (underdevelopment) to B (development). Getting to this desired state is often promised to the population by politicians in poorer countries, and, indeed, by Western countries doing deals with those poorer countries (often referred to as the Global South). Yet it is not simply a "top down" scheme. Rather, becoming "developed" is something that billions of ordinary people believe in and desire, involving as it does a deeply rooted belief in progress, a movement into a brighter future, away from a past ("undeveloped") characterized by poverty, lack of basic amenities, illiteracy, sickness, and so on. It is here that the problem arises for anthropology, for, as we shall see, the true nature of both this past state of un(der)development and the future state of development is fiercely contested and entangled with ethical questions concerning the role of the discipline. It is for this reason that more than any other field of study in anthropology, development is the most politically contentious and morally troublesome. This is also what makes it so fascinating.

THE PROBLEM WITH DEVELOPMENT

Anthropologists have two main problems with development. The first concerns the nature of the past and indeed the future. To understand this, we need to recall the premises of contemporary social anthropology. Rejecting the evolutionism of early "armchair" anthropologists who based their writings on the accounts of missionaries and explorers rather than on their own ethnographic fieldwork, from the 1920s onward pioneering anthropologists such as Malinowski in Britain and Boas in the United States argued against evolutionary theories which posited that non-industrial peoples were irrational savages who would evolve into "modern" or "civilized" people via the interventions of Christian missionaries or colonial reformers. Rather, the newly invigorated discipline showed how such societies had complex and highly evolved forms of social and political organization. Cultural relativity became the discipline's rallying cry. Here, instead of judging the society being studied via one's own cultural norms, anthropologists argued that it should be understood from the local perspective; rather than resulting from "ignorance" or "native irrationality," seemingly inexplicable customs such as polygamy, child marriage, cargo cults, or potlatches were revealed to have their own cultural rationality, with social institutions working together to produce a functioning whole. This theory, structural functionalism, ignored change since it was premised on a notion of cultural logics that worked in harmony with social institutions to produce different types of society which could be classified according to their particular features, such as descent systems or forms of marital alliance.

By the 1960s and 1970s structural functionalism was largely overtaken by structuralism. Within this theoretical paradigm all societies shared an underlying cultural grammar, albeit with different surface manifestations. The premise of cultural relativism remained firmly in place: non-industrialized societies were understood as having internal logics which implicitly were unchanging. Whilst acknowledging that societies were part of global political and economic systems, Marxist anthropology, which developed in the same period, took a similar stance: when change arrived in the guise of a capitalism often imposed by colonialism this was invariably to the detriment of the pre-existing society.

If mid-twentieth-century anthropologists either ignored change or saw it in negative terms, as imposed from the outside by interfering colonial authorities or missionaries, their role was to describe and theorize social diversity, at all times aiming for cultural relativity. For example, Marshall Sahlins argued that though hunter/gatherers had very few material goods, hunter and gatherer societies were "the original affluent society" because they wanted very little. While modern capitalist societies were premised upon scarcity and the need to produce more and more goods, hunter/gatherers followed a "Zen road to affluence" because they didn't want these goods and were able to spend large amounts of time doing very little. This picture of leisured contentment is in stark contrast to what someone who believes in development would perceive: poverty (defined by lack of material goods), illiteracy, lack of health care, etcetera. As this implies, the attitude to the future of developers is inherently different from that of anthropologists; while developers believe in progress and improvement for all, anthropologists such as Sahlins believe in the sanctity of cultural difference, following an ethics of non-interference. From this vantage, in which traditional ways of life are valorized and hunter/gatherers praised for their affluence, planned development is seen in negative terms: the imposition of Western ideals, introduction of capitalism via cash crops or industrialization, settlement for nomadic peoples, and the advent of modernity and all its discontents, which invariably lead to cultural and social breakdown and new forms of impoverishment. As the anthropologist James Ferguson puts it, seen in this light, development is anthropology's "evil twin."

The second problem that anthropology has with development concerns the role of the anthropologist. As every neophyte ethnographer learns, objectivity rather than moral judgment is the goal. To express a need for progress or betterment among the people one is studying is thus inherently problematic. Indeed, work which is aimed at solving social problems has long been seen by the anthropological elite as a lower form of the discipline, nontheoretical and intellectually stunted, certainly not objective. Worse, "applied" anthropologists (who apply their findings to practical ends, such as a development project) are engaging with institutions that the majority of anthropologists are deeply suspicious of: colonial authorities in earlier generations, interfering and "top down" development agencies, and even the military today.

Yet as anthropology shows, moral choices are never simple. To be against change can be deeply conservative, while the promotion of cultural relativism may involve supporting or apologizing for cultural norms or institutions that give one group (the elite, men, older people) power over others. The discipline has moved far beyond earlier generations' assumptions of cultural boundedness and internal harmony; we understand how norms and rules are contested, how change is continual even as the "past" is romanticized, and how all communities and places are part of wider national and global systems. It is no longer possible to talk of distinct social or cultural groups and even if we could, no community or culture is homogenous. We also know, because our interlocutors tell us, that change and progress, the very "development" that anthropologists deride, is often passionately desired.

Anthropological approaches to gender oppression illustrate the dilemmas. Should we merely document institutions involved in gender-based oppression, or should we actively seek to challenge them? While Western feminists might argue that oppression in the form of domestic violence, child marriage, or female circumcision is beyond cultural relativity and that human rights should be universal regardless of cultural relativity, others might retort that this position is ethnocentric and patronizing. Here, anthropologists from the West should be alert not only to the problems caused by their own positionality but also to the reality that not all women in a given community or place will share their emancipatory agenda or solutions. Take, for example, ethnographic research on microcredit in Bangladesh. This has showed that though loans are given to women in order to develop their own businesses, most women pass the loans to their husbands, brothers, or fathers, since local gender norms mean that they are deeply embedded and invested in familial relationships and do not want to set up businesses, seeing this as "men's work." The loans thus failed to have the desired effect of "female empowerment" within Western feminist terms. Instead they were a way in which families accessed much-needed credit, often at the expense of women, who were vilified by the other members of their savings groups if they couldn't repay the loans.

Is this an example of a "failed" project or a culturally appropriate response to the loans? Indeed, should the anthropologist critique the cultural inappropriateness of the program, provide practical suggestions of how to better engage women, or merely document the unintended consequences within this particular context? As this example shows, the study of Big D development (which from now on I shall simply refer to as "development") involves complex ethical and political problems which anthropologists have responded to in a variety of ways. In the rest of this chapter I outline the three main approaches. While elements of these approaches, especially regarding (2) and (3), might appear in a single piece of work, for the purposes of clarity they can be described as follows:

1. Working from within or critiquing projects with an aim of improvement. "Good" development remains possible.
2. Analyzing development as an oppressive postcolonial or neoliberal discourse. Development is bad and should be opposed.
3. Treating development as a field of study like any other, with theoretical implications for the wider discipline and no moral judgement or political agenda on behalf of the anthropologist.

Interestingly, these approaches roughly align to a historical trajectory which begins with the early days of development being treated as theoretically/ethnographically irrelevant, to be left to applied anthropologists working outside of academia (roughly from the 1960s to the late 1980s). From this we move to the use of Foucault to reveal development as a discourse (early 1990s to 2000s), ending with the current phase in which the anthropology of development has emerged as a vibrant field of study, making important contributions to wider theoretical debates.

1. IMPROVING DEVELOPMENT

Development projects in the 1960s–1980s tended to overlook the perspectives of local people, or indeed the differences between them. Culture, often branded as "tradition," was seen as an obstacle to processes of modernization which, it was assumed, would bring social benefits to all. Sudan's Gezira Scheme is a classic example. This started under the British colonial administration in the 1920s, involving irrigation on a huge scale and the mass commercialization of agriculture. Farmers were to be trained in producing cotton as a cash crop and the region's infrastructure modernized. Programs in other parts of the world had similar aims: to radically modernize agriculture leading to increased food production and economic growth. In the "Green Revolution" in India, for example, high-yielding varieties of crops, chemical fertilizers, tractors, and irrigation pumps were introduced via rural extension projects. As anthropologists such as Scarlett Epstein documented in the 1960s, these changes tended to lead to increased differentiation between castes and rural classes; in most cases the elite seized the advantages, accumulating more land and resources in the newly commercialized agriculture, while those with less land, usually the lower castes, tended to sell up and fall into deeper poverty. Other projects failed simply because the local culture was disregarded by planners. In another classic study in the early 1970s Mamdani explained the failure of campaigns of birth control sponsored by the Indian government and the Rockefeller Foundation in a Punjabi village. In direct contrast to the government's aim to reduce the population, villagers desired large families in order to provide them with agricultural labor and future security in their old age. By disregarding the perspectives of its target population the birth control scheme had fallen flat.

While these examples document "why development doesn't work," they also point to ways to remedy the situation: incorporate local perspectives in the planning of projects, understand the disequalizing effects of new technologies, ensure that the poorest are included, and so on. It is not the enterprise of development per se that is critiqued but its poor implementation or negative consequences. This approach is exemplified by work which was originally known as "women in development" and which later grew into "gender and development," in acknowledgment that a focus on gender brings a more nuanced understanding of how roles and relationships are socially constructed and involve men as well as women. Here, insights from feminist anthropology regarding the ways in which development (both Big and little D) had negative consequences for women, ways which were used to design projects aimed specifically at improving women's status. Note that in the earlier period of this work, approximately from the 1970s to 1990s, "women" were assumed to be a largely undifferentiated group, though generational and class differences might be acknowledged. Questions of sexuality or nonbinary gender were not raised and empowerment assumed to involve economic independence and political participation.

Gender and Development, a field of activity including activism, policy making, program design and expertise, emerged over the 1980s in response to ethnographic research which showed how due to pre-existing gender relations and the gender bias of planners, women tended to lose out in development projects. Feminist research by scholars such as Esther Boserup and Barbara Rogers showed how capitalism and the commercialization of agriculture led to women becoming economically marginalized by being pushed into subsistence production to feed their families while men seized control of cash crops. In other instances colonial officials and development planners imported Western assumptions about gender relations into contexts where women were previously central to agricultural production. For example, colonial officials disregarded matrilineal systems of inheritance and women's customary property rights by insisting on formalized land titles, which were given to men. Here, it was not simply that women were a subordinate group, which development should "empower," but that the development process itself discriminated against women.

If applying a gendered lens to development revealed the negative effects on women, the task for feminist anthropologists seemed clear: to "mainstream gender" by incorporating consideration of gender inequality into policy and project planning at every level. Activists working as academics, consultants, and development advisers lobbied for policy change within national and international aid organizations already waking up to the importance of "women's issues" after the UN Decade for Women (1975–85). The late 1980s and 1990s involved a concerted effort to address "the gender problem" within development. This did not merely involve introducing projects which targeted women; gender training was also key. Using feminist anthropological insights concerning the women's reproductive and productive roles, and distinguishing between projects which merely catered for their reproductive needs (for example as mothers) and those that boosted their productive roles (which it was assumed would lead to empowerment), anthropologists working with organizations such as the World Bank, US AID and the British Overseas Development Administration set to work training officials and policy makers to place gender at the center of development policy.

While today this work might be critiqued for its binary approach to gender and over-reliance on first-wave Western feminism, there can be little doubt that gender (often glossed as "women's empowerment") has become mainstream to much development practice. Indeed, by the 2000s gender and empowerment had become development buzz words, constantly repeated, but in danger of losing their political bite, the radical elements of earlier anthropological work falling away, leaving "women's empowerment" as yet another box to be ticked by project planners or NGOs seeking donor funds. This leads us to the second anthropological approach to development, which puts forward a forceful argument as to why development can never be changed from within to become a more radical and politically progressive movement. Rather than working within to improve development, this group of anthropologists regard it as an oppressive discourse, or in the words of James Ferguson, an "anti-politics machine" which can only ever enforce the assumed expertise and superiority of the West over the rest.

2. DEVELOPMENT AS DISCOURSE

While the "aid industry" has long been attacked by critics as a form of imperialist control by the West over the postcolonial world, in the early 1990s a number of anthropologists used the theories of Foucault to show how development works as a form of *discourse* which constructs the world as a field of knowledge and expertise, leading to specific forms of action which omit consideration of structural or political issues and thus silence dissent. In this perspective, development is resolutely a bad thing; the job of the politically and ethically engaged anthropologist is thus to uncover the "hidden transcripts" of what they reveal to be an oppressive discourse. One of the most cited of these anthropologists is Arturo Escobar, who from the late 1980s set out how development functioned as a hegemonic discourse. In his work development is presented in deeply negative terms; working within the system is not possible because the discourse automatically represses political challenges, favoring the powerful institutions and interests that perpetuate it.

To understand how this works we need to briefly consider the work of Foucault. In *The Order of Things* (1970), Foucault focuses upon "fields" of knowledge, such as economics or natural history. While these areas of expertise are represented as objective and politically neutral, Foucault shows how they are socially, historically, and politically constructed and how they work to further the institutions and groups in power. A good example of this are the ways in which peoples colonized by the British were classified and represented by early anthropologists, travel writers, and artists as exotic, child-like and irrational, and in need of governance, their subordination to the colonial authorities therefore justified. Seen in this light, knowledge and representation are acts of power, neither neutral nor objective. The ethnographic or historical task is thus to reveal how the discourse works, and whose interest it serves.

From this, areas of developmental knowledge or expertise can be deconstructed as a historically and politically specific construction of reality. Rather than being objective, understanding places or groups as more or less "developed" or "empowered" is primarily to do with the exercise of power. What is notable is how hard it is to contest the basic assumptions of development because as a discourse it is all encompassing and apparently self-evident: underdevelopment is *obviously* a problem and development projects are *obviously* the solution. Labels such as "women-headed households" or "peasant farmers" become taken-for-granted categories, with assumptions made about the "needs" of each group and the solutions to their poverty. Indeed, Escobar goes so far as to argue that "poverty" was an invention of the postcolonial period, a means for the West to continue to dominate its ex-colonies via a set of technical solutions and expertise that was extended through donor organizations such as the World Bank. By working within development as "experts," anthropologists are therefore complicit in the system, even as they seek to change it from within.

Escobar is resolutely antidevelopment, seeing it only in terms of being a hegemonic and top-down exercise of power. One of the problems with his approach is that, paradoxically, he homogenizes Big D development, presenting it as a monolithic enterprise. Relying on reports rather than ethnographic evidence from within development projects or institutions, he fails to show how the discourse can and does change from within. For example, the work of feminist activists over the 1980s and 1990s has led to real changes in the way that gender is considered in development planning, even if these might not have gone far enough.

James Ferguson takes a similar approach by analyzing the World Bank–sponsored Thaba-Tseka project in Lesotho, arguing that anthropologists of development should reveal the relationship between development projects, social control, and the reproduction of relations of inequality. By analyzing the conceptual apparatus of planned development in Lesotho and juxtaposing this with ethnographic material from a project's "target area," he shows how while development projects usually fail in their explicit objectives, they have another, often unrealized function: that of furthering the state's power. In his work, Ferguson shows how a World Bank report's inaccuracies and mistakes are not the result of bad scholarship, but the need to present the country in a particular way. Lesotho is frequently referred to in the report as "traditional" and isolated, with aboriginal agriculture and a stagnant economy. In reality the country has long been economically and politically intertwined with South Africa. In addition, the report only considers Lesotho at a national level. The implications are first, that development interventions will transform and modernize the country, and, second, that change is entirely a function of the action or inaction of the government.

Ferguson argues that discourses are attached to and support particular institutions. Only statements which are useful to the development institutions concerned are included in their reports; radical or pessimistic analyses are banished. The discourse is thus dynamically interrelated with development practice, affecting the actual design and implementation of projects. In its definition of all problems as "technical" the discourse ignores social conditions, a central reason why the project fails. Crucially too, development is presented as politically neutral. Instrumentally, however, the project unintentionally enables the state to further its power over the mountain areas which it targeted. Rather than this being a hidden aim of developmental practice, and the discourse a form of mystification, Ferguson argues that development planning is a small cog in a larger machine; discourse and practice are articulated in this, but they do not determine it. Plans fail, but while their objectives are not met, they still have instrumental effects, for they are part of a larger machinery of power and control.

While Ferguson's work is not as polemical as Escobar's and crosses the boundaries between types (2) and (3) of anthropological approaches, within his analysis and that of Escobar development discourse can only ever extend governance, either of the state or global institutions such as the World Bank. From this perspective, any attempt to change development from within will fail. Potentially radical ideas, such as "women's empowerment," are subsumed by the discourse, reduced to a training day offered to officials or to be measured via quantitative indicators for audit purposes. Worse, by extending certain forms of governance, development projects can have disastrous effects. To return to the example of microcredit in Bangladesh, Lamia Karim argues that in the contemporary neoliberal era in which the state and donors provide little in the way of real services and people are supposed to "help themselves," savings groups can lead poor women to become dispossessed, losing their social networks and sometimes even their homes. Within the discourse, women should be "helped to help themselves" via loans that empower them to become entrepreneurs with "micro businesses." The reality, Karim argues, is that women face steep interest rates on loans pushed on them by NGOs tasked by donors to disburse untenable amounts of credit on the rural population. Exploiting a culture which makes women more susceptible than men to the social pressure of others in their savings group to repay their loans, the banks that disburse the loans profit while women struggle to repay, losing their social networks and sometimes their homes (which are literally taken apart by NGO workers as collateral) if they fail.

My own work shows similar processes in Bangladesh. In my study of the community engagement program of a multinational energy company extracting natural gas from land surrounded by villages in Habiganj, I argue that development programs which stress "self-help," "sustainability," and "empowerment" are instituted in order for the corporation to make claims of community partnership. This type of "disconnected development" chimes with neoliberal ethics of detachment, in which communities and groups are supposed to be "helped to help themselves" but in which very little in the way of real services or amenities are offered. Rather than the disconnected mantra of "self-help," what the households surrounding the gas field want is connection, to the gas supply, to hospitals and schools, and economic growth.

Like Escobar and Ferguson, within these analyses Big D development (this time in the guise of NGO microcredit or livelihood programs) is presented as part of a wider system of governance and exploitation. Here, the anthropological mission is to deconstruct and critique development discourse, revealing its hidden effects. Whilst apparently opposite from anthropologists who believe that development can be improved from within, those who critique and deconstruct development as discourse tend to share a similar mission, since both groups have a political agenda, using their work to address suffering and, either explicitly or implicitly, calling for change either by improving the projects and policies of development or by denouncing it and thereby encouraging alternative forms of political struggle. Here Big D development is analyzed neither as a practice to be improved nor as an oppressive discourse to be denounced, but simply as a field of human belief and endeavor to be objectively explored. While this may still involve peeling back discursive layers, human suffering is no longer the ethnographic focus and improvement/political struggle no longer its aim.

3. DEVELOPMENT AS AN ETHNOGRAPHIC FIELD

In the final approach, anthropologists approach Big D development in the same way as they would study a religious ritual, political movement, or community, conducting fieldwork within development institutions and projects. Rather than charting the "effects" of development or assuming that it is monolithic and top down, this work reveals inner workings and ethical concerns which complicate the understanding of development as simply a cog in an oppressive machinery. They ask neither "How could this be better?" nor "How does this lead to oppression and suffering?" Instead, they ask: "How does this work in terms of its inner logic?"

In a seminal example David Mosse describes what happens within the day-to-day implementation of a development project. Arising from his experience of working within a British-funded irrigation project in India, the Indo-British Rainfed Farming Project, Mosse takes us deep into its everyday logics. Rather than projects resulting from policy as a rational solution to problems, Mosse argues that the relationship between policy and practice is more complex. Development work has inner logics and rationales in which the ultimate, though hidden objective is not success per se, but the production and appearance of success which is socially produced by the actors involved, be these consultants, project managers, or distant policy makers. "Participation," for example, is turned into a commodity via skillful PR, part of the project brand. In order to continue the appearance of success, VIP visits and publicity material become more important to the daily management of the project than its actual outcomes. Or rather, the appearance of success *is* the actual outcome, a performance for a particular audience, for projects involve conceptual and linguistic devices which inspire allegiance and conceal ideological differences. Through his ethnography of the production of project success, or how development is "cultivated," Mosse is able to show how policy exists to legitimate practice rather than orientate it. Development interventions are driven by the needs of organizations rather than policies; they don't fail "in themselves" but are failed by their networks of support and validation; indeed, "success" and "failure" are policy-orientated judgments.

Mosse's work helps us understand policy in a more complex and nuanced way than those who frame development as a top down, all subsuming discourse. Within his ethnography "Development" certainly involves discursive power, with the attendant framings, ways of seeing, and labeling, but it is nothing like the hegemonic, all-powerful force conjured up by Escobar or Ferguson. It is instead just like other areas of human endeavor: contingent, contradictory, and not always effective. Crucially, rather than culture and social relations existing only for those at the receiving end of Development, we see how both lie at the heart of Development itself. Ironically this had direct repercussions for Mosse when his work caused controversy among other consultants employed by the project. Some of these accused him of being unethical in writing as an insider and in potentially threatening the project's ongoing funding. As this indicates, development work involves a fragile morality, entangled as it is in the varying perspectives and needs of different actors.

That Big D development is itself a cultural and ethical domain is clearly shown by ethnographic work which places aid workers center stage, delving into their motivations and concerns. My final example shows how the moral worlds of aid workers can be at odds; indeed different projects can be based on entirely different and even oppositional premises. In central Uganda, China Scherz analyses the conflicting and yet often interlinked "ethico-moral" assemblages of different projects describing how nuns running a children's orphanage in Uganda are motivated by Christian ideals of charity and love. The nuns, who turn no child away and actively encourage dependency, are disinterested in the bureaucratic regimes required by northern funders and reject their ideals of self-reliance. Meanwhile the orphanage's counterpart, an NGO called Child Hope, follows the ethical imperatives of neoliberal development, embracing ideals of self-help, sustainability, and empowerment via training and workshops. In contrast to the nuns, the NGO accepts only children who are likely to be exemplars of independence. While the sisters' orphanage falls increasingly foul of funders, the NGO is rewarded with increased monies. Rather than deconstructing the ideals of self-reliance, or denouncing the imperatives of Western aid, Scherz's ethnography is primarily focused on the moral worlds of the nuns, who serve God rather than donors. This ethnography, like others that focus on the moral and spiritual underpinnings of charitable and/or aid work, thus takes us in a different direction than work which analyses development discourse in Foucauldian terms as a form of governance or points to cultural difference in explanations of "why projects don't work." Indeed, the point is that Hope Child's programs *do* work, or at least in terms of their ability to create particular representations and bureaucratic practices of audit. Instead, by analyzing development and charitable work as "ethico-moral assemblages," we learn not only of the inner workings of projects, but the relationship between spirituality, ethics, and action. As this shows, human experience and endeavor cannot be delineated into neat categories: development can be understood in terms of ritual or spiritual motivation as much as it can be analyzed as a form of knowledge which keeps the Global South in its place.

CONCLUSION

As the work that I have discussed here shows, the suspicion with which historically some anthropologists have regarded development as a subject of study is short-sighted. While we might have ethical reservations about the workings of the aid industry or the uneven consequences of development projects, this should not mean that we refuse to turn our ethnographic gaze to it, or place it in a silo reserved for applied anthropologists. Instead, as the work that I have described (and a huge amount more that I have not had space for) demonstrates, the anthropology of development is a vibrant field, with myriad theoretical and thematic strands which lead to wider areas within the discipline.

It is not only that the study of development is rich with ethnographic potential. Crucially, it also encourages us to consider our own stance toward the possibility of social progress. While we are unlikely to agree over the role that development might or might not take in improving the world, or, indeed, on whether anthropology can or should contribute to or denounce it, the anthropology of development thus brings us face to face with our professional and personal ethics. Ever controversial, it remains one of the most challenging areas of anthropological work.

SUGGESTIONS FOR FURTHER READING

Epstein, Trude Scarlett. 1962. *Economic Development and Social Change in South India*. Manchester: Manchester University Press.
    An early example of anthropological analysis of the impacts of the Green Revolution, especially on caste relations.
Escobar, A. 2011. *Encountering Development: The Making and Unmaking of the Third World*. Princeton, NJ: Princeton University Press.
    The seminal text which sets out the "Development as colonizing discourse" thesis.
Ferguson, J. 1990. *The Anti-Politics Machine: "Development," Depoliticisation, and Bureaucratic Power in Lesotho*. Cambridge: Cambridge University Press.

An ethnographic classic, showing how a World Bank scheme extends governance over a rural part of Lesotho as an "unintended consequence" of Development.

Gardner. K. 2012. *Discordant Development: Global Capitalism and the Struggle for Connection in Bangladesh*. London: Pluto Press.

Ethnographic study of the effects of gas extraction and corporate social responsibility in a rural area of Bangladesh.

Gardner, K., and D. Lewis. 2015. *Anthropology and Development: Challenges for the 21st Century*. London: Pluto Press.

Wide-ranging and updated discussion of the relationship between anthropology and development, based on *Anthropology, Development and the Post-Modern Challenge* (1996).

Karim, L. 2011. *Micro Finance and Its Discontents: Women and Debt in Bangladesh*. Minneapolis: University of Minnesota Press.

An ethnographically based critique of microcredit programs in Bangladesh, based on theories of dispossession.

Mamdani, M. 1972. *The Myth of Population Control: Family Caste and Class in an Indian Village*. Monthly Review Press.

An early example of how ethnographic analysis shows why family planning projects in India failed.

Mosse, D. 2005. *Cultivating Development: An Ethnography of Aid and Practice*. London: Pluto Press.

Classic study of a development project in North India, building upon discursive approach.

Rogers, B. 2005. *The Domestication of Women: Discrimination in Developing Societies*. London: Routledge.

An early example of the use of gender analysis to understand the unequal gender effects of colonial and postcolonial policy.

Scherz, C. 2014. *Having People, Having Heart: Charity, Sustainable Development and Problems of Dependence in Central Uganda*. Chicago: University of Chicago Press.

Ethnographic study of a Christian charity in Uganda and local conceptions of dependency.

Visvanathan, N., L. Duggan, L. Nisonoff, and N. Wiegersma, eds. 1997. *The Women, Gender, and Development Reader*. Cape Town: New Africa Books.

Useful reader, containing many key texts.

CHAPTER 11

ENVIRONMENT
AND ANTHROPOLOGY

SOCIO-NATURES IN A
POLITICIZED ANTHROPOCENE

James Fairhead and Melissa Leach

INTRODUCTION

Environmental challenges preoccupy humanity as never before. While the political world struggles to negotiate and implement global agreements around
sustainable development goals and climate change, people in the cities, villages,
deltas, rangelands of the world struggle for livelihoods amidst new stresses to
global systems. Anthropologists now grapple with these global phenomena,
however localized, in both material and discursive terms. They are interested
in the inequalities and injustices associated with patterns of production, consumption, and protection that impinge on and use environments and resources
following a broadly political ecological agenda. They engage with discourses
and policy schema, as well as the concepts in which they are wrapped: the anthropocene, planetary boundaries, sustainability, resilience, and more, following a broadly power/knowledge agenda. And they grapple, too, with the
utopias of conservation, whether in calling for half of the earth to be demarcated for wilderness or in "rewilding" landscapes to turn these managed spaces
into simulacra of nature without people, following a critical policy agenda.

To discern the emerging genealogy of anthropological contributions to contemporary environmental dilemmas and their politics, it is instructive to begin, however, with the classic debates and unfolding theorization of people-nature relations, to discern frustrations with this framing. Many anthropologists now reject such binaries and in so doing reject the "anthro" that defines the discipline. They are interested in exploring socialities beyond the human, whether in examining inextricably intertwined social and natural orders, sometimes termed "socio-natures," or by expanding their ethnography to the "more than human," creating a more "multispecies" discipline.

One could track such debates through many possible lenses, whether from the Arctic to the artists of New York; from coral gardens of submerging Pacific islands to car culture in asphyxiating metropolises; or from the favelas of Brazil to the fabrications of biotechnological manipulation. This chapter, however, grounds its route through these debates in a focus on vegetation and land in tropical worlds, where the discipline has its longest genealogy. Forests can provide a starting point as anthropologists have visited forests for as long as they have been studying people. We shall ask, however, what has been the place of "the forest" in their analysis? In many studies, "the forest" is simply a venue for human social relations, albeit at times uncritically imbued by Euro-American authors with ethnocentric symbolism of forest's darkness, secrecy, and mystery. Yet the forest is more dialectically engaged with social worlds, so it becomes important to ask how do we shape it, and it us? Answers are the stuff of both historical ecology perspectives in anthropology and political ecology perspectives that find forests to be more implicated even in shaping social relations. As anthropologists have turned to more multispecies framing, freeing themselves from treating human social relations in separation from relations with animals, plants, and geologies, this also alters the place of these wooded realms in their work.

FROM "FOREST PEOPLE" TO HISTORICAL ECOLOGY AND PERSPECTIVISM

Many anthropological works have treated forests as a venue, and in contrast with more open landscapes. Colin Turnbull's best-selling *The Forest People* documents the relations between the forest-dwelling Mbuti speakers in Central Africa and outsiders who treat them as a kind of property who supply meat, honey and other useful forest foods, as well as, occasionally, labor. Turnbull detailed how outsiders drew Mbuti into their initiation, marriage, and funeral rites. In return, the Mbuti receive farmed food or acquire it surreptitiously but occasionally withdraw into the forest for months. In this work the forest is not simply a refuge and provider, but according to Turnbull it is also personified by Mbuti as a parental force. When awake, the "God of the Forest" cares for its offspring; but when asleep, bad things can happen. Therefore, to address illness and social distress the forest must be woken ritually, in a "voice of the forest" ritual. Critics worry, however, that Turnbull rendered the Mbuti forests as a utopia and that the deification of the forest-as-parent owes more to his own psychoanalytics and Western symbolism than it does to the Mbuti.

The concept of a "forest people" is one commonly deployed by outsiders, often produced in articulation with local political discourses and at times adopted into national nomenclature and conservation policy. The brute category of "forest" also tempts ecologists and publics alike to essentialize these spaces and then either to cast them as "pristine," "virgin," "intact," "old growth," "original," "natural," "primary," "primordial" or to demote them to lesser states, such as "secondary" and "degraded." Yet do those living in treed landscapes identify with anything so simply construed as "forest"? Most dwellers have as many words for their vegetation as the Inuit (or indeed, Scottish people) have for snow.

Several anthropological approaches unpack the "forest" concept. One is historical ecology, associated most with the work of William Balée, whose *Footprints in the Forest* reveals how Ka'apor-speaking Amazonians name, classify, and use the many hundreds of plants they depend on. Their use of the different plants over different timescales also shapes forest composition, and this use is itself shaped by the powers and meanings that people ascribe to different plants. Forests emerge as an entanglement of natural and cultural forces, as a form of socio-nature, and should be read as such. The landscape is an archive that cannot be read simply by "natural historians" but rather requires attention to the meanings and usages of inhabitants that have inflected the ecological dynamics that make it. This is all the more obvious to anthropologists of the forest gardens of Southeast Asia, the palm forests of Benin, and the forest islands in the West African, Central African, and Bolivian savannas where the very existence of wooded vegetation is a product of inhabitation and social life.

Soils may equally be a palimpsest of socio-nature. The dark earth soils that are sought after by Amazonian farmers today are highly fertile, in what ecologists cast otherwise as a counterfeit paradise where poor soils underlie rich but precarious vegetation. These *terra preta* soils are the legacy of pre-Hispanic peoples whose land use and everyday lives enriched them enduringly with char, bone, and other waste materials. We found similar soils to be germane to West Africa and treasured by its farmers, who, in the words of a Liberian woman, exclaimed "God made the soil but we made it fertile." Such soil transformations are perceived locally as more inevitable than intentional. The existence and location of fertile places depend on patterns of settlement and gendered agricultural practices and the social relations shaping these, and unsurprisingly they thus acquire social as well as agricultural significance.

Anthropological works that are framed by ecological concerns can easily give excessive analytical significance to ecological concepts over and above the other ways that people relate to soils, plants, and animals. For example, they can give analytical attention to people's relations with "species" rather than with individuals. Those with interests in ethnopharmacology and biodiversity can miss the potential ethnocentricity of the species lens. Is it species that are relevant to qualities attributed to plants and animals? Or might such qualities be more relational and circumstantial? Brett-Smith's magisterial insights in West African masks and the earth in which they acquire their powers provide an elegant example. She reveals how the Komo masks central to the men's power sodalities are carved from individual trees that are not chosen principally for their species, but for the powers imbued in particular trees when they are associated with termites and their earthen mounds. Termites are transformative: they transform soils, infusing into them qualities of very real benefit for soil and human fertility, and they transform trees, infusing into them powerful qualities that become manifest in the mask. Trees are thus significant not necessarily in themselves but within such assemblages. In similar vein, plants used medicinally or as oracles are not efficacious simply for their species, but for where they grow (on gravesites, in sun or shade); for who collects them, and for the incantations they utter—words being part of the fabric of the world and of these assemblages. When a newborn's placenta is buried near cola trees in West Africa; when cremated remains are buried at the foot of jackfruit trees by Nayar speakers in South India; or when fast-growing trees are planted at birth in Japan for later use in manufacturing dowry, trees are personalized. Trobriand Islanders too speak of helping specific trees overcome their immobility by turning them into swift decorated canoes; an artifact that becomes more alive and vigorous than the original tree.

Approaching "nature" through the lens of "species" carries with it specific modes of relating to the nonhuman world that distance us from the kind of social proximity we might have with particular individuals. It can presume, falsely, that individuals of any given species are interchangeable. This may be compatible with treating them as a commodity, but it does injustice to the relations that we strike up with individuals of the nonhuman world around us. One pet, for instance, cannot simply be replaced by another individual of the species. Instead of making abstract categorizations of the nonhuman in which individuals are subsumed into ordering by species or as part of an ecosystem, the focus is instead on plants, animals, and indeed fungi as individuals living lives entangled with us and others.

It is often not that these "actants" (as Bruno Latour termed nonhuman participants in the network of actors that shape our lives) are somehow "symbolic," standing for something else; it is that they are that something else, configured within perspectives that are unfamiliar—or, in the language of current anthropology, within radically different ontologies. In this respect analysis of ecology has been swept along with the "ontological turn." For example, as de Castro reports it, many Amazonian people do not assume the existence of one nature (of trees, animals, and rocks) that might be interpreted differently by many (human) cultures; rather, they envision but one universal culture (common to people, trees, animals, and even rocks) but which can take many natural forms. These may be people, trees, animals, and rocks that, belonging to one culture, can intercommunicate. Such perspectivism helps to appreciate not only shamanistic practice in Amazonia but also the shape-shifting among specialist hunters in West Africa, who switch natures to take the form of trees and animals, and in New Guinea, where possums might be people in a parallel world to which the dead are transposed. This perspectivism helps respect and report the absolute presuppositions of our interlocutors, without denigrating its truth status as "belief," as "symbolic," or as animistic religion. Some authors take it further. After Kohn's stay among Runa speakers of Ecuador, his hosts prompted him to ask for real: "How do forests think?" And in answering this, questions arise, most notably: What is it to think? To be alive? To be "a forest"? While our commonsense answers may be predicated on our sense that we are fully distinct from all things "nature," Runa people might teach us to be less sure.

It is not just fundamental presuppositions about the order of things that are encoded in socio-natures and what they have to say, but all kinds of social, political, economic, and technological history that have given rise to them. Today's forests in West and Central Africa, for example, are an archive of the slave trade, its conflicts, diseases, and depopulations that left farm and village lands abandoned, leaving their traces in the dense vegetation that profited. Any attempt to read their composition simply through the lens of "natural history" overlooks this and the associated meaning for those who live in them. It would be tantamount to the denial of the holocaust that was slavery. The same can be said of the sparsely inhabited Amazonian forests that research by archaeologists and anthropologists now reveal grew over lands rapidly depopulated by the disease and disruption that rapidly followed Hispanic arrival. The forests and the rich *terra preta* soils of former settlements that often lie under them are an archive to the lives and deaths of many millions of people in the sixteenth and seventeenth centuries. The same can be said, too, of the forests now growing on the many Pacific islands depopulated by the epidemics that traders introduced in the nineteenth century or before. These natures can also carry a technological legacy, such as in the forests that are regenerating on the "no man's land" of the Korean demilitarized zone and that are protected by antitank and antipersonnel mines. These can by understood as "cyborg natures" that combine biological and technological elements.

POLITICAL NATURE

In discerning how lands, all that live on them, and the meanings attributed to them are forged by political relations, anthropological contributions to the field of historical ecology merge with those in an equally powerful political ecology. Our own work has been at pains to see the political relations that shape the anthropogenic forests of West Africa whether for fortification or for the privacy they provide to the initiation societies that dominate regional politics. We have also shown, however, how scientific and policy representation of these forests as "natural relicts" emerges from and embodies the racialist, colonial, and postcolonial relations of production of ecological knowledge. More recently we have made the same points about the anthropogenic soils either overlooked by soil scientists or assumed by them to be natural within discourses that cast human intervention simply as destructive, unless improved by modernist agrochemicals.

The errors in this dominant frame are sometimes appreciated by those more used to the received wisdom, belatedly shocked into a new realization. For example after the veteran colonial forester Don Rosevear returned to the forests of southeast Nigeria in the 1950s some twenty years after his first visit, he captured his own shift in its reading thus:

> What I had in my inexperience looked upon as glorious virgin growth, dating from the Flood, quickly revealed itself to my better experienced and disappointed eye as nothing more than secondary growth of moderately good quality. . . . But there was one curiosity. The abnormally large trees which had so impressed me in 1924 were still there, scattered throughout the forest in sufficient numbers to attract puzzled attention. I was still more perplexed when I discovered that they comprised two—and only two—species, the Sasswood, *Erythrophleum ivorense*, and the Inoit Nut, *Pogaoleosa*. Why these two species? And why this young—in tropical terms—forest, indicating previous widespread destruction in a so markedly underpopulated area? And then it dawned on me. The forest made it clear to me, like reading a book, that the entire region had once

been heavily populated, so densely in fact that the whole, except perhaps for the more inaccessible upper portions of the hills (which I myself never visited) had been intensely farmed, leaving no surplus area of undestroyed forest. What had become of this population; and why the two untouched species, obviously carefully preserved hang-overs from the original forest?

Rosevear was a colonial forester and was otherwise developing what political ecologists Vendergeest and Peluso cast as "political forests." These are forests rendered as such for political reasons and thus their study falls within wider political analytics in anthropology. As in the optic of James Scott's *Seeing like a State* these forests are shaped by scientific, bureaucratic, and institutional practices. They are designated, legislated, demarcated, mapped, and managed by states, conservation organizations, certification bodies, and private companies. They are patrolled and planned as part of assorted state projects: whether to extract value, depopulate for counter-insurgency or to enable oil and mineral extraction, conserve species, and nowadays to store carbon. An environmental anthropology is an anthropology of all these and their social fallout in inequalities and contestation.

Landscapes are thus drawn into contemporary anthropologies of the state, of global environmental governance regimes and their geopolitics, and of the commodification of nature. In our *Science, Society and Power*, we reveal how the rationality of "scientific" management is premised on paradigms of ecological order, stability, and predictability, whereas landscapes in West Africa and the Caribbean that are subjected to "sustainable management" are anything but equilibrial, bearing the legacy both of human footprints and of deep climatic instability in recent history. A forester of Ghana captures this well, observing that its semideciduous forest zone is "not an intricately balanced ecosystem likely to fall apart after minor disruptions but more nearly an ad hoc assemblage of species thriving after millennia of disturbance." Such observations were initially made around rangelands in eastern and southern Africa where the colonial imaginary of stability and "degradation" as pastoralists were thought to exceed "carrying capacity," contrasted sharply with the rainfall-driven shifts in vegetation states that pastoralists appreciated and took advantage of in herd mobility. Rangelands rarely regenerate as predicted by equilibrial ecology, and their "sustainable" management is in practice forever responding to the surprises of a more unruly nature. Alas, the same fate awaits the newer carbon sequestration efforts where the demands of long-term carbon storage financed through global "offset schemes" are upset by ecological unpredictabilities as well as by economic and social ones. Moreover, at the timescales it takes for trees to grow and for carbon to be stored, all kinds of political and policy changes may undermine the eternal rationality encapsulated in dominant ideas of sustainable forest management and forest schemes aiming to reduce greenhouse gas emissions. The latter often fall under the umbrella of "Reducing Emissions from Deforestation and Degradation" (REDD), in which states and land holders are paid to sequester carbon by expanding (or cease reducing or degrading) their forest cover. So while environmental management is predicated on (and justified by) ideas of predictability, it actually unfolds in more ad hoc manners.

Such rationalities, however flawed, have nevertheless instilled in environmental professionals a "will to manage": an imperative that environments be brought under civilizing control that renders the perspectives of inhabitants with interests in those ecologies as outdated, or even as ignorant or vandalistic—in short, a problem. Bluntly, environmental sciences have been a key element of political subjection. Much anthropological study of the relations between people and landscapes from Madagascar to Malaysia concerns a set of core themes: the intersection of economic, political, and discursive forces demarcating and regimenting parks, forests, and land-use zones of all kinds; the evictions and restrictions placed upon existing land users; their contrasting perspectives, and the contestations that result. For much of the twentieth century, these anthropological studies of "political nature" grappled with a host of problems: the social tensions raised by reservation whether for resource production or conservation; sustainable environmental management and its unforeseen consequences; and endeavors to be more collaborative, participatory, and community based, occasionally with undercurrents of counter-insurgency.

Considering ecosystems as orderly was itself the contingent product of British and colonial society and science soon after the First World War and has the same conceptual roots as structural functional anthropology that then attempted to characterize orderly society. In both, constituent structures function in maintaining an overall, higher-order system, be it ecosystem or society, that is "more than the sum of its parts." Given that "scientific forestry," for example, is actually socially and historically contingent, it becomes important to inquire into other cultural logics that might inform environmental management. Knight helps us to an answer. In Japan, he argues, family forestry has a different genealogy, directing tree growth to acquire qualities that are seen as typically Japanese, such as rectitude, endurance, and sturdiness. Socio-natures thus acquire the imprint of different political rationalities.

THE COMMODIFICATION OF NATURE

From the 1980s a plethora of studies appeared in the nascent discipline of environmental economics that purported to show the "real" economic value of forests and other environments around the world. From the 2000s a more systematic identification of "ecosystem services" was made, adding to productive services other valuable services including ecosystem support and regulation, as well as "cultural services," including aesthetics and amenity. These designations disarticulated socio-natures once more so that environments and ecosystem functions and properties were envisaged as separate from and at the behest of humanity. Initially it was argued that due to market imperfections which did not capture these values to wider society, governments and communities should regulate and protect their lands better, taking this broader range of environmental benefits into account. By 2000, however, a different resolution to the problem of market imperfection began to be envisaged: perfect the market. If markets could be established for the carbon storage, biodiversity, aquifer, amenity, and all the other benefits that ecosystems bring, and if people paid for these ecosystem services, then this would fund environmental protection, "selling nature to save it." Indeed with proper markets, valuable environments would pay for themselves and outcompete other land uses. Global policy has embraced this market-based approach, endeavoring to establish the markets in which ecosystem services could be traded.

The establishment of markets for all ecosystem service, sometimes alluded to as the "commodification of nature" or the "neoliberalization of conservation," is fast-moving and has enormous ramifications that are only now being researched. Alongside the emergence of carbon and biodiversity markets, policies and practices of "carbon offsetting" and "biodiversity offsetting" have emerged. Forests, for example, in any particular location have thus acquired new value as part of an emerging global "economy of repair" for damage wrought elsewhere. The forests of Africa and Southeast Asia and South America attract payments for their role in repairing the global climate from fossil fuel emission of greenhouse gases in the "global north," and perhaps for the repair of biodiversity loss wrought by industrial expansion and habitat destruction. Thus, environmental anthropology has expanded to engage with the emergence of globalized markets for nature that ensue in biodiversity and carbon offset markets. Many studies examine REDD schemes as part of these global markets, and questions emerge concerning how offset markets transform relations between these forests, states, and their ancestral inhabitants and claimants. How do the global differences in purchasing power play out in every locality? Answers have given rise to new conceptual lexicons such as "green grabbing" and "CO_2lonization" and call on older analyses of elite capture of lands through enclosure.

This new economy of repair encourages trading so that there ought to be "no net loss." But how do these markets actually operate? Is there really no net loss? These are crucial questions. And as even the most inaccessible parts of the world become tradeable "natural capital," other questions arise: What happens when landscapes are financialized, as the payments that they attract are drawn into speculatory futures and derivative markets? As Sullivan asks: Are we just selling nature to save it? Or are we saving nature to sell it? It may be that one should speak less of "political nature" than of "economic nature" given that the neoliberalism of which this is a part is, itself, a political project.

Recent anthropological interest concerns not only these new political and economic trends, but also the production of new subjectivities that can themselves be understood as novel forms of governmentality, in the language of Michel Foucault. This is what Agrawal casts as "environmentality." The transformations in global discourses that give heightened and globally significant meanings to local landscapes and which thus place localities that had been marginal more toward the center stage in global politics, themselves play into local discursive orders. Again, to take a forest example, Northwest Coast peoples of North America are said to have shifted from being "wood-oriented" to "tree-obsessed." Leaders of "indigenous peoples" have to balance the benefits that, drawing on this identity, bring in terms of rights to land and forest resources with its more negative implications in other political spheres. It is, however, not just the global forest discourses that are transforming local subjectivities, but also global forest economies. The shift to market-based approaches that value forests financially can crowd out peoples' more affective relations within socio-natures, as they come to objectify ecologies in more pecuniary ways, or as Oscar Wilde put it, to know "the price of everything and the value of nothing."

CONCLUSION: THE ANTHROPOCENE AND BEYOND

Anthropological engagements with historical and political ecology have been animated further by escalating interest in the idea of the "Anthropocene": the epoch when human activities began to be significant in altering geologies and ecosystems. Whether one should speak of the "anthropocene," "capital-ocene," "man-thropocene," however, or other geologically significant social forcing remains a pertinent question. Recent works that examine the huge expansion of large-scale commercial farming driving forest transformation or deforestation in Southeast Asia, West and Central Africa, and South America would finger capital. Capital looms large in classic modern ethnographies such as Li's *Land's End* which recall issues that have shaped the interests and conduct of anthropology since its inception in the 1840s; the rising value of land on frontiers, its enclosure, speculation, and often violent "grab"; the social transformations associated with local political collusion, differential ethnic and gendered advantages, outgrower schemes, and proletarianization—and modes of resistance to these things. While the specific permutations in which these play out vary, the underlying logics have long been all too clear.

There are new questions, too. Some concern the crops driving this process in much of the world. Oil palm, soya, and sugar cane have become "flex crops" that can be turned to bioethanol, biodiesel, and other industrial uses, merging food markets with energy markets. Legislation across the world requiring admixtures of biofuels at filling stations for "green" ends accentuates this, so the purchasing power of fuel-guzzling nations now drives land use changes on the frontier. The scale and pace of change on these frontiers is unprecedented. So, despite the discipline's current interest in perspectivism, ontology, and multispecies approaches that, as we have seen, are so important for understanding lived socio-natures, it is no coincidence that it is the *Journal of Peasant Studies*, with its special issues on Soy, Oil Palm, Flex Crops, Land Grabbing, Green Grabbing, Food Regimes, Food Sovereignty, and Agrarian Social Movements, that has become by far the most cited journal in the discipline.

Turnbull was not alone in finding his utopia in forest worlds. Anthropologists have since examined how the alterity of forest Arcadias has become commodified for ecotourists and enrolled in the blockbuster fictive media such as *Avatar*, which promote this interpretive grid. The ironies have not been overlooked. And yet we must also reflect on the subliminal drivers of our own representation. When asking "How do Forests Think?" we might wonder, What, if anything, is specific to forests and to those who live in them? Could we equally well ask "How do Cities Think?" When we appreciate the animal agency in the "companion" species of our new multispecies ethnography, should we forget how structure determines agency; that those we make our companions live in a structural world that tears offspring from parent in a way as brutal as slavery? What refuge do our newfound perspectives that appreciate the radically different ways that people understand social and ecological orders offer against capital and its combined pincer movements of "green grabbing" and land grabbing? And when anthropologists critique the idea of the Anthropocene as overly unifying a single humanity and its planetary predicament, overlooking the multitudinous diversity of socio-natures within it, do they downplay the effect of global capitalist forces, as well as the inequalities and unsustainabilities they produce?

SUGGESTIONS FOR FURTHER READING AND REFERENCES

Agrawal, Arun. 2005. *Environmentality: Technologies of Government and the Making of Subjects*. Durham, NC: Duke University Press.

Balée, William. 1994. *Footprints of the Forest: Ka'apor Ethnobotany — the Historical Ecology of Plant Utilization by an Amazonian People*. New York: Columbia University Press.

Brett-Smith, Sarah. 1996. *The Making of Bamana Sculpture*. Cambridge: Cambridge University Press.

Büscher, Bram, Sian Sullivan, Katja Neves, Jim Igoe, and Dan Brockington. 2012. "Towards a Synthesized Critique of Neoliberal Biodiversity Conservation." *Capitalism, Nature, Socialism* 23 (2): 4-30.

> This work provides a critical evaluation of neoliberal conservation and a shift from considering how nature is used in and through the expansion of capitalism to how nature is conserved in and through the expansion of capitalism.

De Castro, Eduardo. 1998. "Cosmological Deixis and Amerindian Perspectivism." *Journal of the Royal Anthropological Institute* 4 (3): 469-88.

> The classic exposition of perspectivism that reveals the limits of contemporary "Western" framings of the environment for understanding the perspectives of those in Amazonia (and beyond), while falling into other analytical traps.

Fairhead, James, and Melissa Leach. 1996. *Misreading the African Landscape: Society and Ecology in a Forest-Savanna Mosaic*. Cambridge: Cambridge University Press.

> By revealing how colonial and postcolonial science-policy communities have misinterpreted a locally enriched West African landscape as "degraded," this book exemplifies the significance of political ecology and of historical ecology for understanding people-environment relations.

———. 1998. *Reframing Deforestation: Global Analyses and Local Realities — Studies in West Africa*. London: Routledge.

Fairhead, James, Melissa Leach, and Ian Scoones. 2012. "Green-Grabbing: A New Appropriation of Nature." *Journal of Peasant Studies* 39 (2): 237-61. http://dx.doi.org/10.1080/0306 6150.2012.671770.

Fraser, J., M. Leach, and J. Fairhead. 2014. "Anthropogenic Dark Earths in the Landscapes of Upper Guinea, West Africa: Intentional or Inevitable?" *Annals of the Association of American Geographers* 104 (6): 1222-38.

Frausin, Victoria, et al. 2014. "'God made the soil, but we made it fertile': Gender, Knowledge, and Practice in the Formation and Use of African Dark Earths in Liberia and Sierra Leone." *Human Ecology* 42 (5): 695-710.

Kay, Kelly. 2018. "A Hostile Takeover of Nature." *Antipode* 50 (1): 164-83.

> An exemplar of the modes of accumulation unleashed when "nature" becomes recast as "natural capital."

Knight, John. 1998. "The Second Life of Trees: Family Forestry in Upland Japan." In *The Social Life of Trees: Anthropological Perspectives on Tree Symbolism*, ed. Laura Rival, 197-220. Oxford: Berg.

Kohn, Eduardo. 2013. *How Forests Think: Toward an Anthropology Beyond the Human*. Berkeley: University of California Press.

Leach, M., and I. Scoones, eds. 2015. *Carbon Conflicts and Forest Landscapes in Africa*. London: Routledge.

Li, Tania. 2014. *Land's End: Capitalist Relations on an Indigenous Frontier*. Durham, NC: Duke University Press.

Locke, Piers, and Ursula Muenster. 2015. "Multispecies Ethnography." Oxford Bibliographies DOI: 10.1093/obo/9780199766567-0130. https://www.researchgate.net/profile/Ursula _Muenster/publication/294872069_Multispecies_Ethnography/links/56c485f108ae736 e7046ed77.pdf.

This annotated bibliography reveals the difficulty with "anthro" in anthropology, showing why social analysis cannot be limited to the human realm.

Rosevear, Don. 1979. "Oban Revisited." *Nigerian Field* 44:75–81.

Scoones, I. 1999. "New Ecology and the Social Sciences: What Prospects for a Fruitful Engagement?" *Annual Review of Anthropology* 28:479–507.

A clear exposition of the significance of the paradigmatic shift to non-equilibrium ecology for understanding socioenvironmental relations.

Sullivan, Sian. 2013, "Banking Nature? The Spectacular Financialisation of Environmental Conservation." *Antipode* 45 (1): 198–217. DOI: 10.1111/j.1467-8330.2012.00989.x.

Turnbull, Colin. 1962. *The Forest People*. New York: Simon & Schuster.

Vandergeest, Peter, and Nancy Peluso. 2015. "Political Forests." In *The International Handbook of Political Ecology*, ed. Raymond Bryant, 162–75. Northampton, MA: Edward Elgar.

CHAPTER 12

TOXIC LIFE IN THE ANTHROPOCENE

Margaret Lock

The "control of nature" is a phrase conceived in arrogance,
born of the Neanderthal age of biology and philosophy, when
it was supposed that nature exists for the convenience of man.
—Rachel Carson, *Silent Spring* (1962, 197)

PREAMBLE

A December 2016 media report informed Canadians that more than 205 billion liters of raw sewage and untreated wastewater had spewed into Canada's rivers and oceans the previous year despite federal regulations introduced in 2012 to solve the problem. We read that toilet paper washed up on beaches near small towns in Newfoundland and Labrador, and in British Columbia divers reported sick kelp and polluted scallops near sewage discharge pipes. Estimates are that raw sewage mixed with rain and snow runoff that flowed into Canadian rivers and oceans in 2016 would fill 82,255 Olympic-size swimming pools—an increase of nearly 2 percent since 2014, and likely to get worse.

Canada frequently comes in for praise in the media as a well-functioning country, but such reports conveniently ignore the Alberta tar sands, oil pipes and their leaks into pristine water, scores of impoverished communities, and numerous documented cases of contaminated drinking water and untreated waste. The destructive impact of Canadian mining around the world is also set to one side. Peru is Canada's second largest trading partner in Central and South America, but Canadian mining companies operating there have an extremely bad reputation among local communities. A newly proposed mine to extract copper will be situated in a fragile tropical forest and the indigenous population claims that the project will destroy their water resources and livelihood.

A very short list exists of ecologically sustainable countries, including Costa Rica and Iceland, but no country with massive investments in the extraction of basic resources can possibly appear on that list. Globally, this situation is so dire that a new geological epoch has been declared, and the Holocene that commenced 11,700 years ago following the last major ice age is now eclipsed. As of September 2016, we have been living in the Anthropocene. The historian Dipesh Chakrabarty highlights the peculiarity of the current epoch: "The Anthropocene spells the collapse of the Kantian distinction between natural history and human history," for we are now in the first geological epoch in which the force transforming the globe—human-initiated activity—is supposedly *self-conscious* about what it is doing, with profound implications for politics and the allocation of responsibility.

Designation of this new epoch was initiated in the 1980s by the ecologist Eugene Stoermer and taken up again in 2000 by the atmospheric chemist and Nobel Laureate Paul Crutzen at a meeting in Mexico. By 2013 over two hundred peer-reviewed articles had been published airing debates about the looming, epochal transition, and Elsevier had launched a journal titled *Anthropocene*, followed by an e-journal *Elementa: Science of the Anthropocene*.

For a decade or more arguments had taken place as to whether the Neolithic revolution, or perhaps even earlier changes brought about by humankind, evinced the beginning of the Anthropocene. The position of ecologist Erle Ellis and his colleagues is that the transition commenced ten thousand years ago when land clearance for agriculture and irrigation began to have an effect globally on vast swaths of terrain. In recent centuries colonization has further reduced the biodiversity of the planet to a fraction of what it was formerly, as Annie Proulx's recent novel, *Barkskins*, graphically depicts for Canada. Others argue that the industrial revolution that commenced in the late 1700s, epitomized by the steam engine, was the singular moment. But the impact made by humans has increased exponentially over the past half-century and more. Humans have manufactured numerous mineral compounds, including more than 500 million metric tons of pure aluminum since World War II, much of which has sedimented into earth's layers. Even more striking are "mineral-oids"—glass and plastics—300 million tons of which are made annually and are present on the earth's crust and in all the oceans. Concrete, a rock of our own making, encases much of the globe today. Our chemical footprints are every-where, principally in the form of CO_2, nitrogen fertilizer, pesticides, diesel fuel, and electronic trash that has accumulated as toxic waste distributed around the globe. And James Lovelock insists that today the biggest threat of all to Gaia is overpopulation.

The majority recognizes that we now live with dramatic climate change manifest in rising sea levels, extreme temperatures, droughts, floods, and fam-ine. The environment—nature—is exhibiting all the signs of stress, trauma, tox-icity, and abuse usually associated with suffering human bodies—"capitalistic ruins," as Anna Tsing puts it, are all too evident in vast swaths of the globe. But geologists need hard evidence of an *irreversible* transition to identify a new epoch. Their decisions are pegged to a so-called "golden spike"—a marker that appears in ice cores, the oceans, lake sediments, and soils, where recognizable fossilized strata appear that can be hammered, sampled, and/or dug up. Such changes are known as a "time-rock unit."

Following three years of heated exchanges, the notoriously conservative International Union of Geological Sciences convened a group of scholars in 2013 to decide if the Anthropocene should be officially recognized. In a recom-mendation presented to a Congress in Cape Town in 2016 they declared that this was indeed the case. Geologists had showed little opposition to the posi-tion that humans have replaced "nature" as the dominant environmental force on earth, but as to when, *exactly*, the golden spike—the indelible event—took place in order for this force to be recognized as a valid geological turning point caused dispute. The UGS eventually agreed that July 1945, the day when the first nuclear device was exploded, leaving rare isotopes of plutonium distrib-uted throughout the globe, including Antarctica and Greenland, constituted such a spike.

For more than a decade we have been living with another fundamental shift known as the "postgenomic" era, in which the human genome is no longer rec-ognized as the origin of life but, rather, as "reactive" to environments exter-nal and internal to the body. In other words, the very "nature" of what it is to be human has been revised on the basis of knowledge brought to light when mapping the human genome, with enormous consequences for understanding human development, health, ill-health, and possibly our very survival.

In sum, a new geological epoch exists because humans are making over na-ture writ large to such an extent that it is irreparably transformed, and, at the same time, molecular science has shown that the human genome does not determine who we are; on the contrary, the environment that we are constantly remaking is in the driver's seat, bringing about increased inequalities and, for many, intensified misery.

In what follows I set out certain aspects of the field of behavioral epigenetics. The term *epigenetics* literally means over and/or above genetics; it signifies a burgeoning scientific field that investigates how environmental variables bring about changes in the expression of genes in living entities, including humans. More specifically, behavioral epigenetics focuses on the manner in which human behavior and activities trigger such epigenetic changes. At a basic level, involved researchers are steadily exposing the molecular pathways initiated by environmental variables both exterior and interior to the human body that initiate human development and sustain growth and maturation throughout life. The impact of exposure to environmental variables throughout life on human health and well-being and illness causation is also made evident. These emerging insights make obsolete assumptions of genetic determinism (with some minor exceptions for rare conditions) and of a straightforward nature/nurture dichotomy.

Several case studies from various parts of the globe are introduced to illustrate how toxic environments created by humans, characteristic of the Anthropocene, incite specific epigenetic changes in human bodies with long-lasting negative effects that are at times fatal. Certain medical anthropologists are today undertaking ethnographic research tracking the effects of repeated exposures to toxic environments in selected field sites around the world. This research is at times conducted as part of collaborative endeavors undertaken together with other social scientists, epidemiologists, and/or public health workers.

THE EMBODIMENT OF TRAUMA

An article published in the mid-1990s by the epigeneticist Michael Meaney has become iconic of the field of behavioral epigenetics. This research made use of a model of maternal deprivation created in rats by removing young pups from their mothers shortly after birth, thus terminating maternal licking and grooming crucial to their development. The deprivation altered the expression of genes that regulate behavioral and endocrine responses to stress, and hence, indirectly, hippocampal synaptic development. It was found that these changes could be reversed if pups were returned in a matter of days to their mothers. Furthermore, when the birth mother was a poor nurturer, placement of her deprived pups with a surrogate mother who licked and groomed them enabled the pups to flourish. Crucially, it was shown that pups or foster pups left to mature with low-licking mothers not only exhibited a chronically increased stress response but also passed on this heightened sensitivity to stress to their own pups. Hence, variation in maternal behavior results in biological pathways causal of significantly different infant phenotypes that can persist into adulthood and are potentially transmitted to the next generation.

A substantial body of work based largely on animal models, but increasingly in humans, substantiates these findings and broadens their significance. Beginning in the 1990s a literature has accrued showing a strong relationship between "childhood maltreatment" and negative mental health outcomes ranging from aggressive and violent behavior to suicide. Current investigations are gradually exposing how the "biological embedding" of childhood maltreatment comes about. The overall conclusion drawn from this research is that the "epigenome" is responsive to developmental, physiological, and environmental cues that can result in so-called "epigenetic marks."

In 2011 Moshe Szyf titled a presentation he gave at a Montréal gathering "DNA Methylation: A Molecular Link between Nurture and Nature." At the time this talk was given, evidence for such a link had accrued primarily from animal research and from one human study based on a sample of twenty-five individuals who had suffered severe abuse as children and later committed suicide. At autopsy, the donated brains of these individuals showed a significantly different pattern of DNA methylation than did those of a control group of sixteen "normal" individuals. A second control group of twenty individuals who had committed suicide but where no known abuse had taken place was also included in the study. The findings are presumed to substantiate a mechanism whereby nature and nurture meld as one. In this particular case, childhood adversity is associated with sustained modifications in DNA methylation across the genome, among which are epigenetic alterations in hippocampal neurons that may well interfere with processes of neuroplasticity.

The researchers acknowledged that the sample was small and that the study cannot be validated. The absence of a control group that experienced early life abuse and did not die by suicide is another shortcoming. Furthermore, the abuse that the subjects experienced was exceptionally severe. Szyf and colleagues readily agree that deep understanding of these processes is rudimentary. Even so, given that epigenetic markers have been shown to play important roles in learning and memory that may be transmitted intergenerationally, these findings suggest how the trauma associated with events such as colonization, slavery, war, and displacement may be transmitted through time. It is possible that they may also bring about insights in connection with resilience to such events.

SCULPTING THE GENOME

The epigenetic mechanism best researched to date is methylation, a process in which methyl groups are added to a DNA molecule. DNA methylation is found in all vertebrates, plants, and many nonvertebrates. Enzymes initiate such modifications that do not alter the actual DNA sequence, but simply attach a methyl group to residues of the nucleotide cytosine, thus rendering that portion of DNA inactive. Epigenetic researchers are careful to point out that the identification of mechanisms that transmit signals from social environments external and internal to the body resulting in DNA methylation have yet to be fully worked out. But it is incontrovertibly demonstrated that methylation functions so that any given genome is able to code for diversely stable phenotypes. In other words, although every cell at the time of formation is "pluripotent," that is, has the potential to become any kind of mature cell, methylation brings about so-called "cell differentiation," resulting in, for example, liver, neuronal, or skin cells. Furthermore, such changes take place not only in utero and early postpartum years, but continue throughout the life span.

Relatively recently it has been recognized that environmental exposures originating outside the body bring about changes to the three-dimensional chromatin fiber that compacts DNA inside cells. The idea that the epigenome as a distinct layer over and enveloping the genome, is no longer acceptable. Genome and epigenome are now recognized as a single flexible, commingled entity, orchestrated by shape-shifting chromatin that at times results in changes that are hereditable. In addition, small strips of DNA can be altered, often during replication, some of which changes result in mutations that may or may not be hereditable. Epigenetic mechanisms other than methylation also regulate gene expression, but they have yet to be researched to the same extent as has methylation.

In sum, genes are "catalysts" rather than "codes" for development, and it is the structure of information rather than information itself that is transmitted. DNA is not changed *directly* by environmental exposures. Rather, whole genomes respond ceaselessly to a wide range of environments, exposures, and experiences, and chromatin mediates such responses that, in turn, modulate DNA expression. The methylation processes described above are manifest in several time scales—evolution; transgenerational inheritance; individual lifetimes; life-course transitions (including infancy, adolescence, menopause, and old age) and seasonal change modifications. These effects, miniaturized in individual bodies, are researchable at the molecular level.

In the remainder of this essay I highlight the impact of toxins on the physical body, toxins which we all imbibe daily and are exposed to in ever-increasing amounts. Of course, certain populations and individuals are pervasively impacted much more than are others. Accounts given by affected individuals about toxic exposures are in part informed by sensations experienced in the material body itself. Such sensations are necessarily contingent on evolutionary, historical, environmental, economic, political, and social variables that everywhere contribute to the state of individual bodies. Such sensations result from direct exposures throughout life, and/or from attributes inherited intergenerationally.

Embodiment is further constituted by the manner in which self and others represent the body, drawing on local categories of knowledge and experience, including scientific knowledge to the extent that it is available. I utilize the concept of "local biologies" to assist in the explication of reports about the embodied experience of physical sensations, including those of well-being, health, and illness. The body should not be assumed to be universal in kind, simply layered over by sociocultural flotsam, as has happened all too often to date.

The concept of local biologies encourages an analytical sensitivity about the situatedness of knowledge and practice and, furthermore, to the contingency of material bodies. Given the remarkable extent of human movement over time, whether voluntary or forced, local biologies travel, resulting in endless transformations and modifications due to ever-changing environmental variables. Not everyone migrates, certain biologies remain local, but in-migration may bring about changes. Given that environments have always already been subjected to modification by means of human activity and with ever-increasing rapidity today, the concomitant biological responses among humans are on the increase. With these admonishments in mind we turn now to the embodiment of epigenetic effects.

PERMEABLE BODIES AND TOXIC LIVING

For a decade or more, researchers have been working to elucidate the effects on neurodevelopment of exposure to neurotoxins in utero and early life. Recent work has highlighted epigenetic effects and an apparent intergenerational aftermath of such exposures. A 2006 review of an array of 201 neurotoxins, ranging from arsenic to benzene and PCBs, concluded that exposure to hundreds of industrial chemicals are potentially damaging to the developing brains of children worldwide, although it is noted that both timing and the amount of exposure are significant. A 2011 review notes that every year more than 13 million deaths are due to environmental pollutants. Evidence links these pollutants to epigenetic marks associated with a range of disease endpoints. It is emphasized that many of these changes have been shown to be reversible and hence preventive measures are feasible. Lead is the most closely researched toxin to date; it has been shown repeatedly that there is no safe level of exposure during the early years of human development and that exposure results in many epigenetic effects. Decreased brain volume is recognized as lead-related brain atrophy, and is most pronounced in males. Research has also shown negative effects of lead exposure on language function.

Markowitz and Rosner graphically describe the ongoing lead paint scandal in the United States that has steadily unfolded for more than a half-century. Over the years, millions of children have been exposed in their homes to potential lead poisoning, although reliable numbers are not available. It is estimated that today over 500,000 children between one and five years old have lead levels above that which policy makers currently regard as a safe level. Reminiscent of the infamous Tuskegee experiments conducted on African Americans, one hundred children, mostly African American, some less than a year old, living in poor family dwellings where lead paint had been used, have been systematically studied for the effects of lead exposure on their development. A judge who presided over a lawsuit described these young research subjects as "canaries in the coalmine."

It has been shown that lead released from a woman's bones during pregnancy can increase risk for preterm deliveries and low birth weight and, further, affect gene expression in infants involving changes to DNA methylation that may well have lifelong effects. One researcher is quoted as stating: "Lead exposure, rather than a poor social environment, is a key contributor to . . . subsequent cognitive and behavior problems." Such a claim prioritizes one variable over another, causing a distortion. It is highly likely that lead exposure does irreparable harm to all humans, but those individuals who are at the greatest risk of being exposed are almost exclusively economically deprived. In 2014, in the impoverished town of Flint, Michigan, with a population of 100,000, nearly 60 percent of which are African American, a water crisis exploded. It became clear that between 6,000 and 12,000 children had been extensively exposed to lead contamination when, in order to save money, the Flint water source was changed from a safe source to one involving use of aging pipes linked to the Flint River that leached lead into the water supply. As one commentator stated: "Some of the darkest chapters in American industrialization are written in lead."

Thanks to the intrepid battle fought by Rachel Carson, DDT was banned in the early 1970s, first in the United States and then worldwide, although it continues to be used in certain malarial regions. And use of PCBs (polychlorinated biphenyls) is banned or severely restricted in most countries, but about 10 percent of the PCBs produced since the late 1920s remain in the environment today. They are released into the environment primarily from incinerators and build up in the fatty tissues of animals living in water or on land and are passed along the food chain to humans. Dioxins are found throughout the world and accumulate in the food chain, mainly in the fatty tissue of animals. They are highly toxic and cause reproductive and developmental problems, damage the immune system, interfere with hormones, and cause cancer. Dioxin enters the environment primarily from incinerators; of the 419 types of dioxin-related compounds, thirty have significant toxicity.

The effects of PCBs, dioxin, and other toxins in the Arctic are more devastating than elsewhere. Legislation against these chemicals is not effective in the extreme north as yet because toxic residues slowly drift toward the Arctic and accumulate there, making it one of the most contaminated places on earth. The body fat of seals, whales, and walruses hunted for food is highly contaminated, as is the breast milk of many Inuit women. An Inuit grandmother, politically active in circumpolar meetings, is quoted as stating: "When women have to think twice about breast feeding their babies, surely that must be a wake-up call to the world." The situation is exacerbated because the cost of store-bought food is beyond the reach of many Arctic residents.

An article in the *New Yorker* about Tyrone Hayes, a biologist working at the University of California, Berkeley, told a very disturbing story about one of the world's largest agribusinesses, Syngenta. Sales of the herbicide atrazine made by Syngenta are estimated to be around $300 million a year. Hayes's research findings about the toxic effects of atrazine resulted in what appears to be a systematic effort on the part of Syngenta to debunk his findings and destroy his career. Furthermore, the American chemical industry attempted to quash the findings of biologist Frederick vom Saal on bisphenol A, a chemical found in hard plastics and in the coating of food and drink packages, high doses of which have been proven to have a negative impact on health. Moreover, the present partisan government in Canada refuses to legislate effectively against asbestos, although it is the top workplace killer. Clearly, efforts to rid the environment of such chemicals are fraught with dangers other than their toxicity. Rachel Carson encountered great opposition to her work fifty years ago, and it seems that little has changed.

THE INTERGENERATIONAL TRANSMISSION OF TOXINS

An illustration of toxic local biologies is furnished by the mercury-contaminated Grassy Narrows' Wabigoon River system in Ontario, Canada. The government claims that defilement of the river stopped forty years ago when the paper mill was forcibly shut down, after dumping about nine thousand kilograms of mercury into the downstream river. Today mercury levels in the fish near Grassy Narrows are fifteen times the safe consumption limit, and forty times the limit for children, pregnant women, and women of child-bearing age. The Grassy Narrows people have fought for forty-five years for a clean-up of the river, but the Ontario minister of environment reiterated in May 2016 that there is no need for this. Further pressure apparently made the government temporarily change its position, but in late 2016, once again, the provincial government backed down, claiming a lack of funding, despite an official report by mercury experts stating that the river remains badly contaminated. Two generations of people from Grassy Narrows and Wabaseemoong First Nations today exhibit symptoms of mercury poisoning, including loss of muscle coordination, numbness in the hands and feet, hearing loss, speech damage, and tunnel vision. Fetuses are particularly vulnerable to cognitive damage. Extreme cases result in paralysis, insanity, coma, and death.

In the mid-1950s, mercury poisoning was detected in Japan. First, the local cats appeared to go crazy and some "committed suicide" by "falling" into the sea. Thereafter, humans started to report numbness in their extremities, tremors, and difficulty walking; and some appeared to be seriously mentally compromised. By 1959 it had been established that mercury poisoning was causing the symptoms, and the condition was labeled Minamata disease, drawing on the name of the fishing village where it had first occurred. A large petrochemical plant in Minamata, Chisso Corporation, was immediately suspect. Chisso denied involvement, even though it was clear that an estimated twenty-seven tons of mercury compounds was present in Minamata Bay. Protests began in 1959, but it was 1968 before the company finally stopped dumping. Close to three thousand people contracted Minamata disease, more than half of whom have died. Japanese scientists who are experts in mercury poisoning have been summoned to Grassy Narrows, and they state that up to 90 percent of the people show signs of mercury poisoning that may well be intergenerationally transmitted.

Further examples of locally created toxic biologies include the setting of fires to numerous oil wells and a sulfur plant in Mosul, Iraq, by Islamic State supporters, resulting in several deaths and causing hundreds to be exposed to toxic fumes, the effects of which are likely to cause lasting damage and, once infants are born to women presently pregnant, are likely to affect a second generation. Chlorine gas attacks by government troops in Syria are equally devastating and may well have intergenerational consequences.

AGENT ORANGE-LASTING EFFECTS IN TIME AND SPACE

Based on many years of fieldwork that commenced in 2003 in Hanoi, Vietnam, the Danish anthropologist Tine Gammeltoft has documented the devastating effects on reproduction caused by the chemical defoliant Agent Orange that persist more than forty years after the war that lasted from 1962 until 1971. Throughout the war, the US military conducted an aerial defoliation program that was part of a "forced urbanization" strategy designed to force peasants to leave the countryside, where they helped sustain the guerrillas, and move to the cities dominated by US forces. Nearly 20 million gallons of chemical herbicides and defoliants were sprayed onto Vietnam, eastern Laos, and parts of Cambodia, destroying all plant material in two days. In some areas, toxic concentrations in soil and water became hundreds of times greater than the levels considered safe in the United States.

Agent Orange contains the highly toxic chemical dioxin, known to have long-lasting effects on the environment and human tissue. Gammeltoft documents a widespread fear about the so-called dioxin gene, widely believed by many people living in Vietnam today to be increasing in the population over time. It is estimated that at least 3 million citizens in Vietnam suffer from serious health problems due to exposure to defoliants, and the rate of severe congenital abnormalities in herbicide-exposed people is reckoned at 2.95 percent higher than in unexposed individuals. The media has reported cases of third-generation Agent Orange victims, in which individuals exposed during the war have produced apparently healthy children whose grandchildren are born severely disabled. Animal research has shown that, following fetal exposure, dioxin reprograms epigenetic developmental processes the effects of which may become manifest throughout life and intergenerationally.

Vietnam was given membership in the World Trade Organization in 2007, one result of which was heightened concern by the Vietnamese government about the international visibility of the health of the population as a whole. It was at this juncture that extensive use of ultrasonography was introduced—a political tool designed to ensure the birth of healthy children. One result has been that ultrasound is now used repeatedly during pregnancy as part of antenatal care, even though the Vietnam Ministry of Health does not recommend this practice. Reaching a decision to have an abortion if a deformity is detected by ultrasound is not easy, particularly because many affected families think that abortion is an evil act. Furthermore, everyone involved knows that it can be difficult to assess the extent of the deformity from ultrasound images, although it is equally the case that frequently it is all too evident. Some families, reluctant about abortion, and longing for a healthy child, are raising three or four children with deformities, the most common of which is hydrocephalus ("water on the brain"), which causes severe retardation. A few women discover very late in a pregnancy that their fetus is not normal, and some opt for a late termination, to the great discomfort of their doctors.

Gammeltoft's moving interviews with affected families make clear that many people choose not to entertain the idea that an anomalous fetus detected by ultrasound, or the birth of a horribly deformed child, is due to Agent Orange. They are all too well aware that the stigma attached to Agent Orange families ensures that finding marriage partners for healthy members of the family would be virtually impossible. Better to claim publicly that the anomaly resulted from a common cold that the mother had, or from the heavy work she did while pregnant.

A range of severe illnesses is associated with dioxin exposure, including deadly cancers, Parkinson's disease, and spina bifida, in addition to those associated specifically with pregnancy. Vietnamese researchers have reported these findings, but the official US position is that there is no conclusive evidence that herbicide spraying caused health problems among exposed civilians and their children. However, following extensive lobbying over many years, in 2014 the US Congress passed a five-year aid package of $21 million that amounted to a modest sum for each Vietnam veteran. These cases were settled out of court and no legal liability has ever been admitted. The official position to this day is that the government was in effect prodded into settling these legal suits and that no evidence exists that Agent Orange caused harm. This position is supported by its principal makers, Monsanto and Dow Chemical companies. Children born to Vietnam War veterans who have severe birth defects have received no compensation.

In Vietnam, officials were reluctant to press complaints about Agent Orange because uppermost were concerns about the economy as a whole, notably a desire not to damage the marketing of numerous agricultural and aquacultural products made in Vietnam today. In the mid-1990s, Vietnamese writers and artists finally began to express concern about Agent Orange, and eventually Vietnamese citizens filed a class action suit in the US District Court in New York that was abruptly dismissed. But demands for responsibility are increasingly being heard, spearheaded by nongovernmental organizations. This example illustrates how local biologies travel and are not necessarily stable.

FAILING KIDNEYS AND ORGAN SHORTAGES

In Egypt, when considering receiving an organ from a living related donor, patients have been concerned above all about the sacrifice of the donor and their probable loss of health. In addition, the investment in a transplant affects the economic well-being of the family as a whole and, in addition, the majority of potential recipients believe that their own post-transplant lives would in all probability not be improved enough to justify the involved costs. Egyptian dialysis patients come to such conclusions for several reasons, among which is their awareness that a transplant is unlikely to be a lasting success due to excess pesticide usage in daily life and to improper handling of toxic waste. In Sherine Hamdy's words, Egyptian dialysis patients describe a "local biology" that in effect renders organ transplantation inefficacious due to contaminated environments, endemic parasitic infections, poverty, regular intake of poisonous food, inappropriate use of pharmaceuticals, and medical mistreatment.

The numbers of individuals with kidney failure and liver disease are on the increase in Egypt, and nephrologists note that the kidney diseases they see today are more aggressive than formerly and increasingly difficult to treat. Several of these specialists, like their patients, insist that this situation is due to environmental degradation and the regular ingestion of toxins. Compounding matters, formaldehydes are used to preserve milk, hormone-pumped chickens are imported, rather than using local "country" chickens, and pesticides rejected in the West as unsafe are dumped on Egypt. "Aid" packages from the United States ensure that people eat bread made from imported US wheat that, after storage in the hot and humid conditions of Egypt, produces a fungus associated with kidney and liver toxicity and with cancer. Substantial scientific evidence exists to support these claims, and in addition pesticide residues are present in the local crops.

In classical times Egypt was the breadbasket for the Roman Empire and, even though there were on occasion bad harvests, malnutrition, and corrupt regimes in which grain was not equitably distributed, until recently Egypt has been largely self-sufficient in grain production. The building of the Aswan High Dam, completed in 1971, ruined many hundreds of acres of fertile soil, but even so, the country continued to be able to sustain itself. In recent years the situation has changed dramatically. Since the 1970s, a combination of extensive US subsidies that place Egypt under pressure to import US grain, together with the shift in use of locally grown coarse grains for use as animal food, rather than for human nourishment, has left the majority of Egyptians in difficult straits. Furthermore, the meat products that result from the use of grain to feed animals feed tourists, resident foreigners, and wealthy Egyptians, but not the majority of the population.

Current government expenditure on health care amounts to 2 percent of the total GDP, and the cost of health care for Egyptians is increasing rapidly. Given the expense and justified concerns about toxins, many patients conclude that having a transplant will change their lives little, because the new kidney, too, will soon be damaged. And under the present circumstances donors, for all their benevolence, are unlikely to survive on one kidney, no matter what the medical profession claims. Hamdy concludes that when the patients she talked to reiterated "the body belongs to God" this was not a pious mantra, but rather a resigned grievance about state mismanagement of resources, exploitation of the bodies of the poor, corruption at nearly every turn, and an increasingly toxic environment.

The Egyptian story is by no means unique: in Mexico, the leading cause of death for women today is diabetes that frequently results in kidney failure. In addition, kidney disease is caused by exposure to pesticides, exacerbated by the deregulation of agriculture, waste materials from manufacturing, and pharmaceuticals. Millions of agricultural workers in Asia and Central America also have high rates of kidney failure and mortality due to exposure to agrichemicals.

OOZING VITALITY

Cancer mortality rates in China have risen more than 80 percent over the past thirty years, making it the country's leading cause of death. Toxic environments throughout most of the country are well established as the cause. In cities dense smog frequently descends, and toxic particulate matter that people absorb into their systems is suspended in the air. In addition to which, food is often tainted and drinking water is not always safe, particularly in the countryside. More than 70 percent of the rivers and lakes throughout the country are polluted. Paper mills discharge wastewater directly into rivers, and power plants belch smoke constantly. Certain affluent provinces have mobilized for change, with the result that polluting factories are transferred to poorer parts of the country where their pollution goes unchecked. Places where the cancer rate has soared way above the national average are designated as "cancer villages"—in all, more than 450 villages are so labeled, but numerous chemicals are implicated and it has proven very difficult to definitely make cause-and-effect links between specific chemicals and specific types of cancer, some common and others rare. It is estimated that at least 500,000 people die each day in Chinese cities, many of whom have chronic respiratory, metabolic, and cardiovascular problems and cancer of various kinds.

In addition to the alarming mortality rates documented over the past thirty years, a so-called national fertility crisis has been associated by experts with the toxic environment. The Danish anthropologist Ayo Wahlberg carried out episodic fieldwork for over eight years in China, during which time a mix of people to whom he talked stated with increasing regularity that the unremitting drive for sustained high economic growth and associated economic consumption has allowed the current environmental crisis to develop unabated. Massive use of pesticides and bisphenol A are above all else associated with rising rates of infertility among both men and women. Estimates are that fertility rates among farmers and factory workers have dropped by 80 percent in recent years.

Wahlberg argues that sperm banks in China have emerged "quite literally as a sanctuary of vitality" in recent years and that the massive tanks that house sperm have become a "national reproductive insurance protecting the frozen life within from exposure to smog, industrial chemicals and radiation." Wahlberg characterizes this situation as one of "exposed biologies"—a "side-effect" of the toxic process of modernization in China and elsewhere. But he goes to great lengths to make it clear that the crisis is either wholly or in part a media-diagnosed matter, and that no incontrovertible epidemiological evidence exists to validate the claim for this crisis. Of course, infertility is present in China, and heavy smoking, reliably associated with male infertility worldwide, is common. But it is also the case that by far the majority of the Chinese population are today deeply exposed to dioxins, PCBs, and a range of other pesticides and toxic residues from the huge projects undertaken to modernize the country—simply breathing, drinking, eating, and working inevitably expose one to toxins. It would be surprising if fertility had not been affected negatively, quite possibly with intergenerational effects. Following extended research, Everett Zhang has written an ethnography about what he characterizes as the current "impotence epidemic" in China.

Adriana Petryna chose "Life Exposed" as her title when writing about government responses to the explosion of the nuclear reactor at Chernobyl. Only time will tell how the Chinese government responds to "exposed biologies"; thus far, it has been one of largely attempting to concentrate the hotspots in rural areas.

WARFARE AND ANTIBIOTIC RESISTANCE

The US invasion of Iraq involved liberal use of improvised explosive devices and suicide bombs that killed and maimed large numbers of US soldiers. American military surgeons reported an alarming rate of wound and prosthetic infections among these men and women following their return to the United States. Many of these infections were due to Iraqibacter, the name used by the military for

Acinetobacter baumannii, an organism found throughout the world in soil and on the skin that is usually benign. The frequency with which bacterial infections occurred in these veterans was largely a consequence of developments in modern warfare. Soldiers were required to wear strong protective gear in the form of impenetrable Kevlar vests that resisted projectiles, but nevertheless areas of the body remained exposed allowing bacteria to enter. Repeated surgeries, grafts, and attachment of prosthetics by screws provided ideal refuge sites for these bacteria to proliferate. When such wounds fester, the bacteria become increasingly resistant to prescribed antibiotics.

Medical anthropologist and physician Omar Dewachi and his colleagues at the American University of Beirut (AUB) have also documented high rates of antibiotic-resistant Iraqibacter in war-injured civilians from Syria and Iraq who arrive in Lebanon for trauma treatment and reconstructive surgery. These patients have routinely been given high doses of intravenous antibiotics to control their infections while on their way to hospital, a practice that is continued during transfers to Germany and the United States. Making liberal use of intravenous antibiotics in this manner no doubt contributed to the development of drug resistance by killing off the normal bacterial flora resident in humans everywhere that function effectively against many infections. Once the normal flora is disrupted, resistant bacterial strains can thrive.

An exponential increase globally in antibiotic-resistant bacteria is just one example of medically induced toxic environments associated with war. Situated biologies resultant from clusters of antibiotic resistant cases are today dotted everywhere about the world. Misuse of antibiotics for infectious diseases such as TB and for mosquito-borne diseases, including malaria, provide other examples.

FINALE

Ongoing human activities worldwide, notably excess use of pesticides by agribusiness, misuse of antibiotics, and an ever-increasing production of vehicle exhaust and other forms of air pollution, have created environments toxic to human well-being and to that of wild life, domestic creatures, and plants. In addition, endless wars have resulted in untold trauma and destruction. Much of the resultant damage is due to direct toxic exposures but can also result from the intergenerational transmission of epigenetic effects *in utero.* Our future is not bright. We are undergoing a universal abuse of human rights created primarily by a relatively small segment of the population interested largely in their own accumulation of wealth, frequently at the expense of others. This state of affairs necessitates urgent, cooperative attention across borders and boundaries to which anthropologists have much to contribute, involving, at times, research conducted together with historians, sociologists, political scientists, and/or epidemiologists.

A primary goal for anthropologists continues to be, without doubt, to recreate narrative accounts from locally affected individuals about their experience of exposures to toxins. Gammeltoft's discussion of the spraying of Agent Orange in Vietnam makes graphically clear how understanding of the effects of such exposures may be internalized and work to heighten stigma and ostracism locally. Anthropologists can strive to gather members of affected communities together for extensive discussions designed to turn concerns outward and override inappropriate feelings of stigma, shame, or inadequacy. Furthermore, anthropological findings that highlight local corruption allow patients and their families to understand that they should not simply resign themselves to ill health—forces much greater than their own bodies are at work in causing disease and the bad management of ill health.

However, political action has frequently been mobilized locally by members of affected groups such as those in Grassy Narrows, parts of China and Mexico long before an anthropologist arrives on the scene to document the effects of toxicity. Moreover, local and social media keep affected individuals and communities on the alert. Our task as anthropologists then, becomes one of conveying "inside information" about responses to local toxicities to the world at large. In addition, when writing for fellow anthropologists, making explicit the experience of collecting such narrative accounts about our own feelings of frustration, horror, sadness, and guilt is also of importance. Numerous ethnographers do this highly effectively, but we need to ensure that such experiences are made known beyond the boundaries of our profession. The days of the anthropologist as an impartial observer embedded in his or her fieldwork site are long gone. We have all contributed one way and another to the creation of the Anthropocene and its toxic environments. To slow down and hopefully arrest the spoilage of environments and livelihoods, we must become politically astute and find ways to overcome entrenched resistance on the part of so many in power to clean up their act.

SUGGESTIONS FOR FURTHER READING AND REFERENCES

Aviv, Rachel. 2014. "A Valuable Reputation." *New Yorker*, February 10.
Briggs, Charles L., and Clara Mantini-Briggs. 2016. *Tell Me Why My Children Died: Rabies, Indigenous Knowledge, and Communicative Justice*. Durham, NC: Duke University Press.

A graphic account of the response of indigenous peoples in the Venezuelan rainforest confronted by an epidemic that was killing their children but was ignored by the government of Chavez.

Carson, Rachel. 1962. *Silent Spring.* New York: Mariner Books, Houghton Mifflin Harcourt.

Chakrabarty, Dipesh. 2009. "The Climate of History: Four Theses." *Eurozine*, October 30, 1–17.

Crowley-Matoka, Megan. 2016. *Domesticating Organ Transplant: Familial Sacrifice and National Aspiration in Mexico.* Durham, NC: Duke University Press.

Dewachi, Omar, Ngyyen Vinh-Kim, et al. 2014. "Changing Therapeutic Geographies of the Iraqi and Syrian Wars." *The Lancet*, January 20, http://dx.doi.org/10.1016/S0140-6736 (13)62299-0.

Ellis, Erle, et al. 2015. "Involve Social Scientists in Defining the Anthropocene." *Nature* 540: 1092–93.

Gammeltoft, Tina M. 2014. *Haunting Images: A Cultural Account of Selective Reproduction in Vietnam.* Berkeley: University of California Press.

An in-depth ethnography about the long-lasting effects of Agent Orange on families who were exposed during the war in Vietnam.

Hamdy Sherine. 2012. *Our Bodies Belong to God: Organ Transplants, Islam, and the Struggle for Human Dignity in Egypt.* Berkeley: University of California Press.

Hamdy's ethnography makes clear that the practice of organ procurement and transplantation must be understood as inevitably situated and analyzed in specific social and political contexts.

Koch, Erin. 2011. "Local Biologies of Tuberculosis: Insights from the Republic of Georgia." *Medical Anthropology* 30:81–101.

Lock, Margaret. 2001. "The Tempering of Medical Anthropology: Troubling Natural Categories." *Medical Anthropology Quarterly* 15:478–92.

———. 2015. "Comprehending the Body in the Era of the Epigenome." *Current Anthropology* 56:151–77.

Lock, Margaret, and Gisli Palsson. 2016. *Can Science Resolve the Nature/Nurture Debate?* Cambridge: Polity Press.

Markowitz, Gerald, and David Rosner. 2013. *Lead Wars: The Politics of Science and the Fate of America's Children.* Berkeley: University of California Press.

Proulx, Annie. 2016. *Barkskins.* New York: Scribner.

Richardson, Sarah S., and Hallam Stevens, eds. 2015. *Postgenomics: Perspectives on Biology after the Genome.* Durham, NC: Duke University Press.

Roberts, Elizabeth. 2017. "What Gets Inside: Violent Entanglements and Toxic Boundaries in Mexico City." *Cultural Anthropology* 32 (4): 592–619.

Theidon, Kimberly. 2013. *Intimate Enemies: Violence and Reconciliation in Peru.* Philadelphia: University of Pennsylvania Press.

A rich ethnographic account of the resilient response of a Peruvian community to the lived experience of extreme violence.

Tsing, Anna L. 2015. *The Mushroom at the End of the World.* Princeton, NJ: Princeton University Press.

Wahlberg, Ayo. 2010. "Assessing Vitality: Infertility and 'Good Life' in Urban China." In J. Yorke, ed., *The Right to Life and the Value of Life: Orientations in Law, Politics and Ethics.* Aldershot: Ashgate, 371–97.

CHAPTER 13

ANTHROPOLOGIES
OF THE SCIENCES

THINKING ACROSS STRATA

Mike Fortun and Kim Fortun

One cannot look upon the sciences as being only a set of sentences
or a system of thoughts. They are complex cultural phenomena, at
one time perhaps individual, at present collective ones, made up of
separate institutions, separate actions, separate events. Written sentences,
unwritten customs, one's own aims, methods, traditions, development.
Preparation of the mind, cleverness of hands. A special organizational
structure, with its hierarchy, ways of communication and co-operation,
an organizational court, public opinion, press and congresses. A distinct
relation to other aspects of cultural life, to society, to the state, etc.
—Ludwik Fleck, **"Problems of the Science of Science" (1946, 118)**

─────────────

"Shall we go see the equipment?" Huang Wei asked us, before we even had a
chance to sit down in her office at Peking University (PKU) Health Science
Center in Beijing, China, to talk about her research on air pollution and health.
There really was only one possible answer to this question—*Of course!*—not
only for reasons of politeness and anthropological necessity (we were meeting

FIG. 13.1.   Huang Wei in her equipment room, Peking University Health Science Center, November 2016. Photo by Mike Fortun.

for the first time, strangers to each other, each harboring far more questions than answers about the others' work and interests), but also because we are as genuinely excited to examine the many and intricate devices of scientific research as the scientists we travel to meet are to show and talk about them with us. The bonds between scientists and their technologies are strong and complex; scientific technologies allow scientists to do and know new things; they demand the kind of constant care and attention that produce both skill and affective attachment.

We were at PKU in November 2016 to interview Wei (and other scientists) for a multisited ethnographic study of air pollution science and governance in cities around the world, including Beijing. In each city (five in the United States and six in Asia), we are working collaboratively with local researchers, interviewing and interacting with scientists in different disciplines, government officials, environmental activists, and residents. We want to understand how all these people are thinking about the problem of air pollution, but questions about sciences and scientists are a key focus: who is producing air pollution science; how it is commissioned, funded, and used; and what historical, political economic, and cultural influences shape what is known and done about pollution and health. We also want to understand the social formations and connections (between scientists in different countries, for example) that engender and empower improvements to air pollution science and governance. And we want to be able to characterize differences among the cities, drawing out what we think of as signature environmental health governance styles. It is a big, sometimes unwieldy, and experimental study, but also designed to mime and enact the very kinds of research collaboration that we are studying. Through this, we hope to develop ethnographic perspective on collaboration itself, as well as on how sciences of many kinds move through different societies. Experimenting in this way with new methods and study designs has been especially important in anthropologies of the sciences—a response to challenges in adapting traditional anthropological methods to studies of new kinds of communities and practices.

Soon after our arrival at PKU, Wei took us down the hall, past her lab space, to a completely unspectacular room harboring only a few instruments, and a towering rack of data storage devices. One key part of Wei's research concerns the health effects of PM2.5—"particulate matter" of such a small size (less than 2.5 microns in diameter) that it penetrates deeply into lungs, and from there into blood and other tissues. Sometimes, according to recent research, PM2.5 particles may pass directly from the nasal passages to the brain. It's only within the last decade or so that scientists like Wei have even been able to measure atmospheric levels of PM2.5 accurately and routinely, but the known and suspected health effects are piling up in an international scientific literature documenting effects on not only respiratory conditions like asthma but also on heart disease, low birth weight, and (most recently) dementia in the elderly. PM2.5, PM10, and larger particles produced by motor vehicles, factories, domestic heating, wood fires, and other sources are all monitored and regulated by national systems of law like the US Clean Air Act and China's Environmental Protection Act (updated in 2014, through what many observers see as a new level of interaction between the Chinese government, academic scientists, NGOs, and citizens). As anthropologists of the sciences, we are interested in ways new technologies change the way science is practiced. We are also interested in how scientific findings are exchanged: between scientists within and across disciplines, between scientists and lawmakers, and between professional scientists and other kinds of experts (traditional healers, for example, or citizen scientists). Partly because of newly available and affordable scientific instrumentation (such as air quality monitors), "citizen science" projects have really taken off in recent years in many arenas, helping with pollution monitoring, species counts, and astronomy projects, to name only a few.

One of the instruments in Wei's lab is an aethalometer, which converts Beijing's ambient "haze" into daily, hourly, or even minute-by-minute measurements of black carbon (a component of particulate matter). It's an instrument developed initially by scientists at Lawrence Berkeley National Laboratory in California (famous first for its physics research, more recently for its research in genomics), now spun off into a small scientific instruments manufacturing business. Aethalometers are currently used in thousands of locations around the world, from Houston to Antarctica (in addition to its health effects, black carbon is also a significant contributor to global warming). Historians and anthropologists trace how technologies like the aethalometer (earlier, technologies like the microscope and the camera) have moved between settings, sometimes resulting in standardized approaches, but often adapted to local circumstances or used in improvised ways.

A pipe leads to a collector on the roof, where Wei takes us next. (See fig. 13.2.) We can't help taking notice—not only through our eyes, but *in* our eyes, and noses, and throats, and lungs—of the haze surrounding us mid-morning in the heart of Beijing. She begins to talk to us about her research, gesturing toward the nearby hospital where she collects biosamples and other data (complying with human subjects research guidelines similar to but also different from those in hospitals in the United States and Europe). We're familiar with the broad outlines of Wei's research. To prepare for our interview, we've read many of her articles, easily accessible to us in journals like *PLoS ONE*, the *American Journal of Epidemiology*, and the *Journal of the American Medical Association*. Some of these articles list a dozen or so co-authors, not unusual for many scientific fields these days, especially the environmental health sciences, but a fairly recent change in a cultural history where individual achievement and recognition (exemplified by the Nobel Prizes) has long been the norm. These collaborations often cross both national and disciplinary borders, with different people contributing different data sets or helping with the research design, statistical analysis, the interpretation and writing up of results, questions, noting of limitations, and suggested directions for future research.

In the listing of authors of her publications, Wei sometimes is first or last author, the positions to which most credit accrues, but more often, she tells us, she is happy to take the more modest positions in the middle of the list even if doing so may not accurately reflect the importance of her contributions. A key goal for Wei (one we especially admire) is to build environmental health research infrastructure in China that can sustain cutting-edge research beyond her own career. Modesty and a deeply collaborative spirit are critical. That kind of open, collective, and egalitarian ethos has long been part of at least the rhetoric and self-presentation of the sciences, if not always their practice or reality. We've called this style of scientific work, expressly concerned with building durable scientific infrastructure to address social problems, "civic science."

F I G . 1 3 . 2 .   Collecting air quality data on a Beijing rooftop, November 2016. Photo by Mike Fortun.

Wei also exemplifies a kind of cosmopolitan culture that has long character-ized the sciences, whose practitioners have tended to be more "worldly," valu-ing ties and commitments to ideas and ideals beyond local and, importantly, na-tional circumstance. A Beijinger now returned to live and work in Beijing, she lived for years in the United States, first working toward an advanced degree in environmental health and epidemiology, and then as a researcher at the Health Effects Institute (HEI), an important nonprofit research organization estab-lished in the United States in 1980, funded jointly by the US Environmental Protection Agency and the motor vehicle industry. The Health Effects Institute (HEI) was a key player in the now famous "Harvard Six Cities Study," which set the stage for our own multicity project focused on air pollution science and governance. The Harvard study is famous because it made some of the first claims (in the 1990s) about the public health effects of air pollution. The study was challenged by an antiregulatory, energy industry–funded "think tank," the euphemistic Citizens for a Sound Economy, and HEI was tasked to adjudicate. The years-long HEI reanalysis validated the claims of the original study.

But contestation over air pollution science and governance has not stopped.

There are many "stakeholders," including scientists, government agencies, polluting industries, vulnerable people (with asthma, for example), and whoever uses motorized transportation—or simply breathes. Anthropologists of the sciences study how these different groups understand problems and controversies like this, on an immense array of issues with critical scientific dimensions: issues associated with genetically modified organisms in agriculture, for example, or with nuclear power, disposal and cleanup of hazardous wastes, or the development of drones and other technologies of war.

Anthropologists of science also study how scientists themselves form communities, socialize new members, and link with other scientific communities—often dispersed around the world. Like Wei, many scientists today circulate globally, working simultaneously in a particular cultural formation, and constantly called to think and move beyond it. To succeed, Wei and other scientists working internationally need to deeply understand the expectations, opportunities, and constraints of their home settings, while also enacting a scientific persona that makes them recognizable and credible to scientists from other settings. And even more is required. To be a truly effective scientific collaborator, a researcher must understand and respect the conditions that shape the lives, work, and perspectives of those they come to collaborate with—especially if those conditions are very different than their own. Effective scientific collaborators also understand and respect differences across research disciplines—recognizing that a collaborator from another discipline is likely to have a "thought style" different than their own, with a different sense of how (or what) experiments should be run, how (or what) data should be collected, and how results should be interpreted. The latter makes cross-disciplinary scientific collaboration very challenging—but it is certainly easier if involved scientists themselves have cross-cultural insight, thus understanding differences across both geographic boundaries and culture as well as disciplinary ones. Anthropologists of science are interested in how scientists do this work of cultural communication and exchange and in how they cultivate those interests and skills in their students, to both follow and go beyond them. In our ethnographic study of air pollution science, for example, a key focus is on the educational programs that create the "pipeline" of scientists available to work on different aspects of air pollution (sources, health effects, mitigation, etc.).

Like Wei, many scientists today are intensely interested in and committed to the study of phenomena that cross multiple scales of analysis (like rising PM2.5 levels of air pollution and their health effects), from the molecular to the global, and everywhere in between. It is complex, multidimensional research, as full of careful precision and accurate quantitative analysis as it is of uncertainty, modeled parameters and dynamics, analogical thinking and interpretation. One way to think of scientific research like this is as a search for "patterns that connect," the terms that anthropologist Gregory Bateson used to describe a kind of thinking that stretches beyond simple observation and direct causation to understand connections between things that appear disconnected. The challenge, according to Bateson, is to find and characterize connections, and the connections between connections: figuring out what connections matter, and why.

Wei uses her equipment to produce enormous amounts of data; her selection of *which* data to produce is critical and combines her understanding of what isn't yet understood with her understanding of which problems need more science so that they can become more legible to policy makers and other non-scientific audiences. Both science and politics, then, orient what data gets collected and what science gets done. Anthropologists of the sciences are interested in *how* such selection and orientation come about. Interacting with Wei, for example, we wanted to understand how her current research is oriented by her own previous work, by her reading of scientific findings produced by other researchers, by her understanding of what is politically important and possible, and by a particular "thought style" that she has cultivated through interaction with others in her scientific communities. A "thought style" is rather like a cultural frame or worldview. As used in the history and anthropology of science (building on the work of Ludwik Fleck, a microbiologist of the early twentieth century and a keen observer and analyst of his own scientific practices), a thought style develops over time, through interaction among scientists (in a "esoteric" circle of specialists), and between scientists and other kinds of people (in overlapping esoteric and "exoteric" circles), all shaped by the dynamics of a particular sociocultural, political-economic context. A thought style directs the perception of scientists, shaping what problems they investigate, what data they produce, and how they interpret those data.

Wei, for example, is measuring the mix of black carbon, sulfur dioxide, nitric oxide, ozone, and road dust in Beijing's air, trying to connect these (together and separately) to patterns of urinary biomarkers and exhaled gases in the bodies of the city's residents, particularly schoolchildren. And she compares these things across time, using the 2008 Olympics as a "natural experiment" in public health: stricter pollution controls were put in place for the Olympics, allowing her to set up a comparison between that period and more routine, less controlled periods. Wei is working to discern patterns that connect air pollution and health—in ways conditioned by many interlaced factors and forces—historical, sociocultural, political, economic, and technological. Our challenge as anthropologists of the sciences is to discern patterns that connect Wei and her work of connecting patterns to the patterns of her (ever-evolving) cultural context.

As our opening quote drawn from Fleck expresses, the sciences are complex cultural phenomena, and call for study as such. We refer to this as *anthropologies of the sciences* to highlight the need to recognize methodological and cultural differences across scientific fields, geographies, and historical periods (diverting reference to "science" as a monolith). Reference to *anthropologies of the sciences* also highlights the need to cultivate methodological diversity within anthropology itself. The best of contemporary science reinforces a basic tenet of anthropology itself: cultivating and collating different angles on, and styles of thinking about, any complex phenomena will generate more actionable insights than one approach alone.

SCIENCE IN TIME, SPACE, AND POLITICS

On Earth Day 2017, people joined "marches for science" around the world, calling upon their governments to support, as the Society for Social Studies of Science phrased it, "scientific research and education, evidence-based policymaking, and the upkeep and public accessibility of data needed to understand societal problems." The American Association for the Advancement of Science was a leading supporter of the 2017 marches in the United States, along with the American Geophysical Union, and American Sociological Association, and other scholarly societies, including the American Anthropological Association. Universities and scholarly organizations in other countries also played leading roles, as did environmental groups, churches, and citizens of all ages. Anthropologists of the sciences both participated in and critically observed these organizations, and the diverse social and political movements of which they are part.

What did marches for science in 2017 signify, and what do they tell us about ways contemporary sciences are different from the sciences of earlier historical periods? Science circa 2020, it is fair to say, has come to study increasingly complex phenomena (like climate change and air pollution, gene-environment interactions, and emerging infectious diseases) and has itself become more complex in its internal social organization and interaction with the broad social formations in which it operates. Science circa 2020 is complex in every dimension.

It isn't that the sciences were ever simple, unidimensional, and insular; complexities of many kinds have always been the "pattern" in the sciences themselves. But in trying to characterize what makes contemporary science different from, say, the science of Galileo in seventeenth-century Venice, many historians often trace our current moment to changes that accelerate with World War II, when increasing investments (largely driven by military concerns) by the nation-state resulted not only in what came to be known as "Big Science" (primarily in physics) but in a deeper commingling between many sciences and nearly all aspects of social life. In the United States, the National Science Foundation was formed as part of this postwar push, as well as the National Institutes of Health, which funds most biomedical research in the United States; although more economically and infrastructurally damaged by the war, the United Kingdom, Germany, France, the Soviet Union, Japan, and India also began to grow, in different ways and at different paces, their national support for "basic" scientific research. (The distinction between basic and applied research is, it almost goes without saying, much more complicated in actuality than it is often assumed to be, but for our purposes here these broad-brush strokes suffice.) Since then, developments in many scientific fields have led to fundamentally new knowledge about biological processes, ecological dynamics, the atmosphere, chemistry and materials, electronics, evolutionary theory, and so on. Sometimes these developments in basic science are translated into applied sciences and technologies (which also have their own independent development trajectories) with far-reaching social consequences. At other times, sciences are "translated" into policy and law.

Some social scientists refer to the reorganization of science and its sociocultural norms that took shape over the second half of the twentieth century as "normal science," echoing Thomas Kuhn's terminology from his influential 1962 book *The Structure of Scientific Revolutions*. For Kuhn, "normal science" was what most scientists did most of the time: fitting pieces of a puzzle together within established and reliable frameworks or paradigms, as opposed to the paradigm-busting "revolutionary science" done by a few extraordinary figures. The more recent usage of "normal science" refers more to the established framework that we've developed to make sense, not of the natural world, but of the world of science itself as that new postwar system congealed: normal science is "pure" basic science, definitive and determined, disinterested and objective because it is supported by a modern nation-state, in which individual scientists are left free to pursue the logics (often only curiosity-driven) of their scientific fields, and only entering into the different world of politics and policy when asked for their advice, on limited issues relevant to their formal expertise.

The "normal science" of an earlier century is now transforming into what is sometimes called "postnormal science": sciences of complex and even chaotic systems; sciences that are riddled with uncertainties and ambiguities, highly dependent on computer simulations and deeply entwined theories; sciences that are produced in numerous public, corporate, and in-between organizations, in different collaborative and often interdisciplinary organizational forms; and so thoroughly imbricated in matters of political, social, and indeed planetary importance that they defy normal attempts to draw those traditional and comforting lines cleanly separating the natural from the cultural and political. Climate change science is probably the best and most well-known example of a "postnormal science."

Cultures are dynamic and always changing, to put it somewhat differently, and science as part of culture is no exception. What counts as science, how sciences are done, by whom, where, and for what reasons are all matters of culture. And what counts as "anthropologies of the sciences" is similarly context-specific; anthropologists who engage with sciences and scientists now face, in significant ways, different demands, possibilities, and questions than those that shaped the anthropologies of sciences of an earlier generation.

Anthropologies of the sciences, in their most basic conception, work to make sense of the different ways different people make and use different kinds of knowledge, in different times and places. Inevitably, some things and people count more than others. What counts as scientific knowledge also has important social consequences. How things are named and categorized is never a neutral affair, and *always* carries limitations and bias. The politics of naming and categorizing human difference as "racial" is one especially important example — one that has been well studied and thoroughly critiqued by many anthropologists.

Recently, the politics of naming and categorizing has also provoked fanfare in the earth sciences, with some scientists arguing that our current epoch needs to be renamed to acknowledge the profound, destructive effects that humans have had on earth systems and environments. The Holocene, they argue, has transitioned to the "Anthropocene." So far, the scientific bodies (specifically, the International Commission on Stratigraphy and the International Union of Geological Sciences) with the authority to name divisions in geologic time have not approved the name change. But arguments are flying, and many acknowledge the profound importance of what the "Anthropocene" signifies scientifically, politically, and culturally.

Earth systems — soils, waters, energy and natural resources, ecological webs, species biodiversity, and an all-encompassing atmosphere — used to be conceptualized as a strictly natural order, "in balance," independent of humans. No more. Though the beginnings of the Anthropocene continue to be debated — using different data sets and different modes of interpretation — most scientists acknowledge the import of the "Great Acceleration" driven by the industrial revolution, kicked into even higher gear after the 1950s. In this period, human consumption (of food, natural resources, and especially petroleum-based energy) escalated dramatically (in some places much more dramatically than in others), as did use of industrial chemicals (pesticides to drive up agricultural

yields, for example). Nuclear bomb tests also left an indelible, scientifically discoverable imprint (in children's teeth, for example). This is what scientists want to capture in denoting our current epoch as the "Anthropocene."

Naming and categorizing are never innocent acts, as "normal science" would have cast them, and naming our contemporary era the "Anthropocene" sparks disagreement not only among earth scientists but among anthropologists too, some of whom argue that something like the "Capitalocene" would be a more fitting name, assigning causality and responsibility to a more accurately delimited entity than "humans." It's a lively and important conversation across disciplinary circles, but one which we defer here for the sake of aligning with those "postnormal" earth scientists challenging the still-powerful "normal science" trends of their own scientific communities. This apparently small and unimportant insistence on a change of scientific nomenclature from the Holocene to the Anthropocene is an acknowledgment by these earth scientists that their actions are simultaneously acts of science and acts of politics, that the bonds between these two cultural domains are so immediate and strong as to be practically indistinguishable, just as the deep and extensive linkages between "humans" and "the planet" have also become practically indistinguishable.

The tangle of scientific disciplines and politics in debates about the Anthropocene, as in debates about whether scientists should "march for science," points to an exciting and demanding dimension of anthropologies of the sciences: they examine different ways people understand what is going on in the world, differences that dramatically shape their behavior, how they interact with each other, distributions of wealth and injustice, and how futures take shape. Anthropologies of sciences thus zero in on a special activity within societies and cultures, scientific activity, as a powerful way to study cultural formations writ large, focusing on knowledge dynamics as threads that interlace the whole, pursuing the holistic perspective anthropology has long promised.

SCIENCE ACROSS STRATA

So what do anthropologists of the sciences actually study when they are studying "science"? Of course, like other anthropologists, they study people: we are interested in the lives of scientists, how they came to be interested in what they study, what influences their work, and how they understand what influences their work. We are also interested in all those who think about and are shaped by science, and how science operates in and as culture. We study what science becomes in courtrooms, in schools, in the media, and in the lives of citizens in many different settings: how the sciences themselves become powerful forces in society. To learn about this, we talk to people and we watch carefully all that they do—and like any anthropologist would, we note how what people say and do are sometimes different. Attention to practices and material culture has been especially important in anthropologies of the sciences, and in the closely related fields of history and philosophy of science, because of the important role technologies play in science. Because of this, many anthropologists of science refer to what they study as "technoscience."

In our own work, we often use a geologic image of striated rock to imagine and think through the many "strata" where science occurs and can be studied (see fig. 3). An image of many layers, forcefully squeezed together, also reminds that all strata influence all others. As anthropologists have long said: it is a complex whole and all context matters, even at great distance. There are, of course, many other ways of visualizing what anthropologists of the sciences study. Many like Donna Haraway's image of a game of cat's cradle, for example, pointing to the orchestrated and shifting tangled skein of influences from which knowledge emerges. We like the image of striated shale rock because it also points to ways geophysical conditions—and human exploitation and destruction of these conditions through petroleum-based prosperity—are a center of scientific and political concern today.

Thinking in terms of layered strata on and through which the sciences operate first directs attention to what we have called the "meta" strata, the strata where we can observe and analyze how science is operating discursively, as part of dominant discourse, laced into the stories people tell about their lives and worlds. In many settings, what can be called modernist ideas about science are still very powerful: "science" is regarded as a uniquely objective, methodical, rigorous, quantitative, empirical, materialist, neutral, disinterested, and authoritative way of knowing. Other knowledges—philosophical or literary knowledge, for example, or "traditional ecological knowledge" about plants and animals—are, by contrast, characterized (negatively so) as subjective, nonmethodical, nonsystematic, variable, and thus "soft," unreliable, or at least nonneutral, rendering them idiosyncratic, irrational, culture-bound, or simply inferior. Anthropologists of the sciences can identify where such discourse and binaries operate (in school textbooks or legal decisions, for example) and where alternative discourses have emerged (among scientists working to understand the Anthropocene, for example).

Tracking where modernist ideas about science are in play is important, not least because of political implications. In modernist constructs, science is cast as pure, smooth, and "Western" but also as universal, grounded and "hard"—and more suited to men, although that usually goes unstated. Mathematics is cast as the privileged language of science because it was the language of nature (indeed

Querying the Strata of Science

STRATA OF ACTIVITY	EXEMPLARY ANALYTIC QUESTIONS
meta dominant discourses	What discourse traditions shape the way science is talked and thought about—in the media, in schools, in informal conversation? How is science compared to and used along with other knowledge forms?
macro governance, political economy	What events and problems provoke calls for science? How is science used in courtrooms, and by policy makers? How is science itself governed? What drives science in different settings, and how does science drive social and economic change?
meso organizations	What government agencies conduct, sponsor, and disseminate scientific research? What is the organizational culture of labs in different disciplines and places? How are NGOs, businesses, and citizens' organizations involved in the production, use, and authority of science? What social networks connect and control scientists?
micro practices	What do scientists actually do in their laboratories and field research, and what orients their attention? Who is doing science, and whose science has more authority?
edex education, expertise	How are scientists educated, formally and informally? How do they learn to design experiments, and to think about problems that haven't yet been problematized? What gives scientists and other experts authority, and what hierarchies of authority have been established in different settings?
techno equipment, infrastructure	What technologies do scientists use in their work, and how do these technologies shape the questions they ask, what they regard as an answer, and who else will be persuaded? How do scientific technologies circulate, and to what effect?
data infrastructure and visualization	What data and data infrastructure enable science, and its use in governance and other social activities (commerce, education, etc.)? How is data shared, or privatized? How have data visualizations changed over time, and how are they persuasive (or not)?
nano language, subjectivity	What methods and data do different kinds of scientists learn to use and love, and what are their different thought styles? What, and how, do scientists think about ethical and political responsibility? How does science figure in the ethical and political thinking of non-scientists?

FIG. 13.3. Questions to open an analysis of the strata of science.

the language that God, according to Galileo, used to write nature), rigid and geometric in its clarity and determinism. In contrast, interpretation ("hermeneutics") becomes the language of culture, values, and aesthetics—imaginative rather than empirically grounded, subjective, and hard to pin down. In this way of thinking about science, science is largely imagined as free of interpretation and somehow outside of culture, politics, and other domains of human life: a "culture of no culture," in the memorable phrase of Sharon Traweek, one of the earliest anthropologists of science. (Traweek works with physicists and physics, usually accorded exemplary status in the sciences as the purest of the pure, the closest to the ideals of reason, logic, and math.)

Different ways of thinking and talking at this metalevel about what science *is*, especially "good science," are particularly visible today when the topic is climate change. Sometimes what is said to be at issue is whether a particular kind of science—computer model–based science, as is needed to capture the many interlocking processes and timescales involved in climate change—is *sound* science. Peter Huber, a well-known voice for "sound science" (almost always in opposition to regulation) has referred to model-based science as "faith-based," presuming that scientific computer models and "actual observations" are mutually exclusive opposites. Scientists, historians, philosophers, and anthropologists have all explained otherwise—drawing out how scientific computer models can both integrate and be cross-checked with "actual" monitoring data. Such debates over what makes science *good* science recur across domains today, often becoming loud and shrill, often revealing commercial and corporate interests in the sciences. In some cases, arguments about good science result from differences of perspective among scientists, sometimes because of cultural and methodological differences across different disciplines (geology and ecology, for example, a difference that has made a difference in debates about "fracking" and unconventional energy resources). In other cases, arguments about good science are muddied by industries trying to evade regulation (the tobacco industry's manipulation of scientific studies of the health impacts of smoking is one important example).

In our own research we've seen these debates and oppositions play out in efforts to connect air pollution to human health, illness, and death. One basic opposition pits air quality regulation against economic prosperity, arguing (implicitly or explicitly) that regulation undermines economic productivity, a surer means to population health and prosperity. Over the last decade, those arguing against this position have been able to make increasingly fine-grained claims about both the health impacts of air pollution and associated economic costs of *not* regulating. Another opposition—which clearly reflects a difference between normal and postnormal ideals—is between claims that are causal and claims that are associative or suggestive. Many who don't want to regulate air quality insist that evidence of health benefits must be directly causal, with a clear and linear pathway from source to human exposure to a specific health outcome. This kind of claim is difficult if not impossible to make when dealing with many environmental health issues, if only because people experience numerous health stressors or "confounding" factors, like smoking or poor diet, which can't be ruled out as contributors to a particular health outcome. Insistence on direct causal connections between air pollution and ill-health as the basis of air pollution regulation makes it almost impossible to regulate. How people think and talk about science thus has very practical consequences.

What counts as good, sound, or authoritative knowledge also has implications for what we've called the macro strata: a space where laws are enacted or repealed, industries and products are regulated or deregulated, and economies are ordered, always benefiting some people, sectors, or regions more than others. In our air pollution governance study, for example, we are examining the development of laws regulating industrial activity, energy use in homes and transportation, and urban planning—and the various kinds of data and science used to design and legitimize these laws. In the United States, for example, federal law mandates protection for vulnerable communities to offset environmental injustices resulting from uneven distribution of pollution and associated health impacts. This calls for scientific studies that *demonstrate* pollution distributions and health disparities. It also calls for science that can direct air quality improvements.

In Albany, New York, for example, scientists working for New York State's Department of Environmental Conservation are conducting a study to discern the sources of air pollution impacting a mostly African American community near the Port of Albany. These scientists have been surprised to learn that particular routes and patterns of truck traffic are a key pollution source. We, in turn, were surprised to learn how difficult this is to change. Trucks in this area are en route to a federal highway, to which they have a "right-of-access." The rights of trucks are at odds with the rights of people living in the communities that they drive through. But there are different kinds of solutions, and, as anthropologists of science, we are also interested in how such possibilities can be explored and encouraged. Trucks coming in and out of many ports have been required to retrofit their engines so that they pollute less. At the ports of Los Angeles and Long Beach in California (the largest, most active ports in the United States), truckers have borne the cost of these retrofits and recently went on strike in protest. Port managers insisted that the retrofits were a critical component of new commitments to better address climate change. But retrofitting trucks around the Port of Houston, Texas, played out differently. Through a program designed and led by Environmental Defense (a large NGO), truckers received loans to help them transition to cleaner fuels. We've interviewed many of the actors in these controversies (scientists, truckers, environmental activists), working to understand their social and political economic positions, the knowledge they produce and rely on, and their perspective on what needs to happen and why. This kind of controversy analysis is a recurrent thread in anthropologies of the sciences.

Anthropologists also examine dynamics at what we call the meso strata: a layer of organizations and social networks that connect scientists to each other, and to other people and groups in the wider culture. We want to understand how researchers like Huang Wei in Beijing were influenced by and remain connected to key air pollution organizations like the Health Effects Institute in Cambridge, Massachusetts (USA), for example. We also want to understand the organizational culture in state/province-level environmental agencies: in Indian states, Pollution Control Boards; in Texas, the Commission on Environmental Quality (TCEQ). We have learned, for example, that TCEQ is a powerful advocate for industry and is often pitted against both the US Environmental Protection Agency and the City of Houston. A key index of their differences in recent years has been the controversy around federal regulation that put stricter limit on ozone levels in cities. There is a wide, deep, and highly regarded scientific literature demonstrating the negative health effects of ozone, particularly for vulnerable groups (like children and asthmatics). Texas's state toxicologist nonetheless opposed stricter standards, arguing both on scientific grounds (claiming the health data and analyses were "insufficient" and "inadequate") and on political grounds (claiming the burden on industry would be too severe). As anthropologists of science, it is our job to parse how and why such arguments are made, and what weight they carry in the ecology of actors that together govern air pollution in Houston.

We also need to understand the daily practices that result in scientific claims and controversies—watching what science looks like at what can be called the micro level. In the Albany effort to understand pollution from truck traffic, for example, scientists have taken to the streets, with an air monitoring backpack. The data they will collect will be compared to a stationary monitor (running continuously, generating huge amounts of data, averaged for usability). Alternatively, the backpack data may show air pollution hotspots at particular street intersections, or at particular times of the day. This is a new kind of scientific practice, and the Department of Environmental Conservation scientists in New York are well aware of this. (Earlier, this same group of scientists did vehicle emissions testing—testing the pollution created by different kinds of vehicles when put on the [very large] equivalent of a treadmill.) The backpack monitor generates a new kind of data, which they will have to learn to interpret and use. With their backpack study, these scientists are also situated much more personally in the community they are studying, walking the streets alongside community members, trying to learn from their experiences. This recognition of the value of community knowledge in scientific studies has been a key development in the environmental health sciences over the last two decades. Anthropologists of the sciences have both documented and tried to support this development, critically attuned to the value of "explanatory pluralism"—a concept developed to account for the value of gender, race, and class as well as disciplinary diversity in knowledge making.

These kinds of practices occurring on the micro strata always, of course, need to be understood in context, emerging from particular historical conditions. Anthropologists of the sciences thus also examine what we've called the edex strata, where we can observe where and how people are educated, formally and informally, and what credentials experts have *as experts*. In our pollution study, for example, we observe the built effects of particular ideas about how cities should be designed and built and how they should function. And we are observing the emergence and increasing authority of new kinds of city planning expertise, focused more on environmental sustainability and even "just sustainability" that keeps wealth stratification in view, designing against ways that city greening often leads to gentrification and the displacement of poorer residents. Alternative ideas about city planning are often rooted in particular educational institutions—the School of Planning and Architecture in Delhi and the Sir J. J. School of Architecture in Mumbai, India, for example—and almost always involve interdisciplinarity, bringing together urban planners, ecologists, transportation engineers, biking advocates, and residents. Anthropologists of the sciences work to understand how established expertise shapes the world (inevitably delimiting what is seen as a problem and what is seen as a possible solution) and how new forms of expertise (and supporting education) emerge, gain social standing, and sometimes fundamentally challenge the order of things.

Education and expertise, in turn, are enabled and shaped by the technologies available to power them. Consider, for example, how laptops, smart phones, and other electronics have changed how people are educated, and the way people carry out many different kinds of work. We've named the places this occurs the techno strata, where we observe how technological change shapes how and what people know, are interested in, and worried about. The increased availability of air quality monitors affordable to independent citizens is one of the most important technological developments that we've observed in our air pollution study, for example. Some government actors are dismissive of this kind of "citizen science," but others—like the US National Aeronautics and

Space Administration (NASA)—strongly supports it, seeing it as a source of data and insight that won't replace but can supplement that produced by more expensive equipment and professional scientists. NASA and other supporters of citizen science also see it as a way to draw citizens into scientific inquiries, encouraging their support for scientific research and the use of science in decision making. Other technical developments have also transformed air pollution science and governance. Satellite images, for example, are now used to track pollution distributions, as well as the ways pollution can cross borders, and they profoundly challenge governance-as-usual. Efforts to effectively govern air pollution in Singapore and elsewhere in Southeast Asia from fires in Indonesia are largely regarded as a legal and political disaster, for example, in addition to an environmental one.

Technologies of the sciences are important in many different ways, not least because they produce the data on which science turns. Anthropologists of the sciences are increasingly turning to and focusing on what we call the data strata—watching what data is collected, how it is generated and structured, why it is made and shared (or privatized), and to what effect. Indeed, a key part of characterizing the "thought style" of a particular scientist or scientific community is delineating their data practices, infrastructure, and sensibilities— what can be called their "data culture." We are thus interested in how data is or is not shared, and in the epistemological as well as ethical reasons many scientists are committed to "open data." Many scientists are committed to open data as a necessary condition for the "reproducibility" often said to be what makes scientific knowledge precise, trustworthy, good, or robust. Other scientists see open data more in terms of leveraging previous knowledge in the making of new knowledge; open data allows the reanalysis of data from a study of air pollution and the health of rats, for example, with newly available software and statistical techniques deployed in conjunction with new data on human health. It's through data cultures, especially, that one can see how all the strata we've described press and shape one another. Data cultures are both shaped by and drive scientific technologies, which are available and circulate because of supporting law, economies, and social networks, for example; data practices and culture also powerfully shape narratives about what sciences are, and the kind of vital social resource science is. Just think about a recent article you've surely read about how Big Data will solve, or at least provide unexpected and definitive truth about, some previously inscrutable enviro-socio-cultural phenomenon, and you will have spanned all the strata from the data to the meta.

All, also, come together in what we've called the nano strata, perhaps especially familiar to anthropologists, where "worldviews" and "cultural frames" are formed and performed, where language ideologies are harbored and enacted, where ethical imaginaries come together. Anthropologies of the sciences focus here to draw out the thought styles of the scientists they study and to figure out how public discussion and media representation of the sciences (meta discourses) are actually taken up in the imaginations of all kinds of peoples. In our air pollution study, for example, we want to understand how many different kinds of people on the streets of India—auto rickshaw drivers, truck drivers, drivers of personal vehicles, street vendors—understand the (scientific) claims that it is necessary to restrict their movement to improve the air to protect their health, even though restrictions on vehicle mobility will change and possibly undermine the way they do or get to their jobs.

How all these people understand new air pollution laws is, of course, not only a matter of science; it is tangled up in how people think about the actual and legitimate role of the Indian government in their lives, about how and where they can make a living wage, and about how health is best protected and sustained. Anthropologists of the sciences are interested in what people see as usable and valuable knowledge, as expertise, and as appropriate uses of knowledge, data, and other forms of evidence in decision making, dispute resolution, and planning for the future. A key challenge in our air pollution study, for example, is to figure out how the many kinds of experts involved think about the public good and civic responsibility. We also need to understand the many different ways people in different settings, with different social standing, think about "governance" and about the kinds of data and knowledge that legitimately orient governance, always aware that these are shaped by histories of ideas and politics in a given setting, by media dynamics, and by the intricacies of individual life histories. Envisioning all the strata where science is in play helps us get at these entanglements.

Interactively, the many strata we have described produce what science becomes in society and culture. There are many possible ways of focusing work in anthropologies of the sciences, and many reasons why such work advances both anthropological theory and the contributions that anthropology makes to public life. Anthropologies of the sciences address basic theoretical questions about social hierarchies and legitimacy; about how power is distributed within and between societies; about how globalization plays out on the ground; and about how social change happens. Anthropologists of the sciences also speak to many issues of urgent practical concern, offering perspective on how investments in education and research advance societal development, prosperity, and distributions of wealth; how knowledge can move through social formations and into new laws and norms; and how different forms of knowledge can be brought together and leveraged to re-image future possibilities. Anthropologists of the sciences thus provide an especially exciting place to work within anthropology writ large, both as a space of its own and as a dimension of many different kinds of anthropological projects.

CONCLUSION

In our opening story we alluded to the slight awkwardness one often feels at the start of an anthropological engagement with scientists. Often the scientists recognize that anthropologists are fellow *researchers* and respect them as such, but don't fully understand what the anthropologists are up to and why they want to talk to—and analyze—*them*. "So we're your guinea pigs, right?" We've heard this many times. Usually the question isn't hostile, just curious and a show of hesitancy—a call for explanation. Anthropologists of science thus have special demands on them to describe what anthropology is, how and why we do it, and how we move from listening and observation to analysis, interpretation, and the making of (scientific) claims ourselves. Anthropologists of the sciences explain themselves and their work in different ways, and there is a healthy debate among them about whether anthropology itself should be considered a science. Most all, however, at some point have to explain how anthropology moved from the study of lower-tech, other-than-modern societies in remote places to the study of people, practices, and issues at the heart of higher-tech, ultra-complex, globally connected societies. "People are people," although logically impeccable, asks for a bit more anthropological explication when it comes to anthropologies of the sciences.

In our experience, the relative newness of the anthropology of science has made it an exciting place to work, in part because its newness has made it methodologically challenging. The methods, concepts, and theories developed in anthropological research over time and around the world are critical guides to the anthropology of science, but they always have to be translated—becoming something new in process—when focused on the sciences in practice and in culture.

In a move that was notably radical at the time (1969), anthropologist Laura Nader described the challenge as one of "studying up." Nader argued that it was critical to do this not only because people at the top of social hierarchies are indeed part of the "whole picture" that anthropologists strive to capture, but also because this hierarchy organizes and emanates *power*, shaping the lives of all within, in ways that are more or less fair, healthy, and meaningful. Emphasizing the importance of studying lawyers, bureaucrats, and other elites (including scientists), Nader pushed anthropologists toward "'study of the colonizers rather than [just the] the colonized, the culture of power rather than the culture of the powerless, the culture of affluence rather than the culture of poverty."

Nader's early call for studying up literally upended established approaches to anthropological research, foreshadowing the methodological challenges and innovation that would come to be associated with anthropologies of the sciences. Nader's call also reaffirmed Fleck's insights set out in the epigraph, that anthropologies of sciences are also the anthropologies of politics. In studying how science is produced, circulated, legitimated, used, and imagined, anthropologists draw out *who* counts as knowledgeable, *what* counts as knowledge, and *how* knowledge claims shape everyday lives, law, policy, and public discourse—in turn shaping next-generation education, science, and social reproduction writ large. Anthropologies of science are thus best seen not as a topical subfield but as a critical layer in all anthropological research, though depth and scope of attention to different layers will of course vary across projects. Anthropologies of science should also be seen as deeply political in form as well as through specific arguments. In recognizing and exploring *different* knowledge forms—within the sciences, and in comparison with other knowledge forms—anthropologies of science analyze what comes to be seen as important and obvious, who and what gets cut out, and how people are pushing back, reaching for new knowledge forms, attuned to emerging as well as stubbornly enduring problems. Anthropologies of the sciences are thus about how people have figured, and might in the future continue to, in Michael Fischer's phrase, "figure things out."

SUGGESTIONS FOR FURTHER READING

Caduff, Carlo. 2012. "Ethnographies of Science—Conversation with the Authors and Commentary." Curated Collections, *Cultural Anthropology* website; https://culanth.org/cur ated_collections/3-ethnographies-of-science/discussions/3-ethnographies-of-science -conversation-with-the-authors-and-commentary-by-carlo-caduff.

    In an interview format, this piece presents the perspectives of different anthropologists of different sciences in an engaging format with extensive links.

Callison, Candis. 2014. *How Climate Change Comes to Matter*. Durham, NC: Duke University Press.

    This book compares the ways journalists, indigenous leaders, religious leaders, corporate representatives and scientists themselves perceive climate science and the need to address climate change.

Fearnley, Lyle. 2015. "Wild Goose Chase: The Displacement of Influenza Research in the Fields of Poyang Lake, China." *Cultural Anthropology* 30 (1): 12–35. https://doi.org/10 .14506/ca30.1.03.

    This article explores how influenza research moved out of the lab and into the field (in China), referencing other scholars who have explored field sciences (including anthropology).

Marks, Jonathan. *Why I Am Not a Scientist: Anthropology and Modern Knowledge*. Berkeley: University of California Press, 2009.

    This book is a biological anthropologist's witty exploration of the history and culture of the life sciences, with a focus on genetics and race.

Traweek, Sharon. 1988. *Beamtimes and Lifetimes: The World of High-Energy Physicists*. Cambridge, MA: Harvard University Press.

In this early and pioneering ethnography of science, Traweek describes the life-worlds of physicists in the United States and Japan.

REFERENCES

Bateson, Gregory. 2000. *Steps to an Ecology of Mind*. Chicago: University of Chicago Press.

Daston, Lorraine, and Peter Galison. 2007. *Objectivity*. Cambridge, MA: Zone Books.

Droney, Damien. 2014. "Ironies of Laboratory Work during Ghana's Second Age of Optimism." *Cultural Anthropology* 29 (2): 363–84. https://doi.org/10.14506/ca29.2.10.

Dumit, Joseph. 2004. *Picturing Personhood: Brain Scans and Biomedical Identity*. Princeton, NJ: Princeton University Press.

Edwards, Paul. 2010. *A Vast Machine: Computer Models, Climate Data, and the Politics of Global Warming*. Cambridge, MA: MIT Press.

Fearnley, Lyle. 2015. "Wild Goose Chase: The Displacement of Influenza Research in the Fields of Poyang Lake, China." *Cultural Anthropology* 30 (1): 12–35. https://doi.org/10.14506/ca30.1.03.

Fischer, Michael M. J. 2007, "Culture and Cultural Analysis as Experimental Systems." *Cultural Anthropology* 22 (1): 1–65.

Fleck, Ludwik. 1979 [1935]. *Genesis and Development of a Scientific Fact*. Trans. Fred Bradley and Thaddeus J. Trenn. Chicago: University of Chicago Press.

———. 1986 [1946]. "Problems of the Science of Science." In *Cognition and Fact*, 113–27. Boston Studies in the Philosophy of Science 87. Springer Netherlands, doi:10.1007/978-94-009-4498-5_6.

Fortun, Kim. 2001. *Advocacy after Bhopal: Environmentalism, Disaster, New Global Orders*. Chicago: University of Chicago Press.

Fortun, Kim, and Mike Fortun. 2008. "Scientific Imaginaries and Ethical Plateaus in Contemporary U.S. Toxicology." *American Anthropologist* 107 (1): 43–54.

Fortun, Mike, and Herbert J. Bernstein. 1998. *Muddling Through: Pursuing Science and Truths in the 21st Century*. Washington, DC: Counterpoint Press.

Hamdy, Sherine. 2012. *Our Bodies Belong to God*. Berkeley: University of California Press.

Harding, Sandra, ed. 2011. *The Postcolonial Science and Technology Studies Reader*. Durham, NC: Duke University Press.

Haraway, Donna J. 1988 (Autumn). "Situated Knowledges: The Science Question in Feminism and the Privilege of Partial Perspective." *Feminist Studies* 14 (3): 575–99.

Haraway, Donna. 1989. *Primate Visions: Gender, Race and Nature in the World of Modern Science*. New York: Routledge.

Hayden, Corey. 2003. *When Nature Goes Public. The Making and Unmaking of Bioprospecting in Mexico*. Princeton, NJ: Princeton University Press.

Hecht, Gabrielle. 2012. *Being Nuclear: Africans and the Global Uranium Trade*. Cambridge, MA: MIT Press.

Helmreich, Stefan. 2009. *Alien Ocean: Anthropological Voyages in Microbial Seas*. Berkeley: University of California Press.

Huber, Peter. 1993. *Galileo's Revenge: Junk Science in the Courtroom*. New York: Basic Books.

Knorr-Cetina, Karin. 1999. *Epistemic Cultures: How the Sciences Make Knowledge*. Cambridge, MA: Harvard University Press.

Kuhn, Michael, and Hebe Vessuri, eds. 2016. *The Global Social Sciences: Under and Beyond European Universalism.* New York: Columbia University Press.

Latour, Bruno, and Steve Woolgar. 1979. *Laboratory Life: The Construction of Scientific Facts.* Beverly Hills, CA: Sage.

Lock, Margaret, and Vinh-Kim Nguyen. 2010. *An Anthropology of Biomedicine.* Oxford: Wiley.

Marcus, George E., and Michael M. J. Fischer. 1986. *Anthropology as Cultural Critique: An Experimental Moment in the Human Sciences.* Chicago: University of Chicago Press.

Masco, Joseph. 2004. "Mutant Ecologies: Radioactive Life in Post-Cold War New Mexico." *Cultural Anthropology* 19 (4): 517–50.

Montoya, Michael. 2011. *Making the Mexican Diabetic: Race, Science, and the Genetics of Inequality.* Berkeley: University of California Press.

Nader, Laura, ed. 1996. *Naked Science: Anthropological Inquiry into Boundaries, Power, and Knowledge.* New York: Routledge.

Pickering, Andrew, ed. 1992. *Science as Practice and Culture.* Chicago: University of Chicago Press.

Porter, Theodore M. 1995. *Trust in Numbers: The Pursuit of Objectivity in Science and Public Life.* Princeton, NJ: Princeton University Press.

Rapp, Rayna. 2000. *Testing Women, Testing the Fetus: The Social Impact of Amniocentesis in America.* New York: Routledge.

Reddy, Deepa. 2008. "Caught in Collaboration." *Collaborative Anthropologies* 1:51–80.

Rheinberger, Hans-Jorg. 1997. *Toward a History of Epistemic Things: Synthesizing Proteins in the Test Tube.* Stanford, CA: Stanford University Press.

Sunder Rajan, Kaushik. 2006. *Biocapital: The Constitution of Postgenomic Life.* Durham, NC: Duke University Press.

Tousignant, Noémi. 2018. *Edges of Exposure: Toxicology and the Problem of Capacity in Postcolonial Senegal.* Durham, NC: Duke University Press.

Traweek, Sharon. 1993. "An Introduction to Cultural and Social Studies of Sciences and Technologies." *Culture, Medicine and Psychiatry* 17:3–25.

———. 1996. "Unity, Dyads, Triads, Quads, and Complexity: Cultural Choreographies of Science." *Social Text* 46/47:129–39. doi:10.2307/466849.

———. 2000. "Faultlines." In Roddey Reid and Sharon Traweek, eds., *Doing Science + Culture.* London: Routledge.

Verran, Helen. 2001. *Science and an African Logic.* Chicago: University of Chicago Press.

Zhan, Mei. 2009. *Other-Worldly: Making Chinese Medicine through Transnational Frames.* Durham, NC: Duke University Press.

CHAPTER 14

EVERY ERA GETS THE INTERNET IT DESERVES (OR, THE PHASES OF HACKING)

Christopher Kelty

INTRODUCTION

The Internet has a perpetual air of novelty, even though it has been a core part of global culture for close to fifty years. Though much has changed, much has also stayed the same. For as long as it has existed, anthropologists have been trying to make sense of this new technology — as a space, as a medium, as a political technology, and as a danger or threat. The research in this area mirrors not only changes in the role of information technology in society but also changing theoretical concerns central to the discipline: from a concern with the "subcultures" of the Internet to a focus on the Internet and its global publics; from a concern with the approaches of science and technology studies to questions about neoliberalism, global capitalism, and social movements.

By now, the Internet is in the background, if not the foreground, of every anthropologist's research: whether that is the simple communicative aspects of social media, or the information-density of a particular domain (like medical or legal knowledge), or the technical nitty-gritty of the algorithms, data, and software that run everything from our computers to our toasters to the micro-loan payment systems on mobile phones. Like language, the Internet saturates experience, but it consists of many different parts, takes myriad idiomatic forms, and has an agency of its own that puts it in a category similar to other institutions anthropologists study, like law or religion.

Who Does One Study When One Studies the Internet?

On the one hand, anthropologists study how ordinary people are confronting this new medium, adapting it to their culture, history and social lives, and struggling with how it affects them. On the other hand, anthropologists also study the experts who interpret, make, and break the Internet: hackers, engineers, entrepreneurs, software architects, programmers, system administrators, etcetera. The analogy with law and religion is apposite: Just as there are lawyers, judges, priests, or shamans who occupy a special place of interpretation or control in law or religion, so too software engineers have been called a "priesthood" and are perceived as both powerful and dangerous.

But the experts of the Internet are no ordinary bunch. The people who not only use the Internet, but make it and break it, are sometimes also *lay participants*: "hackers." This category of actors has a special status in between the ordinary user and the expert engineer or elite; they participate in aspects of both. Hackers are often opposed to "engineers"—though in some eras, the term has been embraced more enthusiastically by professional engineers than in others—and just as the idea of an amateur surgeon or an amateur magistrate seems absurd to professional doctors and lawyers, many engineers resist the idea that a "hacker" is anything more than a curious tinkerer.

However, cases such as the invention of the Linux operating system, or the creation of Facebook, or the spread of Pretty Good Privacy (PGP) encryption, or the rise of Anonymous all testify to the power of "lay" participation in the technical and political aspects of the Internet. Hackers have a peculiar, recurrent legitimacy that is not true of amateurs or lay participants in many other domains, and this has drawn anthropological attention to them as a special category of the "anthropology of the Internet."

The very term *hacker* is also one of intense debate, by hackers as much as by scholars. Sometimes it implies criminal activity, sometimes it means utopian political intervention through technology, sometimes it means activism. Anthropologists Alex Golub and Gabriella Coleman have proposed that different "moral genres" of hacking exist, all taking up questions of technical skill and political liberalism in different configurations. Luis Felipe Murillo has described the life histories and shared routes of "ethical cultivation" that account for some of these differences, and especially the difference from engineers or formally trained scientists. Hacking is also a phenomenon that has diverse international expressions; anthropologists have studied hackers and hacking in Malaysia, China, Peru, Chile, and Ghana in order to explore how national, ethnic, and gender differences reproduce themselves in hacker cultures just as they do in mainstream cultures.

What is perhaps missing from our account of hackers and the influence of the Internet is that it seems to have a kind of *periodicity* to it: the different forms that hacking takes emerge and dominate public debate and academic investigation in response to larger cultural and political transformations. In fact, it is probably better to think of "hackers" as having phases, like those of the moon. In any given period, one version of "hacker" is waxing, while another is waning; one style of hacking is "gibbous" while another is "crescent." Some may disappear completely, only to return in a later period. The metaphor is useful in that all these varieties of hacking persist through time; it is only in some periods that the light (media, scholarly, or public attention) is clearly shining on one type of hacking; and like most of us, many hackers tend to move to where the light is rather than remain in obscurity.

In what follows I narrate four "eras" of the Internet and the phases of its hackers: new kinds of hackers appear dominant in different eras, and anthropology has investigated different aspects of hackers, technologies and political effects that have emerged from the internet over the last 40–50 years. In each case, I present a lunar chart of the phases of different hackers, along with a cursory indication of the different events and problems that have attracted anthropologists in each era. Of course, all periodizations are untrustworthy, but some are useful. A larger phenomenon is visible when one considers hacking as having phases, rather than as being types of people. Namely, it makes visible tension between expertise and participation in a world saturated with networks, software, data, algorithms, and devices that distribute the power to make and break things more widely than ever before.

THE INTERNET OF TEXT (1970–1994)

PHASES OF THE HACKER (1970-1994)

Phase	Characteristics
F<small>ULL</small>	The hacker as well meaning trouble-maker or Whiz Kid as in War Games (1984); the hacker underground; hacking as exploring and exploiting, as in Robert Morris and the Morris Worm. A world of textual communication.
W<small>AXING</small> C<small>RESCENT</small>	The hacker as amateur maker of software and critic of intellectual property, as in the case of Free software and Richard Stallman.
N<small>EW</small>	The hacker as political actor, activist or resistance.

The Arpanet was established in 1969; UNIX version 1 appeared in 1971; the first personal computers in the late 1970s; and the Hayes smartmodem in 1981, which allowed small-scale Bulletin Board Systems (BBS) to flourish shortly thereafter. By 1984, the Internet was born, and the first major motion picture about a happy-go-lucky hacker who saves the world from himself appeared (*War Games*). It was also the year that the first scholarly books to make sense of this new breed of lay expert appeared: Steven Levy's *Hackers* and Sherry Turkle's *The Second Self*. The former famously reported on the "hacker ethic," and the latter was the first to recognize the intensity with which people were coming to identify with computers as devices for communication, writing, thinking, and interacting. Turkle's work, combining interview and interpretation (influenced by her own psychoanalytic training), gave us a first glimpse into how individuals were changing the ways they understood other humans as a result of the spread of computers and computational thinking. Although there had been speculative works about giant brains and "machines that think" since the 1950s, it was only in the 1980s that networked communication and intensive, joyful immersion came to the fore; children were learning to program with rudimentary languages like Logo; philosophers such as Hubert Dreyfus debated "What computers can't do" and the value of the interactivity of programs such as the "computer psychoanalyst" ELIZA, and console and arcade video games exploded into homes and public places.

Levy and Turkle both placed "hacking" at the center of their analyses, with its peculiar autodidactic forms and underground networks of likeminded enthusiasts. As Turkle put it: "With the computer young people can find paths to a certain kind of virtuosity without passing through the filter of formal education (187)." Anthropologist Bryan Pfaffenberger was one of the earliest to observe in detail how Usenet (an early newsgroup-network organized around shared interests and topics) brought together likeminded hackers and enthusiasts who not only used the technology but modified it, defended it, rebuilt it, and extended it. The denizens of Usenet represented not so much an elite high-tech engineering cadre as they did a motley population of the curious, the obsessive, the underground, the bored, and the over-stimulated: skewing white and male to be sure, but nonetheless unrestricted in a way that empowered many people at the time. Similarly, independent archivist and documentarian Jason Scott has tirelessly documented the period, creating some of the best collections of material about BBS users, early text gamers, and much more (all now preserved at the Internet Archive). And like many other cultures, hackers have self-documented their own subcultural experience in shared text files, zines like *Phrack* and *2600* and magazines like *Mondo 2000* and the early *Wired*.

The meaning of hackers also expanded during this period to encompass anxieties of various sorts. The hacker collective the "414s" emerged in 1983 to a brief spotlight, appearing on the cover of *Newsweek* after breaking into Los Alamos National Labs. But it was the 1988 case of the Morris Worm that captured the attention of security researchers. Robert Tappan Morris (son of the then head of the National Security Agency) was one of the first to be prosecuted under a new US law, the Computer Fraud and Abuse Act of 1986. Morris was convicted and sentenced to three years of probation, four hundred hours of community service, and a $10,000 fine. No doubt because of his status, Morris escaped unscathed: he's gone on to be a very successful entrepreneur and cofounder of the Silicon Valley venture capital firm Y Combinator.

Alongside the Morris worm, however, a range of raids, investigations, and arrests brought a sudden political consciousness to groups like the Berlin-based Chaos Computer Club, the "Masters of Deception," and the "Legion of Doom." One raid in particular, was to have significant effects: the raid of the offices of Steve Jackson Games in Austin, Texas, in 1990. The Secret Service invaded Jackson's Austin offices because they believed he was creating a training manual for computer crime, and they seized all copies of the yet-to-be-released "GURPS Cyberpunk" role-playing game, along with all his computer equipment and floppy disks. The case stirred Mitch Kapor (then of "Lotus 1-2-3" fame) and John Perry Barlow to action. Together they created the Electronic Frontier Foundation (EFF) and made a cause célèbre of the Steve Jackson case (Jackson declared at the time, "I am a horror story"). The EFF has gone on to be a central node in the political monitoring, activism, and defense of a range of hacking, intellectual property, and Internet-related issues—and a frequent location for anthropological participant-observation.

The "Internet of Text" and its cultural significance has more recently been captured most vividly in Fred Turner's 2007 *From Counterculture to Cyberculture*. Turner realized that what had been perceived as distinct subcultures—hippies and their back-to-nature communalism and hackers and their techno-utopian dreams—shared a range of cultural reference points, and even a few key characters, like the cultural impresario Stewart Brand. The continuity of this story has justly reoriented scholars' understanding of some of the small-world influence these cultures have had; but at the same time, the story is all too often used to reduce all forms of hackers, engineers, and computer users to a particular brand of "communalism." Politicized hackers, techno-dystopians, white-collar hacker-by night makers of free software, and others don't fit this mold just because of a particular technical virtuosity. Nonetheless, Turner's work has established the cultural and social history of the period vividly.

Anthropological work on cyberculture in the Internet of Text mirrored existing concerns in academia. A focus on subcultures and cultural studies formed the background to an early influential piece by Arturo Escobar, "Welcome to Cyberia," which assessed then-current claims of a new culture emerging around virtual reality and biotechnology. "Cyberia," though, was not so much specific to the Internet of Text as it was a general label for cultural transformation in the late twentieth century under conditions of "complexity." Very little of the properly ethnographic writing from this period was done by professional anthropologists. Some was done by journalists, for example, Julian Dibbell's "A Rape in Cyberspace." He observed the emergence of legal institutions in the radically free and anonymous spaces, in particular a world called LambdaMOO, where a "virtual rape" turned out to be a very real event in the lives of the residents. But most of the writing about this new culture was carried out by enthusiastic "residents" themselves, often adopting the attitude of an explorer or anthropologist.

And why text? From the perspective of a 1980s cultural anthropology saturated in models of culture-as-text, symbolic forms, grammars of action, structuralisms and poststructuralisms, the Internet of Text could hardly fail to be intriguing, precisely because it so clearly reduced human interaction to one expressive modality: textual communication. Even at this moment, it was clear that interactive textual tools like Internet Relay Chat (IRC), Multi-User Dungeons (MUDs) and MUD Object Oriented (MOOs) gave observers access to a new level of explicitness through which culture emerged. But few works emerged within anthropology that took this new medium seriously. The most well-known is Lynn Cherny's *Conversation and Community: Chat in a Virtual World*, which took an explicitly linguistic anthropology approach to the appearance of online text-based interaction.

The virtuosity of the hacker in particular, in the Internet of Text, was tied explicitly and self-reflexively to this medium. In one widely read paean, science fiction writer Neal Stephenson effused about the command line and its magical power: the strange, seductive power of typing objects and actions into being could not escape being associated with the Christian God. He titled his essay "In the beginning was the command line." The textual Internet was and continues to be a source of endless creativity and play as well. Although computer code and languages have rarely attracted anthropological linguists, the playful invention of the textual Internet was another of the self-documenting features of this period, a famous case of this self-documenting being "The Jargon File," which circulated widely during this period and was later published as *The Hacker Dictionary*.

The vast majority of people using, making, or breaking the Internet in this period were in universities, government labs, and corporate labs. But the Internet was largely perceived and experienced as a "noncommercial" space outside of mainstream media and culture. To be sure, it was expensive, and it drove the purchase of PCs, modems, and other hardware throughout the period, but for many it was understood, narrated, and experienced as underground, sub- or countercultural. While it was mostly a US and European phenomenon, one of its most surprising features was the ease with which it connected the people who were using it around the world. Carl Malamud, a technologist, adopted a quasi-anthropological attitude in his travelogue tracing how nodes of the Internet popped into existence everywhere that a computer science department or a computer firm did; from Malaysia to Brazil to India and beyond. My own fieldwork in India was almost exclusively possible because of connections negotiated with a pioneering set of computer enthusiasts in India who brought the Internet into the country through computer science departments and large corporations. This "instant scalability" would become a core feature of the Internet's ability to warp and blur cultural limits and produced an ongoing fascination with connection and the production of new collectivities that arguably has not waned. Anthropologists (and hackers as well) exploring the Internet in this period encountered it not as a single technology, but as a surprising, rapidly changing, unfolding and complex domain. It was immediately obvious during this period that although the Internet had high-tech military origins and depended on some of the most sophisticated and rarefied engineering expertise in the world, it was also being built, extended, tested, explored, and broken by all sorts of people, not only professional engineers.

THE INTERNET OF UTOPIAS (1995–2006)

PHASES OF THE HACKER (1995-2006)

Phase	Characteristics
 WAXING GIBBOUS	The hacker as maker of Free Software/Open Source; as critic of IP rights; as inventor of new publics and new economic opportunities.
 WANING CRESCENT	Teenage hackers, criminals, the "hacker underground"; the hacker as security researcher; the "cracker"; the "script kiddie".
 WAXING CRECENT	The hacker as political actor (Ricardo Dominguez and Electronic Disturbance Theatre); the hacker as netwar or cybersecurity adversary (Arquilla and Ronfeldt at RAND); the hacker as criminal or spammer.

The Internet of Utopias begins with the World Wide Web in 1994. The web exploded into public consciousness primarily because it was not simply an Internet of Text. A threshold of visibility and usability was crossed when web browsers allowed text and image to be displayed together, along with video, audio, software, and much else. It changed the PC from a stand-alone appliance into a global communication and publishing device for many people. "Websites" piqued curiosity and stoked creativity because of the expectation that "anyone" could access them (though this "anyone" of course generated its own critiques of digital divides and of rights to broadband access). The speed and alacrity of the commercial embrace of this simple change was apparent to everyone: from the makers of browser software like Mosaic to the designers of web sites learning a new visual language (and the artists of 1990s net.art who critiqued that visual language), to businesses of every stripe scrambling to secure a dotcom domain name and a rudimentary ecommerce web site. The story can be (and often is) told through the rise and fall of the dotcom boom and the winners like Amazon and eBay (and the losers like Geocities, Alta Vista, and Pets.com).

Whereas the Internet of Text was approached by anthropologists in a broadly Malinowskian mode—as a novel or emergent culture distinct from that hitherto known or understood—the Internet of Utopias opened up a new problem: the Internet was in fact part of the world, not separate from it. Rather than an atopic place, it became for many scholars a utopic one, perhaps best understood (as Sebastien Broca explains) in Ernst Bloch's sense of the "concrete utopia" lived in the present but always promising a better, more hopeful future. Much of the work that developed in this period, therefore, also mirrored anthropology's concern with the evolving forms of liberalism, neoliberalism, and global political culture, perhaps best captured by the collected volume *Global Assemblages*, the work of Marilyn Strathern and her students (e.g., Annelise Riles, *The Network Inside Out*, and the focus on "multisited" ethnography).

Across the disciplines, theoretical work on the Internet therefore focused more often on its power to transform existing structures and communities, rather than on its distinctiveness. The Internet was characterized as a new public sphere, as a disruptor of markets, as a challenge to bureaucracy, and as the triumph of a new form: the network. It is perhaps not surprising that debates about globalization and about the flows and circuits of labor and capital were also central to the kinds of work initiated in this period. Work in anthropology focused in on how culture intersected with this new medium. Daniel Miller and Don Slater published one of the first in-depth ethnographic accounts of Internet use in 2001, focusing on the case of Trinidad and Tobago. Miller and Slater's work helped establish that the Internet was not a monocultural place, but was taken up differently by different cultures around the world; a point that was especially well demonstrated in Victoria Bernal's study of the Eritrean diaspora and its use of the Internet to stay connected to a specific form of national identity.

Despite the various assertions that "Cyberspace" was an atopic space separate from the world (John Perry Barlow's "Declaration of the Independence of the Internet" was emblematic of this attitude), anthropological work in this period repeatedly and aggressively critiqued the idea that the Internet was another, atopic space. It raised instead fascinating evidence of effects and problems of navigating between on- and offline worlds. One of the most compelling examples of this was Xiang Biao's work on the migration of software engineers: engineers who spent their working days in companies abroad (chiefly in the United States and Australia staring at screens and software code) and their nights as part of an international racialized labor market, with complex ties to the networks of kinship, marriage, and dowry back home in Andhra Pradesh. The Internet facilitated and undergirded this new labor market, remaking the existing patterns of international migration and labor in ways that remain with us in the debates about H1B visas in the United States or call centers in India.

Intellectual property law also emerged as a key object of analysis in the context of the Internet of Utopias. It was from within high-tech cultures that certain forms of critiques would emerge and link up with critiques familiar in at least two other areas: those of biotechnology, on the one hand, and those of indigenous notions of property and ownership, on the other. Software engineers in particular had articulated how the power of collective innovation was being stymied by creator-centric ownership laws that concentrated power in the largest corporate hands, perpetuating forms of imperialism and extraction recognized in other domains. Kim Christen's work on Aboriginal Australians' relationship to openness and circulation of information was a fascinating counter-example to the demands for openness; she demonstrated, both as an ethnographer and as a designer of a web-based archive, how her Warumungu collaborators used different protocols of visibility and accessibility based on cultural ideals, such as which genders can view which pictures and how to deal with pictures of dead ancestors.

From the late 1990s to the early 2000s, anthropological interest in the Internet tracked a related embrace of Science and Technology Studies. This approach emphasized the engineers and hackers who created, maintained, or were otherwise engaged in expert activities, rather than the ordinary users of the Internet. An early case is Georgina Born's study of software engineers at IRCAM in Paris, where she explored the way electronic music was an object of negotiation not only for musicians, but for technologists as well. Later the phenomenon of Free Software/Open Source became a central problem for researchers across the disciplines. Questions about the culture of science and engineering under capitalism set in motion by works like Paul Rabinow's *Making PCR*, Stefan Helmreich's *Silicon Second Nature*, and the works of Donna Haraway, Lucy Suchman, Susan Leigh Star, and others were extended into studies of software, start-up culture, biotech, and elsewhere.

The tensions and affiliations between an anthropology of Internet users and an anthropology of Internet makers, hackers, or engineers is nicely illustrated by two works that appeared around the same time. Tom Boellstorff's *Coming of Age in Second Life* took an explicitly Malinowskian approach to studying Second Life users or residents; it focused on issues of personhood, anonymity, and identity; on the structure of community and the crafting of selves in-world; on making and selling virtual things ("creative capitalism"); and other aspects of being in such alien worlds. Thomas Malaby's *Making Virtual Worlds* was a study of Linden Labs, the makers of Second Life software, and focused instead on the corporate culture of the Silicon Valley firm that makes the software, the ideologies of those who work and manage the firm, and the politics of intellectual property; it made the case that corporate culture was itself being treated much like the experience of being in a persistent virtual world: made and remade from day to day under conditions of a newly precarious industry in Silicon Valley. Together with books by Christine Hine and by Daniel Miller and Don Slater, Boellstorff's work helped establish an ethnographic approach to online and virtual worlds that emphasized a distinctive form of experience and personhood in the contemporary. Malaby's work pointed in a somewhat different direction, towards the hackers and engineers as political actors using this medium to remake the world in new ways.

As the image of the hacker as a well-meaning troublemaker or quasi-criminal waned in this period, the image of the Free Software hacker, entrepreneur of "peer production," the maker, or the advocate of "creative commons" and free culture, rose to prominence. This figure and the general phenomenon of Free and Open Source software, occupied academics across the disciplines because of its surprising, sometimes counter-intuitive existence: thousands of volunteers creating very high-tech software for no apparent salary and doing so with clear passion and joy. Several works explored the life and work of such hackers. My own work in *Two Bits* was oriented toward explaining the emergence of Free Software as an assemblage of different practices (sharing code, writing legal licenses, developing a movement, etc.), and it proposed the idea that the mode of affiliation via technology that brought these hackers together could be called a "recursive public": a public that is vitally concerned with the material and practical maintenance and modification of its own technical existence as a public. Gabriella Coleman's work focused on the joys and craft of hacking, on hackers' free speech advocacy (especially the idea that "code is speech"), and, like other work in the period, challenged assumptions about the atopic space of the Internet with grounded investigations of the social worlds of hackers online and off. Both works made the case for understanding hacking as a lived expression of liberalism, and in particular, as a reinvigoration of those ideas in the form of technical skill, lay expertise, and political engagement in the public sphere. While economists and sociologists largely puzzled over the surprise that hackers "worked for free" (they didn't, most had day jobs) or the "problem of motivation" in peer production, anthropologists have generally been unconcerned (and unsurprised) by the enthusiasm of hackers and unmoved by the lack of a universally rational (or irrational) behavior.

Key events during the Internet of Utopias exemplified this particular brand of hacking-as-liberalism: the moment when Napster was shut down by the US courts; the public arrest of Dimitri Sklyarov by FBI agents at a hacker conference; the birth of the BitTorrent protocol and the launch of the Pirate Bay file sharing website; as well as the maturation of software like Linux, the Apache Web Server, and a number of other key Internet technologies built by collectives of free software makers.

Beyond liberalism and just out of sight, one could also catch glimpses of a style of hacking yet to come into its own. When Subcomandante Marcos and the Zapatistas launched their resistance in Chiapas, Mexico, they did so with a savvy understanding of the Internet and its political power. Many activists joined in these actions. Ricardo Dominguez and the Critical Art Ensemble staged productions of an "Electronic Disturbance Theatre," in particular pioneering a tactic they called "virtual sit-ins" but which would later come to be known in more technical parlance as a "distributed denial of service" attack (DDoS).

The Internet of Utopias was thus a period of intensity of experimentation with new forms of collectivity. New arrangements of expertise and participation exploded into public consciousness and were taken up enthusiastically in business, academia, and government. This utopic enthusiasm would set the stage for what followed, as Internet technologies became ever more ubiquitous. While the dotcom-style enthusiasm for 'disintermediation' counseled replacement of every known structure and remnant of an industrial economy, a similar enthusiasm gripped people in academia around the critique of intellectual property and the promise of Open Access distribution of scholarly productions, and even to the very mode of production itself. From this enthusiasm emerged several new kinds of collectivities; in the world of software and IT engineering, it was becoming clear that the old structures of professionalization and accreditation were being supplemented by a fast-moving, informal process of mutual aid and self-training online; and for those who had been drawn into the world of Free and Open Source software for its critique of political economy, new collectivities of protest, critique, and activism would emerge by the end of this period—culminating in the appearance of new political actors ranging from Anonymous, to Occupy, to the activists of the Arab Spring.

THE INTERNET OF EVERYDAY (2007–2015)

PHASES OF THE HACKER (2007-2015)

Phase	Characteristics
Fᴜʟʟ	The Hacker as Hacktivist, trickster, and political actor: image boards and forums, Anonymous, WikiLeaks; Occupy, Arab Spring, M15.
Wᴀɴɪɴɢ Gɪʙʙᴏᴜs	Free and Open Source software hackers, makers, biohackers, Bitcoin miners; hackerspaces and makerspaces.
Wᴀxɪɴɢ Cʀᴇᴄᴇɴᴛ	Cybersecurity, cyber war, infosec hackers, infrastructure hacking (Stuxnet); state actors; public disclosure hacking.

By the late 2000s, the Internet and its technologies had established themselves globally as a central feature of everyday life and were no longer a curious novelty or cutting-edge emergent technology. A key technology in this respect was one that had remained until this time technically separate from the Internet: the mobile phone. But with the appearance in 2007 of the iPhone in the United States and the astonishingly rapid spread of smart phones generally, the

Internet was now in everyone's pocket. Anthropologists observing this in other places—especially Japan and Korea—had already begun to observe what the Internet of Everyday would come to look like everywhere.

The Internet of Everyday is also fundamentally defined by social media. What was originally touted as "web 2.0"—a "semantic" web that would be more than just a publishing platform but would engage the participation of users in making content, tagging and enriching it, uploading and sharing it—became the super-successful social media industry we have come to love and hate. Facebook was started in 2004; YouTube in 2005; Twitter in 2007. These novel "social media" aimed to remake the experience of the Internet: away from the web page and its more or less publishing-focused imagination of itself and toward sub-networks of connected people engaged in communication and "sharing" of all kinds. What social media promised to do was to repersonalize and re-socialize a medium that had been founded and designed around the potential for anonymity or pseudonymity. It promised to turn a glorified newspaper into a simulacrum of social life itself.

Almost instantly, social media became a site of social research of all kinds. Indeed, the production of research on these media alone far outstrips research on nearly every other aspect of the Internet. Much of it is based on a forced interpretation of social media activity as transparently representative of social behavior; data scientists have been besotted with the sudden and easy availability of "trace data" to be sorted, classified, and analyzed. For some purposes, such data has proven remarkably illuminating: a multibillion dollar advertising economy now depends on its constant collection, corroboration, and intensive circulation and sale. But few insights that one might characterize as transformative of sociological or anthropological theory have emerged. Indeed, quite the opposite: as Noortje Marres and Carolin Gerlitz have described, attention has turned instead to the problem of understanding how the study and use of such data are affecting our experience of the worlds we inhabit.

By the end of this era, it would be much clearer that the combination of data and software necessary to produce a social media ecology came with its own pernicious effects.

As with earlier eras, a split remained visible between studying those who use, inhabit, and make meaning via social media and those who engineer, design, fund, or hack it. In the former category, a wide range of work emerged to make sense of the changes social media was bringing to all aspects of life. Ilana Gershon, for instance, recognized early on that people on Facebook were not only expanding their networks, but severing them as well—and produced a rich account of how couples break up on social media. In 2012, anthropologist Daniel Miller launched a massive project to study social media use ethnographically around the world. Deploying anthropologists in the manner of the great collaborative projects of the 1960s, researchers headed to China, Turkey, Chile, Trinidad, south England, northeast Brazil, south India, and Italy to explore the daily use of social media and Internet technologies embedded in the lives of ordinary people (at https://www.ucl.ac.uk/why-we-post).

Makers and hackers in the Internet of Everyday, by contrast, occupied a different set of anthropological researchers. A key reason for this was not the technical revolution of social media so much as it was an unusual political mutation which happened around 2007, when a new phase of hacking emerged into full view. "Hacktivists" rose to prominence suddenly, most prominently in the case of the Guy Fawkes mask–wearing members of Anonymous. Anonymous emerged directly out of the anonymous and pseudonymous regions of the Internet of Utopias: encrypted e-mail, mailing lists, forums, IRC channels, and most famously, image boards like 4chan and 2chan.

Of all the works in anthropology from this period, one stands out as an instant anthropological classic: Gabriella Coleman's monumental ethnography of the inner workings of Anonymous, *Hacker, Hoaxer, Whistleblower, Spy*. Coleman's work exhibits the core cultural anthropological practice of long-term intensive fieldwork with a new set of actors defined not by territory, kinship, ethnicity, or subjection, but by the fact of their techno-political association as hackers engaged in activities that are at once pranksterish and deeply political. Coleman's ethnographic engagement brought her into direct contact not only with the hackers of Anonymous but with state security (the FBI and the Canadian Security and Investigation Service), the lawyers and advocates defending Anonymous, and the hordes of journalists who suddenly found it necessary to track, talk to, investigate, and understand a kind of actor that few previously had much experience with.

A key feature of being an anthropologist in any setting is combating mainstream media perceptions and stereotypes about whatever population one studies. Often journalists are well-meaning and spirited investigators, but their aim is rarely the kind of reinterpretation and sense-making that the cultural anthropologist sees as her role. Coleman's work illustrates this conundrum explicitly: she trained hundreds of journalists during the course of her research. She taught them how to access hackers via IRC, how to understand the culture, and how to know and judge the validity and value of the information gained thereby, and she has spent countless hours on social media responding to, critiquing, and correcting their work. In some ways, every population of anthropological interest deserves such advocacy (and many anthropologists engage in it), but in the case of Anonymous, Coleman thus helped many journalists and readers see what she saw: a political transformation (a change in phase, perhaps). Hackers had changed from being represented as adolescent white boys or politically agnostic Open Source software makers to visibly political actors on a global stage.

From roughly 2009 to 2014, Anonymous and WikiLeaks participated in, promoted, or enabled a truly stunning range of political actions, ranging from sustained protests of the Church of Scientology, to the Cablegate leaks obtained by Chelsea Manning, to a wide range of Distributed Denial of Service Attacks (DDoS) against everyone from Amazon and MasterCard to various repressive government regimes around the world. Coleman's work brings out the rich, everyday aspects of this process, from the technical details to the biographical and cultural pressures that differ from hacker to hacker, to the climate of fear and suspicion under which any political activist—but especially those threatened with the additional crime of computer hacking—routinely operates.

Anonymous was political not only on its own terms, but in the context of a widespread re-emergence of social media activism. The social movements of Occupy, M15, the Orange Revolution in Ukraine, the Green Revolution in Iran, and the Arab Spring of 2011 were also, for the first time, associated with the Internet and social media, with claims legitimate and spurious for "revolution 2.0." Anonymous often overlapped with those engaged in these movements. Among the anthropologists to engage in the analysis of the nexus of technology and social movements are John Postill, with his work on the Spanish movement of May 15 (the "indignados") and Joan Donovan and her work on the communication infrastructure of the Occupy camps during the 2011–12 emergence of that movement; both scholars embraced these movements as field sites and as well, as moments of solidarity.

While Anonymous occupied the bright light of a full moon, in the waning crescent of light were derivatives of the Utopian hacker era: makers, hardware hackers, biohackers, bitcoin miners, data hackers, and others. "Hackerspaces" and "makerspaces" proliferated in this period, bringing a different set of interests and a largely novel physical expression, globally extensive, but largely restricted to the largest cities. This continued expression of the Free Software/ Open Source era also brought with it some increasingly vocal critiques of the utopian rhetoric, especially around the purported openness and inclusivity of those engaged. It was always apparent that Free Software's gender ratio was appalling, but the tenacity of this ratio only came to be well understood (or documented) slowly.

Christina Dunbar-Hester's work on collectives of geeks who make, break, and repair low-power FM radios stands as one of the most cogent and critical perspectives on hackers in this moment. The makers of Dunbar-Hester's ethnography–who were geeks involved in low-power FM radio—are sympathetically portrayed as activist, creative tinkerers and hackers intent on inclusivity and openness, even as the culture tends to reproduce the exclusions and inequalities of the world around it. Many other works from this period extended these observations and critiques around the world. Lilly Nguyen's recent work on Vietnam demonstrates a very particular aspect of globalization of new technologies by showing how Vietnamese users "jailbreak" their cellphones in an effort to be included in the circuits of capital, to literally get connected to the network of Apple consumers, and not as a transgressive or alternative "hack" of the technology.

At the same time, hacker/maker aesthetics and politics spread into many other areas, from education and science to fashion and art. A key locus of intense scholarly activity was the emergence of synthetic biology, biohacking, and "DIY Bio." Sophia Roosth, for instance, has captured aspects of the hybridization of Free Software/Open Source ideas and practices with work in biological engineering, in her work on the rise of synthetic biology.

The Internet of Everyday also introduced two new objects into everyday life at unprecedented scale: data and algorithms. New social science work has made data and algorithms central objects of scrutiny both for what they are and for how they reconfigure social and economic relations via their use on the Internet and in social media. "Algorithm" is a term which once had a restricted technical meaning as something like a recipe, but which now stands in for the way Internet-based platforms use the actions of users as a real-time stream of input data that determine what and how the technologies themselves respond to us and our actions. From Facebook's timeline, to Uber's surge pricing, to Twitter's trends, algorithms are making decisions constantly all around us; a fact that is unsurprising if one considers the engineering details of the Internet itself, but that now has significant implications for actions and meaning beyond the screen. Nick Seaver, for example, has studied how engineers create "recommendation algorithms" for music and other consumer goods, and how those algorithms mediate between a desire for objective measurement and the requirement of interpretation by both engineers and music lovers. Similarly, Bill Maurer and his students have peeled back the layers of the evolving payment systems that saturate our lives today and require an increasingly sophisticated interface with the Internet to function; to say nothing of their capacity for being hacked and exploited.

The Internet of Everyday began with the enthusiastic embrace of a participatory web filled with social media, new networks of protest, and a transformed meaning of what hackers are and can be. But by 2015 it had also revealed its dark side as well: Snowden's revelations of NSA and GCHQ spying on citizens; the ever-increasing series of breaches of private information demonstrated an infrastructure shoddily constructed and haphazardly maintained in the face of criminal, political, and state hacking. The revelation in 2010 of the StuxNet virus made plain that national actors had begun to engage in offensive hacking (in this case Israel and the United States hacking Iran), and that techniques for hacking physical infrastructure were now possible (in this case, hacking the "SCADA" control systems in a nuclear energy facility). Massive breaches (Target, Home Depot, Anthem, Yahoo, Sony PlayStation, eBay, etc.) became a regularly reported event; a market in "zero day" vulnerabilities (flaws in code that are sold on the black market before being fixed), cybersecurity insurance, and "vulnerabilities disclosure processes" (formal legal processes for governments to disclose what vulnerabilities they know about) all emerged into public consciousness as newly pressing problems.

As a fitting apotheosis of the era, the television series *Mr. Robot* appeared in 2015, with a complicated antihero as protagonist: Elliot Alderson is a politicized hacker (seen targeting and exposing a child pornographer in the pilot episode), suffering from mental illness which he self-medicates with Adderall and other drugs, some combination of which causes him to hallucinate his dead father. The show simultaneously harkens back to a previous phase of the hacker—the late '80s/early '90s hacker crews—as well as a more recent one in the fictionalized version of Anonymous (fsociety) that Eliot leads into ever-larger hacking attacks on the bluntly named Evil Corporation. Coming at the end of the Internet of Everyday it betokens another phase shift, and not necessarily a hopeful one.

The Utopian Kool-Aid of an earlier era revealed in this period, and in concrete terms, both the promise and the threats involved in the Internet and brought with it a clear impact on the global stage, not just economically but politically and emotionally as well. From the Occupy movement to the frightening growth of online abusiveness, the Internet of Everyday exemplifies a moment of participatory experimentation. Citizen journalism, citizen science, open government data mixed with the "lulz" and the protests of Anonymous, the new politics of leaking, and the reconfiguration of power to influence and delude via social media.

THE INTERNET OF SHIT (2016-)

PHASES OF THE HACKER (2016-)

Phase	Characteristics
WANING CRESCENT	Hacker as (leftist/radical) political actor; Anonymous, WikiLeaks.
WAXING GIBBOUS	The Hacker as information security researcher; hacking as exploring and exploiting; cybersecurity, warfare and statecraft; the Internet of Things and infrastructure hacking.
NEW	???

As I write this, under the new Trump administration, Congress has just passed legislation to remove what few consumer protections were in place to stop corporations from doing what we knew they were doing all along: spying on us and selling the details of our online lives to whoever wants them for the purpose (primarily) of advertising to us. A complicated, almost farcical series of events related to Russia and the "hack" of the presidential election has been unfolding for months. New infrastructure hacks of all sorts, involving especially the "Internet of Things," have introduced the possibility of everything from our cars to our toasters to our Amazon Echos being turned into unstable, insecure, physically dangerous spying devices. "Cyberwar" is once again on the lips of every defense contractor, state department employee, and diplomat. Donald Trump's victory is widely associated with a circus of characters including mega-billionaires like Robert Mercer (algorithmic finance genius and funder of Cambridge Analytica), white nationalists, established trolls-turned-nazis like "weev" (Andrew Auernheimer), and a complex network of far right-wing publications accused of creating a nearly impenetrable bubble of propaganda dubbed unhelpfully "fake news." Meanwhile, at home, parents struggle with their ever-increasing addiction to screens and how to help their children avoid the same.

This is the Internet of Shit. From a hopeful utopia of participatory making and a radical, political moment of transformation with Anonymous and Wiki-Leaks, we have turned a corner with the Democratic National Committee leaks and entered a new media ecology within which professional and amateur journalists vie to make good sense of and verify massive dumps of data: from the Panama Papers in 2016 to the DNC e-mails, in which political waters are turbulently rising on the left and the right, and the toxicity of the social media ecology is at an all-time high. WikiLeaks remains at the center of these new controversies, but its politics seem less certain, and the debate about leaking has become much more convoluted. As in the case of our own planet, humans appear to be on the road to ruining the Internet as well.

But maybe it's just a phase. In keeping with the metaphor, the Internet of Shit represents the return of a different kind of hacker: not the maker or the hacktivist so much as the hacker who explores, exploits, and *warns*. The hackers of the "hacker underground" in the 1980s and 1990s return here as "information security researchers," security administrators and architects, privacy advocates, cryptography experts, and so-called black-, white-, and gray-hat hackers. Such explorers represent a long-standing concern with the technical facts of connected life and the problem of helping people maintain both security and privacy. They are at once Cassandras and Samaritans, and if there is to be a different focus on hacking in the Internet of Shit, it is likely to be on figures of this sort, hopefully emerging opposite the increasingly formalized hacking of state military and security services, or the free-market mercenaries in the employ of the largest corporations. As an example consider the case of "Security without Borders"—a volunteer information security project focused on helping activists and journalists secure their information ecologies. This re-emergence tracks a number of events in recent years by which it has become clear just how much *private* surveillance has come to accompany the public surveillance of state actors. High-profile hacking cases like the Stratfor and HBGary hacks of LulzSec, and those of Phineas Phisher, have brought to light the routine private and state surveillance of activists, nongovernmental actors, journalists, and others around the world.

Anthropologists haven't been directly engaged with such issues to any significant degree. However, a range of work is particularly relevant here because it represents parallel developments in other areas. Work by Stephen Collier and Andrew Lakoff on "critical infrastructure preparedness," "vital systems security," infrastructure security, and global health surveillance all help contextualize some of the cultural transformations that are also clearly at work. As the Internet becomes a different problem of governance—not only medium, but vital infrastructure and political battlefield—our understandings of how expertise and participation crisscross its technologies and devices can learn from the work of anthropologists and geographers attuned to problems and challenges in other places, and other infrastructures.

THE NEXT HACK . . .

As the Internet and its vicissitudes infiltrate more and more of our physical, infrastructural, and emotional lives, it is fulfilling its promise as a *medium*, potentially enclosing and transforming our subjectivity in new ways. It is reorganizing our inner lives just as much as our social relations, and as such, problems of technical and engineering specificity blur with those of so-called ordinary life on the viewing/reading/swiping end of the Internet. Both ordinary users (for various values of ordinary) and "hackers" are trapped within an evolving ecosystem of political technologies for which there are neither obvious technical nor political choices.

Perhaps the key reason for anthropology to continue to pay attention to these issues, and what it can offer scholarship broadly, is an explanation of the tension between *expertise* and *participation*. Much of anthropological work concerns itself with this tension—from work on colonial and indigenous encounters and struggles to define legitimate knowledge to studies of biomedical experience and suffering, to work on secularism and religious experience. Expertise and participation are root categories for much of our work, dealing as they do with problems of how knowledge and power are related, how some forms of expertise are suppressed, delegitimated or passed over; and yet they are too often opposed to each other and too often reduced to other categories (like colonizer/colonized; settler/indigenous). Old-fashioned expertise too seems newly threatened, not just in the immediate sense of "alternative facts" in a post-truth era, but in the longer-term sense of a transformed relationship between scientific and technical authority and political decision making. In some cases, a return to a kind of technocracy seems inevitable, even desired; but in other cases an even more radicalized participatory politics seems equally likely.

The play of participation and expertise demands a revival of political theories of knowledge and democratic action that is suitable for making sense of all these cases. Understanding hackers and hacking is one possible way to do so. When seen as emblematic of a larger cultural problem (and not merely as examples of white, Western, male power), hacking reveals some tricky and difficult problems: to what extent do we desire expertise (of any sort) as a guide to political choices, and to what extent can we avoid the necessity of it? Do we have a clear understanding of how expert knowledge and political demands are adjudicated today? For it is no longer "discursive" in some pre-Internet sense, but constitutively technical and "hackerly" in its unfolding. The tactics, strategies, and changing forms of hacking give us a glimpse into not just one peculiar subculture, but into the very transformation of politics as practice today.

SUGGESTIONS FOR FURTHER READING

Amrute, S. 2016, *Encoding Race, Encoding Class: Indian IT Workers in Berlin*. Durham, NC: Duke University Press.

    Although not as well-known as the others, Biao's book is one of the few works to trace the intricate lives of Indian programmers as they migrate from Andhra Pradesh to Australia to Malaysia, while staying connected to the social relations in their home villages. Amrute's work updates the story to the lives of the Indian ex-pats in Berlin.

Biao, Xiang. 2007. *Global "Body Shopping": An Indian Labor System in the Information Technology Industry*. English. Princeton, NJ: Princeton University Press.

Boellstorff, Tom. 2008. *Coming of Age in Second Life: An Anthropologist Explores the Virtually Human*. Princeton, NJ: Princeton University Press.

    Coming of Age is an experiment in classic anthropology in the age of massively multiplayer online games and worlds. It captured the glory that was "Second Life" at its height and draws novel anthropological insights from the experience.

Burrell, Jenna. 2012. *Invisible Users: Youth in the Internet Cafes of Urban Ghana*. Cambridge MA: MIT Press.

Chan, Anita Say. 2014. *Networking Peripheries: Technological Futures and the Myth of Digital Universalism*. Cambridge, MA: MIT Press.

    The everyday life of information technology can be dramatically different around the globe. Burrell shows the life of the internet from Ghana, and how users there navigate globalization, scamming, and basic rights to communicate. Anita Chan's book explores the lives of hackers in Peru, and how their perspective on global capitalism reshapes the meaning of software making.

Coleman, E. Gabriella. 2014. *Hacker, Hoaxer, Whistleblower, Spy: The Many Faces of Anonymous*. London: Verso Books.

    If you want to know what it feels like to be a hacker, in all its gory details, and in a well-told compelling form, this is the book to start with. Coleman spent close to five years deep inside Anonymous—as a kind of gopher between the hackers and the journalists who wanted to know more about them. She chronicles the most important aspects of Anonymous's development from the inside and develops the notion of the hacker as a "trickster" from classic anthropological sources.

Dibbell, Julian. 1993. "A Rape in Cyberspace or How an Evil Clown, a Haitian Trickster Spirit,

Two Wizards, and a Cast of Dozens Turned a Database into a Society." *Village Voice*, December.

> One of the earliest accounts of the dynamics of online life, by a journalist-anthropologist and now lawyer Julian Dibbell. It recounts the way that social and political relations almost immediately reconstituted themselves—even in a bare-bones text-based chat game—despite the hope that it was a space in which people would "leave behind" such concerns.

Eubanks, V. 2018. *Automating Inequality: How High-Tech Tools Prole, Police, and Punish the Poor*. New York: St. Martin's Press.

> The Internet of Shit is already here: Virginia Eubanks documents how new technologies make being poor even worse than without them.

Levy, Steven. 1984. *Hackers: Heroes of the Computer Revolution*. English. Garden City, NY: Anchor Press/Doubleday.

Miller, Daniel, and Don Slater. 2001. *The Internet: An Ethnographic Approach*. Oxford: Berg.

> Daniel Miller and his collaborators have been relentless pioneers in the anthropology of the Internet. This book looks at 1990s experiences of the Internet in the Caribbean Islands of Trinidad and Tobago—much of what he uncovered there has been confirmed and strengthened by his later studies of social media around the world.

Sterling, Bruce. 1993. *The Hacker Crackdown: Law and Disorder on the Electronic Frontier*. English. Reprint edition. New York: Bantam.

> Anyone interested in the history of hacking will inevitably have to read these last three classics. Levy and Sterling form a pair—looking at different "phases" of hacking, the former in its more mainstream history at MIT, the latter among the "underground" of hackers in clubs like Lopht and Cult of the Dead Cow. Turkle's book was then and is still an essential corrective—drawing our attention to the emotional and social nature of being "obsessed with computers."

Turkle, Sherry. 2005. *The Second Self: Computers and the Human Spirit*. English. Twentieth Year Anniversary edition. Cambridge, MA: MIT Press.

Turner, Fred. 2010. *From Counterculture to Cyberculture: Stewart Brand, the Whole Earth Network, and the Rise of Digital Utopianism*. Chicago: University of Chicago Press.

> A history of how the counterculture became cyberculture and the surprising ways in which certain kinds of hippie communalism shaped the Silicon Valley we have today.

REFERENCES

Amrute, Sareeta. 2010. "Living and Praying in the Code: The Flexibility and Discipline of Indian Information Technology Workers (Iters) in a Global Economy." *Anthropological Quarterly* 83 (3): 519–50. George Washington University Institute for Ethnographic Research.

Ananny, Mike. 2016. "Toward an Ethics of Algorithms: Convening, Observation, Probability, and Timeliness." *Science, Technology, & Human Values* 41 (1): 93–117. Sage Publications, Sage, CA.:

Auray, Nicolas. 2003. "Communautés epistemiques d'innovation—La regulation de la connaissance: arbitrage sur la taille et gestion aux frontières dans la communauté Debian." *Revue d'économie politique* 113:161.

Bernal, Victoria. 2005. "Eritrea On-line: Diaspora, Cyberspace, and the Public Sphere." *American Ethnologist* 32 (4): 660–75. https://doi.org/10.1525/ae.2005.32.4.660.

Bloch, Ernst. 1986. *The Principle of Hope*. Oxford: Basil Blackwell.

Boellstorff, Tom, et al. 2012. *Ethnography and Virtual Worlds: A Handbook of Method*. Princeton, NJ: Princeton University Press.

Born, Georgina. 1995. *Rationalizing Culture: IRCAM, Boulez, and the Institutionalization of the Musical Avant-Garde*. Berkeley: University of California Press.

Broca, Sébastien. 2013. *Utopie du logiciel libre: Du bricolage informatique à la réinvention sociale*. Neuvy-en-Champagne: Éd. le Passager clandestin.

Burrell, Jenna. 2012. *Invisible Users: Youth in the Internet Cafés of Urban Ghana*. Acting with Technology. Cambridge, MA: MIT Press.

Chan, Anita. 2013. *Networking Peripheries: Technological Futures and the Myth of Digital Universalism*. Cambridge, MA: MIT Press.

Cherny, Lynn. 1999. *Conversation and Community: Chat in a Virtual World*. Stanford, CA: CSLI Publications.

Christen, Kimberly. 2006. "Tracking Properness: Repackaging Culture in a Remote Australian Town." *Cultural Anthropology* 21(3): 416–46. https://doi.org/10.1525/can.2006.21.3.416.

Coleman, E. Gabriella. 2004. "The Political Agnosticism of Free and Open Source Software and the Inadvertent Politics of Contrast." *Anthropological Quarterly* 77 (3): 507–19. http://www.jstor.org/stable/3318232.

———. 2009. "Code Is Speech: Legal Tinkering, Expertise, and Protest among Free and Open Source Software Developers." *Cultural Anthropology* 24 (3): 420–54.

———. 2012. *Coding Freedom: The Ethics and Aesthetics of Hacking*. Princeton, NJ: Princeton University Press.

———. 2014. *Hacker, Hoaxer, Whistleblower, Spy: The Many Faces of Anonymous*. New York: Verso Books.

Coleman, E. Gabriella, and Alex Golub. 2008. "Hacker Practice: Moral Genres and the Cultural Articulation of Liberalism." *Anthropological Theory* 8 (3): 255–77. https://doi.org/10.1177/1463499608093814.

Coleman, E. Gabriella, and Christopher M. Kelty, eds. 2017. "Limn Number 8: Hacks, Leaks, and Breaches." Vol. 1. 8. Limn. http://limn.it/issues/07.

Collier, Stephen J. 2008. "Enacting Catastrophe: Preparedness, Insurance, Budgetary Rationalization." *Economy and Society* 37 (2): 224. https://doi.org/10.1080/03085140801933280.

———. 2009. "Topologies of Power: Foucault's Analysis of Political Government beyond Governmentality." *Theory, Culture & Society* 26 (6): 78–108. Sage Publications.

Collier, Stephen J., and Andrew Lakoff. 2015. "Vital Systems Security: Reflexive Biopolitics and the Government of Emergency." Vol. 32. 2. https://doi.org/10.1177/0263276413510050.

Crawford, Kate. 2016. "Can an Algorithm Be Agonistic? Ten Scenes from Life in Calculated Publics." *Science, Technology, & Human Values* 41 (1): 77–92. Sage Publications.

Dibbell, Julian. 1993. "A Rape in Cyberspace or How an Evil Clown, a Haitian Trickster Spirit, Two Wizards, and a Cast of Dozens Turned a Database into a Society." *Village Voice*, December.

Donovan, Joan. 2015. "Technologies of Social Change: Mapping the Infrastructure of the Occupy Movement from #Occupywallstreet to #Occupysandy." PhD dissertation, University of California, San Diego.

Dreyfus, Hubert. 1999. *What Computers Still Can't Do: A Critique of Artificial Reason*, 6. Cambridge, MA: MIT Press.

Escobar, Arturo. 1994. "Welcome to Cyberia: Notes on the Anthropology of Cyberculture [and Comments and Reply]." *Current Anthropology* 35 (3): 211–31. https://doi.org/10 .2307/2744194.

Fischer, Michael M. J. 1999. "Worlding Cyberspace: Toward a Critical Ethnography in Time, Space, and Theory." In *Critical Anthropology Now: Unexpected Contexts, Shifting Constituencies, Changing Agendas*, ed. George E. Marcus, 245–304. School of American Research Press.

Freeman, Carla. 2000. *High Tech and High Heels in the Global Economy: Women, Work, and Pink-Collar Identities in the Caribbean*. Durham, NC: Duke University Press.

Gershon, Ilana. 2011. *The Breakup 2.0: Disconnecting over New Media*. Ithaca, NY: Cornell University Press.

Hayden, Cori. 2003. *When Nature Goes Public: The Making and Unmaking of Bioprospecting in Mexico*. Princeton, NJ: Princeton University Press.

Irani, Lilly. 2015. "Hackathons and the Making of Entrepreneurial Citizenship." *Science, Technology, & Human Values* 40 (5): 799–824. https://doi.org/10.1177/0162243915578486.

Ito, Mizuko. 2005. "Mobile Phones, Japanese Youth, and the Re-Placement of Social Contact." In *Mobile Communications*, 131–48. London: Springer.

Ito, Mizuko, et al. 2009. *Hanging Out, Messing Around, and Geeking Out: Kids Living and Learning with New Media*. Cambridge, MA: MIT Press.

Juris, Jeffrey. 2008. *Networking Futures: The Movements against Corporate Globalization*. Experimental Futures. Durham, NC: Duke University Press.

Kelty, Christopher M. 2008. *Two Bits: The Cultural Significance of Free Software*. Durham, NC: Duke University Press.

———. 2011. "The Morris Worm." *Limn* 1:17–19. http://limn.it/the-morris-worm/.

Lakoff, Andrew. 2008. "The Generic Biothreat, or, How We Became Unprepared." *Cultural Anthropology* 23 (3): 399–428. Blackwell Publishing. https://doi.org/10.1111/j.1548-1360 .2008.00013.x.

Levy, Steven. 1984. *Hackers: Heroes of the Computer Revolution*. Garden City, NY: Anchor Press/Doubleday.

Lindtner, Silvia. 2015. "Hacking with Chinese Characteristics." *Science, Technology, & Human Values* 40 (5): 854–79. https://doi.org/10.1177/0162243915590861.

Malamud, Carl. 1992. *Exploring the Internet: A Technical Travelogue*. Computer Networking. PTR. Englewood Cliffs, NJ: Prentice Hall.

Marcus, George E. 1995. "Ethnography in/of the World System: The Emergence of Multi-Sited Ethnography." *Annual Review of Anthropology* 24 (1): 95–117. Annual Reviews 4139 El Camino Way, P.O. Box 10139, Palo Alto, CA 94303-0139, USA:. https://doi.org/10.1146 /annurev.an.24.100195.000523.

Marres, N., & Gerlitz, C. 2016. "Interface Methods: Renegotiating Relations between Digital Social Research, STS and Sociology." *Sociological Review* 64 (1): 21–46. http://dx.doi .org/10.1111/1467-954X.12314.

Maurer, Bill, Taylor C. Nelms, and Lana Swartz. 2013. "'When Perhaps the Real Problem Is Money Itself!': The Practical Materiality of Bitcoin." *Social Semiotics* 23 (2): 261–77. https://doi.org/10.1080/10350330.2013.777594.

Miller, Daniel. 2011. *Tales from Facebook*. Cambridge: Wiley.

Miller, Daniel, and Don Slater. 2000. *The Internet: An Ethnographic Approach*. London: Berg.

Murillo Rosado, Luis Felipe. 2015. "Transnationality, Morality, and Politics of Computing Expertise." PhD thesis, University of California, Los Angeles.

Nguyen, Lilly. 2016. "Infrastructural Action in Vietnam: Inverting the Techno-Politics of Hacking in the Global South." *New Media & Society* 18 (4): 637–52. https://doi.org/10.1177/1461444816629475.

Ong, Aihwa, and Stephen J. Collier. 2004. *Global Assemblages: Technology, Politics, and Ethics as Anthropological Problems*. Malden, MA: Wiley-Blackwell.

Pfaffenberger, Bryan. 1996. "'If I Want It, It's Ok': Usenet and the (Outer) Limits of Free Speech." *Information Society* 12 (4): 365–86. Taylor & Francis.

Postill, John. 2014. "Democracy in an Age of Viral Reality: A Media Epidemiography of Spain's Indignados Movement." *Ethnography* 15 (1): 51–69. Sage Publications.

Raymond, Eric S. 1993. *The New Hacker's Dictionary*. Second edition. Cambridge, MA: MIT Press.

Riles, Annelise. 2000. *The Network Inside Out*. Ann Arbor: University of Michigan Press.

Roosth, Sophia. 2017. *Synthetic: How Life Got Made*. Chicago: University of Chicago Press.

Seaver, Nick. 2013. "Knowing Algorithms." *Media in Transition* 8:1–12.

———. 2015. "The Nice Thing about Context Is That Everyone Has It." *Media, Culture & Society* 37 (7): 1101–9. Sage Publications.

Stephenson, Neal. 1999. *In the Beginning . . . Was the Command Line*. New York: William Morrow.

Turkle, Sherry. 1984. *The Second Self: Computers and the Human Spirit*. New York: Simon & Schuster.

Turner, Fred. 2006. *From Counterculture to Cyberculture: Stewart Brand, the Whole Earth Network, and the Rise of Digital Utopianism*. Chicago: University of Chicago Press.

Weizenbaum, Joseph. 1976. *Computer Power and Human Reason: From Judgment to Calculation*. New York: W. H. Freeman.

Xiang, Biao. 2007. *Global "Body Shopping": An Indian Labor System in the Information Technology Industry*. Princeton, NJ: Princeton University Press.

Ziewitz, Malte. 2016. "Governing Algorithms: Myth, Mess, and Methods." *Science, Technology, & Human Values* 41 (1): 3–16. Sage Publications.

CHAPTER 15

THE PRACTICE OF HUMAN RIGHTS

Catherine Buerger and Richard Ashby Wilson

INTRODUCTION

Human rights are the rights every individual has by virtue of being human. Behind this simple formulation one encounters a vortex of complexity. Human rights are promulgated in international conventions and treaties, in the bills of rights of national constitutions, and even in city municipal codes. Historically, human rights were framed as constraints on the exercise of state power and what acts cannot be done to the individual (e.g., torture, detention without trial), but increasingly they establish positive responsibilities of state and international institutions (e.g., education, health care, a clean environment). Some human rights are legally enforceable by national or international justice institutions, but many are aspirational, and for the latter group, it is unclear who or what body has the duty to fulfill the right. Additionally, human-rights talk circulates outside of strictly legal and legislative contexts. Social movements campaigning for new rights and social justice have altered the very nature of what constitutes a human right. Like any other prominent political and legal ideal, human rights are also a site of fierce contestation and at times have been co-opted by politicians seeking to cloak their own narrow political and economic interests in the language of liberal democracy, individual autonomy, and the rule of law. One persuasive explanation of the global rise of human rights since the 1970s is their definitional slipperiness and their capacity to appeal to radically dissimilar political projects.

Human rights thus articulate a universal set of claims, but they are usually not universal in their application. Instead, the outcomes of struggles over human rights are often local, temporary, and limited. While doctrinally, human rights have an institutional orientation toward the nation-state, their influence is often more social and normative than legal or legislative, in that they shift cultural attitudes and moral norms rather than lead to definite political or legal victories. The social life of rights is a perfect subject for anthropological inquiry, and anthropologists are well placed to look beyond political science and legal scholarship to understand how the moral discourse of human rights overlaps with, but is not confined to, political institutions and the law. Anthropologists can also provide insights into how a political ideology created in the West in the crucible of the American, British, and French revolutions has come to have such a significant impact on decolonization and postcolonial politics in Africa, Asia, and Latin America, and how the conception of human rights has in turn been shaped by its global extension over the last half-century. Given their global perspective that integrates law and society, anthropologists have provided a deeper understanding of this universal language that announces that all persons possess inalienable rights because of their common humanity.

FROM "RIGHTS VS. CULTURE" TO "RIGHTS AS CULTURE"

The ability to see human rights as a practice that extends beyond human-rights law has been one of the most important contributions of anthropology to the study of human rights. But historically, the relationship between anthropologists and the study of human rights has been fraught. After the Second World War, in response to the Nazi Holocaust, there was increased enthusiasm in the idea of an international order that could create and uphold new universal standards and an abstract conception of humanity. This movement coalesced around the establishment of the United Nations in 1945 and in the convening of the Nuremberg Trials of 1946, the first multilateral international tribunal of its kind. Both institutions played a role in establishing a global sense of humanity and a standard of rights to which citizens of the world should be entitled.

In 1946, the UN's General Assembly officially began drafting an "international bill of rights" that all individuals around the world should ideally hold. As a part of its consultations, the United Nations Educational, Scientific, and Cultural Organization (UNESCO) asked the American Anthropological Association (AAA) for an advisory statement. In 1947, the Executive Board of the AAA, largely influenced by Melville Herskovits, submitted their now (in)famous "Statement on Human Rights" to the Commission on Human Rights, rejecting a system of universal values.

The AAA's statement begins with a predicament: The scientific study of human culture (aka, anthropology) has documented that individuals are "inextricably bound" to their societies, and that their lives and values are shaped by the groups of which they are members. Given this understanding of culture, how could a universal declaration on human rights ever truly account for global human diversity rather than simply being founded on Western conceptions of morals and values? The presumption that "the West" (even though some drafters were non-Westerners) could author a truly universal document is especially problematic, the statement comments, given the economic and military power of Western Europe and America along with their evangelizing religious traditions, which have led to Western values being imposed around the world. Therefore, to choose some values (inevitably, Western values) over others and deem them "universal" in a diverse world with varied beliefs would be to impose a new form of moral imperialism.

The "Statement on Human Rights" reflected the historical context of continued (although declining) worldwide colonial domination by "great powers" such as France and Britain as well as the dominant anthropological thinking in the United States. The founding father of modern cultural anthropology in the latter nation, Franz Boas, challenged the widely accepted evolutionary theories of the time. Evolutionism broadly asserted that all societies progressed in a linear fashion along a scale from the most "simple" to the most "complex," with each stage achieving a higher level of moral and societal improvement. In the context of the European colonialism of the time, this social evolutionism involved an explicit ranking of societies that reinforced the colonial project and a sense of Western superiority. In contrast, Boas argued that cultures are unique, with each having its own shared symbols, values, and practices that are dependent on their own particular histories and social environments.

The moral and political position adopted by anthropologists in response to the Universal Declaration of Human Rights is often referred to as "cultural relativism." The "Statement on Human Rights," exemplifies the stance of cultural relativism, suggesting that human rights are not universal. Instead, it argues that what is considered moral or immoral to a person is always relative to that individual's cultural situation. In other words, what is considered to be "right" and "wrong" will vary depending on the culture. As all cultures have diverse sets of beliefs and values, it is inappropriate to make judgements about which beliefs are morally correct or incorrect.

After the publication of the 1947 "Statement on Human Rights" there was little anthropological interest in the international system of human rights. However, in the 1980s, this began to change. Several influential articles were published focusing on human rights, and the AAA Executive Board created a Commission for Human Rights (later converted into a permanent Committee for Human Rights). Some anthropologists campaigned actively on behalf of indigenous peoples, and organizations such as Cultural Survival and the Independent Working Group on Indigenous Peoples became renowned advocates at the United Nations. In the 1990s, sociocultural anthropologists such as Sally Engle Merry and Richard Ashby Wilson moved beyond activism on behalf of indigenous people, on the one hand, and the formal universalism/relativism impasse, on the other, to study human-rights discourses and institutions as subjects of empirical and ethnographic inquiry.

In 1999, the AAA notably reversed its official position, stating its support of international human rights. The declaration stated that the field of anthropology should support the promotion and protection of "the right of people and peoples everywhere to the realization of their humanity, which is to say their capacity for culture." This statement grounded its argument in an understanding of culture and humanity as inextricably linked and therefore understood collective rights to culture as essential to the fulfillment of human dignity and rights.

Just as the 1947 statement reflected anthropologists' understanding of culture at the time, the 1999 statement demonstrated a sea-change in the discipline's conceptualization of culture. Whereas Boasian anthropology viewed cultures as unique, bounded, and relatively static groups with distinct cultural symbols and values, the theory of culture that inspired the 1999 statement conceived cultures as constructed and contested, unbounded and connected to global relations of power. These differing views of culture have implications for how anthropologists conceptualize the relationship between rights and culture. If cultures are viewed as bounded, unchanging, and defined by tradition, then the universalizing goals of human rights would likely present a threat to individual cultures. If, however, cultures are open, fluid, and contested and shaped by long-distance cultural flows and networks, then the human-rights framework becomes part of the global power dynamics that interact with individuals to shape beliefs, meaning, and identity.

The change in the conceptualization of "culture" has also led some anthropologists to develop new ways of thinking about the relationship between rights and culture. The 1947 Statement on Human Rights could be seen as focusing on the potential conflicts between human rights and culture. More recently, however, anthropologists have come to see the human-rights system as having a culture of its own. In the following section, we outline this important theoretical advancement.

RIGHTS TALK, RIGHTS TRANSLATION, AND THE PRACTICE OF HUMAN RIGHTS

In their identification of the human-rights system as a cultural system of its own, many anthropologists point to the fact that human-rights discourse possesses many of the same qualities that anthropologists identify as attributes of culture. The human-rights system compels particular forms of selfhood, requires specific forms of behavioral practice, and creates knowledge that is then disseminated around the world. This view of human rights is empirically rather than normatively driven, meaning that anthropologists are more interested in asking how individuals around the world use and understand international human rights than they are in debating whether universal human rights are possible or desirable.

One essential component of this theoretical understanding is the concept of "rights talk." Rights talk differs from human-rights law in that its focus is on how people speak about rights rather than what the law actually stipulates. Sometimes rights talk echoes the legal understanding of rights. Other times, however, rights talk may reflect a divergent or more expansive understanding of rights. These distinctive uses of human-rights language can potentially spark conflicts among those involved, and it is in closely examining these instances where anthropologists have demonstrated the constructed and contested nature of human rights.

The shift in focus among anthropologists from critiquing the normative concept of human rights to studying human-rights *practice* was largely empirically driven. The hallmark of anthropological research, the ethnographic method, places anthropologists in close contact with individuals around the world who are engaging with the international human-rights system, be it the European Court of Human Rights, the International Criminal Court, or the UN Human Rights Commission. At times, the experiences documented by anthropologists were germane to debates between cultural relativism and universalism, but more frequently, the picture that emerged of human rights in the world was far more nuanced and complicated. In the same way that legal anthropologists working in colonial Africa challenged the accepted thinking of the day that "law" must derive its authority from a central state power, anthropologists studying human rights quickly noted many instances where "human-rights talk" differed from official human-rights law. By focusing on how and why individuals used human rights in the way that they did, anthropologists were able to situate their understanding of this language of rights and dignity within a larger context of globalization and neoliberalism.

This focus on knowledge flows and other transnational processes followed a general trend within anthropology in the 1990s and early 2000s to turn attention to the process of globalization: how cultural notions circulate globally and what difference these exchanges of people and information make in the lives of individuals. The mid-1990s also brought a shift toward the creation of global justice mechanisms that shaped how anthropologists approached the study of rights. From the signing of the UN Declaration on Human Rights in 1948 until the early 1990s, international human-rights law had primarily been a utopian topic with little purchase outside of a small community of academic lawyers. The UN issued human-rights treaties related to topics such as women's rights, the rights of the child, and the elimination of racial discrimination, and these treaties were signed by states that had little intention of ever implementing them. At the time, human rights were primarily situated in the diplomatic realm, hollow rhetoric without any mechanisms of enforcement.

The end of the Cold War and the ethnocidal conflicts in the former Yugoslavia and Rwanda changed all that, bringing about several important events in the history of international human rights. First, the United Nations established two UN war crimes tribunals: one for the former Yugoslavia (ICTY, 1993) and one for Rwanda (ICTR, 1994). Second, there were more UN humanitarian missions in the 1990s than in the previous forty years, and in many cases, these were justified on human-rights grounds. Third, General Augusto Pinochet was arrested in London and placed under house arrest while the chief justice and then the British Law Lords considered the request for extradition by the Spanish magistrate Balthasar Garzón, who had issued an international arrest warrant for Pinochet on charges of torture. Pinochet was eventually released, but not before two important legal precedents had been created: the Spanish Audiencia Nacional court asserted that it had universal jurisdiction to try cases of genocide which had occurred to non-nationals outside of its territorial boundaries, and in Britain, it was ruled that a head of state could not claim immunity for acts such as torture that fell outside of the normal functions of a head of state. Finally, in Rome in 1998, 120 countries adopted the statute to set up an International Criminal Court that would have jurisdiction to try crimes against humanity, genocide, war crimes, and aggression in states that signed its statute. All of these events, along with the trajectory within the discipline of anthropology to study the transnational processes of cultural construction and contestation, proved fertile ground for the anthropological study of human-rights practice.

The concept of studying the "practice of human rights" takes an expansive view of the international human-rights framework. In addition to the actual legal instruments, it also includes the way in which individuals relate to the human-rights system: the way that they talk about it, criticize it, and attempt to use it to meet varying goals. It encompasses the individuals who take part in activities related to human rights including human-rights activists, lawyers, courtroom officials, staff members at international institutions, and so on. This understanding of human rights seeks not only to understand what the system of human rights *is*, but also how human-rights knowledge is produced and transmitted around the world. The concepts of human-rights talk, the practice of human rights, and human-rights vernacularization (which we discuss shortly) provide anthropologists with a unique set of analytical tools with which to better understand how human rights are encountered around the world. In the following two ethnographic examples, one from Ghana and one Guatemala, we illustrate how these concepts shed light on local human-rights practices.

The first example comes from Ghana. As one of the first African nations to gain its independence from colonialism, Ghana has long carried the distinction of being a model of African democracy. Today, the country is heralded around the world for its stability, prosperity, and democratic character, and Ghanaians often note with pride that Barack Obama called Ghana "a model for democracy." Much of this praise stems from the successful transition to democracy that Ghana experienced in the late 1990s. As a part of this transition, the country crafted a new constitution which outlines the "fundamental human rights and freedoms" of all Ghanaian citizens, incorporating many of the human rights described in international treaties and declarations into domestic law. Although human rights play an important role in Ghanaian democracy, there are also many other competing value systems and sources of authority including religion and the customary system of chieftaincy.

The negotiations between these different value systems were particularly apparent in the events surrounding the passing of new antidomestic violence legislation in 2004. The legislation was drafted by a Ghanaian women's rights organization, but was highly contentious. Those who were opposed to the bill complained that the human-rights language it employed was a foreign imposition and that this bill, which sought to move domestic issues out of communities and into courtrooms, would threaten the "traditional" Ghanaian manner of handling family issues. Although the clash over the Domestic Violence Bill was widely reported as a familiar battle between "culture" and "human rights," the anthropologists who studied the issue described a more nuanced situation. Saida Hodzic described how this law began to stand for larger nationalist goals. Although human-rights language was used strategically in the bill to attract support from transnational organizations working on women's human-rights issues, the Ghanaian government saw this network of international solidarity as an incursion. In response, and despite the varied opinions of the populace, government officials claimed to speak for "the people" in rejecting the bill on the grounds of Ghanaian "tradition." Hodzic argues that in the same way that human-rights discourse can add power to claims within the international community, the discourse of cultural sovereignty adds authority to the resistance to expanding rights.

Similar strategic use of discourses of human rights and tradition were documented by Catherine Buerger in her research on human-rights activism in an informal settlement in Accra, Ghana's capital city. Buerger noted that community activists often combined their human-rights claims with more conventional appeals to local chiefs, religious leaders, or political party officials. In one instance, a group of young activists attended a meeting with a government official to assert that their human rights had been violated by the government not meeting the community's sanitation needs. The activists' neighborhood lacked the plumbing required for running water and the installations of flushing toilets. Additionally, a large drainage ditch bisected the community and its poor condition posed a danger to the surrounding homes.

Neither the right to sanitation nor adequate housing are established in Ghana's constitution, but activists drew on their understanding of international human-rights law in their local rights talk. When their claims were met with hostility, however, the activists began addressing the official through language more often reserved for customary practices. "We see you as a father and a leader. You are from the same community as we are. We are prepared to write an apology if our conduct was inappropriate," one activist stated. The emphasis on themes such as apology and patriarchy by the activists signaled a switch away from the strategies commonly associated with human-rights advocacy. By reminding the official that they are from the same community and that they saw him as a father, the youth club was both making a conciliatory statement of respect and also attempting to appeal to the official's sense of community obligation. Despite the fact that some members from the human-rights NGO saw this move as a threat to the human-rights values at the center of the campaign, at no point during this process did the community activists stop seeing their movement as primarily a human-rights campaign. As in the example of the negotiations surrounding the Domestic Violence Bill, rather than focusing on the potential conflict between human rights and culture, focusing on human-rights practice allows anthropologists to identify how power relations come to play a role in the strategic employment of legal discourse. In the latter case, for example, alluding to a patriarchal relationship was not simply a passive acceptance of hierarchy; it was part of the advocacy strategy.

Sally Engle Merry's influential work on human-rights translation or "vernacularization" is useful in elucidating the internal dynamics of the Ghanaian case. Human-rights knowledge may be produced in an international setting, but it then moves to individual communities around the world. In the process, it is adapted to fit with local contexts, value systems, and priorities. As Merry's work outlined, this adaptation is undertaken by "translators," intermediaries who play a critical role in connecting the local with the global, making their goals and values intelligible to each other. Translators take on the task of presenting human-rights knowledge in cultural terms that are appealing to local communities. At the same time, they must frame the concerns of the community within the parameters of the international human-rights system to attract international funding and media attention.

In doing so, translators link local struggles with international networks of interested activists that assist community actors in pressuring their governments. In the case of the Ghanaian sanitation rights campaign, activists used the language of international human rights to frame their claim for improved sanitation, even though this was not one of the human rights explicitly outlined in their country's constitution. The rights discourse allowed them to appeal to an international community of activists and donors concerned with similar issues. At the same time, African activists incorporated more locally recognized notions of kinship obligations into their advocacy. Although somewhat controversial within the larger human-rights community, this strategy of vernacularizing human-rights talk made complete sense to the Ghanaian activists. As the following examples from Guatemala demonstrate, however, this process may also present additional challenges.

The Central American country of Guatemala was once the center of the Maya civilization and over the years, the country has drawn the interest of anthropologists due in part to its large indigenous majority (approximately 60 percent of the country's population) as well as to the high levels of political violence that it has experienced. In the late 1970s and early 1980s, a Marxist guerrilla insurgency incorporated a section of the Maya rural poor and was met with one of the most vicious counter-insurgency policies the Americas has ever seen. According to the UN's Commission for Historical Clarification, during Guatemala's thirty-six-year war, the military razed six hundred villages to the ground, killed up to 200,000 mostly indigenous civilian noncombatants, and forced 1 million people to become refugees.

Moral and cultural relativism seemed inappropriate to these circumstances and many anthropologists denounced the massive human-rights violations and the role of the US government in supporting successive military *juntas*. In denouncing state violence, anthropologists targeted US public opinion and sought to shift the direction of US foreign policy to end covert aid for violent and repressive regimes. As time went on, the focus of the work of anthropologists in Guatemala began to change perceptibly and assume an analytical distance from the mass atrocities. There were fewer direct narrative accounts from victims, and anthropologists began to ask more profound questions about the armed conflict and racial violence. Researchers went beyond denunciations of violations aimed at public opinion to attempting to explain the causes, motivations, experiences, and sociocultural consequences of human-rights violations.

In addition to the local instantiation of human-rights ideals, anthropologists working in Guatemala (and the larger Maya cultural region) also considered the cultural processes associated with the explicit translation of human-rights documents into local languages such as Maya-Q'eqchi'. Richard Ashby Wilson documents one instance where a workshop was convened to discuss the Global Human Rights Declaration that was signed between the Guatemalan government and the Revolutionary National Unity of Guatemala guerrillas. Urban Maya professionals associated with the national Academy of Mayan Languages had translated the document into Q'eqchi', one of the nearly twenty Mayan languages spoken in Guatemala. The workshop attendees, about 150 Q'eqchi' men and women from rural villages in the Alta Verapaz region of Guatemala, received human-rights training on the principles contained in the translated document. The character of this training was significantly determined by the difficult interpretative decisions made by those responsible for translating the document.

For example, as there is no word or phrase in Q'eqchi' that corresponds to a "government accord" or "international declaration," those who translated the United Nations Declaration of Human Rights chose the word *chakrab'* which literally means "law." But in the minds of local Maya-Q'eqchi' speakers, this word denotes the New Testament, which is termed the *Ak' Chakrab'* (literally, the "New Law"). In translating the term "human rights," the translators opted for a phrase (*xk'ulub'em li poyanam*) that means "what all people receive" or "what all people deserve." This phrasing connotes a largely passive reception of rights, as things that one receives from others rather than rights that one actively claims. More vigorous and dynamic possibilities do exist in Q'eqchi' such as *patz'om* ("that which is petitioned") or *titz'om* ("that which is demanded"). Therefore, a textual reading of the direct translation into Q'eqchi' conveys a sense that human rights were laws that carried strong Christian overtones about what one might passively deserve or receive from a benevolent authority.

Despite this rather conservative translation, Wilson's empirical research demonstrates the important role that history and political context play in the actual translation of human rights. Q'eqchi' actors returned to their communities and integrated concepts of human rights into their pre-existing strategy that emphasized petitioning the state and the international community on local development issues. As Rachel Sieder has argued, an active human-rights strategy allowed Maya activists to build connections with international indigenous rights organizations that supported their claims for self-determination. Elevating disputes from the local level to the international, or the "verticalization of conflict," presents both possibilities and obstacles for activists. Mayan activists used their connections with international human-rights organizations to appeal to a larger global advocacy network of indigenous rights activists. This increased the power of local groups in their negotiations with local regional and national state actors and agencies. At the same time, however, in appealing to generalized indigenous rights networks, activists had to portray their group's identity as being harmonious and united in goals, aspirations, beliefs, and practices. A static projection of identity conflicted with the ethnic, religious, and linguistic diversity of the Maya people as well as the dynamic nature of their communities. In this way, the transnational ideals of multiculturalism and indigenous rights both aided activists in reaching their goals and also constrained the possible forms of their activism.

As these examples illustrate, human-rights knowledge does not move between the halls of the United Nations and communities around the world unfettered. Instead, it is refashioned by power dynamics that privilege some voices over others. In Ghana, both "human rights" and "tradition" carry discursive weight, adding power to arguments framed within their parameters. In Guatemala, local activists were able to find support in the transnational community of indigenous rights activists, but only if they presented their claims in particular ways. These examples demonstrate the utility in looking beyond the familiar debate between cultural relativism and universal human rights, to appreciate how discourses of culture and human rights are used strategically by actors in efforts to establish the legitimacy of their claims within the larger political arena.

HUMAN-RIGHTS KNOWLEDGE: EVIDENCE AND INDICATORS

More recently, anthropological scholarship on human-rights culture and practice has turned its attention to the epistemological frameworks of human-rights law itself. This work concerns itself with the global institutions of human-rights accountability, and anthropologists have increasingly focused on courts and the metrics through which accountability is practiced and defined.

This inquiry has taken multiple forms. First, scholars have focused on the international human-rights institutions that emerged in the 1990s. As part of the disciplinary interest in transnational processes and the global production of knowledge, anthropologists shifted their fieldwork from the communities affected by conflict to the halls of international criminal tribunals, truth commissions, and other institutions of transitional justice. These international justice institutions, often developed in the aftermath of political violence, hold individuals accountable for human-rights violations or seek to reconcile the parties and provide an authoritative historical account of the conflict. Anthropologists such as Nigel Eltringham and Richard Ashby Wilson have sought to understand the way in which these institutions construct notions of "justice" and create meaning and knowledge about the origins and causes of violent ethnic and racial conflicts through their trials and hearings.

Anthropologists provide insights into the legal culture of human rights by inquiring into how exactly law knows what it knows about conflict and violence. Legal epistemology centers on the idea of "evidence." Prosecutors and defense attorneys present evidence in a trial regarding the actions and intentions of accused persons, and this evidence is circumscribed by rules of evidence and procedure that steer jurists away from both specialist and nonspecialist forms of knowing into a domain that is uniquely legal. Legal ways of knowing at international tribunals are distinctive in their predilection for documents over other forms of evidence and witnessing. Lawyers prefer documents as sources, and there exists a hierarchy of documents; primary documents are more dispositive than secondary documents, and documents produced by official governmental agencies carry more weight than unofficial ones. In construing documents as the solid basis for objective knowledge about a situation, international courts may overlook the degree to which documents are created by individuals and are therefore just as "subjective" and as historically and culturally contingent as other forms of evidence.

At times, then, it seems as if the law operates within a hermetically sealed textual universe of tightly controlled documentary evidence. Even though the law may officially endorse the scientific method, its ways of knowing diverge widely from science and epistemological realism. International criminal law's conceptions of causality and determination also diverge from those of science, social research, or history. For instance, the causal connections between two acts or events is a richly regulated area of legal inquiry, in which legal actors provide an account of the "chain of causation" that resulted in the crime, and based on these accounts the judges proceed to judgment and, if the accused is found guilty, sentencing. Criminal court judges demand that prosecutors prove linear connections that establish which acts caused which others (and become

"proximate" causes) beyond a reasonable doubt, a level of certainty that no social researcher would claim for their work. Judges also seek a particular kind of
knowledge about the subjective intentions of actors committing the said acts,
with a view to assigning criminal responsibility that corresponds to their level
of criminal intentionality (or *mens rea*).

Anthropologists and other social researchers are usually less concerned with
establishing causality and apportioning responsibility, and when they do see a
link between events, their assertions often acknowledge a greater level of uncertainty. The greatest disparity of all, however, lies in the degree to which social research recognizes multiple and interacting layers of causality and appre-
hends connections between events in a systemic and holistic manner. For social
researchers, it is the ensemble of conditions that are jointly sufficient to result
in an outcome, rather than one particular factor. Lawyers and judges are more
likely to radically pare down the context to isolate only the criminal act and
events that immediately preceded them. While this may be necessary to arrive
at a clear-cut determination of guilt, legal decontextualization comes at a price,
namely a balanced and comprehensive understanding of the conflict.

A related critique has emerged within the anthropological study of global
indicators. As defined by one UN expert body and cited by Sally Engle Merry,
indicators are "statistical measures that are used to summarize complex data
into a simple number or rank that is meaningful to policy makers and the public." Increasingly, governments and NGOs are relying on quantitative metrics
to inform policy decisions. This holds true within the human-rights sector as
well. Anthropologists have argued that the power given to statistical indicators
by governments is a new form of governance, one which relies on soft power
rather than physical force. This form of bureaucratic governance compels behavior by requiring countries to report and be evaluated on various issues,
then either shames or rewards countries as a result of their rankings on various
indicators.

When used at the international level, these metrics enable quick comparisons between countries on topics such as child mortality and literacy rates, as
well as more opaque values such as levels of rule of law, democracy, or freedom. In the same way that anthropologists have critiqued legal procedures for
oversimplification and decontextualization, they have also noted the way that
indicators create streamlined rankings at the cost of obscuring social realities,
which are inherently complex. By squeezing the world into categories, little
space is left for nuance. Anthropologists argue that indicators not only describe
existing conditions but also play a role in shaping social realities. Anthropologists argue further that critical attention must be paid to the use of quantitative
metrics as technocratic tools for global governance and how policy makers de-

cide what to count and what to ignore. For example, by choosing to rank countries on their levels of adherence to human-rights treaties, the values contained in these documents are given precedence over other values that may have relevance locally. As such, human-rights indicators have the dual powers to illuminate and obscure.

CONCLUSIONS

Anthropologists have had a significant impact on interdisciplinary conversations about human rights. At first this was to emphasize the importance of local cultures, but then anthropologists made a major contribution to the theorization of the globalization of human rights. The contribution of anthropology to understanding human rights lies in its documentation and analysis of their practical uses, and in highlighting the degree to which they create and reinforce a cultural matrix of moral norms, political actions, and social perceptions. Human rights promulgate a universal political charter but their meaning lies in their use by social actors, rather than in an abstract theoretical principle. Political and legal theorists may wax lyrical about the inherent, conceptual meanings of rights, but anthropologists provide key insights into how they are contested and instantiated in a variety of real-world settings, and they document their varied (and sometimes unintended) consequences. Thus, as an empirical social research discipline, anthropologists study the social life of rights, understood as the daily political uses to which human-rights discourses and practices are put and the type of knowledge regime they imply.

Anthropological studies inject a much-needed dose of realism into the utopian aspirations of jurisprudence and human-rights activism. They enhance our understanding of the ways in which human-rights movements have resulted in real advancements in social well-being and protections for vulnerable populations, as well as how, like many other policy campaigns, they have failed to attain many of their goals.

SUGGESTIONS FOR FURTHER READING AND REFERENCES

Allen, Lori. 2013. *The Rise and Fall of Human Rights: Cynicism and Politics in Occupied Palestine*. Stanford, CA: Stanford University Press.

   An ethnographic study of Palestinian human-rights campaigns since 1979, illustrating the failed promise of human rights, which became a Western donor-controlled industry instead of a means of popular struggle against the Israeli occupation.

Boas, Franz. 1920. "The Methods of Ethnology." *American Anthropologist* 22 (4): 311–21.

Buerger, Catherine. 2017. "Legal Borderlands: Ghanaian Human Rights Advocacy between the Layers of Law." In *Human Rights Encounter Legal Pluralism*, ed. Eva Brems, Mark Goodale, and Giselle Corradi. Oxford: Hart Publishers.

Cowan, Jane K., Marie-Bènèdicte Dembour, and Richard A. Wilson, eds. 2001. *Culture and Rights: Anthropological Perspectives*. Cambridge: Cambridge University Press.

Systematically reviews the relationship between human rights and culture in anthropology, addresses the universalism vs. relativism debate and demonstrates the various ways in which the concept of culture has been instantiated empirically in human-rights campaigns.

Eltringham, Nigel. 2013. "'Illuminating the Broader Context': Anthropological and Historical Knowledge at the International Criminal Tribunal for Rwanda." *Journal of the Royal Anthropological Institute* 19 (2): 338-55.

Goodale, Mark, and Sally Engle Merry, eds. 2007. *The Practice of Human Rights: Tracking Law between the Global and the Local*. Cambridge: Cambridge University Press.

Examines human rights in practice in a number of political and legal settings around the world, from the Zapatistas of Mexico to customary law in Swaziland, with a focus on the discursive and social aspects of human rights.

Herskovits, Melville. 1947. Statement on Human Rights: American Anthropological Association Executive Board. *American Anthropologist* 49 (4): 539-43.

Hodzic, Saida. 2009. "Unsettling Power: Domestic Violence, Gender Politics, and Struggles over Sovereignty in Ghana." *Ethnos* 74 (3): 331-60.

Merry, Sally Engle. 1997. "Legal Pluralism and Transnational Culture." In Richard A. Wilson ed., *Human Rights, Culture and Context: Anthropological Perspectives*. London: Pluto Press.

———. 2006. *Human Rights and Gender Violence: Translating International Law into Local Justice*. Chicago: University of Chicago Press.

Merry, Sally Engle, Kevin Davis, and Benedict Kingsbury, eds. 2015. *The Quiet Power of Indicators: Measuring Governance, Corruption, and Rule of Law*. Cambridge: Cambridge University Press.

Examines the production, deployment, and contestation of global indicators by international organizations such as the World Bank through case studies, including indicators of human rights, rule of law, and political freedom, and argues that indicators exercise power as "technologies of governance."

Sieder, Rachel. 2011. "Contested Sovereignties: Indigenous Law, Violence and State Effects in Postwar Guatemala." *Critique of Anthropology* 31 (3): 161-84.

Wilson, Richard A., ed. 1997. *Human Rights, Culture and Context: Anthropological Perspectives*. London: Pluto Press.

———, ed. 2001. *The Politics of Truth and Reconciliation in South Africa: Legitimizing the Post-Apartheid State*. Cambridge: Cambridge University Press.

Documents and analyzes the operations of the South African Truth and Reconciliation Commission, illustrating how it sought to manufacture legitimacy for the new post-apartheid regime and neglected to address the demands of victims and profound tensions around race and socioeconomic distribution in South African society.

———. 2008. "Making Human Rights Meaningful for Mayas: Reflections on Culture, Rights and Power." In *Human Rights in the Maya Region: Global Politics, Cultural Contentions, and Moral Engagements*, ed. Pedro Pitarch, Shannon Speed, and Xochitl Leyva Solano, 305-21. Durham, NC: Duke University Press.

———. 2016. "Experts on Trial: Social Science Evidence at International Criminal Tribunals." *American Ethnologist* 43 (4): 730-44, November.

CHAPTER 16

ANTHROPOLOGY AND THE RIGHT TO SELF-DETERMINATION OF FOREST PEOPLES

Marcus Colchester and Tom Griffiths

INTRODUCTION

It is estimated that two-thirds of the world's 6,700 languages are spoken by peoples now referred to in international law as "indigenous peoples." The traditional subjects of anthropological investigations, these peoples continue to suffer persistent discrimination and abuse of their rights, which threaten their physical and cultural survival. One careful review classes some 3,200 of these languages as endangered, noting that about 460 of them are now spoken by less than ten persons each. These stark figures are symptoms of a much deeper set of problems facing such marginalized social groups, who confront simultaneous threats to their lands and livelihoods both from extractive models of development and exclusionary conservation. Yet these same peoples' customary lands cover some of the most valuable and biodiverse ecosystems of the world, including a large proportion of the world's remaining forests.

As roads, dams, loggers, oilmen, miners, planters, colonists, and cash croppers push their way into the frontier areas that are these peoples' territories, the latter's futures are increasingly at risk. According to World Bank and UN Food and Agriculture Organization statistics, some 1.5 billion people still depend on forests for their daily livelihoods and they make up no less than half of the world's very poor.

7 50 - 8 87(c "Forests" are a legal class of lands originally conceived during the Carolingian Empire as royal hunting reserves set aside for the sport of kings and administered by forestry officials subject to special forestry laws with their own courts and jurisdictions. Forestry laws in Europe evolved to heavily curtail the customary rights of local people, restricting their rights of use and access and preventing livelihood activities without permits. As royal power extended, forests came to embrace ever-larger parts of feudal domains. By the time of King Henry II about a quarter of England was defined as "forest"—although maybe only half of this area was actually wooded—and popular resentment against the forestry laws grew proportionally.

"Scientific Forestry" was redefined in the eighteenth century as a state duty to achieve "sustainable forest management." States gradually sharpened forestry laws to further regulate and limit communities' use of forests, while giving preferential access to timber to commercial forestry companies linked to economically strategic enterprises such as shipping, mining, and, later, railway construction. As these resource extraction and management practices extended into colonial territories, in what are now referred to as developing countries, forestry laws became increasingly restrictive. Native peoples' rights to their lands and forests were heavily curtailed and even extinguished. Traditional systems of forest farming, through rotational clearance and forest fallows, were decried as destructive "slash and burn" and banned for posing a threat to timber businesses, while customary hunting was criminalized as "poaching" and a threat to sport hunting and, later, wildlife conservation. Yet despite, or rather because of, this collusive alliance between state forestry bureaucracies and commercial extraction in the name of sustainability, global forest cover has diminished by half since the 1950s.

Forest peoples thus face multiple threats to their existence. Discriminated against as "backward" peoples ill-suited to be productive members of modern states, deprived of rights to their lands and forests by national land and forestry laws, yet they are under intense pressure from corporations given access to their lands in the "national interest" and from conservation and climate mitigation programs, which now seek to control forests for the global good.

INDIGENOUS RIGHTS IN INTERNATIONAL LAW

Despite this extremely challenging and in many places worsening context, international law and policies on indigenous peoples have improved dramatically in recent decades, providing a much more hopeful framework to redress these historical and continuing injustices. Since 1977, when the American Indian Movement sought access to the Decolonization Committee of the UN to seek help in renegotiating their treaty-based relations with the United States of America, there has been an almost permanent presence of indigenous peoples at the UN.

Under the UN framework, human-rights laws seek to reconcile two key principles of international law: that states have a sovereign right to control their own affairs — a notion that historians trace back to the Treaty of Westphalia — and that governments' legitimacy to rule should derive from the "consent of the governed," based on the language of the American Declaration of Independence. The latter principle underpinned President Woodrow Wilson's justification for America's entry into the First World War and was reaffirmed in the Atlantic Alliance, which led to the defeat of Nazism in the Second World War. In reaction to the horrors of genocide and in recognition that state sovereignty should offer no hiding place to crimes against humanity, the UN Charter thus affirms the principle that all peoples have the right to self-determination.

The right to self-determination was more firmly established as a foundational principle of human-rights law when it was articulated in common Article One of the International Covenant on Civil and Political Rights and the International Covenant on Economic Social and Cultural Rights in 1966. This gave prominence to the collective rights of peoples albeit within a legal framework that, by and large and initially, was concerned with affirming the rights of individuals in their relations to states.

Indeed, at the time the Universal Declaration of Human Rights was adopted in 1948 (three years after the UN Charter), the principle of collective rights was submerged. This led to protests by the American Anthropological Association that the declaration was excessively based on Western notions of individual rights and did not provide adequate scope for tolerance of peoples with different social and cultural norms. However, after the International Covenants were adopted, which reaffirmed the principle of self-determination of peoples, anthropologists began to reappraise their views about the human-rights framework, realizing that it could be used to protect the rights of culturally distinctive peoples against the violence, discrimination, or indifference of states.

A notable expression of this changing point of view was the Declaration of Barbados in 1971. The declaration, which derived from a meeting sponsored by the World Council of Churches and the Ethnology Department of the University of Berne, called on anthropologists and others to support the liberation of the "Indians" of the Americas. It also enjoined states and missionaries to respect these peoples' customs and moral orders, their rights to their lands and territories and to self-governance, to enjoy equal rights to other citizens, and to end discriminatory practices designed to force these peoples to adopt religions and ways of life against their will. The Declaration of Barbados affirmed the role of the peoples themselves to achieve their own liberation. It directly gave rise to the founding of the International Work Group for Indigenous Affairs the same year and impelled the human-rights organization Survival International to make self-determination a central principle of its work.

Since the 1970s, as a result of indigenous peoples' own mobilization, with the notable support of nongovernmental organizations, Nordic governments, and applied anthropologists, there has been a marked reframing of international human-rights law, within the confines of its founding principles. This reframing took place through two parallel processes: first, through indigenous participation in the standard-setting committees under the (former) UN Human Rights Commission; second, through the evolution of jurisprudence at the UN treaty bodies which oversee, and make recommendations on, the application of conventions by member states.

The results were dual: the adoption of the UN Declaration on the Rights of Indigenous Peoples in 2007 and the emergence of a substantial body of law which details how these rights should be respected and protected in practice, and how remedies should be made in the case of violations. It is now accepted that indigenous peoples enjoy the same right to self-determination as all other peoples (albeit within the framework of nation-states); and that they have collective rights to their lands and territories, to self-governance, to exercise their customary law, to represent themselves through their own institutions, and to give or withhold their free, prior, and informed consent to measures that may affect their rights. The challenge remains: making respect for these rights effective in practice.

FOREST PEOPLES PROGRAMME: HISTORY, AIMS, AND MODES OF WORK

The Forest Peoples Programme (FPP), set up in 1990 to champion the rights of "forest peoples," is an international human-rights organization with consultative status at the United Nations, which now has a staff of some fifty-two. It works on the ground through partnerships with local NGOs and community-based organizations in about twenty-two countries in Latin America, Central and East Africa, and South and Southeast Asia. The organization employs a wide variety of people including a number of anthropologists, as well as human-rights lawyers, geographers, and environmental scientists, who seek to apply the skills and lessons they have learned in academia and legal practice in service to these beleaguered peoples. The FPP team strives to follow a grounded "bottom-up" approach in full respect of the wishes and decisions of the communities, their representative leaders and organizations and freely chosen spokespersons.

The organization was initially created in order to link the NGOs that founded the World Rainforest Movement (WRM) to the indigenous peoples whose rights they sought to defend. In the mid-1980s a number of international organizations and activists had met at two conferences hosted by the local chapter of Friends of the Earth, Sahabat Alam Malaysia, in Penang. After reviewing the underlying crisis facing tropical forests and the top-down model of imposed development being promoted by international financial institutions and global trade, a group of participants decided to work in alliance to promote an alternative approach to forests based on respect for forest peoples' rights to their lands and ways of life, setting out their vision in the Penang Declaration. The Forest Peoples Programme was then set up to link these activists to the wider movement of indigenous and other forest peoples. Its key aim was to ensure that international advocacy to curb rainforest destruction was supportive of these peoples' right to self-determination.

Two early achievements of FPP immediately had a global effect. The first was creating the context for the emergence of the International Alliance of Indigenous and Tribal Peoples of the Tropical Forests, who then set out their own charter; its demands had a notable influence on the outcomes of the Rio Summit. The second was the publication of a damning critique of the World Bank, United Nations Development Programme, and Food and Agriculture Organization's *Tropical Forestry Action Plan*. This led to the G-7 summit calling for the program to be revamped and then a series of meeting to carry this out. In retrospect the two interventions and ensuing advocacy reshaped international forest policy making so much that it is now the norm for global debates about forests to include forest peoples' representatives; seek to ensure respect for their rights, and acknowledge that solutions to the problem of deforestation should build on their knowledge and initiatives and provide them with secure tenure. Getting these principles to apply on the ground has proven a harder challenge, however.

FPP provides direct support to forest peoples on the ground in South America, Central Africa, and Southeast Asia. It also helps indigenous peoples to engage in international policy forums including with the World Bank, the various UN bodies addressing forests, and the European Commission. This has ensured these bodies have adopted guidelines and "safeguard policies" that, to some degree at least, respect indigenous peoples' rights. The thematic work on indigenous peoples of both the World Commission on Dams and the Extractive Industries Review was led by FPP. By convening hearings of indigenous peoples' testimony, compiling detailed reports, FPP and local partners were able to persuade both to adopt the principle that indigenous peoples' customary lands should not be taken over by dams and mines without the peoples' free, prior, and informed consent (FPIC). Parallel advocacy ensured that similar standards were adopted by the emerging voluntary standards for the certification of commodities such as timber, pulpwood, palm oil, beef, and soya; FPP also helped indigenous peoples engage with global conservation agencies to reform protected area policies. Today, thanks to the combined efforts of indigenous peoples and supportive organizations such as FPP, almost all the major development agencies, conservation organizations, and commodity certification systems have adopted policies which claim to uphold indigenous peoples' rights. Increasingly, the work of FPP focuses on putting these principles into practice, which means working with impacted communities to help them hold states, international development and conservation agencies, and corporations to account against the laws, policies, and principles that they now endorse.

ABORIGINAL TITLE

When the European colonial powers began to compete for control of the lands of native peoples, they were forced to develop legal arguments to justify their usurpations. Colonial possessions, it was agreed among Europeans, were legitimate prizes when acquired by conquest or "discovery." However, these dubious doctrines, while they may have sufficed in European minds to assert the transfer of sovereignty, nevertheless left uncertain how colonial enterprises or colonists were to acquire the native peoples' lands. Two main legal opinions were thus developed. One, the doctrine of *terra nullius*, was to assert that native peoples, who left their land unimproved and had no discernible permanent settlements or authorities, had no rights in their lands. The problem with this approach was that it led to disputes, first with the native peoples themselves but then among the settlers, who thus lacked a means of demonstrating they had acquired rights in land from the natives. Early on in the colonial process, agreement was soon reached on an alternative doctrine which ruled that indeed most native peoples did have rights to their properties, which they could surrender by treaty or sale. Armed with an agreement of cession of land, settlers could then demonstrate the validity of their own property to competing interests. In North America, the Royal Proclamation of 1763 extended this property right to all the hunting grounds of all the native peoples west of the Appalachians and Alleghenies.

Confusions of course remained. In which native persons or institutions were these land rights vested? From what authority did their rights derive? What was the extent of any one person or group's lands? Which indigenous authority could rightfully transfer these properties? Which colonial or state institution or person could rightfully receive them? These legal questions remain relevant to this day but thanks to centuries of litigation and lawmaking the normative framework is now somewhat clearer.

Indigenous peoples, as they are now known, have rights in their lands based on custom. These rights obtain so long as the peoples concerned maintain their connections with their lands, either physically or through cultural association; and so long as they have not been extinguished by due legal process. Moreover, these rights, being derived from customary ownership, occupation, or other use, do not depend on any act of the state, which indeed they very often precede. This legal doctrine, sometimes also referred to as "aboriginal rights" or "native title," gradually emerged in countries with English Common Law jurisdictions. It has now been adopted into international human-rights law, including in the UN Declaration on the Rights of Indigenous Peoples.

Proving to the satisfaction of the courts that a people or community does indeed have customary rights in land is, however, a burdensome requirement. Because courts have tended to prefer written "proof" over oral testimony, indigenous peoples suing for their rights have often called on anthropologists to submit evidence on their behalf, which many have done effectively, although not without some careful re-arranging of the ethnographic data to suit the procrustean concepts of the legal process. Three examples of FPP's anthropologically informed work illustrate these challenges.

SARAMAKA PEOPLE VS. SURINAME

One case concerns the Saramaka people of Suriname, descendants of runaway African slaves who re-created forest-based livelihoods in the interior of the country. During the seventeenth and eighteenth centuries, the Dutch colonial authorities had signed treaties with the Saramaka, and other "Maroon" peoples, in which it was agreed that they should enjoy autonomy in their customary areas on the middle rivers. In exchange they agreed not to raid the sugar plantations along the coast for women or for tools and other goods. Instead the Dutch set up posts on Saramaka lands to trade forest products for the goods they needed.

Suriname's economy has historically centered on the development of sugar plantations along the coast. This has resulted in more than 90 percent of the population residing along a narrow coastal strip, with the forested interior left to the Amerindian and Maroon peoples, who now make up some 25 percent of the national population, many having also migrated to the coast. However, between the 1960s and 1990s, the Dutch and then the newly independent Republic of Suriname promoted large-scale hydropower, mining, and logging operations on the lands of the Saramaka without taking any account of their rights. After appeals by the Saramaka for consideration of their rights were ignored, in 1999 they requested FPP's senior lawyer, Fergus MacKay, to sue the republic for recognition of their rights under the American Convention on Human Rights, to which Suriname is a signatory.

The case took seven years to wind its way through the Inter-American Human Rights Commission, to the Inter-American Court of Human Rights, and so finally to adjudication. In the process the plaintiffs had first to satisfy the requirement that they had "exhausted domestic remedies," that is, they had tried all legal options within Suriname. This was relatively easily proved, as the government, in seeking to have the case dismissed, baldly asserted that the Saramaka had no rights to land under Suriname law.

Proving that the Saramaka do maintain customary connections with their territories was achieved through legal argument, affidavits, and oral testimony in front of judges in the court in San Jose, Costa Rica, and drawing on witness statements of the American anthropologist of the Saramaka, Richard Price. Maps and photographs made by the geographer Peter Poole explained through testimony to the court, demonstrated unambiguously that the logging and mining concessions were undoubtedly within Saramaka territory.

Saramaka People v. Suriname has become a celebrated case in international human-rights jurisprudence; it substantially advanced legal understanding of the basis for forest peoples' rights in land; and it clarified which institutions should exercise rights both to land and, in their dealing with government, to give or withhold their free, prior, and informed consent to operations on their land. The rulings affirmed that the Saramaka, while not originally indigenous to Suriname, as a tribal people with customary rights to their lands should enjoy the same rights and protections under Inter-American law as indigenous peoples. Based on their customs, they have collective rights in land derived from a conjoint reading under the American Convention on Human Rights of their rights to self-determination and to property, as well as the right to collective legal personality as a people. The case determined that Suriname has a legal obligation to respect and protect these rights. It has to pass laws and issue titles to secure Saramaka lands; it has to suspend logging operations in these areas and it has to cease further exploitation of these lands without the free, prior, and informed consent of the Saramaka.

The Government of Suriname sought to overturn this judgment. It asked for a clarification and argued that the *granman*, the Saramaka headman, had consented to the logging. Further anthropological and community testimony was submitted which proved to the satisfaction of the court that the Saramaka have a matrilineal system of inheritance, vest their lands in matrilineal clans, *lo*, and it is therefore the respective *lo* who must give or withhold consent to operations on their lands, not the *granman*. The case has been widely invoked in subsequent judgments, including in the courts in Belize and the Caribbean Court of Justice, which upheld the rights of the Toledo Maya to their lands; and at the African Commission on Human and Peoples' Rights, which upheld the rights of the pastoral Endorois people of Kenya to restitution of their lands from which they had been unlawfully expelled to make way for a national park.

WAPICHAN TERRITORIAL CLAIM IN GUYANA

The Wapichan people in Guyana, South America, have long sought to obtain legal title over their territory covering the rainforest, montane forests, savannah grasslands, wetlands, and dry tropical woodlands in the southwest of the country. In 1976 and 1991 they received titles to a fraction of their land over discontinuous and fragmented areas of forest and savannah around some (though not all) of their villages. However, more than three-quarters of Wapichan land in Guyana remained untitled and vulnerable to government sale or lease to outsider logging, mining, and industrial agribusiness interests. As a result, the Wapichan have suffered repeated land invasions by illegal miners, while "legal" mining and logging concessions have been imposed on parts of their customary untitled lands without their knowledge or prior consent.

In the 1990s, energetic village leaders (known locally as *toshaos*) stepped up community-driven efforts to re-energize the long-standing Wapichan land claim. They engaged in community mapping, action research, and land-use planning projects involving residents and leaders from all the main villages and smaller settlements across the territory. Mobilization involved setting up a community-based organization to implement collective community health and education projects alongside land rights work. This local organization, legally registered as the South Central Peoples Development Association (SCPDA), is run and staffed by local people born and educated in the villages. It serves as a project-implementing organization for Village Councils and the South Rupununi District Council (SRDC), which is the collective representative body for all the communities.

Actions included community outreach to international allies like FPP and

Local Earth Observation (LEO) in order to enable Wapichan access to technical knowhow and funding for their grassroots work. Initial efforts involved training a local mapping team to use hand-held GPS units, map traditional land use, and document cultural meanings attached to the landscape. Work also included the training of one computer-literate Wapichan mapper in GIS software. After several years of fieldwork and extensive mapping trips in the rainforest and savannah, local mappers collected more than forty thousand geo-tagged GPS points alongside detailed records made in field log books. Once the final draft territorial map was completed, it was validated through collective discussions with local land users in multiple workshops and public meetings involving elders, women, youths, farmers, Wapichan ranchers, craftspeople, huntsmen, and fishermen.

In parallel with the mapping project, in 2005–6, a community-selected team undertook action research on their traditional land tenure arrangements and natural resource use. The Wapichan team used "insider research" (as Tuhiwai-Smith calls it) to document customary institutions for organizing tenure and land use as well as beliefs, people's own theories, and customary law on "sensible" use of the land. Information on the collective attachment of communities to their territory was also documented. Again, the draft findings were validated by the authors through community discussions. Copies of the final research report were returned to all communities and the findings were presented in primary and secondary schools in Wapichan territory by SCPDA teams, which stirred much interest and enthusiasm among the school students in their land and culture.

In 2008–11 the SRDC and SCPDA organized and successfully completed collective land-use planning with all the villages to draw up their own vision and plan for their territory and self-determined development. With additional training of more local teams and multiple "write workshops" facilitated by FPP, the action involved over eighty community consultations and collective validation of the final plan by representatives (women, elders, youths) from all the villages. During 2012–14 Wapichan toshaos, councillors, and SCPDA team members presented their plan and digital territorial map to national authorities and land administration bodies in the capital, Georgetown. In 2013–16, the work was further consolidated through participatory approaches to community-based land and forest monitoring. This involved local monitors, trained by FPP with international allies like Digital Democracy, building and using drones and smart phone technology to report land encroachment and violations of human rights.

The Wapichan people's innovative grassroots work, calling for secure land rights and seeking recognition for a 1.4 million hectare Wapichan Conserved Forest, has been shared widely by community leaders with international organizations and UN forums. This has included engaging with government parties and other indigenous peoples' organizations participating in the Convention on Biological Diversity (CBD). As a result, at the Paris Climate summit in 2015, SCPDA and SRDC were awarded the prestigious UN Equator Prize for their work on land rights and forests.

Crucially, the work has led to formal talks with the State of Guyana on the land claim. These started in 2016 and are ongoing in 2018. Major gains so far include formal recognition of the Wapichan digital map and their community studies as part of the evidence to be used in the land settlement process. In 2017 the Wapichan also realized a key vision set out in their territorial plan in securing a government agreement to allow teaching of the Wapichan language in their schools. Mapping, community monitoring and action research have all strengthened collective organization and unity in support of land rights and community development work. The young mappers trained twenty years ago are now elected community toshaos and are active members of the land talks. The indigenous cartographer has continued to teach himself the intricacies of the GIS tool and is able to compile and print off bespoke maps for village councils.

Essential positive elements to success have been long-term and sustained engagement coupled with the use of a multilingual approach to all the work. In the field, most activities are conducted in the Wapichan language. This approach has ensured inclusiveness and bolstered the use of the language among younger people. In all of this, anthropologists working with FPP and other allied organizations have played an enabling and accompanying role. They have respected local decisions and approaches and have built local capacity to undertake "endogenous" research by and for the communities. This has proved empowering and opened important political space for the Wapichan locally and globally.

STOPPING THE PALM OIL JUGGERNAUT

The African oil palm has been a staple crop in West and Central Africa for several thousand years. In the late nineteenth century palm oil began to be traded to Europe and early in the twentieth century plantations of the crop were given trial in Southeast Asia. In the 1970s and 1980s, the World Bank provided numerous loans to the Indonesian government to establish plantations in Sumatra and Kalimantan, thereby reinforcing a colonial model of development by which indigenous peoples' lands were expropriated in exchange for nugatory payments to allow the expansion of capitalist enterprises.

Runaway demand for cheap cooking oil in global markets has led to oil palm plantations extending over 12 million hectares of Indonesia. Their extent will most likely double again by 2030. They have spawned thousands of land conflicts and caused a global controversy as the main driver of deforestation and peat-swamp drainage in the region. Forest loss and peatland drying, plus associated wildfires, have made Indonesia into one of the world's highest per capita emitters of greenhouse gases. Communities who resist expropriation have frequently faced repressive actions by local security forces, often paid for by the companies, with cases of beatings, mutilations, and even killings being all too common. Since national laws only weakly recognize indigenous land rights and the courts are too often corrupt, indigenous peoples lack judicial means to defend themselves.

FPP, working with national and local NGOs and indigenous peoples' groups, has engaged with the palm oil sector to develop voluntary standards consistent with international human-rights law. It has then used these standards to hold companies to account for violations. In 2007, FPP led an international consortium of NGOs which challenged the World Bank's private sector arm, the International Finance Corporation (IFC), for its financing of the world's largest palm oil trader, Wilmar International, after detailed documentation showed the company was expanding its operations without recognizing local peoples' land rights and without their consent. By using IFC's official grievance procedure (Compliance Advisor Ombudsman [CAO]), the communities were able to secure the restitution of some of the lands taken, get compensation for damages, and acquire extra smallholdings. Meanwhile a CAO audit of IFC showed it had financed Wilmar without adhering to its own performance standards. When we complained about the inadequacy of the response to the CAO's findings by IFC management, the president of the World Bank Group agreed. He froze all World Bank funding to the palm oil sector worldwide while a new approach to plantations development was elaborated over the following two years. Since 2011, the World Bank Group has been far more cautious about how it invests in the palm oil sector.

Since then FPP has worked with a number of other communities to file complaints against the operations of major palm oil companies taking over forest peoples' lands without their consent: in Malaysia, Liberia, Colombia, and Peru. In Indonesia a complaint against the largest palm oil company, Golden Agri-Resources (GAR), led the Roundtable on Sustainable Palm Oil (RSPO), a certification scheme of which GAR is a member, to suspend all land clearance and land acquisition by the company while it makes remedy for past violations.

What all these cases expose is that the Indonesian government's national land bureau and plantations department give preferential assistance to companies to take over indigenous peoples' lands while providing no mechanism by which the communities can resist expropriation. Moreover, the law requires that the companies extinguish all community rights in land as a step toward getting a long-term lease on the land. In effect, both parties are obliged to collude in legalized land theft.

Working with its local partners, FPP has filed a series of urgent action appeals to the UN Committee on the Elimination of Racial Discrimination, which has repeatedly called on the Indonesian government to amend its laws so they protect indigenous peoples' rights to their lands and to FPIC. In early 2017, an important precedent was set, in response to a further complaint. The RSPO ruled that Wilmar International's local subsidiary PT PTP 1 in West Sumatra was in violation of the RSPO standard and the law. The ruling stated that Wilmar must hand back lands taken without consent from the indigenous Minangkabau people of the Kapa community and find an alternative way of leasing the Kapa's lands without extinguishing their rights.

Making all these cases effective depends principally on the mobilization and resolve of the communities themselves to defend their ancestral lands. But it also depends on sustained NGO support, detailed documentation of local realities; and technical assistance to carry out participatory mapping of land claims. Justifying communities' claims to lands requires not just maps but also careful study of how communities manage, inherit, and transfer lands under customary law; how they make decisions; and how they resolve disputes. Anthropological skills and training undoubtedly help provide rigor and authority to such work, as do legal training, cartographic skills, environmental insights, and expertise in information technology and communications.

FINAL REFLECTIONS

These examples illustrate the ways some core features of the disciplines of anthropology and law can be usefully applied in support of forest peoples. We have noted how detailed ethnographic data can be used to demonstrate the connections between discernible ethnic groups and their customary lands. "Activist anthropology" can provide solidarity and social science tools for marginalized communities and peoples seeking to legally secure their collective land rights; defend their human rights; obtain justice; and practice self-determined development. Maintaining the distinction between "emic" and "etic" (between what people actually say in their own languages and how these patterns of thought and local theories about the world may be interpreted by outsiders) helps found this engagement on indigenous peoples' own discourses and forms of self-determination. Furthermore, anthropologists' skills in undertaking power analyses and identifying indigenous peoples' institutions help outsiders engage with indigenous peoples with respect for their polities, gender roles, decision-making processes, systems of customary law, land ownership and inheritance, and practices of natural resource management. Anthropological approaches to community engagement and social mobilization help identify the complexities of local social and political organizations. They can reveal how collective representation is multidimensional and recognize that communities and institutions are not homogenous entities, but dynamic and differentiated bodies, which often contain diverse (and sometimes divergent) social, economic, cultural, and political elements. Anthropological discourse analysis can also help reveal the embedded patterns of exclusion and discrimination which frustrate the realization and protection of forest peoples' rights.

The cases summarized above also demonstrate how local communities and collective organizations are using Western writing systems to record their own language, document their culture, and compile evidence for political actions and law suits, to secure redress and realize their right to self-determination. Literate youths are using their school education to practice a form of cultural "jiu-jitsu" (judo) in the service of their communities, where writing is being used to document oral history, customs, traditional knowledge, and local worldviews. Missionary and colonial education that sought to assimilate indigenous peoples into dominant societies (often brutally) is being replaced by intercultural education. Writing is being harnessed by local people and their allies to develop "life projects" organized by and for forest peoples. Anthropologists, human-rights lawyers, and linguists have a key role to play, by working in solidarity with these grassroots movements for the recuperation of language, local knowledge, and cultural identity.

None of this is to say that work in support of self-determination is without its challenges and ambiguities. There is a negotiable continuum between just providing advice and technical assistance to forest peoples—whether it be legal counsel, assisting with mapping lands, or recording indigenous knowledge—and assuming agency in deploying such information through advocacy. Culturally sensitive and mutually agreed mechanisms are needed by which such advocacy efforts are held accountable to the peoples on whose behalf they are deployed, although the rush of land invasions, court processes, and media deadlines can sometimes overwhelm good intentions.

It also needs to be said that not all the tools of the anthropologists' trade are welcomed by indigenous peoples. A widely celebrated case concerns the unhelpful stereotyping of the Yanomami as a "fierce people" chronically addicted to warfare, which hindered efforts to secure protection for their territory. Equally unhelpful have been efforts by some analysts to "problematize indigeneity"—the argument being that by asserting their common "indigeneity" indigenous peoples are reifying and essentializing themselves, thereby obscuring their differences and doing violence to the ethnographic reality. However, a closer reading shows that those most responsible for reification are the anthropologists themselves who invented the term *indigeneity* in order to critique it. The term used in international law is indigenous peoples, which the law has, for good reasons, left purposefully undefined. *Indigeneity* is a term that anthropologists made up only for the purpose of their analysis. For their part most indigenous advocates are profoundly aware that the term *indigenous peoples*, which has been adopted as a catch-all term in international law, embraces a huge diversity of different peoples and cultures with very varied traditions and forms of social organization. They use the term, however, because they claim the same right as "peoples" to self-determination and seek recognition of their collective rights to their lands and territories and to secure their own futures. Forest Peoples Programme seeks to support this movement, while, as thoughtfully as possible, we try to avoid substituting our voice for those of the peoples themselves.

As our Dayak mentor, Pak Nazarius from Indonesian Borneo, once said at a community meeting:

> In my community our understanding is that we have rights to our land and the natural resources both above and below the land. Everything up to sky belongs to us. Several laws and policies have classified our forests as State forests and the minerals as property of the State. We don't see it like that. I have hair on my arm, on my skin. Both are mine. I also own the flesh and bones beneath. They are also mine. No one has the right to take me apart. But the policy has cut these things apart and thus has cut us into pieces. We want the land back whole.

SUGGESTIONS FOR FURTHER READING

Beryl, David B, Isaac P. Percival, Johnny Angelbert, Larry L. Johnson, Maxi Pugsley, Claudine C. Ramacindo, Gavin Winter, and Yolanda Winter. 2006. *Wa Wiizi Wa Kaduzu: Our Territory, Our Custom*, SRDC, Georgetown. http://www.forestpeoples.org/sites/fpp/files/publication/2010/08/guyana10capr06eng.pdf.

Colchester, Marcus, and Sophie Chao, ed. 2013. *Conflict or Consent? The Palm Oil Sector at the Crossroads*, Forest Peoples Programme, SawitWatch, and TUK-Indonesia, Bogor. http://www.forestpeoples.org/topics/palm-oil-rspo/publication/2013/conflict-or-consent-oil-palm-sector-crossroads.

Doyle, Cathal. 2015. *Indigenous Peoples, Title to Territory, Rights and Resources: The Transformative Role of Free, Prior and Informed Consent*. London: Routledge.

MacKay, Fergus, ed. 2005–17). Indigenous Peoples and United Nations Human Rights Bod-

ies—A Compilation of UN Treaty Body Jurisprudence, the Reports of the Special Procedures of the Human Rights Council and the Advice of the Expert Mechanism on the
Rights of Indigenous Peoples. Volumes 1- VII, Forest Peoples Programme, Moreton-in-
Marsh. http://www.forestpeoples.org/topics/un-human-rights-system/publication/2017
/indigenous-peoples-and-united-nations-human-rights-bo.

Price, Richard. 2011. *Rainforest Warriors: Human Rights on Trial*. Philadelphia: University of
Pennsylvania Press.

South Rupununi District Council. 2012. Baokopa'o wa di'itinpan wadauniinao ati'o nii—
Thinking Together for Those Coming behind Us: An Outline Plan for the Care of Wapichan Territory in Guyana, SRDC, Georgetown. http://www.forestpeoples.org/sites/fpp
/files/publication/2012/05/wapichan-mp-22may12lowresnomarks.pdf.

Tuhiwai Smith, Linda. 2012. *Decolonizing Methodologies: Research and Indigenous Peoples*.
Second edition. London and Dunedin: Zed Books and Otago University Press.

World Rainforest Movement. 1989. *Tropical Deforestation: Causes, Effects and False Solutions*,
Penang: The Ecologist and Sahabat Alam Malaysia.

For more information about the Forest Peoples Programme, see www.forestpeoples.org.

CHAPTER 17

ANTHROPOLOGY/MEDIA

Faye Ginsburg

Igloolik Isuma is the world's first Inuit production company, cofounded in 1990 in the village of Igloolik, Nunavut, by Zacharias Kunuk, the late Paul Apak Angilirq, and Norman Cohn; their goal—which they met with considerable success—was to produce independent locally based Inuit media for themselves and audiences worldwide. They are perhaps the most well-known of indigenous media groups in the world, through years of groundbreaking work created through their distinctive community-based production process: most notably with the global success of their multiple prize-winning film *Atanarjuat: The East Runner* (2001), the first Inuit/Inuktitut-language feature film, winner of the prestigious Camera d'Or at the Cannes Film Festival, the first indigenously directed film to win this prize. As Zach Kunuk remarked: "Look at us. What we have, we went all over the world. We've stopped Cannes for five minutes when I spoke Inuktitut. We did all this." Isuma's second feature, *The Journals of Knud Rasmussen* (2006), was the opening-night film at the 2006 Toronto International Film Festival and was nominated for a Canadian Genie. Their 2008 film, *Before Tomorrow* (coproduced by Isuma and the Arnait Women's Video Production Collective), won best first feature at the Toronto International Film Festival.

Since its inception, Isuma turned televisual technologies into vehicles for the rendering of Inuit lives and histories, a counterpoint to mainstream media's introduction into the Canadian Arctic, not only through their remarkable creative work as filmmakers, but also because of their innovations in reimagining distribution. Frustrated by the difficulty of showing their work to other Inuit communities across the Arctic, in 2008, they launched a groundbreaking alternative for indigenous distribution, Isuma TV, a free internet video portal for global indigenous media, available to local audiences and worldwide viewers. A year later they launched a digital distribution project, bringing a high-speed version of Isuma TV into remote Nunavut communities where the bandwidth can at times be inadequate to view even a single YouTube. Isuma TV allows films to be rebroadcast through local cable or low-power channels, or downloaded to digital platforms. The bigger story here concerns the unanticipated possibilities for reinventing media from the so-called cultural periphery at moments of media innovation. As Isuma veteran Norm Cohn explained to me:

> We saw the historical technological "moment of opportunity" for the Internet, the way we saw the analog video moment in 1980, and the Atanarjuat digital/ film moment in 1998: the brief window in the technology of communication where marginalized users with a serious political and cultural objective could bypass centuries of entrenched powerlessness with a serious new idea at a much higher level of visibility than usual in our top-down power-driven global politics. In 2007, Internet capacity allowed us to end-run the film industry entirely and launch a video website that could take aspects of YouTube to a much higher level of thematic seriousness, and see what happens. So this is a serious experiment in the history of alternate media experiments since the early '70s, as Isuma has been from the start, helping viewers see indigenous reality from its own point of view.

Despite their remarkable success as one of the most robust, creative, and staunch of indigenous media groups in the world, Igloolik Isuma went into receivership in 2011 after a quarter-century of astonishing work, although Isuma TV was sheltered from this collapse. It continues as an online international media distribution channel for Inuit and indigenous cultures worldwide. Their extraordinary archive, however, was acquired by the National Gallery of Canada (NGC). In 2015, Geronimo Inutiq, an accomplished younger multimedia Inuit artist, active in digital video production, electronic music, and deejaying, was invited by the NGC to be a resident artist to untangle and assess the Isuma archive. Inutiq worked to remediate elements of Isuma's work in a contrapuntal critical response to Canadian musician and celebrity Glenn Gould's iconic 1967 radio documentary "The Idea of North," which failed to include the voices of any First Nations or Inuit participants, mirroring the settler colonial imaginary of the time. In the show he produced for Vancouver's artist-run grunt gallery, ARCTICNOISE, Inutiq disrupts this absence with screens featuring digitally manipulated scenes from Isuma films, repositioning the archive to literally speak back (in Inuktitut) to the shocking lack of Inuit voices in Gould's earlier work. The project unsettles not only the settler colonial narrative of destruction and erasure of indigenous lives, but also disrupts conventional expectations of archival indigenous media by foregrounding *noise* and *glitch*, calling attention to the place of random and difficult-to-interpret interference. Thus, prior indigenous media works are repurposed through intergenerational collaboration, creating sites of community building and recognition through projects that simultaneously mobilize and reconsider indigenous pasts and futures. Nonetheless, the question remains: where does Igloolik Isuma stand on this resignifying of their work far beyond their purview?

This brief chronicle of innovation in both legacy media and new virtual forms, as well as the difficulties of containing control over cultural and intellectual property in a digital viral medium and a neoliberal political economy, is emblematic of many of the epistemologically challenging issues that have been raised in the field of media anthropology over the last three decades. It reminds us that they are not only academic but also, of course, have consequences in the lives of people we study, many of whom are avid producers and consumers of media of all kinds. In the process, they have become increasingly aware of how Western cultural protocols regarding media—valorizing free and open access—are at times very different from those in local indigenous worlds where certain forms of mediation may be restricted in their circulation.

These notes on Isuma represent one moment in my ongoing, multisited research project on indigenous media that began in 1988. They indicate how crucial it is to understand media worlds as complex sites of cultural production, exchange, and debate, tracking how they acquire meaning and value over time through multiple circuits of circulation. This underscores, in turn, the importance of bringing the methodological and theoretical tools of anthropology to the study of contemporary media of all sorts, particularly for those of us working with indigenous communities where such media of all sorts play a transformative role.

MODES OF IMAGINING

In the twenty-first century, the anthropology of media has emerged as a new and increasingly robust field that has taken shape in tandem with a general reconceptualization of anthropology that addresses our changing relationship with our interlocutors as our cultural worlds grow ever closer. This is increasingly the case as the social domains we track to understand how contemporary lives across the globe are shaped by processes of late capitalism, and how the stunning acceleration of global social media require multisited research strategies as we imagine what our work can contribute to worldwide transformations wrought by media. These range from cell phones to Facebook, to feature film industries and local video collectives, to the dizzying circulation of photographs across countless platforms, from Instagram to Weibo. Additionally, we have the emergence of indigenous television stations across the planet linked by the World Indigenous Broadcasters Network and virtual reality viewing that ranges from the voyeuristic to the therapeutic. Audio includes radio- and music-streaming services, dubbing and translation practices, as well as spectatorial and sonic "noise" that reveals the limitations of an allegedly perfect world of technology.

All these forms, and more, that comprise the geometrically expanding media universe have been subject to the ethnographic gaze and analysis. Indeed, it's hard to imagine a time, only a few decades ago, when doctoral students had to justify the study of such practices to their dissertation committees. Now, it is virtually impossible to carry out research anywhere without addressing these rapidly proliferating forms of mediation. Even in remote communities where these technologies may be harder to find, the very fact of their isolation from dominant media forms requires attention as an exception to the seemingly insatiable invention of communication forms designed to demand our attention.

The anthropology of media, still a relatively new field, is informed by several intertwined legacies of thought. A number of scholars link their work on media to the field of visual anthropology, often bringing a critical revision of that field through the lens of postcolonial scholarship and the production of a variety of alternative and diasporic practices. Another, related strand of thought emerged from those interested in how processes of modernity, postmodernity, and globalization actually work on the ground, tracking the cultural effects of transnational flows of people, ideas, and objects mediated more and more by digital media of all kinds that are instrumental in creating a sense of a social world that is rapidly respatializing culture and power. This scholarship builds, in particular, on the foundational work of Benedict Anderson's foundational insights into the role of print and other media in the creation of the "imagined communities" of nation-states, and the extension of Anderson's frame to a broader notion of the social imaginary. Equally influential is Jürgen Habermas's articulation of the historical emergence of the public sphere (and the ensuing debates and critiques of that model). The work of Arjun Appadurai has been particularly influenced by these thinkers, and in turn has been influential in synthesizing their frameworks with anthropological concerns and methods. In his model, media are a central part of public culture, particularly important to the articulation of the national and transnational with local processes. His early but still influential essay on "global ethnoscapes" points to the significance of the spread of media throughout the world, arguing for the increasing significance of the "imagination" in the production of culture and identity in the contemporary world. Finally, Pierre Bourdieu's framing of the "field of cultural production"—the system of relations (and struggles for power) among agents or institutions engaged in generating the value of works of art, while creating cultural capital for themselves—has been especially effective for those whose emphasis is on the institutional sites that provide the infrastructure for the production of media work.

One might think of these linked processes of the cultural production of media, its circulation as a social technology, and the relationship of mediated worlds to self-fabrication as existing on a continuum. On one end is the more self-conscious cultural activism in which cultural material is used and strategically deployed as part of a broader project of political empowerment, providing a "third space" for indigenous and minoritized groups, often created in circumstances where choices are heavily constrained and political mobilization is incipient. In the middle range are reflexive but less strategic processes in which the imaginative encounter with cinematic or televisual images and narratives may be expressive and/or constitutive of a variety of social worlds such as the transnational links that cell phones, Skype, video, television, films, and computer networks and digital streaming capacities provide for diasporic communities. On the other end of the continuum are the more classic formations of media which require institutional framings and imply some dimension of social segregation between producers and audiences. Anthropological research on these mediations focuses on the complex and divergent ways in which national/regional/transnational cinemas and television operate, tracking the frictions that emerge, the often unstable relation between intention and effect as these media are put to the service of constituting modern citizens, through a variety of forms, notably in popular soap operas, telenovelas, melodramatic serials, action films, and how these are intended and *understood* in relation to larger conjunctures and in many different settings from production to distribution to consumption.

Because anthropologists so frequently locate themselves in non-Western and "out of the way" places, our research offers not only a thick, vertically integrated, and multisited sense of the social life of media, but also engages with how this occurs outside the circuits of first-world settings which have provided an ethnocentric frame for most academic discussion of media until the twenty-first century. Ethnographers and fellow travelers in media studies are attending increasingly to the circulation of media in settings not dependent on Western hegemonic practices, such as the export and wide circulation of Hindi cinema or of Mexican telenovelas, or YouTube sensations that circulate widely and wildly, regardless of their place of origin.

At the same time, anthropological research on media reiterates the insufficiency of once-current, bounded concepts of culture as a way of understanding contemporary lives in our own or other societies. Scholars developing ethnographies of media usually begin with an interest in understanding questions generated by the phenomenon itself, often motivated by a desire to comprehend the popularity, power, and/or passion attached to certain kinds of media production and viewing (e.g., why is Indian cinema so popular in Nigeria? How do the people in Anonymous interact online?). Answering these questions leads to an appreciation of the complexity of how people engage with media in a variety of social spaces and the resulting shifts in the sense of the local as its relation to broader social worlds becomes almost a routine part of everyday life. Understanding the social relations of media production, circulation, and reception in this way entails a grounded focus on the everyday practices and consciousness of social actors as producers and consumers of different forms of media. Their interests and responses shape and are shaped by a variety of possible subject positions: cultural, generational, gendered, local, national, regional, and transnational communities of identity, requiring an ever-more complex and plural notion of audience. Indeed, these multiple identities may be part of a single social subject's repertoire of cultural resources. While our work is distinguished by an effort to track qualitatively and with the kind of cultural knowledge that enables what Geertz called "thick description," the practices, consciousness, and distinctions that emerge for people out of their quotidian encounters with media are also always situated within the context of a broader social universe and often so widely distributed that one scholar has identified his fieldwork across widely distributed media domains as "thin description." Whether in our own societies or elsewhere, ethnographers look at media as cultural artifacts enmeshed in daily lives, to see how they are imperfectly articulated with (and sometimes created as a counter to) larger hegemonic processes of modernity, assimilation, nation-building, commercialization, and globalization, but in terms that draw attention to how those processes are being localized in cultural fields and particular political economies.

THE ACTIVIST IMAGINARY: INDIGENOUS MEDIA

Much of the work on media follows popular cinema and television soap operas and melodramas, interrogating how these apparently hegemonic forms have a more diverse interpretive life on the ground. Another substantial body of research addresses counterhegemonic fields of cultural production, most notably in the small but influential study of media such as the amateur video and cellphone films being produced by minoritized people as a culturally protective/productive response to the introduction of dominant forms. For First Nations people, indigenous media which developed in the late 1970s in North America, the 1980s in Australia and New Zealand, and the 1990s in most of Latin America was especially attractive to our profession because of its association with people in remote locations. Such formations seemed particularly well-suited for anthropological inquiry: small in scale and apparently a world apart from the mass media industries that dominate late capitalist societies, they occupy a comfortable position of difference from dominant cultural assumptions about media aesthetics and practices, one that paralleled the place indigenous people are meant to occupy in traditional anthropology. Indeed, the initial anthropological research on such work, which began in the 1960s with Sol Worth and John Adair's now classic study, *Through Navajo Eyes*, set out precisely to explore the impact of cultural difference on the way the world is envisioned, by teaching young adult Navajo who had never made or used motion pictures to make their own work for the first time, to see if their films would reflect a distinctively Navajo film grammar. Like much of (American) anthropology at that time, the work was guided in part by the possibility that Navajo filmmaking might offer both a scientific insight into another culture's literal vision of the world, as well as an alternative view, a kind of embedded cultural critique, of Western presumptions about the way media should look and how it might produce meaning. Recent efforts on the part of Navajo scholars to return to that project, repatriate film and photographs, and to engage with contemporary Navajo filmmaking in more meaningful ways reveal the remarkable possibilities of a decolonized archive.

In the last two decades, indigenous people have had to deal with the threats and possibilities of media entering their lives and have struggled to find ways to turn that circumstance to their advantage. As anthropologists study the impact that media such as video might have on their communities, indigenous media makers are busy using the technologies for a variety of purposes, sometimes as legal documents in negotiations with encompassing settler states or to assert their presence televisually within national imaginaries. For their own communities, these works are aimed at cultural preservation through the documenting of ceremonies and traditional activities with elders or creating works to teach young people literacy in their own languages; communicating among and between communities on issues such as how to confront loggers and gold prospectors; or long-distance communication among relatives separated by vast Arctic expanses.

Much of the writing and research on this topic has focused on remote communities in the Amazon, the Australian outback, and Canada's Arctic where media are produced and consumed primarily by members of the same community (although the work circulates to other native communities as well as to non-aboriginal audiences via film festivals and broadcasts). Indigenous people who live in or closer to metropoles also have been aspiring to be recognized as part of the broader world of media imagery production and circulation, yet feel their claim to an indigenous identity within a more cosmopolitan framework is sometimes regarded as inauthentic, as if their comfort with aspects of modernity, including filmmaking, erased their legitimacy. Māori filmmakers were the first to break that barrier with films based on contemporary Māori life such as *Te Rua* (Barry Barclay, 1990) and *Once Were Warriors* (Lee Tamahori) which, in 1994, became the first indigenously made feature to become an international hit, followed by Chris Eyer's now classic Native American coming-of-age drama *Smoke Signals* (1998). In 2001, the aforementioned Inuit feature *Atanarjuat* won the Camera d'Or at Cannes; in 2009, indigenous Australian director Warwick Thornton won that award for *Samson and Delilah*, his harrowing and extraordinary account of the lives of aboriginal teens living in remote Central Australia, indexing the growth and significance of indigenous media. The remarkable creativity of "the Indigenous New Wave" has placed this work on the world stage beyond hegemonic regimes of value such as Cannes or Toronto, with robust festival circuits governed by First Nations curatorial committees, such as Canada's imagineNATIVE.

While such forms of cultural production clearly differ in scale and style from local community-based video, these media makers insist that there is no absolute dividing line that establishes one arena of indigenous production as somehow more authentic than another. These range from the early remote experiments in low power TV in indigenous languages, to feature films and now national indigenous television channels meant to appeal not only to viewers from their own communities, as well as to a diversity of audiences worldwide. Such works are all part of the efforts of indigenous people living in a variety of situations to claim a space that is theirs in the world of modernity's representational practices: what Native American scholar Beverly Singer refers to as *Wiping the Warpaint off the Lens*.

This activist engagement with media encompasses not only indigenous work but media being produced by a variety of other minoritized subjects—black

British and African American filmmakers, for example—who have become involved in creating their own representations as part of a counter-public. One might think of this creative and self-conscious process of objectification as a form of cultural activism in which media are used by subaltern groups not only to pursue traditional goals of broad-based social change through a politics of identity and representation, but also to represent a utopian desire for emancipatory projects, part of much larger processes of social transformation.

OBJECTIFYING CULTURE

More broadly, this work is on a spectrum of practices engaged in the self-conscious mediation and mobilization of culture. This is not to deny that the presence of media technologies in cultural peripheries is part of a global process of the penetration of media which has multiple and sometimes contradictory effects on local communities. However, the assumption that the center always dominates the so-called periphery has too often meant that, as Ulf Hannerz pointed out, we get the history of the impact of the center on the periphery, rather than the history of the periphery itself. In the case of indigenous media, for example, one might read this not simply as an adaptation of Western visual culture, but as a new form of collective self-production that is being used by indigenous producers to mediate historical and cultural ruptures within their own societies and to assert their presence in the polities that encompass them.

Objectified and mediated, culture as such, especially for minoritized people, can become a source of values that can be converted into political assets, both internally as bases of group solidarity and mobilization and externally as claims on the support of other social groups, governments, and public opinion all over the globe, as Terry Turner has shown regarding the work of Amazon-based Kayapo media makers with whom he worked for several decades. It is the unpredictability and often vitality of such media practices that has generated much recent interest in what anthropology might offer in terms of an understanding of how these restructurings are taking place.

PARALLEL MODERNITIES

Joining a slew of social theorists theorizing the place of media in the emergence of alternative modernities all over the globe, a number of projects have exemplified the value of anthropological research on this topic. In his study of media in northern Nigeria, for example, Brian Larkin uses the trope of parallel modernities to account for those who are not mobile but who nonetheless participate in the imagined realities of other cultures as part of their daily lives, through circuits in which Western media are only one of many choices which might offer Hausa youth the choice between watching Hausa or Yoruba videos, Indian, Hong Kong or American films, or videos of Quranic *tafsir* (exegesis) by local preachers. The popularity of Indian cinema is evidenced not only by cinema attendance but also by a burgeoning local culture industry of *littatafan soyayya* (love stories): pamphlet-type books in which the imagined alternative of Indian romance is incorporated within local Hausa reality. The intense interest in the spectacle and plot of Indian films and their indigenization in these *soyayya* books as well as in locally produced videos offers Hausa youth a medium through which they can consider what it means to be modern and what may be the place of Hausa society within that modernity. The point, of course, is not to assume that power is lodged in the West, but to track how and why media is now so closely associated with power and its embodiment, such that states everywhere attempt to control the mediation of their own representations and that of others through regulation, censorship, and efforts to contain the means of distribution. A number of anthropologists engaged with media are grappling with the effects of the increasing respatialization and privatization of cultural production and flows, querying when and whether the national offers an appropriate frame of analysis, providing helpful periodizations of shifts in mediation with the increasing impact of neoliberal privatization.

In a number of cases, digital media are still tied to national structures of feeling as well as structures of state, a dynamic that has taken on a somewhat surreal cast with the use of Twitter by President Trump in unprecedented ways. Such phenomena raise questions once again regarding the significance of the national and the nation-state, under destabilizing conditions and accelerating technological change.

CIRCULATING CULTURE

It is the ever more evident necessity of linking media production, circulation, and reception in broad and intersecting social and cultural fields—local, regional, national, transnational, networked—that characterizes the anthropology of media. In most anthropological studies of media, audiences are varied and situated in a broad context which strategically includes both producers and audiences in the query, as well as intertextual sources through which meaning is constituted.

Some scholars argue not only that producers and audiences should be encompassed in the same frame; they are calling for a radical rethinking of the very divide between production and reception and for more attention to the important but theoretically and empirically neglected area of distribution as a central process through which media help to constitute and reflect social difference, as power and status are signified through spatial and temporal dimensions of exhibition, as well as the increasingly individualized medium of the cell phone. Film festivals are emerging as important sites for the analysis of new cultural formations. These studies provide important insights into the relationship of media practices to public culture beyond the proverbial living room that has dominated reception studies as a site of analysis. They also offer an important counterpoint to Foucauldian and Marxist frameworks that point to discourses of power as causative, but fail to locate them concretely in the lives and motivations of social actors and the processes of everyday life.

PRODUCING CULTURE

If media has presented a kind of forbidden object to anthropologists in non-Western settings, the final boundary (breached by Powdermaker's prescient study of Hollywood in the 1950s) was fieldwork in the social worlds and cultural logics of media institutions where dominant ideologies are produced, in our own as well as other societies bringing new methods and insights to the territory already established by a small but significant body of work by sociologists of media, a tradition which Bourdieu joined in his lectures and subsequent book on television. Recent ethnographies of media as a field of cultural production focus on a variety of forms, including work on journalism's "back stories," and "image brokers," as well as the hazards of news making in the digital era. Others offer deep insights into the transformation of the Hindi film industry into Bollywood and into the lives of workers haunted by risk in the Hollywood and Hong Kong film worlds, while others examine the introduction of media technologies and infrastructures into Nigeria and the religious, political, and cultural changes they bring about. All of these provide grounded analyses and critiques of how media production is balanced between logics of recognition, audience appeal, aesthetics, and cultural and commercial imperatives.

Ethnographies of cultural production open up the media to interrogation as anthropologists track the ways in which structures shape the actions of professionals who are in the business of making representations of other cultures, and how structures of power affect image-making practices. Increasingly, these works underscore that oppositional logics are insufficient for grasping media practices; rather, our models must allow for what theorist Martin-Barbero calls "mediations" in which media are imbricated in everyday practices, creating the thick texture of hegemony/subalternity, the interlacing of resistance/submission, and opposition/complicity.

COMPLICITIES

Many ethnographers studying media often find themselves implicated in their object of study, in a relationship of complicity that places us more and more often in the same social universe as our subjects: if not in an activist relationship, then at times in an unanticipated reversal of authority over the representation of culture. Anthropologists have found themselves working as production assistants, extras in films, or as momentary celebrities on popular shows.

Perhaps because of the intensity and self-consciousness of the concern with media's possible deleterious effects as well its utopian possibilities, most of us carrying out research on media with indigenous or other subaltern groups have an activist engagement with this work while serving as supporters and even catalysts of activity: bringing cameras to communities and assisting in the logistics of projects or helping to develop visibility, funding, and circulation systems for the work. Some have argued that these projects go beyond advocacy as authorial relations are reversed, underscoring the ways in which we are increasingly complicit with our subjects, as we find ourselves jointly engaged in the project of objectifying and representing culture.

One can see a trajectory in the theorizing of the relationship between culture and media over the last half-century as the objectification of the category of culture becomes ever more widespread and the observer becomes more implicated as a participant. In the early work on media, culture operated as a kind of unconscious Durkheimian indicator of the national which was interpreted in metaphors of personality types in the work of Margaret Mead and others in the 1950s. When, in the 1990s, anthropologists began to turn their attention to film and television once again, they looked at media not so much as a reductive mirror but as a social force in which culture is a resource in struggles for political and/or economic hegemony over the representation of society in media. Most recently, scholars are developing research that will help us rethink abstract notions such as globalization or social media, to see how new technologies and economies of late modernity are being framed both by the new international division of cultural labor as people at every end of the social spectrum are engaging with mediascapes that increasingly escape the control of national political structures and economies, rearranging the ways in which cultural formations are spatialized and imagined in the process. For many social theorists interested in media as a site for either social possibilities or cultural decay, the question is still open as to whether even alternative media practices inevitably "eat their young." The lack of resolution is undoubtedly healthy for intellectual debate, an unanticipated dimension of continued research during an era of ever-widening penetration and availability of media. We are increasingly implicated in the representational practices of those we study, a social fact that brings absolute and welcome closure to the tendencies of the field to situate those we study as being profoundly different than we are.

Anthropologists are finally at home with the inescapable presence of media as a contemporary cultural force engaged with the mediation of hegemonic forms and resistance to them; the growth and transnational circulation of public culture; the creation of national and activist social imaginaries, with the development of digital media as new arenas for political expression and the production of identity; and the wildly accelerating forms associated with digital/social media in non-Western as well as Western societies.

SUGGESTIONS FOR FURTHER READING

Appadurai, Arjun. 1996. *Modernity At Large: Cultural Dimensions of Globalization*. Minneapolis: University of Minnesota Press.

Askew, Kelly, and Richard Wilk, eds. 2002. *The Anthropology of Media: A Reader*. Oxford: Blackwell Publishing.

Banks, Marcus, and Jay Ruby, eds. 2011. *Made to Be Seen: Perspectives on the History of Visual Anthropology*. Chicago: University of Chicago Press.

Boyer, Dominic. 2007. *Understanding Media: A Popular Philosophy*. Chicago: Prickly Paradigm Press.

Ginsburg, Faye, Lila Abu-Lughod, and Brian Larkin, eds. 2002. *Media Worlds: Anthropology on New Terrain*. Berkeley: University of California Press.

Horst, Heather, and Daniel Miller, eds. 2011. *Digital Anthropology*. Oxford: Berg.

Larkin, Brian. 1998. "Indian Films and Nigerian Lovers: Media and the Creation of Parallel Modernities." *Africa* 67 (3): 406–40.

Pertierra, Anna Cristina. 2018. *Media Anthropology for the Digital Age*. Cambridge: Polity Press.

Powdermaker, Hortense. 2013 [1950]. *Hollywood, the Dream Factory: An Anthropologist Looks at the Movie-Makers*. New York: Martino Books.

CHAPTER 18

READING TIME

AN ANTHROPOLOGY OF CLOCKS
IN THE HISTORY OF PHOTOGRAPHY

Christopher B. Steiner

The clock, not the steam engine, is the key-machine
of the modern industrial age.
—**Lewis Mumford (1934)**

. . . cameras, in short, were clocks for seeing.
—**Roland Barthes (1981)**

———————

For a brief fashion moment during the mid-1980s cheap plastic stopwatches
worn around the neck became a must-have style accessory for New York's
urban youth. What began as a trend in some of the city's predominately African American neighborhoods spread quickly to other teenage communities
across the five boroughs. "You get running time, regular time, Army time and
an alarm that beeps," said one early adapter of the fashion trend. "It makes life
less complicated." Several months after the launch of the stopwatch craze in
urban black culture, the lead rap-singer of the hip-hop group Public Enemy,
Flavor Flav, upped the fashion ante by wearing around his neck a full-size wall
clock (fig 18.1). "Before I started out wearing these clocks," he explained in a

FIG. 18.1.   Hip-Hop artist Flavor Flav at the 34th Annual American Museum Awards in Los Angeles. Photo by Lisa O'Connor/ZUMA Press. Copyright 2006 by Lisa O'Connor. Reproduced by permission of ZUMA Press, Inc/Alamy Stock Photo.

1994 interview on MTV, "we started off with little stopwatches, and one day I just wanted to do something out of the ordinary." The clock-around-the-neck became an iconic symbol of Flavor Flav's stage persona and celebrity identity. "The reason why I wear this clock is because it represents time being the most important element in our life," he said. The clock is a reminder to everyone that "I'm paying attention, so you can't get fast on me because I know what time it is." In 2013, when he was inducted in the Rock and Roll Hall of Fame, one of Flavor Flav's signature clocks was accessioned into the collection and put on permanent display.

This essay is about clocks and their visual representation in the history of photography. It is an exploration of how a visual anthropologist like myself might approach the representation of "time," and how clocks figure prominently into the social construction of power in both colonial and postcolonial contexts. It is about the circulation of a specific object of material culture in the channels of global trade. It is about a long, complicated history of "clock symbolism" that precedes by nearly a century Flavor Flav's bold adoption of the wall clock as fashion accessory.

CLOCKING IN

The origins of anthropology coincide more or less with the beginnings of photography in the mid- to late nineteenth century. In many cases, the changing function of photography in anthropology can be traced in tandem to the ebbs and flows of major trends within the discipline—from the use of photography in assembling visual evidence for racial typologies in the nineteenth century, for example, to documenting human behavior, ritual practices, and material culture in the twentieth century. For most anthropologists, until fairly recently, photography was viewed as an uncomplicated instrument within the repertoire of tools and methodologies available for ethnographic inquiry. In more recent years, however, anthropologists have come to understand that photography is far from being a simple technical means with which to record "reality"; it is fraught instead with inherent bias and open to endless possibilities for distortion, manipulation, and misunderstanding. To study photographs through the lens of anthropology reveals a great deal about the history of visual representation, since the image often tells us far more about the maker than about its subject.

Like the invention of photography in the nineteenth century, the advancement of small portable clocks also coincides with the development of ethnographic fieldwork, as well as with the associated rise in international travel to far-flung destinations by European and American anthropologists, colonial agents, missionaries, and excursionists. In 1847, French inventor Antoine Redier was the first to patent an adjustable mechanical alarm clock, which allowed its users to set their own time to wake. In the following decades, clock companies in both Europe and the United States worked to miniaturize Redier's large mantel-size alarm clock to a much smaller and more portable design. At the Paris Exposition Universelle of 1878—where France paraded its colonial troops and first displayed "exotic" subjects from its burgeoning colonies in Africa—the Ansonia Clock Company of New York introduced in the Palace of Industry the first portable, spring-powered alarm clock designed to run one full day with a single wind. Marketed under the name "One Day Bee," the sturdy nickel-plated timepiece was sold in a compact lithographed tin, making the clock safely transportable to even the most remote corners of the earth. Some two decades after the "One Day Bee" was introduced at the Exposition Universelle, an Ansonia clock of similar design wound up in the hands of one Reverend George Brown as he traveled in the summer of 1902 across the Solomon Islands, to bring Christianity to what he regarded as its backward and "heathen" inhabitants whom time had forgotten.

A CLOCK IN THE EAR

In 1860, British-born clergyman Reverend George Brown enlisted as a Methodist missionary assigned to the islands of the South Pacific. Over a period of almost fifty years, Brown traveled extensively throughout the Pacific region while representing the Wesleyan Methodist Missionary Society. He spent time on the islands of New Britain, Tonga, Fiji, Samoa, as well as making frequents visits to the Bismarck Archipelago and the Solomon Islands. Like many colonial evangelists stationed across the globe at this time, Brown also considered himself something of an amateur anthropologist. He assembled a collection of over three thousand ethnological artifacts, which were acquired after his death in 1917 by the Bowes Museum at Barnard Castle in Brown's home town of Teesdale, England. In 1910, Brown published a monograph entitled *Melanesians and Polynesians: Their Life-histories Described and Compared*, which detailed the "manners, customs, and folklore" of the people he came to know through his ministry. As is typical of this particular ethnographic genre, Brown offers in his book firsthand observations on such topics as family life, childhood, food, disease, religion, magic, government, language, and beliefs about death. Because Brown's ethnographic inquiries were largely done in relation to his primary goal of converting indigenous people to Christianity, he often stressed, in his reporting, the most abhorrent or sensational practices espoused by the men and women he encountered. As an avid photographer Brown used his own images to document what he and his fellow missionaries felt were inappropriate or "savage" modes of dress and behavior, especially female nudity and extreme forms of body ornamentation, including perforation of the earlobes and septum, tattoos and scarification, and other forms of bodily mutilation. In nighttime lantern-slide shows, which he presented to potential converts, Brown showed the people what the Gospel had done to "improve" the lives of other people like themselves.

In the summer of 1902, Reverend Brown, his daughter, and a team of missionary coworkers traveled from Sydney, Australia, aboard the steamship *SS Titus* to Rovania Lagoon in order to establish a new mission station along the coast of New Georgia in the Solomon Islands. Brown took a series of photographs during that summer journey in Melanesia which document various examples of vernacular village architecture, "head-hunting" canoes, as well as

FIG. 18.2.   Man with clock inserted in distended ear lobe, New Georgia, Solomon Islands. Gelatin silver print. Photograph by Reverend George Brown, 1902. British Museum Oc,B36.16AN380876001. Reproduced with permission of the British Museum.

portraits of men, women, and children sporting various modes of indigenous attire and styles of body ornamentation. One photograph from that series depicts an unidentified man posing in frontal view for Brown's camera (fig. 18.2). The subject is positioned in such a way as to show not only his beaded shell ornaments and bare chest, but to highlight especially his left distended ear lobe. As in other groups throughout Melanesia, it was customary for adult men and women in the Solomon Islands to have significantly enlarged earlobes as marks of both beauty and status.

Beginning at a young age, spool-shaped plugs were inserted into perforations in the lobes of the ears, with the gradual increase in size of the plugs over time until, in adulthood, the lobes were distended to three or more inches in diameter. These distended contours of the earlobes were adorned traditionally with hollow ebony loops or with incised wooden discs inlaid with mother-of-pearl and ground shell beads. In Reverend Brown's photograph from New Georgia, however, rather than an indigenous ornament, the man's left ear holds instead a Western industrial-manufactured mechanical clock supported in place by the large pendulous loop of his distended earlobe. Since the clock is located at almost the exact center of the composition, Reverend Brown was clearly trying to draw the viewer's eye to the man's dramatically enlarged earlobe distension — a feature Brown must have considered to be his subject's most fundamental mark of "primitiveness" and alterity. In his 1908 autobiography, Brown describes his photograph as "Man with clock placed in the lobe of his ear to show the size of the orifice. Circumference of clock, thirteen inches."

Without the descriptive caption that gives context to this photograph one might have assumed, incorrectly, that Brown had unwittingly stumbled upon an inhabitant of New Georgia island who had seen fit to appropriate a modern clock as a substitute for the traditional earlobe ornament. Yet there are no references in any of Brown's journals, diaries, or letters indicating that he ever encountered anyone during his time in the South Pacific wearing appropriated European objects (including mechanical clocks) as forms of personal adornment. The actual clock which appears in the field photograph is among the three thousand or so objects accessioned by the Bowes Museum in 1917 when they acquired Brown's ethnographic collection (fig. 18.3). Though missing its bezel glass and hands, the inscription on this clock allows us to identify it as having been manufactured by the Ansonia Clock Company of New York around 1901; a paper label affixed to the side of the clock reads: "Clock placed in lobe of ear."

Unlike the hollow loops or inlaid discs which men and women traditionally wore to shape the distended contours of their earlobes, the mechanical clock would have been a familiar object for Brown's intended Western audience — providing them with an easily "read" gauge of dimension and size. Thus, the clock would serve in this example essentially as a scientific measure of "primitiveness," like the scales of a measuring rod in an anthropometric or forensic image. Since Reverend Brown was in the process of establishing a new mission station during the summer of 1902 in a region of Melanesia where no European or American missionaries had previously worked, he was probably quite eager to justify the need for an imposition of Christian values in a locale he considered to be particularly "backward" and as yet untouched by "civilization." It is likely for this reason that he sought to photograph some of the most extreme forms of

FIG. 18.3.   Clock seen in figure 2, manufactured by the Ansonia Clock Company, New York. Missing clock bezel glass and hands. Paper label on side reads "Clock placed in lobe of ear." The George Brown Collection, National Museum of Ethnology, Osaka, Japan. H0138197.

body modification he could find. I would argue also that the clock was undoubtedly intended to provide an element of humor, as Brown's photograph is surely meant to highlight what he perceived as a stark contrast between the apparent "primitiveness" of a shirtless man with natty hair and the inherent "modernity" symbolized by the latest model windup mechanical alarm clock.

Brown's biographers agree he had mixed attitudes toward the various people he tried to convert. He deeply admired and was fond of Samoans, and other Polynesian peoples, but he was less generous or kind toward Melanesians, particularly those he encountered from New Georgia. Brown had little respect for what he perceived to be the Melanesian's "grotesque" body modifications, their culture of warfare and violence, and, especially, their practice of head hunting and cannibalism. It is no accident, then, that Brown juxtaposed in the photograph what he considered the most "savage" of his heathen flock with the most modern trope of "civilization" and modernity. The clock, here, is not a randomly chosen signifier of measurement and scale, but rather it serves as a key symbol of modernity, of structured work and labor schedules, and of the imposition of European regulations and mechanical timekeeping onto a society that was deemed by colonial evangelists as culturally backward, lazy, and stagnating. Walter Benjamin described industrialized modern time as a decisive break with precapitalist modes of time, which he called "messianic time." For him, modern or capitalist time structures past, present, and future (as well as the workday itself) in a linear fashion; while "messianic" or precapitalist time suggests the simultaneity of past, present, and future united across time by an "eternal" foundation. Indeed, like Reverend Brown himself, the clock is a mark of "whiteness" which is meant to be read against the grain of "blackness" signified by the man in the photograph.

THE VANISHING CLOCK

Between 1896 and 1930 American photographer Edward S. Curtis captured over forty thousand photographic images among more than eighty indigenous tribes throughout North America, from the Mexican border to the Bering Strait. He took portraits of men and women, young and old, and documented indigenous clothing, ceremonial costume, habitations, industries, games, rituals, funeral customs, and material culture. In 1907, Curtis published the first volume of *The North American Indian*, a portfolio series of large photogravures accompanied by narrative text which, by 1930, would ultimately become a massive twenty-volume leather-bound set containing almost 2,500 original photographic plates. Curtis believed that his project represented the last possible "authentic" documentation of Native Americans before they were destined to lose the "traces of their aboriginal character" and would "ultimately become assimilated" with, what he called, the "superior race."

Influenced heavily by Social Darwinism, Edward Curtis, like many of his contemporaries, believed that cultures were locked in an irreversible evolutionary battle where the "strongest" would force those who were less "developed" toward extinction. For Curtis, extinction was not necessarily defined as physical death, but rather as capitulation to external influence, where traditional lifeways would be corrupted, in his view, by assimilation to Anglo-American social practices and material cultures. For Curtis, and many others of his generation, "Indians" were only "real Indians" when they behaved as they were imagined to have behaved prior to contact with Anglo-Americans. As a direct result of these assumptions and beliefs about Native American identity and authenticity, the vast majority of photographs in *The North American Indian* depict native people as Noble Savages—as yet "untouched by civilization." But in truth, of course, by the time Curtis undertook his photographic expedition, the vast majority of Native American subjects who stood before his lens had already undergone significant transformation and change since the precontact era. Suffering eco-nomic, social, and physical deprivation on reservations, and falling victim re-peatedly to disease, violence, and neglect, the Native Americans that Curtis photographed were in a state of upheaval and flux, not harmony and balance. Thus, Curtis's "scientific" mission to photograph and document traditional life in its unfettered reality was, in fact, largely an exercise in fiction, fantasy and myth-making.

Interest in Edward Curtis's photographs declined soon after the comple-tion of *The North American Indian* in the early 1930s. By the time of his death in 1952, Curtis was largely forgotten and penniless. A brief obituary in the *New York Times* ended with the simple statement that "Mr. Curtis was also known as a photographer." With the rise of Native American activism and the Civil Rights movement in the late 1960s, Curtis's work began to gain new interest and attention. A decade later, by the late 1970s, anthropology took what has been called "the reflexive turn," in which writers like Ruth Behar, James Clif-ford, Vincent Crapanzano, George Marcus, and Paul Rabinow among others began to question the "scientific objectivity" of ethnography and the practice of anthropological fieldwork. The "reflexive turn" implied a figurative "look in the mirror" by anthropologists who started to question seriously their own biases and the entanglement of anthropology itself in the legacies of colonialism and imperialist expansion. Influenced by this "crisis of representation," and a grow-ing sense of self-criticism and epistemological angst within the discipline of anthropology, studies of Edward Curtis's photographic oeuvre, beginning in the late 1970s, took on a greater tone of skepticism and mistrust with regards to the objectivity of his photographic record. In early 1982, historian Christopher Lyman curated an exhibition entitled *The Vanishing Race and Other Illusions: A New Look at the Work of Edward Curtis*, which ran for several months at the Smithsonian's National Museum of Natural History. Featuring over 115 original prints and photogravures, the exhibition and its accompanying catalog set forth a provocative argument suggesting that Curtis routinely manipulated both his subjects and the photographic process to present distorted and glorified images of Native American life at the turn of the last century.

In the catalog to *The Vanishing Race and Other Illusions*, Lyman presents a broad examination of how Curtis altered his photographs to eliminate signs of modernity and outside influence. In some cases, Curtis dressed his subjects in buckskin jackets and feather headdresses that he carried with him in a trunk of costumes. In other cases, Curtis manipulated his glass negatives by adding or removing various elements in the composition of a scene. In what has now be-come a classic case of photomanipulation, Lyman presents two versions of the same image taken by Curtis in Montana around 1909 among the Piegan tribe

FIG. 18.4.   Little Plume (right) and Yellow Kidney (left) seated inside a lodge, Montana, ca. 1909. Photograph by Edward S. Curtis. LOT 12322-C. Library of Congress, Prints and Photographs Division, Washington, DC.

of the Blackfoot Confederacy—one being a print from the original glass dry-plate negative (fig. 18.4) and the other a photogravure from volume six of *The North American Indian* published in 1911 (fig. 18.5). In the original print, the two men, Little Plume and Yellow Kidney, are seated in a well-appointed tepee surrounded by an array of traditional artifacts, including buffalo-skin shields and deerskin articles. On the ground, between the two men, rests a ceremonial pipe and tobacco cutting board. By their sides, the men are flanked by an eagle-wing fan and a large quillwork medicine bundle. Near the center of the image, standing in stark contrast to its other material surroundings, is a mechanical peg-leg windup alarm clock typical of the kind manufactured in the United States in the first decade of the twentieth century. The fact that the clock is still housed in its original pasteboard box offers an intriguing detail, suggesting perhaps that it was valued more as a marker of status than as a functional time-keeping device.

Sometime between 1909, when Curtis is thought to have taken this photograph in the Piegan Lodge, and its publication in 1911, Curtis decided to excise the clock from the image Though faint remnants of the clock's form are still discernible in the published version, the clock was scratched off when the

FIG. 18.5.   *In a Piegan Lodge.* Plate 188. Photograph by Edward S. Curtis. Published in *The North American Indian: The Piegan. The Cheyenne. The Arapaho* (Cambridge, MA: University Press, 1911).

photographic negative was transferred to the copper plate that was used to etch the photogravure. Although Curtis left no record of why he removed the clock from the published image, one can only imagine that he did so in an effort to preserve (or further) his mythologizing of an authentic, untouched indigenous Other. The clock in the Piegan Lodge represents not only the proliferation of industrial manufactured commodities within Native American communities by the beginning of the twentieth century, it also signifies a period in world history when time itself became a commodity within the context of industrial capitalism. In contrast to the symbols of "ritual time" signified by the presence in the Piegan Lodge of the ceremonial pipe and the medicine bundle, the clock represents "secular time," characterized by regularity, order, and self-government. Thus, Curtis's erasure of the clock functions to banish time itself from the image and ultimately to deny the Piegan their contemporaneity with the viewer of the photograph. For Curtis, the "vanishing clock" was a necessary prerequisite to fulfilling his mission to document the "vanishing Indian."

Just one year after the publication of Curtis's photogravure *In a Piegan*

FIG. 18.6. "Indian" alarm clock. Manufactured by E. Ingraham Co., Bristol, Connecticut. Patent date 1912. Private collection.

Lodge, Connecticut-based clockmaker E. Ingraham Company introduced in 1912 its latest alarm clock model called the "Indian" (fig. 18.6). The company boasted that its new product, with an internal alarm and spring-action windup mechanism, "adapted to a low-priced clock the high-priced features hitherto applied only to expensive alarm clocks." Lower-priced clocks such as this one meant that they were now more readily available to middle-income families. One year after its introduction to the market, a weekly trade journal for hardware retailers reported in 1913 that the "Indian" clock's "departure from old methods were immediately recognized by the public" and that "the demand for the Indian has been so tremendous as to tax its manufacturing facilities to the utmost." Ingraham's newly designed alarm clock appropriated not only the name "Indian" but also adopted as its logo an image of a Native American warrior. On the clock's face appears a profile view of a Native American man in Plains-style eagle-feather war bonnet and what looks to be the shoulders of a fringed buckskin jacket.

The fact that just one year after Edward Curtis had scrubbed away the presence of a mechanical clock from his photograph of Little Plume and Yellow Kidney, a clock of nearly identical design was introduced to the marketplace under the name "Indian" is, to say the least, ironic. While it was not uncommon for images of Native Americans to be used as logos or motifs in American advertising by the end of the nineteenth century, these cultural appropriations usually aligned themselves with some "logical" connection between the product and its Native American referent—Black Hawk cigars, which evoked a connection to native tobacco, or Eskimo Ice Cream Pies, which suggested an affinity to the blustering cold of the Circumpolar North. But to include the profile of a Native America man on the logo of a mechanical clock seems to confound any rational logic between the product itself and its symbolic referent.

Yet, if considered in relation to the overall goals of Edward Curtis's photographic project, the "Indian" clock makes perfect sense. Curtis's primary agenda was to document and preserve in photographic images Native American peoples before their "disappearance" into the melting pot of Anglo-American cultural assimilation. By 1912, when E. Ingraham Company released its "Indian" model clock, Native Americans had lost most of their indigenous land and rights; they were thus no longer perceived as a threat to Anglo-American ambitions for westward expansion, conquest, and hegemony. As is the case with other indigenous populations who have been successfully colonized and "neutralized," it is common for the colonizing culture to memorialize the vanquished through sentimental and nostalgic representations of those very "traditional" cultures they have altered or destroyed. The "Indian" clock thus serves as an ideal example of the argument made by anthropologist Renato Rosaldo in 1989 in his coining of the phrase "imperialist nostalgia" to refer to this paradoxical phenomenon in which people mourn the passing of what they themselves have destroyed or transformed. Denied the presence of a clock in Curtis's photographic representation of indigenous "reality," the Native American is now relegated instead to a stereotypical logo on the face of a mechanical clock—a clock almost identical to the one Little Plume and Yellow Kidney attempted to include in the staging of their self-representation.

THE CLOCK AS STUDIO PROP

Born around 1921 in Bamako, Mali, at the height of French colonial occupation, Seydou Keïta developed an interest in photography at a young age. Returning from a trip to Senegal in 1935, Seydou's uncle, Tiémoko Keïta, brought back for his young nephew a Kodak Brownie camera manufactured in Stuttgart, Germany. Just over a decade later, in 1948, Keïta set up his first studio near the family house in Bamako, situated behind the city's main prison and near the train depot. At the time there existed only a handful of portrait studios in Bamako, some still run by colonial French expatriates, and a few newer ones owned and operated by up-and-coming Malian photographers. Keïta's studio was located in a prime and lively section of Bamako, where people disembarking from the train would routinely visit his studio to have their portraits taken. As Keïta continued to build his professional photography business into the 1950s, Bamako had become a bustling metropolitan center experiencing, since the end of World War II, a period of rapid growth and urbanization.

What started mostly as an enterprise for taking photographs for government identification cards—necessary for the official documents marking colonial identity in the big bureaucracy of what was then still called French West Africa—eventually transformed into a proper "artistic" portrait studio where men, women, and children posed against decorative or flowery backdrops sometimes surrounded by props and various accessories. Unlike the identification photographs, which were by definition dreary and whose composition was dictated by the tyranny of bureaucratic standards, the studio portraits were meant to express individual personalities and an eccentric sense of aesthetic beauty. Portraits such as these were commissioned by men and women as keepsakes, given to loved ones as romantic mementos, sent to relatives back home in rural villages, or carried by soldiers into battle.

In developing his unique style of photo portraiture, Keïta was keenly aware of the relationship between himself and his clients. Unlike French colonial photography, which was structured largely around a model of inequality—where colonial subjects were dragged (metaphorically, but sometimes literally) and stripped of their dignity in front of the camera—Keïta's studio was based on mutual respect and an equal transaction between portrait-taker and portrait-sitter. In colonial photography the intended viewer was not the subject of the photograph itself, but rather the audience was likely located at a distance, back in Europe. In a parallel manner to the type of photographs taken by Reverend George Brown in the South Pacific, colonial photography in Africa was largely aimed at taxonomizing and devaluing African men and women, with the ultimate goal of justifying imperialist exploitation, conversion to Christianity, and what the French called the "civilizing mission."

For Seydou Keïta, the photographic studio was not conceived as a theater of exploitation but on the contrary as a theater of aspiration. His sitters were consenting, not coerced. Keïta's photo sessions involved a lively collaboration between himself and his sitters; his clients were free to express themselves and made extensive use of costumes, props, and various poses to construct their own desired identity and individuality. Whereas colonial photography sought to emphasize the subject's "primitiveness" (especially through its focus on nudity), Keïta's studio photography emphasized the sitter's modernity, urbanity, and fashion savvy. These portraits were commissioned as allegories of wealth, status, romance, beauty, and respectability. Since many of the clients who posed for their portrait in Keïta's studio did not yet possess the attire or accoutrements they aspired to someday own, they instead borrowed many of the outfits and props seen in the studio portraits from Keïta's stock of lendable supplies. "I had several suits available in my studio," Seydou Keïta told an interviewer in 1996, "including straight ties, bow-ties, breast-pocket handkerchiefs, shirts, hats, and even a beret. . . . I also had accessories available for them: watches, fountain pens, watch-chains, plastic flowers, a radio, a telephone, a scooter, a bicycle, and an alarm clock."

In an undated portrait, likely taken in the early to mid-1950s, Keïta photographed in his studio a young man wearing stylish gray slacks, a dark pin-striped jacket, and brown leather shoes and sporting a fine wristwatch (fig. 18.7). The man, who is leaning with self-confidence toward the camera and looking directly into the lens, rests his right arm on a large tabletop tube radio—a 1946 Ducretet-Thomson model D736 housed in a Bakelite case. Sitting on top of the radio, like a totem pole for prized commodity fetishes, is an elegant mantel clock. The clock is an OBLIC model eight-day windup alarm clock from 1935–37 manufactured by the JAZ company, one of France's premiere clockmakers, which was the company's top-of-the-line alarm clock in the 1930s. Boasting an almost silent mechanical movement, the OBLIC was marketed as a "*reveil de luxe*," and housed in an Art Deco Bakelite (or, as it was branded, "Jazolite") case with polished chrome trim (fig. 18.8). This was by no means an inexpensive or common clock. Designed with what were called "*buildings*" clock hands (shaped to evoke the pointed form of New York's newly constructed skyscrapers), this JAZ-brand clock epitomized a contemporary metropolitan ethos and streamlined modernist design.

In the 1930s, when this clock was manufactured, French Art Deco style signified the height of innovative design and cool sophistication. At the 1931 International Colonial Exposition in Paris—where France continued its tradition, initiated at the Exposition Universelle of 1878, to display representative subjects from its global empire in *faux* villages and so-called "human zoos"—the French metropolitan pavilions were designed in the Art Deco style to signal unmistak-

FIG. 18.7. Seydou Keïta, Untitled, Bamako, Mali, ca. 1950s. Gelatin silver print. Pigozzi Collection, Geneva.

Clish Parh of
Identity

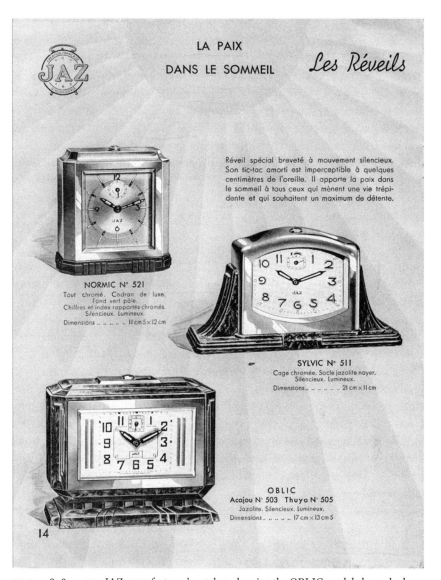

LA PAIX
DANS LE SOMMEIL

Les Réveils

Réveil spécial breveté à mouvement silencieux.
Son tic-tac amorti est imperceptible à quelques
centimètres de l'oreille. Il apporte la paix dans
le sommeil à tous ceux qui mènent une vie trépi-
dente et qui souhaitent un maximum de détente.

NORMIC N° 521
Tout chromé. Cadran de luxe.
Fond vert pâle.
Chiffres et index rapportés chromés.
Silencieux. Lumineux.
Dimensions .. .. 11 cm 5 × 12 cm

SYLVIC N° 511
Cage chromée. Socle jazolite noyer.
Silencieux. Lumineux.
Dimensions.. .. .. 21 cm × 11 cm

OBLIC
Acajou N° 503 Thuya N° 505
Jazolite. Silencieux. Lumineux.
Dimensions.. .. .. .. 17 cm × 13 cm 5

14

FIG. 18.8. 1937 JAZ manufacturer's catalog, showing the OBLIC model alarm clock. Collection of Denis Raquin.

ably that they represented the values and domains of French culture in sharp contrast to the exposition's non-European venues, which were meant to show the enigmatic riot of "primitive man" in his chaotic "natural state." One of the rooms in the metropolitan pavilion's Musée des Colonies, the so-called Salon du Ministre, was designed by Emile-Jacques Ruhlmann, regarded as one of the best Art Deco decorators of the time. In describing the room in a contemporary account, one observer noted that "the strict order of metropolitan civilization has arrived at a stage where the predominance of simplicity and practical sense feels repugnance for superfluous ornaments and uselessly complicated forms." In the hierarchy of French imperialist logic, its colonized subjects in French West Africa represented the bottom of the evolutionary scale, while the modernism of Art Deco, and its physical manifestation in the JAZ clock, represented the pinnacle of civilization.

The JAZ clock's entanglement in the baggage of French colonialism and its theories of racial hierarchy may not have been fully appreciated, or even deemed relevant, by those who chose to pose with the clock in Seydou Keïta's studio. Yet by incorporating within their photographic portraits imported commodities from the European colonial metropole, Keïta's clients were expressing their alignment with French cultural values, and their desire for economic and class status in the urban culture of mid-century Bamako. Many of those who commissioned portraits at this time had recently migrated to the city from their rural, agricultural homes, arriving in Bamako in search of income, upward mobility, and a desire to partake in the promise of French colonial prosperity and growth. Even if they had not yet achieved their goal (and many never would), the photo studio offered an opportunity for men and women to fantasize about material prosperity and reimagine themselves as members of Bamako's cultural elite. The man photographed by Seydou Keïta standing aside the "tower" of modern French technology is signaling not only his association with urban modernity but also his access to Western culture and material objects. It is not insignificant, I think, that his left hand is positioned in such a way that it appears he is adjusting the tuning knob on the radio's control panel. With this simple gesture of his hand, he suggests to the viewers of the portrait that he is "tuned in" or, as the French say, *branché* to the latest trends in technology and to the marketplace of modern luxury consumption items.

THE CLOCK IS STILL TICKING

James Luna, a resident of the La Jolla Indian Reservation who traced his descent to California Luiseño, Pooyukitchchum/Ipai, and Mexican-American ancestry, passed away unexpectedly on March 4, 2018, at age sixty-eight. Regarded as one of the most important contemporary Native American artists of his generation, Luna's internationally recognized artistic practice included photography, video, performance art, and sculptural installation. One of Luna's earliest and perhaps most iconic and significant works is *The Artifact Piece*, which was performed at the San Diego Museum of Man in February 1987. The performance consisted of Luna, wearing only a modest loin cloth, lying motionless on a bed of sand in a museum exhibition case. His vulnerable, unclothed body was surrounded by didactic museum labels that explained the scars on his skin—results of "excessive drinking," "bar-room brawls," and "falling drunk into a campfire." Alongside the display of his "installed" body was a small glass case exhibiting mundane artifacts drawn from his daily life—cassette recordings and record albums by the Rolling Stones and Jimi Hendrix, political campaign buttons, a book of Allen Ginsberg's poetry, personal family photographs, Luna's college diplomas, a basket, a rattle, and his divorce papers. In this piece, James Luna reimagines the historical encounter between audience and indigenous body, and, in transforming his body from "artifact" into "art," he reclaims agency for his own representation. *The Artifact Piece* is a direct critique of a long legacy of museum representations of Native Americans in which indigenous people are portrayed as dead, silent, or passive subjects only able to express themselves through the intermediary voice of non-native museum curators speaking on their behalf. Luna's performance is also framed as a challenge to the lingering trope of the "vanishing Indian," as championed by Edward Curtis and others alike. The juxtaposition of Luna's "extinct" motionless body and the cache of 1980s college-dorm-room artifacts and memorabilia speak directly to the dilemma of where to position Native American identity in contemporary American culture.

In his performance *Take a Picture with a Real Indian*, James Luna engages even more directly with the legacy of photography and the work of Edward Curtis. While the piece was performed several times in both museum and outdoor venues since 1991, in the final version of this performance on Columbus Day 2010 Luna placed three life-size, black-and-white cardboard cutouts of himself at the foot of the Columbus Memorial in Washington, DC. Each cutout represented Luna in different attire. In the first, he wears a buckskin breechcloth and moccasins; in the second, he dons a feather headdress and beaded breastplate, regalia associated with Plains Indian ceremonial dress or fancy attire; and in the third, he presents himself in "casual work apparel," wearing khaki pants and a dark polo shirt. Through the course of the performance, Luna stepped onto the makeshift platform on which the cutouts had been positioned wearing, each time, one of the three versions of the costumes represented in the cutout photographs. With each appearance on stage, Luna recited the same monologue: "Take a picture with a real Indian. Take a picture here, in Washington, DC, on this beautiful Monday morning, on this holiday called Columbus Day. America loves to say "her Indians." America loves to see us dance for them. America likes our arts and crafts. America likes to name cars and trucks after our tribes. Take a picture with a real Indian. Take a picture here today, on this sunny day here in Washington, DC."

After delivering his speech, Luna invited visitors who had gathered around the performance space to have their picture taken with whichever version of the costumed figure they felt represented the most "real" or authentic Indian. Most audience participants chose the figure sporting full Native American war dance regalia, thereby underscoring the point of the performance: the persistence of Native American stereotypes in the mind of the non-native participants. Using the medium of photography itself as a vehicle to explore the cultural history of representation, Luna reappropriates, here too, his agency in staging his own spectacle of Otherness.

In 2010, the same year in which Luna performed the last iteration of *Take a Picture with a Real Indian*, he also produced a series of three photographic diptychs entitled *Apparitions 2*. These photographs were included in Luna's last one-man exhibition, *Performagraphic*, held at the TRUCK Contemporary Art Gallery in Calgary, Canada, in 2016. Each of the three diptychs consists of a black-and-white photograph of a historical Native American figure juxtaposed with a color self-portrait of Luna imitating, in some fashion, the pose of his ancestral "double." In one of the three diptychs (fig. 18.9), Luna has selected an "anthropological" photograph, from around 1936, of William Ralganal Benson, a master basket maker and storyteller of the Eastern Pomo tribe from the region of Ukiah, California. William Benson and his wife, Mary Knight Benson, also an expert basket maker, worked together in the first decades of the twentieth century to create what are regarded today as some of the most exquisite and high-quality Pomo-style baskets ever made. The Bensons were members of a small group of "celebrity" Native American artists who emerged in the early 1900s, commanding high prices and garnering significant public recognition. Benson-made baskets were especially coveted by Anglo-American collectors because they were thought to represent the last "authentic" or "real" examples of Eastern Pomo basketry. Yet, ironically, and perhaps unbeknownst to these early collectors, both William and Mary Benson were in fact of mixed-blood ancestry — each the descendant of a Native American mother and Anglo-American father.

William and Mary Benson traveled in 1904 to participate in the St. Louis World's Fair. They were invited by the head of the fair's Anthropology Department, William J. McGee, to represent the Eastern Pomo. Mary Benson demonstrated basket-weaving techniques, while William Benson showed his skills at flint knapping. The Bensons' trip to St. Louis was a huge financial success;

FIG. 18.9.   James Luna, *Apparitions 2*, 2010. Reproduced with permission of Joanna Bigfeather.

they sold as many baskets as they could produce, as well as everything they had brought from Ukiah. In the archival photograph of William Benson, selected by James Luna for one of the diptychs in *Apparitions 2*, Benson holds in his hands what was probably one of his own baskets—a coiled willow gift basket adorned with applied feathers and white clamshell beads. In the color self-portrait of James Luna which forms the other half of this diptych the artist is dressed in dark pants, white jacket, and a white printed t-shirt. Luna tilts his head, like Benson, slightly to the right while looking directly into the camera's lens. Instead of a basket, Luna displays in his hands a large wall clock with white trim and a black face. What is the significance of the clock? One interpretation might be that Luna has chosen to hold a mechanical, industrial object to position himself at the opposite end of the technological spectrum from Benson's hand-coiled natural fiber basket. Benson's portrait in this piece, which appears to show a traditional native artist, would certainly fit more comfortably with Curtis's "imagined Indian" than would Luna's hybrid, confrontational intervention in his presentation of himself.

Yet at the same time, Luna's visual juxtaposition in this diptych from *Apparitions 2* may also be inviting the viewer to look more critically at the photograph of the famous Pomo basket weaver. Benson, after all, made a very successful living from his work by marketing his baskets to Anglo-American patrons who were eager to collect "authentic" Native American art that appeared to be traditional and showed no evidence of "corruption" from external influences. Yet William and Mary Benson were very much a part of the period of rapid cultural change experienced by the Pomo people in the late nineteenth and early twentieth centuries. Their creation of "traditional" Pomo baskets was not the product of an unbroken linear trajectory that could be traced from their ancestors directly into the present. It was instead the result of a disjointed and hybrid process of cultural "reinvention," in which the Bensons were able to produce the kind of work that satisfied their patrons' stereotypical expectations of timeless, authentic Native American art. So perhaps Luna's clock is signaling that "time is money"—the clock he holds is a metaphor for the "timeless" tradition of Pomo artistry and for the now priceless Pomo basket held in Benson's hands.

One final reading of this diptych may be that in his self-portrait Luna is directly referencing the "missing clock" from Edward Curtis's photograph of the Piegan Lodge and the lingering myth of the "vanishing Indian." Large and bold in its presence within Luna's self-portrait, the clock he holds may refer back to Curtis's excised clock, signaling that native presence cannot so easily be purged from history. Just as Benson's traditional identity and artistic genius was not erased by the disruptions to Pomo life caused by social and environmental upheavals at the end of the nineteenth century, so too Luna asserts in his juxtaposed self-portrait that the Native American artist remains present through the passage of time. And while Luna's t-shirt is mostly obstructed by the clock, the full graphic (visible in another of the diptychs from the *Apparitions 2* series) shows a black-and-white image of Elvis Presley's face printed above the words in hot pink "I'M DEAD." Although official records certify that Elvis died at age forty-two on August 16, 1977, popular culture continues to embrace the belief that Elvis is actually alive and enjoying life in hiding outside the limelight of fame. Could James Luna be drawing an ironic parallel here between the myth of the "vanishing Indian" and the conspiracy theories driven by die-hard Elvis fans? How can one reconcile the absurdity of widespread theories that Elvis is alive while at the same time denying the contemporaneity of Native American people and their cultures?

CLOCKING OUT

Although each image discussed in this essay was selected because it features the presence (or absence) of a clock, the meaning and value of the clock in each image is significantly different. In the case of Reverend George Brown, the presence of the clock signals an alien intrusion into the subject's physical space and social world. Here the clock was imposed into the image by the photographer to provide a "scientific" measure of body modification and, more importantly, to underscore the structural difference between the "savage" and the "civilized." Unlike Reverend Brown, Edward Curtis did not insert modern technology into his photograph of the Piegan Lodge. On the contrary, it was the two subjects of the portrait themselves who likely positioned the clock on the ground between them while staging the mise-en-scène of their own self-representation. Curtis's intervention occurred after the fact, when he erased the clock's presence and thus denied the existence of modern technology in what he imagined was an "authentic" Native American world uncorrupted by outside influence.

Unlike the first two examples, which demonstrate how a British and an American photographer each respectively used a mechanical clock to help define the nature of their encounter with indigenous people, the last two examples illustrate the power of the photographic subject to reassert control over their own self-representation. In the case of Seydou Keïta's photograph of a young man in his studio, the staging of the scene was likely directed entirely by the portrait sitter. The man's sophisticated attire and his selection of technological icons used as studio props animate his desire to embrace cosmopolitan modernity and the material culture of high style and status. The image is a testament to the subject's engagement with modern life and to his ambition of belonging to the modern urban world of mid-century Bamako. Inasmuch as Seydou Keïta's portrait represents a desire to position oneself within the world of materialist modernity, it is also a gesture of defiance—a refusal to be represented as colonial subject, without agency or access to metropolitan power.

James Luna's diptych *Apparitions 2* likewise represents an act of defiance, in which the artist inserts himself into the history of photography and its legacy of encounters with indigenous peoples. The obvious dissimilarity between the objects held by William Benson and James Luna in the diptych—a traditional hand-woven basket, on the one hand, and a mass-produced factory clock, on the other—may invite an initial response that focuses on narratives of progress and evolution. But the message of difference and change is immediately undercut by the striking similarity between the two men—their posture, their expression, and even the uncanny similarity of their mustached faces. They could be brothers. In pairing these two images, one must consider if Luna is inviting us to critically reassess the relationship between tradition and modernity, authenticity and inauthenticity, past and present.

One of the challenges for anthropology today is to re-examine the legacies of its own past and to develop new ways to better engage with an overwhelming deposit of visual images that form a permanent sediment of archival knowledge distributed up and down the strata of the discipline's history. Countless fleeting moments of encounter between lens and subject have been rendered permanent by the camera's technology of visual inscription. By tracing the "social life" of different clocks through photographic records spanning over a century, I have tried to suggest ways in which one might begin to (re-)engage with a particular set of photographic images and genres. While the basic character of photography itself has been defined by the assumption of its precise, mechanical, and impersonal rendering of "reality," what emerges from an anthropological interrogation of these photographic records is the inherent tension between fact and fiction, objectivity and subjectivity, realism and fantasy.

The study of photography in the history of anthropology is usually compartmentalized within the subdiscipline of "visual" anthropology. By definition, the study of the visual assumes that the topic of investigation is inherently visible to the observing eye. Yet, I would suggest that the most significant points of analysis to emerge from this investigation of "clock" photographs are not the traces of visual/visible culture but rather the elements that are invisible and that lie hidden just below the surface of visual analysis and observation. Like the internal mechanisms of the clock itself, which operate in the background behind the clock face, each of the four photographs analyzed here can be understood only by analyzing what is not represented in the image—agendas, motivations, desires.

ACKNOWLEDGMENTS

I am very grateful to Rebecca C. Steiner for her careful reading of earlier drafts, and for her insightful editorial guidance throughout. My thanks also to Denis Raquin for his assistance in identifying the clock and radio in Seydou Keïta's photographic portrait, and for his permission to reproduce a page from the 1937 JAZ catalog from his personal collection. And finally, I am indebted to Joanna Bigfeather for granting permission to reproduce James Luna's *Apparitions 2*.

SUGGESTIONS FOR FURTHER READING AND REFERENCES

Barthes, Roland. *Camera Lucida: Reflections on Photography*. Trans. Richard Howard. New York: Hill & Wang, 1981), 15.

Brown, George. 1908. *George Brown, D.D., Pioneer-Missionary and Explorer: An Autobiography*. London: Hodder & Stoughton.

Edwards, Elizabeth. 2011. "Tracing Photography." In *Made to Be Seen: Perspectives on the History of Visual Anthropology*, ed. Marcus Banks and Jay Ruby. Chicago: University of Chicago Press.

A history of photography in anthropological practice, which identifies three primary functions of visual representation traced along an arc of shifting theoretical approaches within the discipline.

Fabian, Johannes. 1983. *Time and the Other: How Anthropology Makes Its Object*. New York: Columbia University Press.

In this landmark book, Fabian argues that anthropology constructs its subject by positioning the "Other" as existing in different times from anthropologists and the cultures they represent. He calls this phenomenon the "denial of coevalness" and links it to a political agenda that seeks to justify colonial domination and also assumes a universal model celebrating the positive attributes of Western progress.

Freedman, Samuel G. 1986. "Beep Beep: Stopwatch Gets Hot," *New York Times*, October 11, p. 33.

Gladstone, Mara, and Janet Catherine Berlo. 2011. "The Body in the (White) Box: Corporeal Ethics and Museum Representation." In *The Routledge Companion to Museum Ethics: Redefining Ethics for the Twenty-First-Century Museum*, ed. Janet Marstine. London: Routledge.

An important review essay on the representation of the indigenous body in museum representations, which demonstrates the transformative influence of James Luna's 1987 performance of *Artifact Piece*.

Gonzalez, Jennifer A. 2008. *Subject to Display: Reframing Race in Contemporary Installation Art*. Cambridge, MA: MIT Press.

An exploration of the visual culture of race and identity through an analysis of the work of five contemporary installation artists, including James Luna.

Hawley, Elizabeth S. 2016. "James Luna and the Paradoxically Present Vanishing Indian," *Contemporaneity: Historical Presence in Visual Culture* 5 (1): 5-25.

Hutchinson, Elizabeth, 2009. *The Indian Craze: Primitivism, Modernism, and Transculturation in American Art, 1890-1915*. Durham, NC: Duke University Press.

A history of collecting Native American art and artifacts in the United States during the early twentieth century. The author demonstrates the relationship between artifact collecting and popular attitudes toward tradition and modernity.

Johnson, Billy, Jr. 2013. "Flavor Flav Explains Why He Wears a Clock as a Necklace." *Hip-Hop Media Training*, April 18.

Keller, Candace M. 2013. "Visual Griots: Identity, Aesthetics, and the Social Roles of Portrait Photographers in Mali." In *Portraiture and Photography in Africa*, ed. John Peffer and Elisabeth L. Cameron. Bloomington: Indiana University Press.

Lyman, Christopher M. 1982. *The Vanishing Race and Other Illusions: Photographs of Indians by Edward S. Curtis*. New York: Pantheon Books.

One of the first critical commentaries on Edward S. Curtis's work and legacy, it explores the biases and stereotypes that influenced his photographs.

Magnin, André, ed. 1997. *Seydou Keïta*. Zurich: Scalo.

An excellent catalog of representative photographs by Seydou Keïta from the collection of Keïta's work in Bamako, Mali, during the early 1990s.

McLendon, Sally. 1993. "Collecting Pomoan Baskets, 1889-1939," *Museum Anthropology* 17 (2): 49-60.

Morton, Patricia A. 2000. *Hybrid Modernities: Architecture and Representation at the 1931 Colonial Exposition, Paris*. Cambridge, MA: The MIT Press.

Combining architectural history and postcolonial theory, this book offers an important analysis of the 1931 Colonial Exposition in Paris, suggesting that the colonies were considered simultaneously as sites of decadence and rampant sensuality and as laboratories of Western rationality.

Mumford, Lewis. *Technics and Civilization*. New York: Harcourt, Brace, 1934. 14.

Nanibush, Wanda. "The Epistrophy of James Luna." http://www.jamesluna.red/about-hay den/ Accessed 3/20/2018.

O'Barr, William M. 2013. "Images of Native Americans in Advertising," *Advertising & Society Review* 14 (1): 1–51.

Parezo, Nancy J., and Don D. Fowler. 2007. *Anthropology Goes to the Fair: The 1904 Louisiana Purchase Exposition*. Lincoln: University of Nebraska Press.
    A careful historical analysis of the role of anthropology in the representation of non-Western cultures at the 1904 St. Louis World's Fair.

Pinney, Christopher. 2011. *Photography and Anthropology*. London: Reaktion Books.
    An account of the histories of photography and anthropology which documents both the parallels and a shifting relationships between the two disciplines.

Pinney, Christopher, and Nicolas Peterson, eds. 2003. *Photography's Other Histories*. Durham, NC: Duke University Press.
    A collection of essays exploring photographic practices around the world, one which demonstrates how a globally disseminated technology has been locally appropriated by non-Western photographers around the world.

Rosaldo, Renato. 1989. "Imperialist Nostalgia." In *Culture and Truth: The Remaking of Social Analysis*. Boston: Beacon Press.
    A very influential essay that introduced the concept of "imperialist nostalgia"—a phenomenon that Rosaldo defines as a mode of representation in which the West longs for "lost" traditional cultures which the West itself intentionally altered or destroyed.

Slater, Don. 1995. "Photography and Modern Vision: The Spectacle of 'Natural Magic'." In *Visual Culture*, ed. Chris Jenks. London: Routledge.

Webb, Virginia-Lee. 1995. "Manipulated Images: European Photographs of Pacific Peoples." In *Prehistories of the Future: The Primitivist Project and the Culture of Modernism*, ed. Elazar Barkan and Ronald Bush. Stanford, CA: Stanford University Press.
    An important essay that grew out of a more critical approach to the history of ethnographic photography in the 1980s and 1990s. Webb demonstrates how stereotypes of non-Western cultures were perpetuated through subtle photo retouching and carefully crafted studio arrangements.

Zamir, Shamoon. 2014. *The Gift of the Face: Portraiture and Time in Edward S. Curtis's "The North American Indian."* Chapel Hill: University of North Carolina Press.
    The author seeks to rethink and challenge the critical reception of Curtis's work which began in the 1980s. Zamir argues that Curtis's subjects were indeed active agents and engaged "co-authors" of Curtis's photographic project, who used their visual representation to negotiate a rapid transformation in indigenous culture and ideas of selfhood.

CHAPTER 19

CRITICAL ANTHROPOLOGIES AND THE RESURGENCE OF CULTURE MUSEUMS

ALTERNATIVE HISTORIES

Anthony Alan Shelton

In 1949 extolling its radical potential, Clyde Kluckhohn famously wrote, "Anthropology holds up a great mirror to man, and lets him look at himself in his infinite variety." Kluckhohn's use of the mirror metaphor affirmed anthropology's ability to invoke and sustain a self-critical and reflexive attitude able to upset everyday dogmas and presuppositions and inform a critical sensibility with which to distinguish truth from falsity and better understand the world from multiple perspectives. His early work promoted an applied anthropology that in the late twentieth and early twenty-first centuries has increased awareness of the relativism of ethics and values; the positional status of knowledges; and the ideal of an open society. These perspectives, taken together, have contributed to the rethinking and democratization of museums; they have also increased their receptivity to organizational restructuring, governance, the adoption of new curatorial models, and their re-engagement with diverse audiences and indigenous and minority communities.

Kluckhohn's mirror, like the better-known works of his colleagues Margaret Mead and Ruth Benedict, marked one of the mid-century turning points in the development of anthropology as a critical discipline. Kluckhohn contrasted five aspects of society across different cultures: morality, ecology, action (being, becoming, materialist, spiritual, goal orientation), social relations, and time, in what he described as the "value orientations" method. Whether intentional or not, his conclusions contested the competitive, acquisitive individualism of American society and thereby denied the assumed naturalism and unquestionable virtue of capitalist values.

TWO PARALLEL GENEALOGIES

American anthropology was not alone in realizing the critical potential of anthropology in promoting social critique and re-evaluation of the way the world is seen and understood. In France, Marcel Mauss and his circle, Henri Hubert, Maurice Halbwachs, Robert Hertz, Henri Beuchat, and others, synthesized the ethnographic knowledge accumulated through the intensive fieldwork of their American and British colleagues to construct a comparative analytical approach to the understanding of Western-defined categories such as space; the body and law; ritualized actions like gift exchange and sacrifice; and the mechanisms of recording, transmitting, and structuring the past through social memory and embodied forms of knowledge. Whether demonstrating the limitations of established Western categories, actions, and technique, mapping their unsuspected diversity, or deepening awareness of their significance, Mauss, like his American colleagues, developed perspectives that effectively de-privileged and challenged the authority of any singular way of seeing the world. Kluckhohn and Mauss's positions encouraged the later development of a skeptical anthropology which systematically interrogated the basis of fundamental Western assumptions on rationality, ethics, belief, and social organization.

The period 1840-90 has been termed anthropology's museum age, when exhibitions were dominated by mechanistic theories of cultural evolution, espoused in Britain by Alfred Cort Haddon and in the United States by Otis Mason and John Wesley Powell. In contrast, during 1890-1920, the museum university period, museum exhibitions adopted the culture area approach, championed by Franz Boas. In Britain the codification of ethnographic collecting and the elaboration of classificatory systems during both periods were guided by institutional handbooks like the successive editions between 1874-1951 of *Notes and Queries*, compiled and published by the Royal Anthropological Institute, and Brian Cranstone's Section Four entry on Ethnography, for the 1958 edition of the *Handbook for Curators*. Other systems of classification included those by Augustus Pitt Rivers, Haddon, and Beatrice Blackwood, and in the United

States by George Peter Murdock. More surprising, given his more radical approach, Marcel Mauss in his 1926 *Manuel d' ethnographie*, also contributed to this intellectual appropriation of indigenous cultural meaning by proposing a classificatory system of his own. In all cases, indigenous knowledge or the agency of objects was ignored in favor of a focus on the accumulation, classification, and sometimes exhibition of objects within pre-established Western theoretical frameworks.

So irrelevant and anomalous had many ethnographic museums in the United States become that in a landmark article published in 1954, Tschopik and Collier insisted that museums needed to reassess their means of communicating knowledge and use new technologies to refocus displays on contemporary issues like cultural assimilation. Skepticism on the relevance of ethnographic museums, within the profession, was echoed in William Sturtevant's much-quoted 1969 article "Does Anthropology Need Museums?" and in the Netherlands by H. Frese's erudite but less well-known 1960 monograph on *Anthropology and the Public*. For more than a century, between the 1870s and the 1970s, museums, far from embracing anthropology's more radical interpretive implications, relinquished its critical potential in support of the constraining influences of Western prescriptive classifications. In the process museums ignored indigenous knowledge systems, stripped objects of their ascribed agencies, and imposed a scientific conservatism that blunted the discipline's radical potential.

THE CRITICAL GAZE

By the 1970s anthropology museums, like the discipline itself, faced wide and multiple criticisms. While anthropology feared the extinction of its subject and was assaulted by accusations of its colonial origins and unsettled by epistemological doubt, anthropology museums had to face the anger of the indigenous people they claimed to represent, a multicultural society whose existence they ignored, and critical theory they ill understood. In the United Kingdom, *The Hidden Peoples of the Amazon* exhibition at the Museum of Mankind, London (1985), met protests from indigenous peoples, derision from public media and human-rights organizations, and public outrage for failing to include indigenous voices and idealizing the social and political conditions under which indigenous communities suffered. In Canada, the Lubicon Cree, who were to be celebrated in Calgary's Glenbow Museum's exhibition *The Spirit Sings: Artistic Traditions of Canada's First Peoples* (1988), condemned the petroleum company funding the exhibition for exploiting their land and asked museums to boycott loan requests. At the Royal Ontario Museum, Toronto, the exhibition *Into the Heart of Africa* (1989) was condemned by African Canadian protestors as insensitive and supportive of former colonial regimes. While all three museums at the time defied the demands made on them, the public recognition of their global and ethical responsibilities and the need for respectful and meaningful consultation later exerted a significant impact in changing exhibition methodologies. The Museum of Mankind's successive exhibitions, including *Madagascar: Island of the Ancestors* (1986) and *The Living Arctic: Hunters of the Canadian North* (1987), collaborated with local peoples and institutions, acknowledged the Western economic impact on those societies, and incorporated first-person voices into exhibition texts.

In Canada, in 1989, the Assembly of First Nations and the Canadian Museums Association responded to their own crises by instigating a task force to examine and recommend reforms on the relations between museums and indigenous peoples. Its report, which appeared in 1992, had a deep and enduring impact on the adoption of collaborative methods in curating First Nations exhibitions. While it was successful in returning the right of self-representation to communities, it failed to restore management over cultural property or to appreciably increase the number of First Nations curators and senior managers in permanent positions in Canadian museums. Demands for control, interpretation, and management of cultural property were again reasserted in 2015, in the influential Report of the Canadian Truth and Reconciliation Commission. This resulted in a second task force (Indigenous Council) being established by the Canadian Museums Association in 2017 to assess the progress of the first task force and to propose criteria and means to instigate intellectual decolonization and the establishment of effective mechanisms for power sharing between museums and communities. During this same period, twenty-eight years after the exhibition opened, in 2016 the ROM finally issued a formal apology to African Canadians for the hurt caused by their *Into the Heart of Africa* exhibition.

CONTEMPORARY RESPONSES

Because the growth of ethnographic museums has differed at distinct times in their history and in discrete parts of the globe, this section will examine three recent practices through which some museums have sought to reinvent themselves and regain contemporary relevance, ethical propriety, and intellectual integrity. The first practice focuses on the application of collaborative methodologies; second, the reconfiguration of ethnographic into world culture museums focused on glocalization; third, the development and museum application of critical museology.

Anthropology is by its nature a collaborative discipline, and it is more instructive to examine the power relations between museums and communities than it is to identify changes in methodology, to assess their degree of decolonization. This has provided a useful measure at the Museum of Anthropology at the University of British Columbia, where curators acknowledge at least three types of collaborative methodology, participant action research, when the museum fully relinquishes responsibility for an exhibition to an originating community, leaving the in-house curator as facilitator; dialectical collaboration, when a curator engages with community artists or knowledge keepers and the dialogue itself, in all its heterogeneity, structures the exhibition; and the consultation model involving community meetings and advisory panels. All three variants are collaborative, but involve the mobilization of very different types of relationship and result in different levels of empowerment. These current approaches, particularly participant action research, were instigated by Michael Ames, who, influenced by Dell Hymes and Paulo Freire's radical pedagogy, distanced the museum's methods and interests from mainstream disciplinary anthropology to embrace open, politically committed relationships that still guide many of its exhibitions.

The democratization of museums and knowledge mobilization with indigenous communities has further been accelerated by some nation-states assuming multicultural or plurinational identities and adopting the UN Declaration on the Rights of Indigenous Peoples (2007). Canada implemented policies to protect and enhance its multicultural and bilingual heritage as early as 1971, before enshrining them in the 1982 Charter of Rights and Freedoms and the 1988 Canadian Multiculturalism Act. Ecuador and Bolivia adopted new constitutions in 2008 and 2009, respectively, which recognized their plurinational composition, not only protecting their multicultural and multilingual legacies, but agreeing to a level of indigenous self-government within the wider state polity. The adoption of the UN Declaration of the Rights of Indigenous People, signed by Canada in 2016, is expected to bring substantial organizational and curatorial changes to heritage management. Social and political changes like these will not necessarily threaten the museum's commitment to anthropology, but they do give renewed support to the adoption of the discipline's more radical strands discussed earlier.

The collaborative turn in museum anthropology has received especially strong intellectual leadership from Mexico, despite its government's disregard of the 1996 San Andrés Accords with the Zapatista Army of National Liberation (EZLN) on constitutional reform, and despite its backtracking on the adoption of a plurinational state model. Regardless of governmental cynicism, Mexican anthropologists have long been major international advocates of indigenous rights and reform over control of museum collections. Guillermo Bonfil Batalla, director of the Instituto Nacional de Antropologia e Historia, INAH (1972–76), edited many of the most important documents from Latin America on indigenous political thought (for example, *Utopía y Revolución*, 1981). Six years later, he published *México Profundo: Una Civilización Negada*, where he argued that, despite more than five hundred years of repression and marginalization, an indigenous civilization with roots in the pre-Columbian past continued to exist side by side with Euro-American civilization in a common national territory. Bonfil's museology was devoted to returning voice to Mexico's indigenous, minority, and working–class populations, which, if impossible to execute through the INAH's vast network of national repositories of the country's official history, might, he suggested, be achieved through the establishment of a new organization, the Museo de Culturas Populares, which he founded in 1982. The collaborative methodology he developed was clearly embodied in the museum's first exhibition, *El Maíz: Fundamento de la Cultura Popular Mexicana*, which sought not to abstract maize from its historical and cultural contexts and reduce it to a scientific category or commodity, but to understand it as shaping culture just as culture shaped the plant's domestication and cultivation. The project team worked with communities throughout Mexico recording history and myths, techniques of cultivation, harvesting and storage, its religious and social significance, rituals, preparation and recipes, linguistic designations, and metaphorical associations. This compendium of indigenous knowledges was published as *Nuestra Maíz: Treinta monografías populares* (1982). The books were distributed among the participating communities along with poster-board exhibitions based on the museum's displays. Bonfil did not envision the Museo de Culturas Populares as developing a collection of its own, but as committed to political action and indigenous empowerment, which through community-based research undertaken for temporary exhibitions, might reverse the usual one-way flow of knowledge from local rural communities to metropolitan institutions. The museum also worked closely with existing institutions and community museums to build capacity and promote collaborations. Through his museum practice, written works, and the journal *Civilización: configuraciones de la diversidad*, Bonfil closely interwove museums, anthropology, and political activism, bringing to fruition one of the radical potentialities always endemic to anthropology.

The development of world culture museums began in the late 1990s as some major northern European ethnography museums began to redirect their primary associations away from the nations in which they were situated toward international intergovernmental organizations like ASEMUS (Asia-Europe Museum Network), and geopolitical blocs such as the European Union through which new regional identities were coming to supplant or coexist with national identities.

Between 2009 and 2013 the European Commission launched a research project, Ethnography Museums and World Cultures (RIME). Divided into two sections, First Contacts and Modernities, the project reiterated some of themes first discussed by Tschopik and Collier in 1954, albeit in a markedly different geopolitical and intellectual context. The themes covered: the relationship between anthropology and ethnography museums; collecting foci and methods; the uses to which colonial collections could be put, as well as new questions on how to incorporate indigenous perspectives into exhibitions, and the relationship between ethnography and contemporary art. These were all issues central to the ongoing emergence and development of world culture museums as well as others which had provoked areas of dispute with more traditional ethnographic museums. The project incorporated ten of Europe's largest and oldest ethnography museums, some of which had already reinvented themselves as world culture museums, and others which were in the process of doing so.

The rise of world culture museums coincides with our second practice intimately connected to changing definitions and significances of ethnographic collections. What was classified as "primitive art" before the 1970s was redesignated world art in the 1980s and global art in the 1990s. These redesignations coincided with different interpretive frameworks and the incorporation of certain categories of ethnographic materials into different art worlds. Ethnographic or "primitive art" had been clearly distinguished from Western art and attributed its own qualities. World art, although then accepted as comparable to Western art, both in its expressive power and through its accelerating commodification, was still separated from Western art. Global art, however, incorporated Western and non-Western artists as equals. The changing significance of ethnographic collections was mirrored in differences in its institutionalization and expressed in defining exhibitions. *Sacred Circles. 2000 Years of North American Indian Art* at London's Hayward Gallery, in 1976–77, exemplified the essence of "primitive art" objects by grafting a cultural area approach to the presentation of what its curators deemed to be highly refined art works. The New York Museum of Modern Art's *'Primitivism' in 20th Century Art: Affinity of the Tribal and the Modern* exhibition in 1984 juxtaposed anonymous non-Western art objects with named European avant-garde artists to demonstrate the supposed affinities that connected them. Finally, the exhibition *Magiciens de la Terre* (1989) at the Centre Georges Pompidou and La Villette, Paris, dissolved the categories of artist, artisan, and aesthetics to affirm the works, regardless of their place of origin, as specially endowed objects made by a common class of fabricators, or "sorcerers"—a move that many have criticized as a new form of appropriation of non-Western cultural expressions. The world of global art created a division between historical ethnographic collections which have remained in ethnography museums, or, in a few cases, have been subsumed by art museums, and contemporary ethnographic objects, which when redefined as global art, with named artists, became increasingly commodified and distributed through galleries and art shows. Global art avoids institutionalization through the mobilization of new forms of exhibition such as biennales and art shows to escape the prescriptions of ethnographic classification.

Some world culture museums, such as the once-controversial Musée d' quai Branly, are a complex mixture of objects which fall into this historically disjointed net of categories and others which freely mobilize multiple exhibition genres regardless of their disciplinary affiliation. The quai Branly represented a radical break from its parent, the Musée de l'Homme, an ethnographic museum dependent on the National Museum of Natural History. In contrast other world culture museums have maintained a contemporary anthropological affiliation. However, one of the things that distinguish them from "unreformed" museums is their reconfiguration and sometimes reinstitutionalization of previously established collections. Sweden's Världskultur Museerna, the National Museum of World Culture in Stockholm and Gothenburg, established in 1999, combines the former independent museums of Middle Eastern and Asian art and archaeology with the country's two ethnographic museums to establish a new consortium whose wide collections encourage more interdisciplinary presentations. Liverpool Museum, redesignated a world museum in 2005, combined ethnographic, archaeological, historical and Western science collections but avoided any new synthesis, while the former Antwerp Museum of Ethnography was amalgamated with the city's European ethnography museum and maritime museum in the new Museum aan de Stroom (MAS). Frankfurt am Main's Museum für Völkerkunde, renamed Museum der Weltkulturen in 2001, attempted to reconfigure its collections through acquisitions of contemporary art, provoking a crisis in its identity and purpose which will be slow to heal. Nevertheless, the majority of these museums, including Rotterdam's Wereldmuseum (renamed 2000) and Vienna's Weltmuseum (renamed 2013), although mainly depositaries of ethnographic collections, depend on loans and new acquisitions to shift their exhibition focus and drive an agenda that concentrates on global and glocal themes. This new focus enables them to move away from the old dichotomy between tradition and modernity and employ different disciplinary lenses to substantially reshape their identity and profile.

Ethnographic institutions, collections, and exhibitions have become much more complex and heterodoxical than in the 1970s and can no longer be understood independent of the larger art world and the mixed institutions that comprise it. Many have also revived their popularity. World cultures are seen as dynamic, connected, and open-ended, and exhibitions like *Secret Love* (2012–13, Världkultur Museerna), *Fetish Modernity* (2011, Royal Museum for Central

Africa, Tervuren), *Dazzling Desire* (2017–18, Museum aan de Stroom) mark this new shift to global themes. These museums have also shed their close relations to museum ethnography, with its emphasis on older concepts of history, functionality, material culture, and provenance, to re-engage with more wide-ranging anthropological themes and related issues.

The third practice I want to discuss is that which stems from critical museology. Critical museology espouses its radical and essential break from operational or practical museology. Together with its means of reproduction embedded in wider heritage regimes, university courses and professional organizations, operational museology constitutes critical museology's subject of study. Critical museology grew out of the multiple social, political, and intellectual critiques, disquietudes, and experimental exhibitions and installations that have been aimed against museum operations since the 1970s. Its codification and methodological precepts have been heavily influenced by practices stemming from the application of the more radical anthropological perspectives applied by practitioners Charles Hunt, Jacques Hainard, Marc-Olivier Gonseth, Fernando Estévez, Nuno Porto, Klaus Schneider; and by various exhibitions curated in different institutions by Mary Bouquet, Nicola Levell, Anthony Shelton, Boris Wastiau, and others.

Between 1981 and 2004 Hainard curated or co-curated twenty-two exhibitions that applied anthropological insights to the examination of a wide variety of cultural subjects which formed the basis of what he called a museology of rupture. The exhibitions curated during this period have been divided into three categories: (1) those thematic exhibitions that focused on the deconstruction of cultural and social categories and classifications, (2) experimental exhibitions that sought to deconstruct the sociocultural dynamics that condition everyday life, and (3) reflections on the passions and politics involved in collecting objects, their exhibition, and their institutionalization. Hainard's museology envisaged the museum as a laboratory to examine the translation and revelatory power of visual languages to express the contradictions and unexamined values and assumptions underlying the performance of everyday life. Hainard and Gonseth at the Musée d' etnographie Neuchâtel, created a dynamic and restless, reflexive museology that ensured the museum remains critical of its own position and mindful of the limitations and contradictions within its own processes of collecting, cataloging, and displaying. For Hainard the world and the laws, rules, and norms surrounding its perception are always culturally constructed and should never be assumed to be natural, universally applicable, or transcendentally guaranteed. Through his museology of rupture, the political strategies and purposes which mobilize them can be decloaked and the simulacrum of the everyday revealed.

The potential of anthropology to provide methodologies and themes for museum exhibitions is recognized by a number of other critical museologists. Bouquet in her 1992 exhibition, *Man ape—Ape man* at the Pesthuis, Leiden, explored the context of Eugene Dubois's discovery of the missing link, Pithecanthropus, in human evolution. Instead of focusing on the fossils themselves, however, Bouquet constructed a cultural history of the period, concentrating on their depiction in cartoons and illustrations, advertising media, even re-creating Dubois's library to provide the social and intellectual context of his interpretation. Another room compared the West's fascination with evolutionary or genealogical classificatory systems with the systems of other societies where contemporaneous kinship terms are more important. Another of her exhibitions re-presented the history of the University of Oslo's ethnographic collections, while yet another focused on the significance of two sets of labels attached to a collection of Melanesian objects at the University of Porto. The collection had been acquired from German museums at the outbreak of World War II and the two sets of labels clearly expressed divergent German and Portuguese translations and variant understandings of the objects once they entered European collections.

For Estévez, memory, forgetting, and the personal and state objects and instruments through which it is modulated, provide a re-occurring theme of the installations he curated at the Museo de Antropología y Historia, Tenerife. Shelton's 1995 *Fetishism: Visualising Power and Desire* used Congo minkisi figures and modern and contemporary art to deconstruct the different historical uses to which the term *fetishism* had been used. The exhibition began with the term's nineteenth-century use to describe the earliest phase in the evolution of religion, before examining its incorporation into psychiatry and psychoanalysis and then finishing with its Marxist conception in the theory of commodity fetishism and alienation. Wastiau's 2000 *ExitCongoMuseum* sought to similarly deconstruct the aesthetic works in the Museum of Central Africa, Tervuren, to reveal their individual histories and the colonial history of their accumulation. This deconstructive turn was further adopted by Nicola Levell in the Centennial Gallery at the Horniman Museum (2001–16), where she laid bare the history of different visual languages through which the museum's collections had been mediated. In a later exhibition, *The Marvellous Real: Art from Mexico 1926–2011* (2013–14), Museum of Anthropology, University of British Columbia), Levell deconstructed and replaced a French surrealist view of Mexican art with a classification devised by the Cuban ethnomusicologist, critic, and novelist Alejo Carpentier to examine the significant differences in perspective generated by the adoption of a Latin American interpretive framework.

Other experimental exhibitions, usually eluded from the history of ethnographic displays, were also curated in the United Kingdom in the 1980s–90s. My own redisplay of the ethnographic and archaeological galleries of Brighton Museum and Art Gallery in 1993 attempted to promote a dialogue between the ideas and values of different cultures with those of Western collectors. The Cultures Gallery assembled complexes of objects under the heading of action words—worship, exchange, conflict, the exercise of power and authority, and gender ascription—to present part of the multitudinous ways different cultures conceptualized and visualized them. A second gallery presented parts of the museum's larger ethnographic collections classified according to the assumptions and narratives recorded by their nineteenth- and twentieth-century collectors: a yachtsman who sailed the Pacific, a reporter and graphic artist for the *London Illustrated News* stationed in South Africa; a collector fascinated by the use of natural materials by indigenous societies; and a female anthropologist who had made extensive collections from Papua New Guinea. A smaller third gallery in this exhibition complex intended for temporary displays focused on issues that emerged from the juxtaposition of Western and non-Western worldviews, questions of hybridity, the politics of collecting, and the impact of anthropological views on contemporary art. Artists' intervention, though unpopular with some curators, were also encouraged in these galleries. In one intervention in the Cultures Gallery, *Peep*, the artist Sonia Boyce covered the vitrines with cut-outs of the tracings of the shadows cast by the objects, creating oblique peepholes on to the exhibits which forced viewers to bend their heads and bodies to see what lay obscured by the opaque paper coverings. In so doing she transferred the subject of the visitor's voyeuristic gaze away from the exoticized objects on display to the actions of the Western visitors in their attempt to penetrate and see beyond the paper screens.

A more ambitious project, which followed similar premises, informed my 1999–2002 redisplay of the ethnographic collections at the Horniman Museum, London. The museum's large central South Hall, surrounded by a high balcony, was transformed into Britain's first permanent exhibition of African art. This time a committee of curators (ACP) brought from Africa and Trinidad, together with two African curators based in the United Kingdom provided the criteria for the exhibition and advised on how best we could enlarge collections to include objects from French-speaking Africa, a region usually missing from United Kingdom collections. Display criteria included categories like patronage, different natures, men/women, ancestors and morality, royalty and power, text, image history, cycles of life, parody and humor, and creation and recreation. Although not based on the action-word approach, the ACP chose these themes to upset established anthropological categories. *Different Natures* was intended to present masquerade as part of wider African concepts of nature;

patronage was incorporated to historicize the changing relations of production and consumption that resulted from colonialism; and text, image, history were meant to undermine the dichotomy between literate and oral cultures. Objects were described using different sets of categories contained within this list. A second level of interpretation was provided by the Voices Project, which reached out to London's and Brussels's diverse African communities to request they share their memories of similar objects to those exhibited. This strategy was intended to de-exoticize the works in the gallery even more by locating them through diasporic memories to real Africans living among us. A third level of interpretation was provided by British, French, Belgian, Nigerian, Malian, Benin, Brazilian, and Trinidadian anthropologists, traditional knowledge holders and collectors whom the ACP contracted to enlarge the collections and increase their inclusiveness. Third-level interpretations were provided as texts or in video form. The importance given to narrative authenticity expressed in the several levels of voices, narratives, and audiovisual presentations contrasted starkly with the alienation we wanted to create in the design of the gallery itself. A postmodern pastiche of aluminum and glass cases enclosed in soaring ochre- and sand-colored structures rejected any feat of imagination that the gallery intended to transport visitors to an imaginary Africa. This was a London Gallery and without recognizing its distance and removal from Africa, it would have been impossible to acknowledge the colonial and neocolonial histories that had helped move these collections (and the voices and narratives of the people quoted in the exhibition) from their places of origin to where they are today. The intimacy of memories and words contrasting with the spatial alienation of the design conjured objects as transnational envoys, problematically located with disjunctured meanings, agencies, and purposes. If once they were part of more elaborate ceremonial, religious, or political assemblages, now they were abstracted. Instead of once possessing religious-legal life cycle functions or transforming and modulating supernatural powers, the works took on a didactic functioning which in the eighteen years since it was opened, dramatically increased the number of African British visitors to the museum, many of whom were anxious to share these powerful icons of their identity with their children and families.

As in the Brighton experiment, a second gallery in the Horniman Museum, curated by Levell, was devoted to the history of the larger collections from which the works in *African Worlds* had been drawn. However, instead of focusing on private collectors, the gallery drew attention to the museum's founder and subsequent curators to understand the growth of the collections and the motivations behind different historical genres of exhibiting it. This was much more complex than the Brighton version and adopted a Mondrian-like grid attached to the gallery's ceiling to help suspend four large internally sculptured exhibition cases. The ceiling grid acted as a physical device that descended to partition the cases in increasingly complex compartments. In this way, the grid was intended to denote the various narrative uses and increasingly specialized classifications used by the museum to legitimate the growth of the collections and their deployment in changing genres of exhibition. The first case, *Scholars, Travellers and Traders,* gave an unrestricted view of the diversity of the ethnographic collections, idealized as prior to their classification and mobilization within the museum. The second case, on John Horniman's original collection and exhibitions, *The Gift,* cut deep furrows and acutely angled spaces and platforms into the case, so different aspects of the original collection, including police batons, meerschaum pipes, metal helmets and chain mail, cascading cases of butterflies and insects, plains Indian headdresses, Benin ivories, Sri Lankan masks, Hindu and Buddhist deities and a life-sized papier-mâché statue of Kali were ascribed discrete positions. The grid held the case but hardly penetrated it, consistent with the idea of a cabinet of curiosities in which the spectacle of wonder dominated all else. The third cabinet, *The New Museum,* a long wall case, was dedicated to the period 1901–46, when Haddon had been the museum's external adviser and rearranged the displays to represent a didactic exposition of the laws of cultural evolution. Mainly focused on the museum's Oceanic collection, here the grid descended to determinedly dissect space and make ever-increasing prescriptions on the arrangement and display of the collections by tracing similarities and differences in decoration and arranging objects according to the evolution of artistic decoration from abstract to naturalistic motifs. The fourth cabinet, the Material Culture Archive, conjured the period from 1946 onward, when anthropological functionalism was adopted and collections assembled through fieldwork. During this period, first under the curatorship of Otto Sampson and later Keith Nicklin and Ken Teague, collections representing aspects of distinct cultural and social practices were assembled to illustrate ethnographic strategies: Naga tattooing instruments; masks from Ibibio, Ekoi, and Anyang secret societies; models of the markings on Indian caste heads; and London tradespeople. Here the grid dissected the case into sections which isolated each set of objects, while large text reduced the importance of the objects to illustrations of set textual exegesis. The parody was completed by a system of drawers arranged alphabetically, each of which contained the fragments of a specific culture. As with the Brighton experiment, the two galleries were mobilized through a series of provocations engineered through a program of African artist residencies who critically responded to both displays.

These exhibitions share a common set of interests and perspectives neatly described by Gonseth's threefold classification of Neuchâtel's own exhibitions. However, critical museology has wider interests. Nuno Porto's *Offshore* (2006, Museu de Antropologia, University of Coimbra) was a visually hard-hitting comparison of the free, unencumbered circulation of objects as icons of ethnic identities throughout the world to the legal impediments that restrict the movement of peoples between Africa and Europe. Wastiau's *Amazonie: Le chamane et la pensée de la forêt* (2016–17, Musée de Ethnographie, Geneva) used an elaborate scenography and employed multiple indigenous voices which, along with Brazilian artists, attempted to explain indigenous concepts of the forest, humans, and animals and their parallel "reality." Wastiau's exhibition ended with recordings made by a number of the Amazon's indigenous people's delivering messages to museum visitors about the challenges that threatened them. Like Porto, Wastiau told a brutal story about the history of the destruction of culture and habitat and implicitly adopted Ames's precept that knowledge is never neutral.

The importance of structuring exhibitions using indigenous categories is crucial to the development of critical museology and essential in moving the power of interpretation from monographic to dialogical presentations, and from curators to traditional knowledge holders and indigenous artists and intellectuals. Wastiau's Amazonie marks an important intersection between collaborative and critical museology, and it makes equally important points about the form of a future postcollaborative museology, when the binary opposition between Western and Amerindian institutionalized museums and community centers and their different visual systems might be superseded. The work of indigenous curators and thinkers like Jisgang Nika Collison, Claudio Alvares, and Paul Wangoola is, against enormous odds, beginning to map some of the strategies and practices to ensure these alternative museologies continue to move forward. The UBC Museum of Anthropology, after a visit by Wangoola, attempted in 2010 to adopt the idea of multiversity to a new eighteen-thousand-square-feet gallery, which, with mixed success, aimed to redisplay large parts of its worldwide collections following the classifications and themes proposed by different indigenous communities.

INTERNATIONAL PERSPECTIVES AND INTELLECTUAL DIVERSITY

This essay seeks to demonstrate the coexistence of a potential radical anthropology which has subsisted alongside its various scientific articulations from earliest times. Scientific anthropologies dominated museum displays from the 1880s to the 1920s. Anthropology museums in Britain sluggishly adopted functionalist and monographic displays after the 1920s, but increasingly lost popular appeal, eventually falling into crisis in the 1960s–70s. Only then after a period of intense criticism did some museums again find relevance through rediscovering and applying the radical potential of anthropology and new, related disciplines to rethink and produce critical and contemporary displays.

Outside of the Anglo-centric world, as in Mexico, anthropology and museums have long enjoyed a closer relationship. In Europe it is no accident that all those museums which have adopted critical museology are closely associated with universities. Museums outside the English-speaking world have incorporated radical and conservative streams of anthropology and consequently established both museums that supported national identity and museums of resistance. It is this latter type of museum I have sought to give prominence to here.

The change that has transformed so many ethnography museums into world culture museums in northern Europe has coincided with a move from a focus on national to European and multicultural identities and global vistas. This transformation also rests on reconfiguring collections, exhibitions, and disciplinary affiliations to adequately describe new global relations which in many cases have been prefigured in anthropology's particularly radical nature. Nevertheless, it has also been the move from a disciplinary anthropology to a broader anthropological imagination composed of a raft of cultural sciences including the new art history, cultural geography, cultural history, cultural studies, Indigenous Studies, critical theory, and the history of ideas that has recharged and redirected ethnography museums to again become vital social institutions. What has changed most is that many museums have expunged scientific anthropology and museum ethnography for a humanistic anthropology and in so doing have constructed a potential bridge between themselves and local, indigenous, and world communities.

SUGGESTIONS FOR FURTHER READINGS AND REFERENCES

Ames, M. 1992. *Cannibal Tours and Glass Cases: The Anthropology of Museums.* Vancouver: University of British Columbia Press.

Augé, M. 1999, *An Anthropology for Contemporary Worlds.* Stanford, CA: Stanford University Press.

Belting, H., A. Buddensieg, and P. Weibel, eds. 2013. *The Global Contemporary and the Rise of New Art Worlds.* Karlsruhe: ZKM. Center for Art and Media.

Bouquet, M. 1993. *Man-ape Ape-man: Pithecanthropus in Het.* Pesthuis, Leiden: Nationaal Naturhistorisch Museum.

Bouquet, M., and J. Freitas Branco. 1988. *Melanesian Artefacts, Postmodernist Reflections / Artefactos melanésios, reflexões pós-modernistas.* Lisbon: Instituto de Investigação Científica Tropical / Museu de Etnologia.

Bouttiaux, A-M, and A. Seiderer, eds. 2011. *Fetish Modernity*. Turvuren: Royal Museum for Central Africa.

———. 2012. *Museo Nacional de Culturas Populares*. Mexico D.F.: Universidad Autonoma de México.

Bonfil Batalla, G., ed. 1981. *Utopía y Revolución: El pensamiento politico contemporáneo de los indios en América Latina*. Mexico D.F.: Editorial Nueva Imagen.

Boyce, S. 1995. *Peep*. London: Institute of International Visual Arts.

Burrow, J. W. 1966. *Evolution and Society: A Study in Victorian Social Theory*. Cambridge: Cambridge University Press.

Clifford, J. 2013. *Returns: Becoming Indigenous in the Twenty-first Century*. Cambridge, MA: Harvard University Press.

Colombres, A. 1982. *La hora del 'bárbaro': Bases para una antropologia social de apoyo*. Tlahuapan: Premiá Editora.

Cranstone, B. A. L. 1958. *Ethnography: Handbook for Museum Curators*. London: The Museums Association.

Estévez Gonzãlez. F., and M. de Santa Ana, eds. 2010. *Memorias y Olvidos del Archivo*. La Lagunilla: Museo de Historia y Antropologiaa de Tenerife.

Estévez Gonzãez, F., ed. 2004. *El Pasado en el Presente*. Tenerife: Museo de Antropología de Tenerife.

Frese, H. H. 1960. *Anthropology and the Public: The Role of Museums*. Leiden: E. J. Brill.

-Gonseth, M-O. 2005. "Un atelier expographique." In M-O Gonseth, J. Hainard, and R, Kaehr, eds., *Cent ans d' ethnographie sur la colline de Saint Nicolas 1904-2004*. Neuchâtel: Musée d'ethnographie, pp. 375-96.

Gonseth, M-O, J, Hainard, and R. Kaehr. 2002. *Le musée cannibal*. Neuchâtel: Musée d'ethnographie.

Harrison, R. 2013. "Reassembling Ethnographic Museum Collections." In R. Harrison, Sarah Byrne and Anne Clarke, eds., *Reassembling the Collection: Ethnographic Museums and Indigenous Agency*. Santa Fe: School for Advanced Research Press, pp. 3-35.

Isaac, G. 2007. *Mediating Knowledges. Origins of a Zuni Tribal Museum*. Tucson: Arizona University Press.

Kluckhohn, C. 1949. *Mirror for Man. The Relation of Anthropology to Modern Life*. New York and Toronto: Whittlesey House, McGraw Hill.

Kovach, M. 2009. *Indigenous Methodologies: Characteristics, Conversations, and Contexts*. Toronto: University of Toronto Press.

LaRocque, E. 2010. *When the Other Is Me: Native Resistance Discourse 1850-1990*. Winnipeg: University of Manitoba Press.

Levell, N. 2001. "The Poetics and Prosaics of Making Exhibitions: A Personal Reflection on the Centenial Gallery." *Antropologia Portuguesa* 18:151-94.

Mauss, M. 1967. *Manuel D'Ethnographie*. Paris: Editions Payot.

Morales Moreno, L. G. 1995. *Orígenes de la museología Mexicana: Fuentes para el studio histórico del Museo Nacional, 1780-1940*. Mexico D.F.: Universidad Iberoamericana.

Penny, H. G. 2002. *Objects of Culture. Ethnology and Ethnographic Museums in Imperial Germany*. Chapel Hill: University of North Carolina Press.

Phillips, R. 2011. *Museum Pieces: Towards the Indigenization of Canadian Museums*. Montreal: McGill-Queens University Press.

Porto, N. 2009. *Modos de Objectificação da Dominação Colonial: O Caso do Museu do Dundo, 1940-1970*. Lisbon: Fundação Calouste Gulbenkian.

————. 1999. *Angola a Preto e Branco. Fotografia e Ciência no Museu do Dundo 1940–1970.* Coimbra: Museu Antropólogico da Universidade de Coimbra.

————. 2002. *Museums and Modernity: Art Galleries and the Making of Modern Culture.* Oxford: Berg.

Shelton, A. A. 1992. "The Recontextualisation of Culture in UK Museums." *Anthropology Today* 8 (5): 11–16.

————. 1997. "The Future of Museum Ethnography." *Journal of Museum Ethnography* 9:33–48.

————. 2013. "Critical Museology. A Manifesto: Museum Worlds." *Advances in Research* 1:7–23.

————. 2016. "European Ethnography and World Culture Museums." Museumskunde. *Herausgegeben vom Deutschen Museumsbund* 81 (1/16): 20–27.

Shelton, A. A., ed. 1995. *Fetishism: Visualising Power and Desire.* London: Lund Humphries.

Stocking, G., ed. 1985. *Objects and Others: Essays on Museums and Material Culture.* Madison: University of Wisconsin Press.

Sturtevant, W. 1969. "Does Anthropology Need Museums?" *Proceedings of the Biological Society, Washington* 82:619–50.

Tschopik, H., and D, Collier. 1954. "The Role of Museums in American Anthropology." *American Anthropologist* 56 (5, part 1): 768–79.

Wastiau, B. 2000. *ExitCongoMuseum: An Essay on the Social Life of the Masterpieces of the Tervuren Museum.* Tervuren: Royal Museum for Central Africa.

————. 2016. *Amazonie: Le chamane et la pensée de la forêt.* Paris: Somogy éditions d'art.

CHAPTER 20

PARADISE POSTPONED

THE PREDICAMENTS OF TOURISM

Jeremy MacClancy

"Tourism?' the student scowled, when I introduced the topic of next week's class. "*Tourism*? But that's something you just do, and enjoy yourself, and not think about. It's not something you *study*." The attitude is widespread, but still misguided. For the tourism and leisure industry is now the largest in the world. And that's no joke. The United Nations World Tourism Organization has estimated that in 1950, across the world, there were 25 million tourists; by 2016 that figure had risen to 1,235 billion, an increase of almost 50,000 percent. Further, between 2010 and 2016, the World Travel and Tourism Council has calculated, the contribution of travel and tourism to global Gross Domestic Product outpaced the world economy year on year. By 2016 this sector constituted 10.2 percent of global GDP, and it sustained over 290 million employees, that is, just over one in ten of all jobs on the planet.

So, just because tour operators try to sell us sun, sea, sand, sex, and fun, fun, fun does not mean we should not cast a serious eye over the whole business. Indeed, the very opposite: it's all too easy to hide the seamier side of the trade behind the glossy promises of unbridled pleasure in foreign settings. Operators may want us to buy into prefabricated dreams, but who is really paying the price?

Indigenous groups in Thailand know the answer, and it is not a pretty one. Squeezed out of their sylvan homelands by the accelerating deforestation of the logging companies or pushed away by beachside developers, they are forced to enter Thai society at the very lowest rung. There they have the choice of working for local planters or merchants at punitive rates or joining a human zoo for tourists to gawp at. Uprooted, much of their culture now but a memory, they perform "characteristic" tasks—tree climbing, corrupted versions of their rituals, pig killing—for the visitors to video. Some also sell their crafts. Some simply beg.

This sort of story is all too common for indigenous and tribal groups throughout the world. Coastal peoples may be banned from their beaches, recently privatized, and fishing communities denied their hitherto traditional access to coral reefs, now parts of government-run marine parks. Pastoralists may see their homes razed, and their livestock expelled from their customary grazing areas, all in the name of developing eco-tourism. Elsewhere, those who survive by agriculture might be turfed off their land for the sake of hotel construction. In the process, water can become a scarce resource as the constant tourist demand for showers and baths overburdens local supplies. In sum, it seems that wherever the needs of locals clash with others' greed for the tourist dollar, it is the locals who lose the contest.

The tribulations of tourism are not, however, restricted to embattled indigenes. In Europe, many locals today face similar, though admittedly lesser onslaughts from the peering eyes of intrusive tourists who now come to their hometowns in massed groups. As shown by the Dutch anthropologist Jeremy Boissevain, many harassed locals choose to resist covertly, by being sullen and obstructive, by parodying or ridiculing the visitors. Resentment toward the interference of affluent outsiders is commonplace. Classifying them into derogatory national stereotypes is one way of assuaging the pain they cause, as are emotional outbursts. As one Maltese woman complained angrily to Boissevain, "We are used as carpets! . . . The residents have a right to live. We want to live. When we air our views, outsiders tell us that (our city) is not ours but it belongs to the Maltese population. But we live here! We have a right to our city."

In Jerusalem, the tale is similar, though here the story takes a slightly different twist. There, Palestinian shopkeepers feel demeaned by the condescending style of affluent visitors to their tourist-goods stores. They compensate by yarning to each other tales of their sexual conquests. More fantasy than reality, these tales serve to reset the moral balance, otherwise so gravely upset by the self-assumed superiority of affluent outsiders only all too well aware of their monetary might. Through sex (albeit more narrative than enacted), the financially exploited turn the tables on their exploiters. Slaves of capitalism they strive, through their stories, to regain some modicum of mastery over their dominators. But the more insightful of these merchants realize that any success is also a sign of their failure: the sex is fleeting, the structural inequities perdure. The orgasm over, the woman is still a wealthy tourist, and he a petty trader in a saturated market. She can continue to travel, picking up pretty boys as she goes; he remains bound up with the daily struggle in the overcompetitive streets of Jerusalem's Christian Quarter. Her financial clout makes her the potent consumer and his lack of it makes him the consumed, whose only recourses are stories for his peers and the occasional sex for himself. According to Glenn Bowman, who studied this trade, in local parlance the men wish to "fuck" the visitors but it is they who, in the end, are truly "fucked."

Some Europeans choose to hide aspects of their culture from the tourist gaze. Though they continue to stage their major festivities, which draw in the crowds and ensure locals' prosperity, they start to concentrate their efforts on previously minor ceremonies, either held away from main tourist areas or outside the tourist season. These revitalized events take on a new significance for their participants, becoming locally private opportunities to celebrate community, free from the stare and questions of inquisitive outsiders. For instance, in the north Spanish city of Pamplona, the annual June fiesta of Sanfermines was made famous by Hemingway, who was fascinated by its daily bull-running, bull-fighting, and sustained ambience of public revelry. Thanks to his writings and the efforts of his imitators, however, the fiesta has now become so large, so drunken, and so riotous that many locals who do not profit directly from the presence of the crowds quit town for the period and leave the festivities to the incomers. Instead they prefer to participate in "little" Sanfermines, a late September celebration of one of the areas within the Old Quarter of the town. As locals said to me, this four-day fiesta was so pleasurable because there was such an atmosphere of people enjoying themselves "at home." They do not have to worry about the observations of outsiders and they all know how to behave.

If these strategies of covert resistance, fantasy, and hiding fail to secure local life against the depredations of the intruders, they can always turn to organized protest, active campaigns against unwanted changes. In the mid-2010s, anti-tourist graffiti started to appear in Barcelona: "Tourist you are the terrorist," "All tourists are bastards," "Why call it tourist season if we can't shoot them?" In 2017 Spain received a record number of tourists. Some locals felt too many: 34 million in Barcelona alone, a 25 percent increase in four years. Activists produced lists of depredations caused by tourists and staged mass demonstrations; the movement spread to Palma de Mallorca and elsewhere. The national government said it would consider peoples' demands.

So far, so bad. Worse may be yet to come.

It's complicated

The examples given above suggest that the predicaments of tourism can be drawn in the stark terms of good versus bad, of the upright against the voracious, of locals versus developers. However, closer examination reveals that the encounter with organized tourism cannot always be portrayed in black and white: far more common that the picture must be painted in diverse shades of gray. And it is here perhaps that social anthropology can make its greatest contribution to the study and understanding of tourism and its effects.

Analysts of tourism have convincingly claimed that its market is so vast and so complex, so differentiated and diffused, that generalizations about its nature and process cannot be easily made. Some have tried to argue that because of its commonly exploitative character, of the non-Western poor by the Western wealthy, tourism should be seen as "the new imperialism." But others have counter-argued that the industry is in fact so heterogeneous that terms like "neocolonialism" are not adequate labels for it. It is true, new kinds of imperialism are emerging with the tourist industry, but so many other things are happening within it at the same time. Given this complexity, anthropologists are well placed to tease out the threads of different tourist knots. For their training in long-term fieldwork primes them, in any particular ethnographic setting, to listen to the competing voices of members from different interest groups, to compare their words with their deeds, to disentangle the overlapping realities, and to clarify the various misconceptions and consequent confusions.

Malcolm Crick, who studied the industry in the ancient Sri Lankan city of Kandy, found that some middle-class locals thought tourism was seriously "polluting" their culture. These critics castigated tourists as the cause for apparently increasing levels of heterosexual prostitution, homosexual prostitution of young boys, dishonesty by locals, drug abuse (especially among the young), and irresponsible behavior by youths keen to emulate Western ways. They also complained of the rise of tourism as creating a system of apartheid. They thought their compatriots were being treated as second-class citizens in their own homeland and they complained about the way hotels employed security guards to keep locals out. The arrival of more and more Westerners brought some money into the country but it also pushed prices up, making domestic tourism too expensive a prospect for many middle-class Sri Lankans. Members of local elites did profit from tourism, as they had the capital to do so, but most

Sri Lankans were powerless to do more than watch the cash flow. In Kandy, the feeling most associated with tourism was "deeply-felt resentment and social jealousy."

Sri Lankan critics' claims about the decline in public morals might have appeared cogent. But they always relied on idealized images of the Sri Lankan past, which could not withstand historical scrutiny. In other words, tourists were being made the scapegoats of a variety of social ills, with critics fabricating a past to suit their purposes. These critics were at the same time ignoring the fact that tourism was only one force for social change among several others. Tourism, when it arises in a particular place, does not spring from nothing, as though the contemporary contexts of that place were irrelevant. The advent of tourism in any one area is deeply affected by the current social and economic situation of that area. It is true the coming of the industry may exacerbate already-established phenomena, such as young women selling access to their bodies, and may transform local morals, such as codes of hospitality to visitors. But these changes may well have already been set in motion by other forces whose arrival predated that of tourism, for example, the expansion of a cash economy, the creation of plantations and factories, the rise of labor migration. Tourism has its sins but it should not be made to bear all those consequent on more general socioeconomic development. Local elites might be the only Sri Lankans who make substantial money out of tourism, but this is not an especial evil of tourist development itself, just part of the general capitalist process in that country.

There is no doubt tourism can have a devastating effect on local cultures, drowning them in tsunami after tsunami of new ideas and new money. But there is also no doubt the introduction of tourism can have precisely the opposite effect, serving to boost or even revitalize local ways. A pair of very different examples here will illustrate two possible modes of this process.

The first, and perhaps the most spectacular example comes from the southern end of Pentecost Island, part of the southwest Pacific archipelago of Vanuatu (formerly the Anglo-French colony of the New Hebrides). There, since at least the early nineteenth century, locals have performed the annual ceremony of *gol*, "land-diving," to celebrate the yam harvest. The male members of each village which chooses to hold the event cut down trees to make poles. These are lashed together to make a tall tower. A series of platforms are constructed down one side of the tower. Each man who elects to dive selects his own pair of lianas. Each pair is then secured to the end of a platform and the other end of the pair tied to the ankles of the diver. To the accompaniment of women and some men dancing and singing at the foot of the tower, the divers then take turns, proceeding from the lowest platform to the highest, to drop. The elasticity of the lianas takes the strain of the dive when the diver reaches his lowest point and the vines are stretched to the maximum. Other men then rush quickly forward to catch the diver and prevent him hitting the ground. According to the Guinness Book of Records the g-force experienced by the divers is the highest reached by human activity outside of the industrialized world.

Since the late nineteenth century missionaries, predominantly Anglicans and Catholics, have worked in the area, in a largely successful bid to persuade the locals to adopt Christianity. Locals who converted were forced to abandon their rituals and to don Western dress. Members of one village (Bunlap) stubbornly resisted these changes. Instead they vigorously asserted their commitment to customary ways. They did not let their penis-wrappers or grass-skirts rot, and they continued to perform the *gol*. In the 1960s these villagers began to enjoy an unexpected pay-off for their cultural resilience. Tourists started to attend the land-diving. In order to control the movements of these Westerners, the chief of the village allowed them to visit only during the days surrounding the event, and entry to the tower area was very strictly supervised, so that no visitor could avoid paying the hefty entrance fee (in 1981—the year I attended—the price was fifty Australian dollars). Well aware of their desires, the chief allowed those with cameras to climb the tower. He knew they liked to take photos from directly behind the platforms as divers let themselves go. These tourists attending the event were expatriates from the mini-capital of the archipelago, Australians visiting the islands, and Americans, touring the Pacific on their yachts, who had specially sailed in. The chief of Bunlap, moreover, was quite prepared to solicit actively more tourists when he visited the main town on a nearby island. The money recouped was divided equally among the villagers, with a certain proportion kept aside for spending on communal projects.

In the mid-1970s educated locals began to lead a call, throughout the archipelago, for independence from their colonial masters. In a bid to unite all islanders, they campaigned for a positive revaluation of *kastom* ("traditional ways") and, where necessary, for its revitalization and even for its revival. According to them, *kastom* was no longer to be seen as backward and evil but as a great cultural asset, compatible with Christianity. Once independence was achieved, in 1980, the new government began actively to promote tourism to the country. The number of visitors started to rise steadily. People in villages neighboring Bunlap, seeing that traditions were back in vogue and mindful of the money being made by the land-divers, revived the ceremony in their own territory, though as fervent Christians, they did not swap their shorts for penis-wrappers, to the disappointment of tourists.

So, by the early 1980s, in Pentecost a particular kind of cultural tourism, based on brief stays at a certain time of year, dovetailed successfully with already-established local ways. It boosted the resistant stance taken by the villagers of Bunlap and brought them tangible material benefits without at the same time creating great internal division. Carefully controlling the process, they accepted tourists on their terms and at their price levels. A few other villages had also begun to profit. And in a further twist south Pentecost chiefs, supported by the Vanuatu attorney general, attempted to seek recompense from bungee-jumping organizations for cultural theft. But by the 2010s land-diving, ever more practiced, had become a victim of its own excess.

The example of Bunlap was too enticing to resist for the people of many south Pentecost villages. By 2011 land-diving ceremonies were being held three times weekly, between April and June, in one locale or another. Also, contemporary construction could be slapdash: in 2008 a local cameraman died when a badly made tower collapsed on him. Though staging the ritual remained highly profitable, the rate charged to tourists dropped, and the income that was generated fomented division, as locals argued over an equitable distribution of the spoils, with certain "big-men" being accused of pocketing the proceeds. The ambience of competition and dispute continued to worsen: in 2015 the chiefs of south Pentecost were so concerned to maintain their monopoly that they dispatched over a hundred villagers to cut down a tower adjoining the airstrip in the center of the island, on the morning it was to have been used. The gathered tourists, a report of the incident stated, "watched in disbelief."

In sum, tourism has revitalized, then transformed an indigenous ceremony. Local revenue has certainly been boosted but at the cost of social cohesion, while for all but the most traditionally timed *gol*, the link of the ritual to a particular point in the agricultural calendar has ended. The leaders of south Pentecost villages, pushed by a popular desire for money and lacking other equally profitable economic opportunities, have turned their celebration of the yam harvest primarily into an exotic spectacle for camera-toting Western tourists. In other words, they have converted a key aspect of their own *kastom* into a commodity for consumption by outsiders. My query: is that a price worth paying?

The second example comes from the province of Alicante, southeastern Spain. In this part of the country, in particular, the major annual fiestas are *Moros y Cristianos* ("Moors and Christians"), where locals enact a fantasy version of the Moorish invasion and the subsequent Catholic Reconquest.

These events are so well known because many locals form into *comparsas*, fiesta-centered social clubs; all are exclusively *moro* or *cristiano*; never mixed.

These can be so popular that in certain villages, over 70 percent of all adult inhabitants are members, while over ten thousand expensively outfitted *moros* and *cristianos* parade every year in the celebrations staged by the small Alicantine city of Alcoy. The primary purpose of a *comparsa* is its members' collective participation as a group in the festive activities. *Comparsistas*, dressed in Disneyland interpretations of medieval garb, parade slowly through the streets. Formed into files, they advance very gradually, raising each leg in a theatrically slow manner, while swaying from side to side, with an almost military precision. The brass band hired by each *comparsa* lends a theatrical gravity to this costumed slow-step: most tunes call for massed drumming, akin to the sonorous soundtrack of Hollywood historical epics, *Spartacus*, for instance, or *Cleopatra*. Onlookers, standing by the side or sitting in hired chairs, clap each file and cheer the most spectacular. The first day the *comparsas* simply parade, which can last several hours. The second day the parade ends with the *Cristianos* occupying a tall plywood set they call the "castle"; the *Moros* dispatch a mounted embassy commanding the *Cristianos* to surrender. They refuse. To the sound of blunderbuss-simulacra firing into the air, the *Moros* then attack and gain control. The third day the parade ends with the *Cristianos*, again to blunderbuss accompaniment, regaining castellar control.

Comparsas can be very long-standing: some were founded in the nineteenth century, while others may have formed in the last few months. All but the most poorly organized have their own club premises where, during fiestas, members gather to breakfast, lunch, and dine, and to drink at any time. Membership is transgenerational, and youths will often choose to join the *comparsa* of their parents. Most *comparsas* also hold a series of events, outside of fiestas, throughout the year: fund-raising dinners, elections of office-holders, or simply communal meals to mark the midpoint of the festive calendar: as they say, "Only six months left before fiestas!"

The popular logic of these fiestas is sanctioned excess. The rule is to go beyond the usual rules, or indeed energetically break them. The paraders wish their costumes to be as showy as can be, the deep notes of brass bands to stir others and reverberate as far as possible. Vehicles are banned: the people have retaken control of their streets, where public drunkenness is smiled at and the smell of dope often pervasive. Villagers, normally careful with their money, spend without seeming concern. Strangers can broach one another. It is said sexual license, within or without marriage, does not lead to postfestive recrimination. As one villager said to me, "You get dressed up, leave shame at home, lock the door, and go out."

Regional journalists add to the ambience. At the start of a municipality's fiestas, provincial newspapers may well carry several articles or indeed whole

FIG. 20.1. "El beso. A young *moro* leader takes advantage of the festive ambience. The woman grants his petition." Castalla, Spain, September 2017. Photo by Jeremy MacClancy.

supplements on the upcoming events, with pages of collective portraits of all the local *comparsas*, fully kitted-out, ready to parade. Subsequent articles assess how well the fiestas are going. The tone throughout is one of superlatives: the costumes magnificent, winning new tunes of the bands, the parades even better than last year. Above all, the journalists may praise the *comparsistas* and other locals for their demonstrable commitment to making their fiestas as profoundly festive as they can. Thus they will eulogize parades which continue despite downpours, or nocturnal frolickers who go on reveling in the face of a small-hours power cut.

Mayors and town-councilors wish to stay in office, and so to please as many voters as possible. Hence they support the fiestas of their electorate greatly; most town halls have a dedicated councilor for fiestas, who negotiates the significant municipal subsidy for the events and helps coordinate their management. If the fiestas of a town are big enough, the papers will run a piece by its mayor boasting how exceptional its events are and how welcoming to outsiders. That last point is key, for the more visitors the fiestas attract the more money is spent in the locale during these days of serious fun. To that end, town halls will pay for groups of the more showy *comparsistas* to file and dance publicly in major Spanish cities, and in affluent countries from which people already come to holiday in the peninsula. Town halls will also bid for their fiestas to be officially classified by external bodies as an event of provincial, regional, or national importance. The acme of municipal aspirations is to have their event recognized by UNESCO as having "World Heritage Status." But these classifications come with qualifiers: for each level of approval, the fiestas have to fulfil a set of criteria, and the higher the level sought, the more demanding those criteria are. Thus these criteria may be seen to be as restrictive as they are enabling, for they confine the fiestas to a certain format, while official recognition of their quality is publicized as a plum to pull in yet more tourists. One danger to this inter-municipal competitiveness is that it's a zero-sum game. The number of fiestas with some external validation continues to rise, e.g. the UNESCO program is today far bigger than was originally forecast, and there is as yet no foreseeable endpoint to this classificatory inflation. Yet if the fiestas of all but the smallest villages come to proclaim their certified distinction, wherein, exactly, lies their individual distinctiveness?

There are competing logics in play here. Local businessmen who stand to profit from fiestas are keen that visitors fill their town to the utmost; municipal representatives state they want the same. Many villagers think differently and do not wish to regard their annual period of excess in the terms of a narrowly bounded economic rationality. They are happy that people from neighboring villages and towns come to observe and participate in their fiestas. That is part of a local, long-standing competitiveness, people of close-together sites informally vying with one another to see which place can boast the most memorable fiestas. For these people, the attendance of the odd tourist is, at best, of marginal importance. But they do not want hordes of foreigners: they don't know how to participate and, by weight of numbers, threaten to dilute that central concern: the festive ambience. Some of these villagers argue that mayors are caught in the tension between the two logics: to forestall criticism from local businessmen, these elected representatives have to be seen promoting their fiestas, but privately, as integral, lifelong members of their own community, they would prefer more homely excess, like the majority of their codenizens. As far as I can judge, based on my own long-term fieldwork in Alicante Province, this tension so far remains without resolution.

Another tension within fiestas can also be perceived in reactions to an extremely ugly gang-rape committed in the early hours of Sanfermines in 2016. Two years later five young men, styling themselves "La Manada" ("the wolf-pack"), were found guilty of serially assaulting a young woman and videoing sections of the event. Journalists of the trial said the men linked their actions to the "Todo vale" ("Anything goes") attitude some associate with fiestas. The majority of commentators and female demonstrators who took to the streets counter-argued that this was gender-based violence, unjustified by reference to the anarchic component of fiestas. The town hall responded with an online publicity campaign reminding viewers that Sanfermines was a fiesta for all, where participants respected each other. Fiestas might be touted as opportunities to collective frenzy, but there are legal and moral limits to that behavioral excess. One might leave shame at home, but machista aggression is meant to stay there as well.

All the worse then, that days after the trial, five other young men, deliberately styling themselves "La Nueva Manada" ("the new wolf-pack"), were charged with gang-raping a sixteen-year-old during fiestas in the Canary Islands. As of late June 2018, a date for the trial has yet to be fixed. At what cost fiestas, and who bears it?

The days when a culture could be regarded as static, clearly bounded, and uncontested are long gone. Today, if the concept can even be maintained, "cultures" are seen as permeable, dynamic, negotiated, contested. For tourists, like other travelers such as labor migrants, visit other cultures but take some of their own with them at the same time. Thus tourists might go to visit another culture, but that way of life is already modified, sometimes slightly, sometimes grossly, by its admission of tourists. What can then occur is that the passage of foreigners through an area becomes an accepted, standard aspect of a broadened conception of local ways. Thus in places such as the Bahamas, Venice, and other much-visited parts of the traveled world, tourism becomes a "traditional," if begrudged, part of regional life. Tourists, by their very presence, change what they have come to see.

In some cases locals, keen to feed the market, may invent traditions to satisfy visitors' desire for seeing memorable difference. But this deliberate fabrication of folkloric custom need not necessarily be seen as a cultural lie. In Malta, locals did not mind performing novel dance routines for the tourists. In fact, many came to enjoy them and now regard them as part of their own contemporary traditions. In other words, because of tourism they had exaggerated the distinctiveness of their way of life and found a new source of pleasure, maybe even of pride, in the process.

Tourists' sustained gaze makes locals conscious of their actions, not as appropriate means to certain ends, but as objects of significance and curiosity in themselves. Let me give a personal example. One Sunday a few years ago, I drove into a local Oxford hypermarket for my weekly shop. A coachload of Italian tourists followed me into the parking area. I entered the store, went straight to a large pile of apples, and began to fill a plastic bag. I then realized the Italian group had come in, and most had stopped to observe me, as though my selection of Golden Delicious were particularly worthy of scrutiny. I started to feel more absurd than uncomfortable. What to me was the most normal and near thoughtless of trivial, quotidian acts was being adjudged a noteworthy local performance, perhaps to be compared and calibrated. The anthropologist had been anthropologized by visitors turning my home-patch into their field site. I also wondered whether my observers were regarding me, the son of a proud Irishman and a Maltese mother, in national terms, as a stereotypical British consumer. Was this encounter of tourists with a supermarket shopper being turned into a mundane surreality? Were they converting my ordinary into their extraordinary?

If, as some claim, tourism is a willed meeting of the Self with the Other, this does not equate to the West checking out the Rest, for today tourists can come from any corner of the world populated by people with disposable income. For instance, the increasing number of Indians visiting Bali are not pulled by the promise of ethnic difference. Rather, they journey to the island to confirm the international reach of Hindi devotion. They are not in search of the exotic but the reaffirmation of a common spiritual legacy. For similar reasons, the Malaysian government is today working to rebrand its country as a center for Islamic tourism in its successful bid to attract planeloads of the faithful from the Middle East.

Those Western travelers who do seek an encounter with an "authentically" different way of life will always be disappointed, or mildly self-deluding. This holds true as much for British backpackers keen to outdo their peers by venturing into the more dangerous zones of southeast Asia as it does for middle-class Americans visiting the lesser developed parts of Eastern Europe. The common concept of authenticity held by almost all these wanderers is a mythical one grounded in a pretourist world, linked to ideas of unchanging cultures unaffected by the outside. So all today's tourists get to see are performances of "staged authenticity," where the fact that the event has to be put on for or mindful of the visitors robs it of the very quality so many have traveled to seek. Perhaps, to use the vocabulary of Rupert Stash, the best they can achieve is a mutually derived "working misunderstanding" or "productive miscommunication." At this rate, the paradise they search for is forever postponed.

SUGGESTIONS FOR FURTHER READING AND REFERENCES

Adams, Kathleen M. 2016. "Tourism and Ethnicity in Insular Southeast Asia: Eating, Praying, Loving and Beyond." *Asian Journal of Tourism Research* 1(1).

Boissevain, Jeremy. 1996a. "'But we live here!' Perspectives on Cultural Tourism in Malta." In L. Briguglio et al., eds., *Sustainable Tourism in Islands and Small States: Case Studies*. London: Pintar.

Boissevain, Jeremy, ed. 1996b. *Coping with Tourists: European Reactions to Mass Tourism*. Oxford: Berghahn.

   A good collection demonstrating the power of anthropology to analyze European tourism.

Bowman, Glenn. 1989. "Fucking Tourists: Sexual Relations and Tourism in Jerusalem's Old City." *Critique of Anthropology* 9(2).

   An excellent, early paper on sex tourism.

Cohen, Erik. 1996. "Hunter-Gatherer Tourism in Thailand." In Richard Butler and Tom Hinch, eds., *Tourism and Indigenous Peoples*. London: International Thomson Business Press.

Crain, Mary M. 1996. "Contested Territories: The Politics of Touristic Development at the Shrine of El Rocío in Southwestern Andalusia." In Boissevain 1996b.

Crick, Malcolm. 1994. *Resplendent Sites, Discordant Voices: Sri Lankans and International Tourism*. Chur, Switzerland: Harwood Academic.

   Though published over twenty years ago, it remains the exemplary ethnography of tourism.

Keefe, Jean, and Sue Wheat. 1998. *Tourism and Human Rights*. London: Tourism Concern.

Stash, Rupert. 2015. "Introduction: Double Signs and Intrasocial Heterogeneity in Primitivist Tourism Encounters." *Ethnos* 80:4.

Tabani, Marc. 2017. "Development, Tourism and Commodification of Cultures in Vanuatu." In Elizabeth Gnecchi-Ruscone and Anna Paini, eds., *Tides of Innovation in Oceania: Value, Materiality and Place*. Canberra: ANU Press. Free download via https://press.anu.edu.au /publications/series/monographs-anthropology/tides-innovation-oceania.

Waldren, Jacqueline. 1996. *Insiders and Outsiders: Paradise and Reality in Mallorca*. Oxford: Berghahn.

   A perceptive, historical ethnography of the establishment of a famed literary colony amidst tolerant but distanced locals.

CHAPTER 21

RESOUNDING POWER

POLITICIZING THE ANTHROPOLOGY OF MUSIC

Matt Sakakeeny

My research in ethnomusicology, the anthropological study of music, has focused on musicians in brass band ensembles who provide music for funerals and parades, festivals, and concerts in New Orleans. When I began conducting fieldwork in 2006, participation and observation meant marching behind the drums and tuba for miles through the city streets, or standing amidst the dancing crowds at a nightclub while the trumpets, trombones, and saxophone played the melodies of an old jazz standard or a recent pop song. On festival stages, brass bands appeared alongside jazz, blues, soul, and funk bands, hip-hop artists, and Mardi Gras Indian "tribes." Because these black performance traditions are integral to New Orleans' identity as a musical city, black New Orleanians serve as ambassadors of local culture and yet they remain vulnerable to the patterns of marginalization that define life for people of color in countless other urban centers.

My conversations with musicians and other New Orleanians about this push-and-pull of precariousness and possibility eventually led me to interview Cherice Harrison Nelson. Cherice was nearing retirement as a public school teacher and dedicating her time to directing a cultural center in her Upper Ninth Ward neighborhood. I explained to Cherice my method of collecting stories from practitioners so that their own words would not just stand alongside my own but drive the direction of my research and the theories developed in the writing. Looking at me with the suspicion of schoolteacher to student, interlocutor to interloper, black woman to white man, she asked "But what stories are you going to choose to tell?"

Any form of qualitative research begins with a design plan that is then modified as data is collected, the results not only providing answers but also calling for new questions. An ethnographer conducting research through interactions with living people has a usually high degree of agency in crafting their observations into writing or other forms of dissemination. Cherice was acutely aware of the power anthropologists have in representing others, as both an anthropological subject — a "culture-bearer" — and a scholar. Her father, Donald Harrison Sr., was the Big Chief of the Guardians of the Flame, one of the many black Indian "tribes" that parade through the city's neighborhoods on Mardi Gras day, wearing elaborate feathered suits and beaded masks, singing chants to the rhythm of tambourines and cowbells. Anthropologists, folklorists, and journalists were a familiar presence around the family home, following sibling Donald Jr. as he developed into a leading saxophonist and bandleader, and eventually visiting the Mardi Gras Indian Hall of Fame that Cherice founded with her mother, Herreast. Cherice refers to my "tribe" as "talking heads of tradition," and she agreed to speak with me because I had demonstrated a commitment to collaboration by volunteering at her school and the Hall of Fame. She was the authority in our meetings but she knew I could exercise ultimate authority in determining what would be written, and she exercised her influence to direct me toward the social problems that condition the lives of so-called culture-bearers.

This chapter uses Cherice's intervention into my overall research design as a starting point for prompting anthropologists to consider what stories they choose to tell in their musical studies. Her question highlights the relative degree of autonomy that ethnographers have in choosing who to engage with, how the power dynamics of those engagements are scaffolded, and how the lives and experiences of interlocutors and collaborators structure the plans, methods, and outcomes of our research. I will describe the process that ultimately led to organizing my book *Roll With It: Brass Bands in the Streets of New Orleans* around racial justice issues that musicians face as young black men in a twenty-first-century American city. That meant situating the microlevel of musical performance and audience reception within the macrolevel of antiblack racism, economic exploitation, neighborhood gentrification, and interpersonal violence. The larger point of telling you this story is that all forms of musical expression, from the latest hit song to the traditional chants of hunter-gatherers, are imbricated within structures of power that cannot be bracketed off from rigorous ethnographic research.

WAYS OF ENGAGING WITH MUSIC

I begin with this claim because music is commonly fetishized as a safe space of uncritical pleasure, an escape from the political, social, and economic forces that shape society in all its strenuous gravity. This is a legacy of Romanticism, the nineteenth-century European philosophy of aesthetics that locates the power of music in its ineffable beauty, offering individual listeners a portal to "take us out of the everyday into the realm of the infinite," as E. T. A. Hoffmann described in 1814. In this tenacious formulation, the idealized figure of the music listener is characterized "by its attentiveness and interiority," writes Jairo Moreno, "and by the fact that for it musical experience is inescapably immediate." Environments that draw heightened attention to music—whether lost in contemplation listening to Beethoven in a concert hall, dancing to trance-like rhythms in a ritual space such as a nightclub, or "tuning out" with headphones and mobile devices—can invite an abandonment of social responsibility. And distracted listening—of radios murmuring in the background, "Muzak" in retail shops, or classical music at bedtime—facilitates disengagement of other types.

In the anthropological realm, where methods of cultural comparison and participant observation were designed explicitly as forms of engagement, scholars have analyzed the relationship of sound structure and social structure and demonstrated the power of music in the formation of social identity. With comparative musicology in the early 1900s and then ethnomusicology since the 1950s, researchers demonstrated the integral role of music at weddings and funerals, for work and for play, in spaces public and private. In Alan Merriam's paradigmatic textbook *The Anthropology of Music*, he argued that musicological analysis of "the music itself" must be situated within and against anthropological analysis of "music as human behavior," for "[w]ithout people thinking, acting, and creating, music sound cannot exist." The emphasis on human behavior has since been expanded to include multispecies sounds such as birdcalls, environmental "soundscapes," and noise "pollution," as well as the technological mediation of recording and broadcast mediums. Ethnographic and comparative studies have attested to the universality of music while underscoring the relativism and cultural specificity of its production and reception, eventually tracking how cultures and places are reconfigured through the transnational flows of music and people.

In the most general and generous sense, the related disciplines of cultural anthropology and ethnomusicology were founded on the tenuous premise that an ostensibly objective evaluation of difference would challenge Eurocentric presumptions of biological, cultural, and religious superiority. If research on the music of indigenous, racialized, and otherwise marginalized peoples has sustained an implicit politics of inclusion, ethnographic writings have been criticized for reproducing cultural essentialisms, enabling cultural appropriation, and isolating cultural practices from societal infrastructures. In those cases where there has been an explicit engagement with macrolevel politics, it has been largely limited to specific areas of extreme violence or negligence, resistance or struggle. In South Africa, ethnomusicologists Louise Meintjes, Gavin Steingo, and others have uncovered political dimensions of music in apartheid and post-apartheid states. Studies of music deployed as a weapon in US detention camps by Suzanne Cusick and Martin Daughtry have not only questioned the association of music with beauty and transcendence; they have also revealed how militaries use sound to shatter the will of fellow humans.

In the wake of the Fukushima nuclear disaster in March 2011, Japanese activists relied on music as a medium for mobilizing diverse counterpublics in antinuclear demonstrations, alternative festivals, and the virtual contact zones of cyberspace. Noriko Manabe tracked the emergence of protest songs on YouTube that were then re-voiced by activists in street demonstrations, which in turn were documented and posted online, creating a cycle of sonic and visual accumulation. Mostly suppressed in mainstream media, and subject to government censorship and other constraints, antinuclear music circulated through backchannels to "voice anxieties that many Japanese were feeling but could not express in the atmosphere of silence that prevailed after 3.11." A parallel study by David Novak focused on the Project Fukushima! festival, a performative assembly in which collectivity was expressed through disruptive noise rather than explicit messages of protest in song lyrics. Through the participatory acts of singing, dancing, and creating experimental music, Project Fukushima! attempted to build "the ambivalence of regional culture into a platform for amplifying the noise of political community in the disaster zone."

To situate music within the expansive and invasive territories of power, ethnographers have undertaken interdisciplinary approaches to integrating data drawn not only from participant observation of expressive culture but also public policy documents, archival materials, geopolitical studies, activist discourse, multisited ethnography, and other resources. In her study of the songs of Rongelapese women from the Marshall Islands, Jessica Schwartz finds references to politics and ethics, health and survival across a spectrum of source materials. Recently declassified documents reveal how survivors of the 1954 "Castle Bravo" thermonuclear test, the largest hydrogen bomb detonation in

US history, were used as human subjects for studying the effects of radiation by the Atomic Energy Commission. Every March 1, on the anniversary of the bombing, the Rongelapese hold a "remembrance day" ceremony and perform songs like *"Kajjitok in aō ñan kwe kiō"* ("These are my questions for you now"), which recall the deception and renew the demand for answers to ongoing health problems. Because women are more susceptible to thyroid cancer than men, Schwartz integrates methods of medical anthropology to show how "vocal articulation of this suffering . . . [serves] as a barometer of communal health." The songs recuperate memories and articulate ethical demands through the sound of the voice as well as the meaning of the text. These examples of music in post-nuclear crises are part of a long, if not exactly robust, legacy of scholars attending to music as a diagnostic of imbalanced power relations.

This politically engaged body of literature extends to studies of social identification—race and ethnicity, nationality and religion, gender and sexuality. In the musical study of black Americans, there is an unbroken lineage that situates performance, recording, and reception within transnational structures of enslavement, segregation, and institutional racism. The formative writings on slave spirituals—such as *Narrative of the Life of Frederick Douglass, an American Slave* (1845), *Slave Songs of the United States* (1867) by scholar-abolitionists William Francis Allen, Lucy McKim Garrison, and Charles Pickard Ware, and *Souls of Black Folk* (1903) by sociologist W. E. B. Du Bois—laid a foundation for contextualizing musical study in explicitly political realms. Methodical ethnographic study did not begin until the 1930s with the work of Melville Herskovits, Zora Neale Hurston, John and Alan Lomax, and other cultural anthropologists and folklorists who were primarily located outside of music studies. As research on black American music has expanded, politically engaged study has been concentrated in historiography, cultural studies, and literature, with dedicated ethnographers such as Kyra Gaunt and Cheryl Keyes working the periphery. As is always the case with anthropological studies of music in any area, ethnographers must assemble a "toolkit" of analytical materials and methods drawn from multiple disciplinary locations in order to contextualize aesthetic practices within the machinations of power.

MUSIC AS A DIAGNOSTIC OF POWER IN NEW ORLEANS

When I began my research I did not see it as grounded in one particular area so much as distributed across scattered terrains of social theory, critical race studies, anthropological methods, New Orleans history, and research on music and sound. After Hurricane Katrina struck in August 2005, the disproportionate effects of the devastation on black New Orleanians directed me toward studies of disaster, social suffering, and structural racism. Katrina deeply politicized my work because the musicians I was preparing to research were victims of disaster profiteering and urban restructuring. I undertook a fieldwork study that was heavily revised so that the everyday experiences of musicians could be contextualized within the structures of power that condition their lives. On the one hand, the city needed "culture-bearers" to rejuvenate a tourist economy based on music and food, while on the other hand the systems of public housing, education, and healthcare were being entirely dismantled, privatized, and downsized in ways that specifically harmed people of color. How to go about situating such joyful music against such debilitating infrastructures without reducing the complex negotiations of power to rigid binaries of resistance or accommodation? Early in my field study I attended an event that became a launch pad for an inquiry into the political dimensions of musical performance and bodily assembly in the public spaces of New Orleans.

On November 11, 2006, I attended the funeral for Adrienne "Shorty" Chancley, who had passed away from congenital heart failure at the age of thirty-two. She was memorialized with a jazz funeral, a burial procession that begins with slow marching to a mournful dirge and ends with up-tempo music and dancing to celebrate the life of the deceased. As the band led a crowd of a hundred or so family, friends, and onlookers away from the St. Jude Shrine and back into the Tremé neighborhood where Chancley lived, the musicians ratcheted up the tempo with the upbeat hymn "Jesus on the Mainline." By the time the procession reached Chancley's house, a dozen musicians were playing an instrumental arrangement of "Shorty Was the Bomb" by rapper DMX and the participants chanted the chorus until the hearse stopped in front of the family home. The band planned to end the funeral there, and Chancley's daughter was hoisted up onto the coffin while they played a final dirge, "Just a Closer Walk with Thee." But when the musicians shouted "Let's send her away!" and pointed to the interstate overpass looming over the nearby intersection, the crowd moved quickly under the concrete decks, shaking the casket in the air and dancing exuberantly to the Mardi Gras Indian chant "Hoo Na Nae." After this improvised ending, the casket was put back in the hearse, the cortege drove away to the cemetery, and the rest of the crowd disbanded.

What are the political dimensions of an event in which a young woman of color who died from a birth defect is honored with a musical funeral in the public spaces of her hometown? Unlike an antinuclear demonstration, a funeral procession does not project an explicit politics of assembly, or at least none was clear to me as I walked away from the scene with a few observations scribbled in my notebook and some pictures and videos on my point-and-shoot camera. It was around this time that I first met Cherice and she had asked what stories was I going to choose to tell. As a New Orleanian with firsthand knowledge about the black experience and local culture, Cherice was deeply invested in areas that were unknown and even unknowable to me. Mapping the power relations embedded in a funeral procession of the type that occurs hundreds of times per year, her prompt led me beyond participant observation to draw upon numerous other resources: archival data, urban planning documents, media reportage, and studies of racialized geographies.

Having first moved to New Orleans in 1996, I had accumulated a decade of experiences that I began to review in light of the new information gleaned from the funeral procession. In 2002, the funeral for saxophonist Harold Dejan, leader of the Olympia Brass Band, also reached its ecstatic culmination "under the bridge," as locals refer to the strip carved out beneath the overpass. Come to think of it, nearly every funeral and brass band parade I had attended in the downtown district hit peak intensity in this semi-enclosed space where bodies are pressed close together and the sound of the instruments echoes off the huge concrete slabs and columns. The day after Chancley's funeral, the Tremé Sidewalk Steppers Social Aid & Pleasure Club hosted their annual neighborhood parade, which paused under the overpass while a crowd of thousands danced ecstatically to the horns and drums of the Rebirth Brass Band. What was the significance of the bridge and why did the sound of the brass band in this particular spot "get everybody hyped," as Rebirth bandleader Philip Frazier told me?

Urban planner Robert Moses designed the interstate in 1946 and construction began two decades later, with the primary aim of serving white commuters who were relocating to the suburbs after the forced integration of the city school system. In addition to Moses's plans, I reviewed oral histories of black residents who recalled the demolition of a tree-lined commercial thoroughfare and the construction of the hulking concrete structure. From newspaper articles and other historical sources, I learned that planners had advanced a multistage urban development scheme in the Tremé at the height of the Civil Rights era. The city forced the relocation of hundreds of black families in the name of fighting "urban blight" that, in actuality, was caused by a dwindling tax base in a shrinking city. This racialized incursion of space had been analyzed by urban geographers and other scholars, and their work provided an interdisciplinary frame of reference for the cultural displays I kept witnessing under the bridge.

In the fields of urban theory and human geography, scholars unpack how space is produced through the dialectic of city planners controlling the built environment and everyday people using those spaces in unintended ways. Henri Lefebvre theorized urban public space as "abstract space," or bureaucratically shaped space, which can be reappropriated as lived space, or "concrete space." The physical and sonic presence of musicians and parade participants in contested public spaces could be interpreted as a way of staking claims on those spaces, commanding what Lefebvre termed a "right to the city." Conjoining theories of sound and space led to a politicization of soundscape studies or an acoustification of theories of public space. More precisely, the musicians and marchers provided the grounds for analysis, compelling me to assemble a theoretical apparatus that could help me explain what was happening with sound, bodies, and space under the bridge.

Philip Frazier is the tuba player and founder of Rebirth, an internationally renowned brass band that I had seen perform at festivals, in concert halls, onstage at their weekly gig at the Maple Leaf Bar, and parading in the streets. When I interviewed "Tuba Phil" in 2006 he explained how he directs the mobile ensemble to regulate the movement of the parade as they move through space. "When you get to a certain intersection or a certain street where there's an opening, if the street is really wide, you know that's more dancing room for everybody, you want to keep everybody upbeat. When you get to a street where it's more closed, and the parade might slow down at a pace, you slow it down because you know everybody's trying to get through that small street." When the Sidewalk Steppers parade began in the narrow streets of the Tremé, Tuba Phil dialed back the music to keep the large crowds under control, but when the parade turned onto Dumaine Street, past Shorty Chancley's house and toward the bridge, the tempo was rising. "When you get under an overpass, because of the acoustics, you know the band's going to be loud anyway, and the crowd knows that's going to be like some wild, rowdy stuff and you want to get everybody hyped." This is a sonic and embodied practice for retuning abstract space as concrete space, and it was the reflections of Tuba Phil and other musicians that directed me to seek out Lefebvre and other theorists to unpack the complexity of the ethnographic event.

There is a substantial body of academic literature on the relation between sound and space, with a debt to Murray Schafer's influential conception of the "soundscape," or sonic environment. In Schafer's terminology the bridge would be a "soundmark," or "community sound which is unique or possesses qualities which make it specially regarded." But Schafer would not have considered the highway overpass a suitable soundmark: New Orleans exemplifies the "lo-fi soundscapes" of congested areas that "suffer from an overpopulation of sounds," and he condemned urban noise "pollution" while praising the serene "hi-fi soundscapes" of natural environments. Steven Feld retooled the soundscape concept in developing his theory of "acoustemology," stripping away Schafer's judgment in a more inclusive understanding of "local conditions of acoustic sensation, knowledge, and imagination embodied in the culturally particular sense of place." However, Feld's foundational case study was of an indigenous egalitarian society in the rural rainforests of Papua New Guinea, leaving open the question of how people experience place through sound when those people are socially stratified and those places are contested.

A comparison to the soundmark of the bridge and the racialized sound-scapes of New Orleans can be found in the "Islamic soundscapes" analyzed by Andrew Eisenberg in a Muslim neighborhood in Mombasa, on the Swahili coast of Kenya. In this postcolonial African metropolis, where the liberal-democratic logic of the state maintains public space as an arena of "neutral principles," the explicitly religious soundscape of the Muslim quarter is emblematic of the symbolic struggle over their right to the city. The key soundmark in Old Town is the *adhān*, the call to prayer broadcast five times each day. Emanating from loudspeakers perched on the rooftops of dozens of mosques, the *adhān* reso-nates in polyphony with Qur'anic recitations, religious songs, and sermons in Arabic, Swahili, and sometimes English. Eisenberg highlights "the centrality of ritual sounding and listening practices for Muslim subject-formation . . . through which denizens of the coastal city of Mombasa negotiate the literal and figurative place of a Muslim community within the bounds of a hetero-geneous Kenyan metropolis." This lo-fi soundscape does not signify a shared sense of place; there are disagreements over the status of public space enacted through competing acoustemological commitments to space. Subjects with dif-fering orientations must "strategically navigate and negotiate multiple logics of public space," and sound is a central site of navigation and negotiation.

TOWARD A PUBLIC ANTHROPOLOGY OF MUSIC

Scholars affiliated with musicology, ethnomusicology, the anthropology of music, and sound studies are redirecting intellectual lineages that have roman-ticized music as an aesthetic and affective mode of expression, autonomous from the mundane and profane domains of society and politics. They offer a progressive response to the question every author faces: What stories are you going to choose to tell? In my own work, I followed musicians into the spaces of their everyday lives, tracking how their physical and social mobility was condi-tioned by racial marginalization. My discussions with Bennie Pete, bandleader of the Hot 8 Brass Band, alerted me to the economic obstacles that brass band musicians navigated in their attempts to earn a livable wage within a local cul-ture industry that exploits their labor. The tragic murders of other members of the Hot 8 led me back to the jazz funeral, this time to focus on young musicians who were memorialized after suffering violent deaths. The police killing of an unarmed twenty-two-year-old musician and the murder of his twenty-five-year-old bandmate underscore how young black men who are celebrated as culture-bearers are not free from the incapacitating effects of structural and interpersonal violence.

In *Roll With It*, stories about the perilous lives of black New Orleanians pushed me to analyze music as a diagnostic of power relations within imbalanced racial hierarchies. After completing the manuscript in 2012, a black teenager named Trayvon Martin was murdered in the Florida community where he lived by white "neighborhood watchman" George Zimmerman. When Zimmerman was cleared of all charges on July 13, 2013, protesters organized demonstrations using the social media hashtag #BlackLivesMatter, which grew into a national movement in 2014 after the police killings of Michael Brown in Ferguson, Missouri and Eric Garner in Staten Island, New York. Though my research in New Orleans preceded the movement, the experiences of musicians and the stories they told me support the central claim made in the "Movement for Black Lives Platform": "Despite constant exploitation and perpetual oppression, Black people have bravely and brilliantly been the driving force pushing the U.S. towards the ideals it articulates but has never achieved." As I continue to become more attuned to music's entanglements with political and economic forces, my research about expressive culture becomes increasingly inseparable from research about social justice.

For all my commitment to foregrounding race and racism, my work thus far has generally not attended to intersections with gender and sexism. Brass bands in New Orleans are almost exclusively male, with one all-female band disrupting the gendered norms of this patriarchal community. Subsequent research by Kyle DeCoste focused on this band, The Pinettes, to demonstrate how "gender identity has been neglected as a category of analysis, reproducing the bias of the scene at large." Disregarding the intersectionality of race and gender, as I acknowledged in my book, closed off an entire domain of power relations in a way that "perpetuates the marginalization of black women in scholarly studies." It is a story that needs to be told and by choosing not to tell it I failed to provide a full and accurate accounting of struggles over power.

Cherice's provocation underscores the agency of scholars in choosing their objects of study, structuring their interactions with subjects, and sustaining engagement throughout the process or research and writing. If my book was based on the premise that picking up an instrument is a political act, it was Cherice and others who urged me to model my own creative work as a call to action. These are stories of people and events caught up in contemporary critical issues that are central to public policy and discourse but have mostly hovered above the purview of musical ethnography; that is, governmentality and the lives of individuals shaped by its most powerful institutions. Philippe Bourgois urges anthropologists not only to take up contemporary struggles over power but to use writing itself as a form of activism to "engage with political stakes that matter to the people who bear a disproportionate toll for suffering caused by the inequalities that power imposes." In the book *Why a Public Anthropology?* Rob Borofsky calls upon scholars and students to undertake ethnographic study in service of the public and advocate for the communities and societies granting the privilege of studying them. In each of these formulations, music studies would provide a kind of limit case for engaging with the contemporary and creating publically engaged scholarship because for so long the discipline has curated a space for disengagement.

In stressing the potential for ethnographers who make uniquely intimate engagements with people to open up more possibilities for social justice, I am not making a grand claim for the power of academic writing to transform society. Like many other scholars loosely affiliated with "applied ethnomusicology," I have collaborated with musicians and activists to combine research with community engagement. I consult with the Music and Culture Coalition of New Orleans (MaCCNO) to advocate for equitable pay and better working conditions for local musicians. I am a board member for the nonprofit organization Roots of Music, an afterschool music program for middle school students, and I coordinate students from my university for volunteer tutoring. I teach courses on "Music and Politics," "Black Music, Black Lives," and my class on "New Orleans Music" is structured around the complex history of racial identity in the city my students and I live in. I mention these activities only to highlight some ways in which music research, writing, and teaching can be integrated within broader initiatives aimed at ameliorating suffering and building equity. These initiatives can be undertaken in even the most unlikely places, including music studies.

SUGGESTIONS FOR FURTHER READINGS

Cusick, Suzanne. 2008. "Musicology, Torture, Repair." *Radical Musicology* 3. Accessed November 30, 2016, at http://www.radical-musicology.org.uk/2008/Cusick.htm.
 Cusick's study of the use of music in torture challenges asks us to consider at what point does music shed its association with beauty and become "sheer sound"?
Feld, Steven. 1988. "Waterfalls of Song: An Acoustemology of Place Resounding in Bosavi, Papua New Guinea." In *Senses of Place*, ed. Steven Feld and Keith Basso, 91–136. Santa Fe: School of American Research Press.
 Feld's research on the Kaluli in the rainforests of Papua New Guinea shows how different cultures have different understandings of what constitutes music.

Gaunt, Kyra Danielle. 2006. *The Games Black Girls Play: Learning the Ropes from Double-Dutch to Hip-Hop*. New York: New York University Press.
    A deep ethnography of black music and dance from the perspective of a scholar and practitioner.
Schwartz, Jessica A. 2012. "A 'Voice to Sing': Rongelapese Musical Activism and the Production of Nuclear Knowledge." *Music & Politics* 6(1).
    Schwartz situates song lyrics and performances alongside policy documents to show how survivors of nuclear disasters use music as a form of social activism and healing.
White, Bob M. 2008. *Rumba Rules: The Politics of Dance Music in Mobutu's Zaire*. Durham, NC: Duke University Press.
    White's ethnographic study of Congolese music, which under the Mobutu dictatorship could both contest and support regimes of power.

REFERENCES

Allen, William Francis, Charles Pickard Ware, and Lucy McKim Garrison. 1867. *Slave Songs of the United States*. New York: A. Simpson & Co.
Borofsky, Rob. 2011. *Why a Public Anthropology?* Honolulu: Center for a Public Anthropology.
Bourgois, Philippe. 2006. Foreword to *Engaged Observer: Anthropology, Advocacy, and Activism*, ed. Victoria Sanford and Asale Angel-Ajani, ix-xii. New Brunswick, NJ: Rutgers University Press.
Charlton, David, ed. 1989. *E. T. A. Hoffman's Musical Writings*. Cambridge: Cambridge University Press.
Cusick, Suzanne. 2008. "Musicology, Torture, Repair." *Radical Musicology* 3. Accessed November 30, 2016, at http://www.radical-musicology.org.uk/2008/Cusick.htm.
Daughtry, Martin. 2015. *Listening to War: Sound, Music, Trauma, and Survival in Wartime Iraq*. New York: Oxford University Press.
DeCoste, Kyle. 2017. "Street Queens: New Orleans Brass Bands and the Problem of Instrersectionality." *Ethnomusicology* 61 (2): 181–206.
Du Bois, W. E. B. 1903. *The Souls of Black Folk*. Chicago: A. C. McClurg.
Eisenberg, Andy. 2013. 2013. "Islam, Sound, and Space: Acoustemology and Muslim Citizenship on the Kenyan Coast," In *Music, Sound, and Space: Transformations of Public and Private Experience*, ed. Georgina Born, 186–202. Cambridge: Cambridge University Press.
Feld, Steven. 1988. "Waterfalls of Song: An Acoustemology of Place Resounding in Bosavi, Papua New Guinea." In *Senses of Place*, ed. Steven Feld and Keith Basso, 91–136. Santa Fe: School of American Research Press.
Gaunt, Kyra Danielle. 2006. *The Games Black Girls Play: Learning the Ropes from Double-Dutch to Hip-Hop*. New York: New York University Press.
Keyes, Cheryl. 2004. *Rap Music and Street Consciousness*. Urbana: University of Illinois Press.
Lefebvre, Henri. 1991. *The Production of Space*. Cambridge, MA: Blackwell.
Manabe, Noriko. 2015. *The Revolution Will Not Be Televised: Protest Music after Fukushima*. New York: Oxford University Press.
Meintjes, Louise. 2003. *Sound of Africa! Making Music Zulu in a South African Studio*. Durham, NC: Duke University Press.
Merriam, Alan. 1964. *The Anthropology of Music*. Evanston, IL: Northwestern University Press.

Moreno, Jairo. 2004. *Musical Representations, Subjects, and Objects*. Bloomington: Indiana University Press.

Movement for Black Lives. 2016. "Platform." Accessed November 30, 2016, at https://policy .m4bl.org/platform/.

Novak, David. 2017. "Project Fukushima! Performativity and the Politics of Festival in post-3.11 Japan." *Anthropological Quarterly* 90(1).

Sakakeeny, Matt. 2010. "'Under the Bridge': An Orientation to Soundscapes in New Orleans." *Ethnomusicology* 54 (1): 1–27. Videos of the funeral and parade discussed are available at https://www.youtube.com/playlist?list=PLB9FA66F89B338772.

———. 2013. *Roll with It: Brass Bands in the Streets of New Orleans*. Durham, NC: Duke University Press.

Schafer, Murray. 1977. *The Tuning of the World*. New York: Knopf.

Schwartz, Jessica A. 2012. "A 'Voice to Sing': Rongelapese Musical Activism and the Production of Nuclear Knowledge." *Music & Politics* 6(1).

Steingo, Gavin. 2016. *Kwaito's Promise: Music and the Aesthetics of Freedom in South Africa*. Chicago: University of Chicago Press.

ACKNOWLEDGMENTS

In 2000 Jonathan Benthall, then director of the Royal Anthropological Institute, asked me to produce the first edition of this book: I accepted gladly. It was broadly and positively reviewed, and sold well. So it was not difficult to persuade David Shankland, the present director of the RAI, to support production of a second edition, which he has done, throughout. Priya Nelson, the editor at the University of Chicago Press whose brief includes anthropology, immediately rose to the challenge. She and the others on the team for this book, Dylan Montanari and Mark Reschke, have all provided exemplary support and, most importantly, a degree of patience only lightly laced with a sense of urgency. I am also grateful to all the contributors, who rose to the occasion: of course, we are all indebted to the peoples—scientists or slum-dwellers, hackers or nostalgic socialists—with whom we have spent so much time; they have taught us so much.

I am not a priest. My rites of absolution are secular, not sacred. Should you disagree with any statement in this book, do not email, text, or whistle at any of the above. Best to blast your blame at

Jeremy MacClancy
Oxford Brookes University

CONTRIBUTORS

Ruben Andersson is an anthropologist and associate professor of migration and development at the University of Oxford.

Philippe Bourgois is professor of anthropology and director of the Center for Social Medicine and Humanities in the Semel Institute of the Department of Psychiatry at the University of California, Los Angeles.

Catherine Buerger is research associate at the Dangerous Speech Project, Washington, DC.

James G. Carrier is an associate of the Max Planck Institute for Social Anthropology and adjunct professor of anthropology at Indiana University, Bloomington.

Marcus Colchester is the founder, former director, and now senior policy adviser of the Forest Peoples Programme.

James Fairhead is professor of anthropology at the University of Sussex.

Kim Fortun is professor and chair of anthropology at the University of California, Irvine.

Mike Fortun is associate professor of anthropology at the University of California, Irvine.

Katy Gardner is professor and chair of anthropology at the London School of Economics.

Faye Ginsburg is the David B. Kriser Professor of Anthropology at New York University.

Roberto J. González is professor and chair of anthropology at San Jose State University.

Tom Griffiths is a social anthropologist working with the Forest Peoples Programme.

Chris Hann is a director at the Max Planck Institute for Social Anthropology (Halle/Saale, Germany) and a Fellow of Corpus Christi College, Cambridge.

Susan Harding is professor emerita of anthropology at the University of California, Santa Cruz.

Faye V. Harrison is professor of African American studies and anthropology at the University of Illinois at Urbana-Champaign.

Laurie Kain Hart is professor of anthropology at the University of California, Los Angeles.

Richard Jenkins is professor emeritus of sociology at the University of Sheffield.

George Karandinos is an MD-PhD doctoral candidate in anthropology at Harvard University.

Christopher M. Kelty is professor at the University of California, Los Angeles, in the Institute for Society and Genetics, the Department of Anthropology, and the Department of Information Studies.

Melissa Leach is professor of anthropology and director of the Institute of Development Studies at the University of Sussex.

Margaret Lock is the Marjorie Bronfman Professor Emerita in the Department of Social Studies of Medicine at McGill University, where she is also affiliated with the Department of Anthropology.

Jeremy MacClancy is professor of anthropology at Oxford Brookes University, where he is also director of the Anthropological Centre for Conservation, the Environment, and Development.

Sally Engle Merry is Silver Professor of Anthropology at New York University.

Fernando Montero is a PhD candidate in anthropology at Columbia University.

Matt Sakakeeny is associate professor of music at Tulane University.

Anthony Alan Shelton is professor of art history, visual art and theory and director of the Museum of Anthropology at the University of British Columbia.

Christopher B. Steiner is Lucy C. McDannel '22 Professor of Art History and Anthropology and director of the museum studies program at Connecticut College.

Richard Ashby Wilson is Gladstein Distinguished Chair of Human Rights and professor of anthropology and law at the University of Connecticut.

INDEX

Page numbers in italics indicate figures.